DICTIONARY OF BUSINESS

K.C.S. Ranganayakulu

ATLANTIC
PUBLISHERS & DISTRIBUTORS (P) LTD

Published by

ATLANTIC

PUBLISHERS & DISTRIBUTORS (P) LTD

7/22, Ansari Road, Darya Ganj,
New Delhi-110002
Phones : +91-11-23273880, 23275880, 23280451
Fax : +91-11-23285873
Web : www.atlanticbooks.com
E-mail : info@atlanticbooks.com

Branch Office
5, Nallathambi Street, Wallajah Road,
Chennai-600002
Phones : +91-44-64611085, 32413319
E-mail : chennai@atlanticbooks.com

Printed in India at Nice Printing Press, A-33/3A, Site-IV, Industrial Area, Sahibabad, Ghaziabad, U.P.

indispensible reference source for students, research scholars, academicians, professionals and executives in the field of business and commerce. Anyone seeking a better understanding of economics and business terminology will also find it interesting, informative and inculcating.

K.C.S. RANGANAYAKULU

PREFACE

Business is the backbone of any society. The world of business is varied and diverse. This *Dictionary of Business* provides a wealth of information about the major functional areas of business, namely accounting, economics, finance, information systems, law, management and commerce. It encompasses concepts, terms, applications, innovations and ideas that together constitute the various components of business. In addition, terminology relating to business theories, international monetary and welfare schemes, various business laws and acts and different abbreviations have also been included in it. Considerable emphasis has been given to include all the key terms used in the field of business, public finance, international trade and development.

The *Dictionary* is the result of the painstaking efforts to bring together a forbiddingly complex and astounding terminology that defines the world of buying and selling, trading and trucking, exporting and importing from the very beginning when the barter and exchange system was in vogue, to the modern times marked by man's relentless quest for novel and precious goods and commodities. It provides a comprehensive vocabulary of terms used in business. All the entries have been judiciously selected and comprehensively dealt with. The entries included in the book have been presented in a clear and explanatory style to furnish straightforward information.

The *Dictionary* is planned to serve as a companion to the readers. All efforts have been made to make it comprehensive, more informative, useful and relevant to the users. It is an

A

Abilene Paradox. A situation occurring when members of a group publicly agree on a course of action even though there is an underlying consensus agreement that an alternative course is preferred.

Ability. Stable characteristics responsible for a person's maximum physical or mental performance.

Ability Tests. Paper and pencil quizzes, usually multiple choice, that measure an applicant's knowledge of specific work content or cognitive ability.

Above Par. The par value of a share is its face value. When the share price is above its face value it is said to be above par.

Absentee Ownership. Exists when the owners of a business firm do not take active part in its operation.

Absolute Advantage. When a country has monopoly on producing a product or is able to produce it at a cost below that of all other countries.

Absolute Price Thresholds. The lowest and highest prices that buyers are willing to pay for a particular good or service.

Absolute Priority Rule. Rule establishing priority of claims in liquidation.

Absoluteness of Responsibility. *See* Responsibility.

Absorption Costing. A type of product costing that assigns fixed manufacturing overheads to the units produced as a product cost. Contrast with direct costing.

Accelerated Cost Recovery System. A system of the internal revenue service that requires depreciation deductions to be based on arbitrary 'recovery periods' instead of useful lives.

Accelerated Death Benefits Rider. A rider that allows insureds who are terminally ill or who suffer from certain catastrophic diseases to collect part or all of their life insurance benefits before they die, primarily to pay for the care they require.

Accelerated Depreciation. Any pattern of depreciation that systematically writes of depreciable costs more quickly than the ordinary straight-line method based on expected useful life.

Acceptable Price Range. Those prices that buyers are willing to pay for a good or service.

Acceptable Quality Level. A concept of quality control whereby managers are willing to accept a certain level of production defects, which are dealt with repair facilities and service centres.

Acceptance Theory of Authority. The theory that, in informal organizations, authority flows up, because the decision as to whether an order, or communication, has authority lies with the person who receives the communication:

Accident. A loss causing event that is sudden, unforeseen, and unintentional.

Accidental bodily injury. Bodily injury resulting from an act whose result was accidental or unexpected accommodating to satisfy another person's objectives.

Acceptance. The paying of the first call on a rights issue, thereby accepting the allotment.

Accommodating Style. A style exhibiting low assertiveness and high cooperation.

Account. A stock exchange's dealing period is usually two weeks. All deals done for the account during the period are due for settlement on the settlement day relating to that account.

Account Statement. When an account with a broker is active, he periodically issues a statement to his client, featuring all transactions, including long and short positions.

Accountability Practices. Focus on treating diverse employees fairly.

Accounting. The recording, classifying, summarizing, and interpreting of financial events and transactions to provide management and other interested parties the information they need to make good decisions.

Accounting Cycle. A six-step procedure that results in the preparation and analysis of the two major financial statements: balance sheet and income statement.

Accounting Method. *See* Accounting Rate of Return.

Accounting Principles Board. The top private sector regulatory body, which existed from 1953 to 1973, when it was succeeded by the financial accounting standards board.

Accounting Rate of Return. An expression of the utility of a given project as the ratio of increase in future average annual net income and the initial increase in required investment, also called book value rate and unadjusted rate.

Accounts Payable. Debts that are owed to others and payable within a short period.

Accounts Payable Period. The time between receipt of inventory and payment for it.

Accounts Receivable. The claims against debtors generally arising from the sale of goods or services on open account, usually a current asset.

Accounts Receivable Financing. A secured short term loan that involves either the assignment or factoring of receivable.

Accounts Receivable Period. The time between sale of inventory and collection of the receivable.

Accounts Receivable Turn-over Ratio. This is obtained by dividing the total credit sales by the account receivables. The ratio shows how many times the receivables have been collected.

Accrual Basis. A matching process whereby revenue is recognized as services are rendered and expenses are recognized as efforts are expended or services utilized to obtain the revenue, regardless of when cash is received or disbursed.

Accrual Method. An accounting method that describes a method of keeping accounts whereby expenses incurred and income earned for a given financial year are shown in the books even though they may not have actually been paid or received during that period.

Accrue. Accumulation of a receivable or payable during a given period though no explicit transaction occurs.

Accrued Income. The amount of dividend or interest deemed to have accrued during the period since the last distribution of income.

Accrued Interest. Interest accumulated on debentures since the last interest-payment date.

Accumulated Depreciation. The cumulative sum of all depreciation recognized since the date of acquisition of particular assets described.

Accumulated Dividend. Dividend due to preference shareholders, not paid and carried forward on the balance sheet as a liability till it is paid. Skipped or passed dividends do not accrue to equity shareholders.

Accumulation. When the price of a share rises as a result of increased buying pressure it is said to be under 'accumulation'.

Accumulation Area. A term used by technical analysts when the price of a share moves within a narrow range of ups and downs over a period. Technical analysts interpret this as accumulation or buying activity.

Achievement Test. A test which measures skill or proficiency.

Acid Rain. Naturally occurring rain that contains dilute solutions of nitric acid and sulphuric acid that are formed when nitrogen oxide and sulfur oxide combine with atmospheric water vapor.

Acid Test Ratio. The sum of cash accounts receivable and marketable securities divided by current liabilities.

Acquired Advantage. A form of trade advantage due to technology rather than the availability of natural resources, climate, etc.

Acquired Group Memberships. Affiliations not determined by birth, such as religions, political affiliations, professional and other associations.

Acquirer. The acquirer includes any individual company or any other legal entity who intends to acquire or acquires substantial quantity of shares or voting rights of target company or acquires or agrees to acquire control over the target company along with Persons Acting in Concert (PAC) with him.

Acquisition. The purchase of one company by another company.

Acquisition Cost. The original historical cost of an asset acquired usually includes directly associated costs such as freight and installation.

Across the Board. Any movement in share prices which affects all the shares in the same direction up or down. An 'across the board settlement' with the employees of a company affects all of them from the highest paid to the lowest paid.

ACRS. *See* Accelerated Cost Recovery System.

Acting in Concert. When two or more investors act together with the same goal, e.g. buying or selling shares of a particular company to push the price up or down, or accumulating stocks with the eventual purpose of securing a controlling interest in a company. They are acting in concert.

Action Research. An approach to change that involves an ongoing process of joint (with clients) problem discovery, diagnosis, action planning, action implementation, and evaluation.

Action/Negotiation Teams. A highly differentiated or highly integrated team.

Active Bond Management. It means that increased volatility brings both greater opportunities as well as risks in managing fixed income securities.

Active Corp of Executives (ACE). SBA volunteers from industry, trade associations, and education who counsel small businesses.

Active Income. Income of a CFC that is derived from the active conduct of a trade or business as specified by the U.S. internal revenue code.

Active Listening. Accepting responsibility for the accurate understanding of a message by helping the sender clarify its meaning.

Active Market. Characterized by frequent and large volume of trading of a particular share or shares in general. In such a market the gap between buying prices and selling prices is narrow. Also in such a market the buying or selling activities of financial institutions tend to have a lower impact than in a dull market.

Active Monetary Policy. When the Federal Bank increases the money supply in an attempt to bring down interest rates, thus pruning investment and aggregate demand.

Active Rule. A monetary policy rule that prescribes changes in the money supply in response to changes in the economy.

Active Shares. Shares in which transactions take place everyday can be called 'active shares'. The other shares can be relegated to the 'partially active and inactive categories'.

Activity. The work necessary to complete a particular event in a PERT network. An activity consumes time, which is the paramount variable in a PERT system. In PERT networks, three time estimates are used for each activity; an optimistic time, a pessimistic time, and a most likely time.

Activity Accounting. *See* Responsibility Accounting.

Activity Based Costing. A cost accounting system that ties actual costs to the direct performance and value of activities. Costs are traced and assigned to specific activities rather than by formula.

Actual Cash Value. Value of property at the time of its damage or loss, determined by subtracting depreciation of the item from its replacement cost.

Actual Costing. The method of allocating costs to products using actual direct materials, direct labour, and overhead.

Actual Loss Ratio. The ratio of incurred losses and loss-adjustment expenses to earned premiums.

Actual Maturity. The number of days between today and the date of loan or security is redeemed or retired.

Actuarial. Calculation of premiums and matters connected with pension funds.

Actuarial Tables. Tables that give the probability of death for particular age groups. These tables are based on past experience with separate tables for men and women of different racial groups and for certain hazardous occupations. Such a table might indicate that at age 25, a white male would have 1 chance in 350 of dying within the next year and could on the average expect to live 36 more years (to age 72) for a 65-year-old white male it might list his chance of dying in the next year as 1 in 10 and his future life expecting as ten years (to age 75).

Ad hoc Coalition. Any informal and temporary group organized to lobby for or against a law of government regulation.

Ad hoc Margin. When a member of a stock exchange has an usually large outstanding position, the exchange collects this margin from him.

A-D Index or Advance-Decline Index. A useful tool for detecting bullish or bearish trend in the stock market in which one divides the number of traded shares which have risen in prices by those which have fallen.

For example, if 200 shares have advanced and 100 declined on a particular day the A-D Index is 2. Index more than 1 indicates a bullish trend and less than 1 a bearish trend.

AD Referendum. Ad referendum indicates that while the contract has been agreed and signed, there are some matters to be discussed.

AD Valorem. Ad valorem means 'according to the name' used to describe the rates of transfer stamp duty payable on a transaction as stamp duty.

AD Valorem Duty. A duty (tariff) assessed as a percentage of the value of the item.

AD Valorem Tariff. A tariff levied as a proportion of the value of an imported good.

Adaptive Expectations Hypothesis. Views expectations as evolving relatively slowly over time and being revised in the light of past experience.

Adaptive Perspective. Assumes that adaptive cultures enhance a firm's financial performance.

ADB. Asian Development Bank.

Add Back Method. The practice of beginning a statement of changes in financial position with net income and then adding or deducting income statement items not affecting working capital.

Add-on Plan. Pays benefits to an accident victim without regard to fault, but the injured person still has the right to sue the negligent driver who caused the accident.

Additive Tasks. Tasks where productivity is measured by adding together the output of each group member.

Add-on Rate. A method for calculating the interest charge on a loan when the interest bill is added to the principal amount of the loan. That sum is then divided by the number of installment payments required to determine the amount of each payment needed to eventually payoff the loan.

Adhocracy. A centralized, informal, but complex organization which tries to maintain flexibility in the face of rapid environmental changes by using a matrix or network formal structure.

Adjourning Stage. The stage in which task forces complete their task and disband.

Adjustable Life Insurance. Insurance contract that permits certain changes to be made in amount of life insurance, premiums, period of protection, and duration of the premium paying period.

Adjustable Mortgage Instrument. A home mortgage loan under which some of the term of the loan, such as the loan rate or the maturity of loan, will vary as market conditions change.

Adjustable Peg. An exchange rate which varies from time to time when it is pegged or tied to another or other currencies. India's Currency has an Adjustable peg.

Adjustable Rate Mortgage. A mortgage in which the interest rate is tied to some market interest rate. Thus, the required monthly payments can change over the life of the mortgage.

Adjusting Entries. The records made of an accounting transaction giving effect to the correction of an error, an accrual, a write-off, a repayment, a provision for bad debts or depreciation, or the like.

Adjustment Bureau. Organization for adjusting insurance claims that is supported by insurers using the bureau's services.

Adjustment Credit. Loans made to depository institutions to allow them to more gradually adjust their reserves and loan portfolios in response to changes in deposits.

Adjustments. The key final process (before the computation of ending account balances) that assures the accountant that the financial effects of transactions are assigned to the appropriate time periods.

Administered Distribution System. A distribution system in which producers manage all of the marketing functions at the retail level.

Administered Price System. A system in which the price is set without close regard to the costs. Obviously, it must be above the break-even price. It generally occurs in the oligopoly models and it tends to remain steady across variations in prices.

Administrative Agencies. Institutions created by congress with delegated power to pass rules and regulations within their mandated area of authority.

Administrative Costs. The direct costs incurred in running government regulatory agencies, including salaries of employees, equipment, supplies, and other such items.

Administrative Learning. A stage in the development of social responsiveness within a company during which managers and supervisors learn the new practices necessary for coping with social problems and pressures.

Administrative Management. The universality of management as a function that can be applied to all organizations.

Administrative Model of Decision Making. A descriptive approach, recognizing that people do not always make decisions with logic and rationality, that outlines how managers actually do make decisions; also known as the organizational, neo-classical, or behavioral model.

Administrative Trade Policies. Policies typically adopted by government bureaucracies, that can be used to restrict imports or boost exports.

Administratively Guided Market Economy. An economic system in which there is a great deal of cooperation among government, management, and workers to achieve growth and full employment with low job turnover on a non-mandated basis.

Administrator. *See* Manager.

Admission to Dealing. When a particular share of a company is allowed to be entered in the official list of a stock exchange, it is said to be admitted to dealing.

Adoption Level Price. The price a buyer uses as the basis of a comparison with a product or service's actual price.

Adoption Level Theory. Assumes that stimuli are judged with respect to internal norms (adaptation levels) representing the combined effects of perceived as members of categories and are evaluated relative to the individual's adaptation level for that category.

Advance Corporation Tax. Sum paid by a company to the inland revenue equivalent to the tax credits/issued to shareholders with their dividends as an advance payment of corporation tax for the relative trading period.

Advance Decline Line. It is one of the most important technical indicators of the condition of the stock market. It is the most common measure of market breadth. It is derived by taking the difference between the number of advancing issues and the number of declining issues each day. This daily figure is then added or subtracted each day to a cumulative number in order to determine the advance decline line. It is a measure which will often signal a major change in the direction of the market. Its purpose is to tell whether the market as a whole is gaining or losing strength.

Advance Funding. Pension-funding method in which the employer systematically and periodically sets aside funds prior to the employee's retirement.

Advance Premium Mutual. Mutual insurance company owned by the policy owners that does not issue assessable policies but charges premiums expected to be sufficient to pay all claims and expenses.

Advance Purchase Discount. Discount given to customers who purchase or make reservations early.

Adverse Impact. Occurs when there is a substantially different rate in hiring, promotion, or other employment decisions which works to the disadvantage of members of protected groups.

Adverse Selection. Tendency of persons with a higher-than-average chance of loss to seek insurance at standard (average) rates, which, if not controlled by underwriting, results in higher than expected loss levels.

Adverse Selection. In the loan market the situation that occurs as the interest rate rises and honest borrowers decide not to borrow. The bank is left with an adverse pool of borrowers—those who know they are more likely to default.

Advertising Agency. An independent business which specializes in planning and carrying out the ventures or campaigns for other business firms.

Advertising. Paid, non-personal communication through various media by organizations and individuals who are in some way identified in the advertising message.

Advertising. A sales presentation which is of a non-personal nature and is paid for by a sponsor.

Advice/Involvement Team. A team formed to generate input from a broad base of employees.

Advisory Sentiment. It is often best used as an indicator of contrary option. It is common knowledge that stock market investment advisors tend to be trend followers. They tend to be bullish quite quickly after the market prices start rising. Conversely, when the market has been declining, advisors tend to get over pessimistic. The degree of advisors' pessimism can best be determined by the 'Sentiment index'.

Aesthetic Pollution. Any thing that detracts from the beauty of nature.

ADB. African Development Bank.

Affiliate Action Programs. Policies designed to increase OB opportunities for minority groups through analysis of the present pool of workers, identification of areas where women and minorities are under-represented and establishment of specific hiring and promotion goals along with target dates for meeting those goals.

Affiliate Power. Power that is derived by virtue of a person's association with someone else who has some source of power.

Affirmative Action. Employment activities designed to 'right past wrongs' by increasing opportunities for minorities and women.

Affirmative Action. A positive and sustained effort by an organization to identify, hire, train if necessary and promote minorities women, and members of other groups who are under-represented in the organization's workforce.

AFIC. Asian Finance and Investment Corporation.

AFTA. Asian Free Trade Agreement.

AFTR. *See* ASEAN Free Trade Receipt.

After Tax Interest Rate. The interest rate minus the amount of the interest payment that is due in income taxes. Calculated as the interest rate minus the interest rate times the tax rate.

After Tax. When a tax-payer is investing in loan investments like debentures or bonds or fixed deposits, it is the after tax return which is the real return not the rate(s) of interest. The relevant rate(s) of interest on the investor's slab of income should be decided from the earnings and the actual return compared with returns from tax sheltered instruments, such as tax free bonds, or debentures which enjoy an interest exemption, under section 80 of the Income Tax Act.

Agency Costs. The agency problems arising from the conflicts between shareholders, debenture-holders and managers are handled through monitoring and restrictive covenants which involves cost. These costs are agency costs.

Agency Factoring. This type of factoring is basically used as a method of financing book debts under this the client continues to administer credit and operate sales ledger and the factor finances the book debts.

Agency Problem. The possibility of conflict of interest between the owners and management of a firm.

Agency Shop Agreement. Agent agreement says that employers may hire non-union workers who are not required to join the union but must pay a union fee.

Agency Shop. A shop agreement in which both union and non-union employees pay union dues but a worker does not have to join the union in order to be or remain employed.

Agenda. Details of business to be transacted at a meeting. An agenda has to be sent to every equity shareholder before a company holds the AGM.

Agent. Someone who legally represents the insurer has the authority to act on the insurer's behalf, and can bind the principal by expressed powers, by implied powers, and by apparent authority.

Aggregate Demand Curve. A relation between the price level and aggregate quantity of goods and services demanded holding other things such as interest rates and the money supply constant.

Aggressive Style. Expressive and self-enhancing, but takes unfair advantage of others.

Aging Schedule. The aging schedule breaks down according to the length of time for which they have been outstanding.

AGM or Annual General Meeting. Meeting held once a year where the Directors of the company report to the shareholders' on the year's performance and any vacancies in the Board of Directors are filled by taking shareholders' consent. The chief of the company comments on the future outlook of the company and answers questions from shareholders. Notice of the meeting along with a copy of the annual report has to be compulsorily sent to every shareholder, who may send a PROXY to attend on his behalf. Shareholders can insist that all resolutions on company policy be voted upon by the equity shareholders of the company. This meeting also receives the auditors' report.

Agrarian Society. A society in which agricultural activities dominate work and employ the largest proportion of the labour force.

Agreeableness. The degree to which a person possesses such traits as courtesy, flexibility, trust, good nature, cooperativeness, forgiveness and tolerance.

Agreed Value Policy. It is the sum to be paid out in the event of claim in insurance policy. It is often used for antiquities, jewellery and classic cars.

Aided Analytic. Using tools to make decisions.

Air Pocket Stocks. Due to sudden and unfavourable news affecting a company or an industry (such as price control or liberalization of imports) there is a steep fall in the price of a share, creating a large gap between a day's closing price and considerably lower opening price on the following day. An air pocket appears and the stocks are said to be air pocket stocks. Shares which are particularly prone to such falls are usually over priced in the first instance.

Air Pollution Rights. A legal right to exceed established emission limits such right may be bought, sold or held for future use with the approval of government.

Air Pollution. Gaseous elements or particles in the air.

ALADI. *See* Latin America Integration Association.

All-channel Network. Communication network in which information flows upward, downward, and laterally among all members of the group.

All or None. Instruction to the broker, fill the entire order: no partial execution; if you can't, let go.

Allocation. Assigning one or more items of cost or revenue to one or more segments of an organization according to cause, benefits received, responsibilities, or other logical measure of use.

Allocation Model. This type of management science model is used in a situation where several candidates or activities all compete for limited resources. It enables the user to allocate scarce resources to maximize some predetermined objectives.

Allotment. The number of shares or amount of stock forming part of a new issue due to an applicant or existing holder.

Allotment Advice. Letter sent to a successful applicant for shares and debentures of a company informing him that he has been allotted.

Allotment Letter. The document evidencing an allotment. It is a provisional letter in the case of a rights issue.

Allotment of Shares. Allotment can be made after the minimum sub-subscription stated in the prospectus has been fulfilled. In the event of over subscription the basis on which the shares are to be allotted is decided by the principal stock exchange in consultation with the company. Approval of the other stock exchanges where the shares are proposed to be listed is also required.

Alpha Factor. The concept which measures the inherent volatility of a share. A share with an alpha factor of 1.5 (say) is slated to rise in price by 50% in a year on its inherent strength, such as growth in earnings per share regardless of the behaviour of the market (*See* Beta Factor).

Alpha Shares. The most frequently traded shares are also called specified shares also called a group securities (*See* Blue Chips).

Alternative Delivery Procedure (ADP). A delivery mechanism in which the long and the short agree to carry out physical delivery under terms and conditions that are different from the standardized contract rules prescribed by the exchange. The ADP is available only after the end of trading in a futures contract and after the longs and shorts have been matched by the clearing house.

Altruism. An ethical standard which places highest value on behavior that is pleasurable and rewarding to society.

Ambulance Stocks. Securities recommended to an investor whose portfolio has done badly.

American Depository Receipt (ADR). A negotiable certificate issued by a U.S. bank in the United States to represent the underlying shares of a foreign corporation's stock held in trust at a custodian bank in the foreign country.

American Dream. An ideal goal or vision of life in the United States usually including material abundance and maximum freedom.

American Federation of Labor. An organization of craft unions that championed bread and butter of labor issues.

American Option. An option that can be exercised at any time prior to the contracts expiration date.

American Stock Exchange. 86 Trinity Place, New York, the second largest stock exchange in America. Till 1921 it was known as the Kurb Exchange. Stocks and bonds listed at amex are usually those of medium to small-sized companies as also of a large number of oil and gas companies. It is dealing in foreign shares, more than any other exchange.

Americans with Disabilities Act of 1990. An anti-discrimination law aimed at integrating the disabled into the workforce. There are now estimated to be approximately 43 million Americans with some type of disability.

AMEX. The American Stock Exchange.

Amortization Schedule. Schedule showing how the monthly mortgage payments are split between principal and interest payments full pay off the mortgage by its maturity date.

Amortization. The systematic reduction of a lump-sum amount.

Amortize. The process of writing off expenditure for capital equipment by prorating costs over a period of time, such as an asset's depreciation period.

Amortized. A mortgage is amortized when the fixed principal and interest payments fully pay off the mortgage by its maturity date.

Analogue Computers. Computers which are primarily measuring devices, measuring quantities on a continuous scale.

Analyst. An investment professional, who makes buy or sell recommendations. Successful analysts not only influence the fortunes of their employees, but of the shares listed on the stock market as well.

Analytic Process. A production process in which raw materials are reduced to form products.

Analytic System. Manufacturing system that breaks down raw materials into components to extract other products.

Anarchy. A society with little or no government or social controls in which each person pursues individual interests without regard for others.

Anchoring and Adjustment Effect. Perceptual bias that involves making an insufficient adjustment from a given value (an anchor).

Anchoring Effect. *See* Anchoring and adjustment effect.

Anchoring Prices. Prices used by individuals to make perceptual judgments about other prices.

Andean Group (ANCOM). A South American form of economic integration involving Bolivia, Colombia, Ecuador, Peru and Venezuela.

Andean Pact. A 1969 agreement between Bolivia, Chile, Ecuador, Colombia, and Peru to establish a customs union.

Annual Equivalent Value. The value is calculated by dividing NPV by the annuity factor.

Annual Meeting. A yearly meeting called by a corporation's board of directors for purposes of reporting to the company's stockholders on the current status and future prospects of the firm.

Annual Percentage Rate. The actually determined rate on a consumer loan that the federal truth-in lending law required lenders to communicate to borrowers.

Annual Report. A yearly statement of the financial condition and progress of an organization covering one year period. Formal financial statements, the Auditors' Report, together with the Directors' Report issued by a company. These financial statements are usually prepared at the end of the company's financial year.

Annualized Basis. Statistical computation, whereby com-pany figures covering periods of less than a year are extended to cover a full year. The computation takes into account seasonal variations, if any.

Annuity. A series of fixed payments starting at the beginning of each period for a specific number of periods is called an annuity.

Annuity Due. An annuity for which the cash flows occur at the beginning of the period.

Annuity Due Value. Ordinary annuity value × (1+r).

Annuity FV Factor = (future value factor–1)/r.

Anomaly. The situation where the price of a stock or share is out of line with other similar stocks or shares indicating an opportunity for a purchase or sale.

Anthropology. The behavioral science that studies learned behaviors of individuals. It seeks general laws, which explain intercultural and extracultural behavior. This includes social, technical, and family behaviors. It is often defined as the study of man and his works.

Anticipated Inflation. The amount of inflation that is expected.

Anti-dumping Policies. Policies designed to punish foreign firms that engage in dumping and thus protect domestic producers from unfair foreign competition.

Anti-dumping Regulations. Regulations designed to restrict the sale of goods for less than their fair market price.

Anti-group Roles. Behaviors that disrupt the group to draw attention to individual rather than group functioning and detract from positive interactions.

AOL-Time Warner. AOL-Time Warner received approval for their $ 106 bn merger in December 2000. For the first time after receiving approval they reported combined earnings. The media and Internet company has a net loss of $ 1.09 bn. While the total revenues of the combine were around $ 10.2 bn. However, AOL's Internet and cable services reported good growth.

APB. *See* Accounting Principles Board.

APB Opinions. A series of thirty-one opinions to the accounting principles board issued during 1962-73.

Application Form. A written summary of the applicant's background—education, age, marital status, and work experience.

Application Money. The amount an investor is asked to pay along with the application for new issues, usually less than the full value of shares. The remainder being either fully or partly collected on actual allotment.

Application of Cash. A firm's activities in which cash is spent.

Application of Funds. A term featuring on the balance sheet of a company showing how the total funds of the company, i.e. share capital, reserves and surplus and loans are deployed. A part of it constitutes NET FIXED ASSETS; another part goes into investments; another towards CURRENT ASSETS, loans and advances and the remainder is miscellaneous expenditure like technical know-how or royalty on the use of patents and processes.

Applied Factory Overhead. The excess of actual factory overhead over the factory overhead applied to products.

Appreciation. When the dollar appreciates it buys more units of foreign currency than before.

Apprentice Programs. Training programs involving a period during which a learner works alongside an experienced employee to master the skills and procedures of a craft.

Apprenticeship. A combination of classroom training and on-the-job training.

Apprenticeship Training. Training which involves learning a skilled trade, and includes both principles and practices of the specific skilled trade.

Approach to Management. McKinsey's 7-s framework. An analysis of management which organizes managerial knowledge around the following categories: Strategy, Structure, Systems, Style, Staff, Shared values and Skills.

Approach to Management, Contingency or Situational Approach. An analysis of management that emphasizes the fact that what managers do in practice depends upon a given set of circumstances or the "situation" and that there is no single "best way" to manage.

Approach to Management, Empirical or Case. An analysis of management as a study of experiences from instances of managing.

Approach to Management, Group Behaviour Approach. An analysis of management as a study in group behaviour patterns.

Approach to Management, Managerial Roles. A means of analyzing management by observing what managers actually do and from such observations come to conclusions as to what managerial activities (or roles).

Approach to Management, Mathematical. An analysis of management primarily as a matter of developing mathematical models of managerial decision areas.

Approach to Management, Operational. An analysis of management which draws together knowledge that is unique to managing and knowledge from other fields pertinent to managing and relates it to the task of managing in a way most useful to the managerial practitioner. It is thus a summary of the central core of knowledge which exists in management situations.

Approach to Management, Socio-technical Systems. An analysis of management viewing managerial situations as involving a combination of interacting social and technical systems.

Approach to Management, System Approach. An analysis of management which emphasizes looking at managerial knowledge from the point of view of system.

Appropriability Theory. The theory that companies will favour foreign direct investment over such non-equity operating forms as licensing arrangements so that potential competitors will be less likely to gain access to proprietary information.

Appropriation. A term featuring on the balance sheet of a company showing how the net profits are deployed in distribution of dividends on preference shares or equity shares, transfer to general reserves, and balance carried forward.

Approved List. A list of various investments in which a mutual fund, the LIC, the Unit Trust of India, pension funds, etc. are allowed to make investments. The list also specifies in what proportion investments are to be made from the instruments so approved.

Approximation Process. The process by which Arabic or verbal numerals are first converted into an internal magnitude representation. The input mode such as dollar is then ignored and the numerical quantities are represented and processed similarly to other physical magnitudes such as size.

Aptitude. The natural capacity to learn an ability.

Aptitude Test. A test to measure the potential ability a person possesses to learn a new job.

Arbitrage. The purchase of securities in one market for immediate resale in another to profit from a price discrepancy.

Arbitragers. Buyers and sellers who try to take advantage of temporary profit opportunities caused by discrepancies between prices in various markets.

Arbitrageur. Arbitrageur would buy the relatively cheap and sell the relatively expensive one.

Arbitration. Process where by an impartial entity determines the relative merit of different viewpoints and makes a decision called an "award". Settlement of claims differences or disputes between one member and another between a member and his clients, authorized clerks, sub-brokers, etc. through appointed arbitrators. It is a 'quasi' judicial process that is faster and is an inexpensive way of resolving dispute. The exchange facilitates the process of arbitration between the members and their clients. The disputes between the parties are resolved through an arbitration in accordance with the bye laws of the exchange.

Area Division. *See* Geographic division.

ARIEL. (Automated Real time Investments Exchange). Computerised dealing system for large scale investors by passing the stock exchange.

Arithmetic Mean. The sum of all items divided by the number of items.

Arm's-length Price. A price between two companies that do not have an ownership interest in each other.

Arm's-length Transaction. Assumes that the parties to it are unrelated such parties may be the main company and its group of companies or subsidiaries or members of the same family. This is done so that neither normal advantage to either party is surrendered, nor extra advantage gained.

Arms Index. It measures the relative strength of volume entering advancing stocks against the strength of volume entering declining stocks, and is calculated as follows: Divide the number of advancing stocks by the number of declining stocks. Then divide the upside volume by the down side volume. Finally divide the first answer by the second result. Readings below 100 are bullish and above are bearish. Extreme readings of 1.50 or higher are very bearish and of 0.50 or lower very bullish. Climax readings would be at 2.00 and 0.30.

Arrangement Regarding International Trade in Textiles. An agreement among government establishing rules on textile trade also known as the multi-fibre arrangement (MFA).

Arrear Age. If interest on bonds or dividends on cumulative preference shares are not paid, the company is said to be in arrear age. Dividends on ordinary shares can't be paid until cumulative dividends on preference shares are paid.

Arrears. Interest and dividends payable on a fixed interest bearing security that were not paid when due.

Art. Practice; skill acquired by experience.

Articles of Association. Drafted along with the MEMORANDUM of association by the promoters of a company. The articles lay down the detailed rules and regulations for managing the companies affairs. This has to be submitted to the Registrar of Companies for approval. The articles are contractual terms between shareholders and directors.

Articles of Co-partnership. A written agreement between partners which sets the relationship between the partners as to contribution, profit, share, authority, etc.

Artifacts. The organization's visible structures and processes that express its culture.

Artificial Intelligence. Programs that seek to make computers able to work—to 'think'—as much like the human mind as possible.

Artificial Person. Though the shareholders own the company, the company has an independent legal existence of its own, distinct from that of its shareholders. It is regarded by law as an independent entity. It is considered to be an 'artificial person' and is attributed by law with most of the legal rights and obligations which normally devolve on an individual person.

Ascending Right Angle Training. It is characterised by a top-line boundary that is horizontal and bottom line that is sloping upward. This formation occurs when demand is growing yet continues to meet supply at a fixed price. If demand continues the supply being distributed at that price will eventually be entirely absorbed by new buyers, and prices will then advance rapidly.

Asch Effect. Giving into a unanimous but wrong opposition.

Ascribed Group Membership. Affiliation determined by birth, such as those based on gender, family, age, caste, and ethnic, racial or national origin.

ASEAN. Association of South-East Asian Nations.

ASEAN Free Trade Area (ASEAN). A free trade area formed by the ASEAN countries on January 1, 1993, with the goal of cutting tariffs on all intra-zonal trade to a maximum of 5 per cent by January 1, 2005.

Ask Price. *See* Average option.

Asked Price. The price at which a share is offered for sale on the floor of the stock exchange. It is the price at which the Jobber will sell. This is countered by the BID price.

Aspirin Count Theory. A light-hearted approach to the market behaviour which states that if aspirin consumption rises in the country about a year later the market will fall and *vice versa*.

Assembly Process. Production process that puts together components.

Assented. Description of stocks or shares where an offer to acquire them or to modify their rights has been accepted.

Assertive Style. Expressive and self enhancing, but does not take advantage of others.

Assessment. Collecting information about employees' behaviour.

Assessment Year. An income tax year, known as the assessment year, is the period of twelve months beginning April of each year and ending on March 31st the next year.

Assessment Centre. A technique to aid the selection and evaluation of potential managers whereby candidates are subject to various tests and exercises and their performance is observed and evaluated by assessors.

Assessment Center Tests. Programs that typically simulate managerial tasks.

Asset Based Lending. Conventional loans made to the extent that they can be secured with tangible assets pledged as collateral.

Asset Financing. This converts assets of a company into liquid cash in exchange for a security interest to be paid to a bank or a financing company, distinct from borrowing from banks. Usually it takes in the form of loans against accounts receivables (which is an asset) but inventories and fixed assets are being mortgaged to raise loans.

Asset Securitization. The packaging and selling of loans and other assets backed by securities issued by a financial institution.

Asset Specific Risk. A risk that affects at most as mall number of assets.

Asset Stripping. Selling off the assets of a company for quick profit, rather than running the company for steady gain. The asset stripper is usually left with a shell company which keeps alive, not for regular business, but for other, usually dishonest purposes, such as tax evasion.

Asset Transfer. Financial claims issued by an FI that are more attractive to investors than the claims directly issued by corporations.

Asset Turnover. The ratio of sales to total assets available.

Asset Value Per Share. The value of the assets of a company on balance sheet after allowing for the repayment of creditors, divided by the number of equity shares in issue.

Assets. Tangible or intangible possessions that have value to a business including cash, accounts receivable, inventory, real estate, patents, trademarks, service marks, copyrights and goodwill.

Assets = Liabilities + shareholders' equity.

Assignment. The purchase of a share in loan syndication with some contractual control and rights over the borrower.

Assimilation. Organizational practices that force minority groups to accept the norms and values of a majority group.

Assimilation Contrast Effects. When comparing prices against a reference price, buyers first judge whether the price being evaluated belongs to the same category as the reference price, then the buyer judges that it is similar (assimilation effect). If the buyer judges that the price belongs to another price category, then the buyer evaluates it as different (contrast effect).

Assimilation Effect. The tendency to bias current judgments in the direction of past judgments.

Associated Company. An associated company is a company owned jointly by two other companies.

Associating Cause and Effect. According to this principle certain costs expire in a particular accounting period because they can be directly associated with specific revenue recognized during that period. Raw material, consumed power, fuel and wages are examples of such costs.

Association of South-East Asian Nations. A free-trade area involving the Asian countries of Brunei, Indonesia, Malaysia, Philippines, Singapore, and Thailand.

Association Power. Power arising from a close relationship with a powerful person.

Asymmetry. The financial marketplace contains pockets of inefficiency in the availability and use of information relevant to the value (price) of assets.

Asymmetric Competition. The situation when buyers respond differently to similar price changes of different com-petitors. A dominant com-petitor (brand) may induce buyers of other brands to switch to it with a price promotion, but price promotions by the other brands may not induce buyers of the dominant brand to switch.

Asymmetric Information. A situation where parties engaged in a transaction have different information. For example, in the loan market, when borrowers have better information about their ability to repay a loan than does the bank.

At a Premium. When a well established company issues new shares, to the public, it may ask for a higher price than that printed on the share certificate, *i.e.* above par.

At Par. When the offer for sale of 'rights' is made at the face value of the shares, they are said to be issued 'at par'.

At the Opening. An order to buy or sell at the opening of trading. This has a much better chance of being executed.

ATPA. Andean Trade Preference Act.

Attention. Being consciously aware of something or someone.

Attention Directing. That function of the accountant's information supplying task which focuses on problems in the operation of the firm or which points out imperfections or inefficiencies in certain areas of the firm's operation.

At-the-money. A term referring to an 'option' when the market value of the asset on which the option is written is equal to the 'strike price' of the option.

Attitude. A person's tendency to feel and behave towards some object in some way.

Attribution. An inference made about one's own feelings or another person's feelings, based on observed behavior.

Auction. An auction is a mechanism utilized by the exchange to fulfil its obligation to a counter party member when a member fails to deliver good securities or make the payment. Through auction the exchange arranges to buy good securities and deliver them to the buying broker or arrange to realize the cash and pay it to the selling broker.

Auction Companies. Do not take title to goods which they offer for sale at public auction to highest bidder.

Auction Method. A method used to sell securities in which buyers file bids and the highest bidders receive securities.

Audit. An examination that is made in accordance with generally accepted auditing standards. Its aim is to give credibility to financial statements.

Auditing. The job of reviewing and evaluating the records used to prepare a company's financial statements.

Auditor's Report. The written description of an auditor's finding together with the auditor's professional opinion regarding the credibility of management's financial statements. Auditor's report informs the shareholders whether the accounts of the company give a true and fair view of the state of the company's finances at the close of the company's accounting year, and of the profits made by the company for the said year.

Authority. It is the right to use resources to accomplish goals and the right to make decisions and to take action acquired to complete an assignment.

Authority, Organizational. *See* Organizational authority.

Authority, Parity with Responsibility. The principle that responsibility for action should not be greater than the authority delegated, nor should it be less. Authority is the discretionary power to carry out assignments and responsibility is the obligation owed a delegate to accomplish these activities.

Authorized Share Capital. The maximum number of shares that a company may issue, stated in the memorandum and articles of association of the company. A company may initially issue fewer shares. The authorized capital can be increased with the consent both of the shareholders and SEBI.

Authorized Unit Trust. A Unit Trust authorized by the development of trade under the provisions of the Preventions of Fraud (Investments) Act 1958.

Autocratic Leader. One man rule.

Autocratic Leadership. Leadership style that involves making managerial decisions without consulting others.

Automated Teller Machines. Machines that give customers the convenience of 24-hour banking at a variety of outlets.

Automatic Debit Transfer. Service provided in the UK by Giro Bank that, for a small charge, allows a business to collect regular sums of money from a large number of customer.

Automatic Rate. Reduction mortgage—mortgages in which the lender automatically lowers the rate on an existing mortgage when prevailing rate fall.

Average. Properly weighted and adjusted arithmetic mean of certain shares to represent general market behaviour of a particular class of shares.

Average Accounting Return (AAR). An investment's average net income divided by its average book value.

Average Collection Period. The average number of days an account receivable is outstanding. A measure of the liquidity of a firm's accounts receivable, calculated as follows.

Average Indeed Monthly Earnings (AIME). Under the OASDI program, the person's actual earnings are indexed to determine his or her primary insurance amount (PIA).

Average Option. An option in which the final payoff is determined by the average price of the asset during a specified period. In a fixed strike average option, the payoff at maturity depends on the difference of the average and a fixed strike price. In a floating strike average option, the payoff at maturity depends on the difference of the spot price and the average.

Average Revenue. Total revenue divided by the number of units sold.

Average Tax Rate. Total taxes paid divided by total taxable income.

Average Total Cost. Total cost divided by the number of units produced and sold.

Averaging Down. The purchase of further holding of shares at lower price (averaging down) or at higher price (averaging up).

Avoidable Cost. Those costs that will not continue if an ongoing operation is changed or deleted.

Avoidance. The act of strengthening a desired behavior by allowing individuals to avoid negative consequences by performing the behavior.

Avoiding Style. A style displaying low assertiveness and low cooperation.

B

B Group. The list of group B shares contains a few active shares, but the vast bulk consists of partially active and inactive ones.

Baby Bonds. Bonds offered by registered friendly societies to minors. The funds are tax exempt.

Baby Boomers. Generation born between 40 and 64 which comprises of 3 out of every 10 Americans today are called baby boomers.

Back End Fee. The fee charged on the unused component of a loan commitment.

Back to Back Lease. Equipment which is leased to a leasing company and then sub-leased to the actual user.

Back Up. When the stock market has backed up it shows a sudden reversal of trend, *i.e.* a sudden fall in a rising market, or a sudden rise in a falling market.

Back-end Load. A kind of redemption charge, that an investor has to pay for withdrawing his money before the date of maturity, applies to time deposits, to discourage investors from withdrawing funds pre-maturely.

Back-to-back Loan. One method of borrowing foreign currency. A deposit in one country is used to obtain a loan in another, financed by a reciprocal transaction.

Backward Induction. A technique used in pricing derivative securities. The value of the option is fist determined at maturity, and then, by working backwards the current value of the derivative is calculated.

Backward Integration. Taking over of a company which produces raw materials or ancillaries by another company, which uses these products to manufacture finished goods. Backward integration guarantees, to a certain extent, quality control, an uninterrupted supply of raw materials and components at a fair price, and timely deliveries.

Backwardation. The carry over charges in the case of the seller is called 'backwardation'.

Bad Account. An account financially very weak and high risky customer.

Bad Debts. Accounts receivable that cannot be collected.

Badla. *Badla* in Hindi means "something in return". This is a process where the buyer who has bought shares in the settlement does not wish to take the delivery of shares but wishes to carry over his purchase to next settlement. The consideration, which he pays (in case of *Sidha Badla*) or receives (in case of backwardation or *Undha Badla*) for such a carry over, is called *badla*.

Bagging the Street. It is concealment of information about the sale of stock from dealers and specialists by institutional investors or broker. Such an information may include reasons why the stock is being sold off, and the number and price of the shares in question.

Bail Bond. Bail bond is an extension of motor insurance, taken out in the UK, that can be used to pay the bail of a UK motorist taken into custody in Spain.

Baile's Customer Policy. Policy that covers the loss or damage to property of customers regardless of a Bailey's legal liability.

Balance. The difference between the total debits and the total credits in an account at any particular time.

Balance Certificate. Certificate representing balance of stocks or shares back to vendor after sale of part only of holding.

Balance Charge. The difference between the sale proceeds and the tax written down value of equipment for tax purposes.

Balance of Goods and Services. The value of a country's exports of merchandise trade minus imports.

Balance of Payments Accounts. National accounts that track both payments to and receipts from foreigners.

Balance of Payments. (1) The difference between money coming into a country (from exports) and money leaving the country (for imports) plus money flows from other factors such as tourism, foreign aid, military expenditures, and foreign investment. (2) An accounting summary of the value of payments between households, firms, and government in one country and the rest of the world.

Balance of Trade. Difference in value, over a period of time, between a country's imports and exports of merchandise. When exports exceed imports, the country has a favourable balance of trade, and when imports exceed exports the balance is unfavourable. Often shortened to BOT.

Balance on Services. That part of the balance of payments accounts that consists of exports and imports of services including such things as military expenditures, tourism, transportation services and investment income such as dividends, interest income and royalties.

Balance Sheet. A financial statement showing the nature and amount of the assets owned by the company, the liability it owes prepared on a given date.

Balance of Trade. The relationship of exports to imports.

Balanced Funds. It is a mutual fund which invests in equity shares, debentures, government bonds, and unit trust certificates so as to balance gain with risk. A balanced fund usually offers a higher yield than a fund which consists only of equity shares (as the yield from good equity shares is usually lower than debenture or bond yields), but its share price rises slowly. In a bear market a balanced fund performs well, whereas in a bull market all-equity shows a faster capital appreciation.

Balanced Schemes. Mutual Fund schemes that aim to provide both growth and income by periodically distributing a part of the income and capital gains they earn. They invest in equities and fixed income securities in the proportion indicated in their offer documents. In a rising stock market, the NAV of these schemes may not normally keep pace. The scheme suits investors looking for a combination of income and moderate growth.

Balance-of-payments Deficits. An imbalance of some specific component within the balance of payments, such as merchandise trade or current, account, that implies that a country is importing more than its exports.

Balance-of-payments Surplus. An imbalance in the balance of payments exists when a country exports more than its imports.

Balloon Maturity. Long-term deposits or investments in which larger repayments are due in the later years.

Balloon Mortgage. Mortgage in which lump has to be paid at the end of the mortgage period to pay off the outstanding principal and interest. It is also called non-amortizing mortgage.

Balloon Options. A Balloon Option is an option that "Balloons" in size once a certain trigger is reached. It is most commonly used in FX markets but can also be used in interest rate, equity and commodity markets.

Balloon Payment Mortgage. Mortgage that requires a fixed monthly interest payment for a three- to five-year period. Full payment of the mortgage principal (the balloon payment) is then required at the end of the principal.

Balloon Payment. A final payment of debt instalment which is considerably larger than the previous payments.

Balloon Stocks. Loans, which are not repaid in fixed instalments. They are repaid as and when funds come in.

Ballot. A random basis of allotment of shares when a new issue has been over subscribed. A typical announcement of allotment on the basis of a ballot works like:

No. of shares applied of	Basis of allotment	No. of shares allotted	No. of allot-tees
100	1 : 37	100	27344
200	1 : 28	100	26532
300-500	2 : 49	100	15641
600-1000	1 : 20	100	10897
and so on			

The above chart shows the allotment in a highly over-subscribed issue.

Band Ke Baad. The prices offered by unauthorised dealers in stocks outside the official hours of the stock exchange.

Bank Borrowings. Banks provide funds for financing a firm's fixed assets. Such loans will be grouped under long-term liabilities. In India, it is a common practice to include both short and long-term borrowings under loan funds.

Bank Charter. Approval from a regulatory agency to form a bank granted by the comptroller of the currency or state banking commission.

Bank Credit. Bank credit includes loans, cash/credits, overdrafts, inland bills, foreign bills purchased, discounted. Bills exclude those re-discounted with RBI and IDBI.

Bank Deposits. A firm can deposit its temporary cash in a bank for a fixed period of time. The interest rate depends on the maturity period. For example, the current interest rate for a 30 to 45 days deposit is about 5% and for 180 days to one year is about 8%. The default risk of the bank deposits is quite low since banks in India are owned by the government.

Bank for International Settlements (BIS). A bank in Basel, Switzerland that facilities transactions among central banks, effectively the central banks.

Bank Loan Sale. Sale of loan originated by a bank with or without recourse to an outside buyer.

Bank Note. A written document issued by a bank and promising to pay the bearer on demand. A note issued by a bank which is payable to the bearer on demand and is intended to circulate as money.

Bank Panic. A period during which banks throughout the banking system face an increased desire for currency by depositors which manifests itself as a widespread withdrawal of deposits from the banking system.

Bank Rate. The rate of interest at which the Reserve Bank of India will lend to the other banks in the country's banking system. It is also known as the minimum lending rate or the base rate.

Bank References. Another source of collecting credit information in the bank where the customer maintains his accounts.

Bank Run. A sudden and unexpected increase in deposit withdrawals from a bank.

Bank-discount Method. The procedure by which US Treasury bills, commercial paper, and bankers' acceptances are calculated. A 360-day year is assumed and there is no compounding of interest.

Banker's Acceptance. A written demand, which has been accepted by a bank, to pay a specified amount on a future date.

Banking Crisis. A loss of confidence in the banking system that leads to a run on banks, as individuals and companies withdrew their deposits.

Banking Holding Companies. Corporations that hold one or more banks.

Banking Structure. The number, relative sizes, and type of banks in a given market or in the industry as a whole.

Bankruptcy. The legal state of being insolvent, incapable of paying debts. Through bankruptcy proceedings under one of several laws, persons or corporations can obtain court-adjudicated relief from certain creditors.

Bar Chart. A chart, using either vertical or horizontal bars, for data presentation.

Bar Trustee. One who holds an asset to the order of the owner. Usually used where a trust has ended permitting a new owner to take control of the asset (*See* Nominee).

Bargain Purchase Option. A provision allowing the lessee, at his option, to purchase the leased asset for a price which is sufficiently lower than the expected fair market value (at the date such option becomes exercisable), the exercise of the option appears, at the inception of the lease, to be reasonably assured.

Bargain Renewal Option. A provision allowing the lessee, at his option, to renew the leased for a rent sufficiently lower than the expected fair rental for the property (when the option becomes exercisable) the exercise of the option appears, at the inception of the lease, to be reasonably assured.

Bargain. A transaction carried out by a stock broker with a jobber.

Bargaining School Theory. A theory holding that the negotiated terms for foreign investors depend on how much investors and host countries need each other's assets.

Bargaining Zone. Range of options between the initial and final offer that each party will consider before negotiations dissolve or reach an impasse.

Barometer. Economic and market data which represent larger trends used in economic forecasting. The more significant data are consumer spending, start in housing and interest rates.

Barometer Stock. A share, usually a blue chip, which is taken to show the state of the stock market. Share is widely held, frequently traded with a stable price record.

Barrier Option. A path dependant option the payoff of which depends on the payoff to an ordinary option and whether a pre-specified barrier has been crossed. Common examples include down-and-in options, down-and-out options, up-and-in options, and up-and-out options.

Barriers of Trade. Practices of nations which restrict the international exchange of goods—quotas, embargoes and tariffs.

Barriers to Entry. Factors that make it difficult or costly for firms to enter an industry or market.

Barter. The exchange of goods and services directly for other goods and services without the use of money.

Base Capital Accord. The Basel Committee on Banking Supervision is a Committee of banking supervisory authorities, which was established by the central bank governors of the group of ten countries in 1975. In the Basel Capital Accord of July 1988 explicit reference is made to off-balance-sheet netting vis-à-vis the same counter party, but not to the offsetting of on-balance-sheet assets and liabilities. Over recent years, certain methods of on-balance-sheet netting have developed and the Basel Committee has decided that the time has come to establish certain principles for the guidance of its members and of other countries.

Base Currency. The currency whose value is implicitly 1 when a quote is made between two currencies. For example, if the cruzeiro is trading at 29692.5 cruzeiros per dollar, dollar is the base currency and the cruzeiro is the quoted currency.

Base Line Data. Pre-intervention data collected by someone other than the target person.

Base Market Value. Average market price of a group of shares at a given time, used for plotting changes in the market indexing.

Base Portfolio. Specific portfolio against which the performance of a managed fund can be compared.

Base Rate. A loan rate used as the basis or foundation determining the size of the current interest rate to be charged to a borrower, such as the prime rate or LIBOR.

Basel Accord. An agreement that requires the imposition of risk-based capital ratios on banks in major industrialized countries.

Basic Balance. The net current account plus long-term capital within a country's balance of payment.

Basic Research Centers. Centers for fundamental research located on regions where valuable scientific knowledge is being created; they develop the basic technologies that become new products.

Basis. The purchase price of an asset for tax purpose. The taxable gain is the difference between the sale price and the basis (usually purchase price plus other expenses less depreciation).

Basis Point. A basis point equals 0.01 per cent or one-hundredth of a percentage point.

Basis Price. The price on which an investor calculates his capital gains when he sells his shares or bonds.

Basle Accord. An inter-national agreement to establish capital adequacy standards for banks.

Bathtub Analogy. The advance-decline line can best be understood by the 'bathtub analogy'. Imagine the market as a bathtub and the water level as represented by the advance decline line. Advancing stocks raise the water level and declining stocks lower the water level.

Bear. A bear is a speculator who takes a pessimistic view of the future. He expects the price of a particular share to fall in the immediate future. He sells the shares which he does not possess at their current market price.

Bear Cycle. An extended period, usually shorter than a bull cycle, when share prices generally keep falling and the stock market indexes keep going down.

Bear Hug. Term used in takeover situation, meaning an indication to the board of a target company that an offer of takeover is under consideration. A strong bear hug is a formal notice to the target company of an intended takeover. A steady bear hug is an indication from a target company that it will favourably consider a takeover, but at a higher price than offered.

Bear Market. A market in which stock prices are moving downward.

Bear Raid. Manipulation by a group of investors or bears selling a large number of shares 'short' in an attempt to bring down their prices. They then keep the difference between their selling price and the new lower price.

Bear Slide. General downward movement of share prices towards conditions characterised by BEAR MARKET.

Bear Speculator. A bear speculator is one who sells the shares in expectation of a fall in price.

Bear Trap. An erratic movement of share price downwards, encouraging investors to SELL SHORT. When the market corrects itself and prices go up, unwary investors get caught in the bear trap. *See* Bull Trap.

Bearer Bond. A bond on which the owners name is not registered but is the property of whoever holds them at a specific time.

Bearer Bonds. Bonds with coupons attached to the bond. The holder presents the coupons to the issuer for payments of interest when they come due.

Bearer Instrument. An instrument in which the holder at maturity receives the principal amount and interest.

Bearer Security. A security does not require the registration of the owner's name in the company's book. The owner's name is not shown on the security certificate also. The transfer of such a security takes place by mere delivery.

Bearish. When the market is dominated by a lot of bear activity and there is a falling trend in prices, the market is said to be 'bearish'.

Beating the Market. Getting a higher return on investments higher than the market average is possible, but difficult, as the market beats, more often than not.

Bed and Breakfast. The selling of a security one day and buying it back on the following day in order to establish a capital gain or loss for tax purposes.

Behavior. Any observable response given by a person.

Behavior Based Appraisal. A subjective evaluation of the way an employee performs job tasks.

Behavior Chart. Program evaluating graph with base line and intervention data.

Behavior Modification. An approach to motivation that uses operant conditioning: operant behavior is learned on the basis of consequences. In management, if a behavior causes a desired outcome (for managers), then it is reinforced (positively rewarded); and because of its consequences, it is likely to be repeated. Thus, behavior is conditioned by adjusting to its consequences.

Behavioral Approach. A view of management that emphasizes understanding the importance of human behavior, needs, and attitudes within formal organizations.

Behavioral Approach to Job Design. The design of jobs based on the view that workers are independent parts of the production process whose individual characteristics should be taken into account in forming jobs.

Behavioral Approach to Management. A body of literature characterized by its concern for human behavior in the work environment. The school's primary means for acquiring knowledge is the scientific method, with emphasis on research. Chronologically, the behavioral approach to management though followed the classical approach. Its first phase was identified with human relations, theory, popular in the 1940s and early 1950s. Its second phase was the behavioral science approach, which came into popular use in the early 1950s.

Behavioral Change. Planned change in the attitudes, skill, and knowledge of organizational personnel.

Behavioral Contingencies. Antecedent >behavior>consequence (A>B>C) relationships.

Behavioral Motivation Theory. The behavioral approach to management advocates the pluralistic view of motivation, which emphasizes that many different needs influence behavior and that man is motivated by the desire to satisfy many needs.

Behavioral Science Approach. This approach to the study of management can be thought of as the study of observable and verifiable human behavior in organizations, using scientific procedures. It draws especially from psychology, sociology, and anthropology.

Behavioral Self Management. Modifying one's own behavior by managing cues, cognitive processes, and consequences.

BARS. Behaviorally Anchored Rating Scales.

Bell Whether Stock. Bell whether literally means a sheep that leads the herd, often bearing a bell, hence a share which assumes a position of market leadership. If it moves up the market is buoyant and if it declines, the market falls. It is not, as some people suppose a share that is supposed to hold firm in stormy conditions.

Bells and Whistles. They are the extras, like options added to a financial product to make it more attractive.

Belly Up. A company in its last stage of existence, likely to go bankrupt soon looks like a dead fish which floats with the belly up.

Below Par. A price lower than the face value of a share.

Bench Marking. Process by which a company compares its performance with that of high performing organizations.

Benefit Cost Ratio. The present value of an investment's future cash flows divided by its initial cost.

Benefit Period. A period of time, typically one to three years, during which major medical benefits are paid after the deductible is satisfied. When the benefit period ends, the insured must then satisfy a new deductible in order to establish a new benefit period.

Benefits. These are rewards available to an employee or group of employees as a part of organizational membership.

Bermuda Option. An option that can only be exercised at a fixed number of intervals over its life. It is a cross between a European and an American option.

Best. An instruction to a broker to deal 'at best' means to deal at the best price obtainable, *i.e.* without imposition of a limit.

Best Efforts Underwriting. An underwriting in which the investment banker acts as an agent rather than a principal that bears risk. The underwriter does not guarantee a price to the issuer and acts more as a placing or distribution agent on a fee basis related to its success in placing the issue.

Best Fit Line. The line drawn through the points on the scanegram that is chosen by a statistical procedure to fit the best straight-line to the scatter of points.

Best Terms. Broker's commission at rates which do not include sharing with an agent.

Beta. Beta is a measure of the percentage change in the price of a stock relative to the percentage change of a market index.

Beta Coefficient or Beta Factor. A measure of performance of a particular share or class of shares in relation to the general movement of the market. If a share has beta of 1 its rise and fall corresponds exactly with the market; with a beta of 2 its rise or fall is double, *i.e.* when the market falls by 10 per cent it falls by 20 per cent with a beta of 0.5, the particular share will rise by only 5 per cent if the market rises by 10 per cent and falls by 5 per cent if the market falls by 10 per cent. Shares with negative beta coefficients are CONTRARIAN SHARES.

Beta Ratio. Relates stock performance to market performance. For a Z per cent change in the market, a stock will tend to change by bZ per cent where b is the stock's beta ratio.

Beta Shares. Listed but infrequently traded, shares of companies with generally low equity capital.

Bid. The offer by a jobber to buy a stock or share. Hence, 'bid price' is the price at which stocks, shares or units in a unit trust can be sold by a holder. (*See* Offer)

Bid and Asked. A 'bid' is the price a prospective buyer is willing to pay whereas 'asked' is the price a seller is willing to accept.

Bid and Offer. Bid is the price of a share prospective buyer is prepared to pay for a particular scrip. Offer is the price at which a share is offered for sale.

Bid Price. It is the price a prospective buyer of a share is prepared to pay on the floor of the stock exchange at a particular auction. This is in response to the jobber's ASKED PRICE.

Bid Spread. The difference between Bid Price and Asked Price.

Bid-ask Spread. *See* Bid Spread.

Bid-up. When demand exceeds supply the trend will be up as buyers 'bid up' the price.

BIFR. Board of Industrial Finance and Reconstruction.

Big Board. The name for the New York Exchange.

Big Eight. The eight largest American Accounting Firms. Arthur Anderson and Co., Coopers and Ly Brand, Ernst and Whinny, Delistle Haskings & Sells, Peat Marwick Mitchell and Co., Price Water House and Co., Touch Ross and Co. and Arthur Young and Co.

Big Ticket Lease. A lease in which the asset's capital cost is very high.

Bill of Exchange. A written order by one party to another party (usually a bank) to pay a third party a specified sum of money. (Also *see* Commercial Bill of Exchange.)

Bill of Lading. A document that is issued to a shipper by a carrier, listing the goods received for shipment. Information on a document issued by a carrier to cover a shipment of merchandise.

Bill of Materials. A specification of the utilities of direct material allowed for manufacturing a given quantity of output.

Bills Discounting. Bills discounting consists of the client drawing bills of exchange for goods and services on buyers, and then discounting it with bank for a charge. Thus, like factoring, bill discounting is a method of financing.

Bills Payable. They are the promises made in writing by the firm to make payment of a specified sum to creditors at some specific date.

Binary Option. *See* Digital Option.

Binary System. A two-digits number system, 0 to 1 used in the digital computer to represent various quantities.

Binder. Authorization of coverage by an agent given before the company has formally approved a policy which provides evidence that the insurance is in force.

Bi-nomial Modal. A model that describes the random evolution of the price of an asset over time. The model assumes that at the end of each interval the asset price can have one of the two possible values.

Bio-degrade. A process of natural decomposition in which a substance is slowly absorbed back into the natural environment.

Bio-feedback. A technique, usually involving the use of instrumentation in which the user attempts to learn to control various bodily functions such as heart rate and blood pressure.

Bio-mass. Any plant or animal material or waste by-products such as wood chips or municipal solid wastes that can be used to generate energy.

Bio-sphere. The land, air, water and natural conditions on which life on earth depends.

BIRPI. *See* International Bureau for the Protection of Industrial Property Rights.

Birth. The initial state when the product is introduced.

BIS. *See* Bank for International Settlements.

BIT. A binary notation, one (1) represents the presence of a value and is called a bit while a zero (0) represents the absence of a value and is defined as a no bit.

Black Book. It refers to the company's pre-planned strategy to be put into action in the event of a hostile take-over bid.

Black Knight. An un-welcomed take-over bidder.

Black Market. The foreign-exchange market that lies outside the official market.

Black Trading. Stock market disaster so named as the first such took place on Friday 24 September 1869.

Black's Model. A model for pricing a futures option using a lognormal distribution for the underlying futures price.

Blackout Period. The period during which social security benefits are not paid to a surviving spouse—between the time the youngest child reaches age 16 and the surviving spouse's sixtieth birthday.

Black-scholes Model. A model for pricing stock options using a lognormal distribution for the underlying stock price.

Blank Sales. Sale of securities by BEARS who do not possess the securities at the movement of selling, but hope to buy them at a lower price when the market has fallen.

Blank Transfer. A blank transfer is made when the seller fills in only his name and signature in the transfer form and does not fill-in the buyer's particulars or the date of sale. The buyer can then sell these shares without registering them in his name. This process may be repeated many times without the shares being sent to the company for making changes regarding their ownership. A record of such transactions can be found on the reverse of the transfer deed where the delivering broker writes his name and the date. It must, therefore, be checked that valid transfers forms have been delivered as the transfer deeds have a limited life of one year or till the date of closure of the register of members, whichever is later.

Block. Fixed assets are referred to as block.

Block Trade. A trade involving 10,000 shares or more often handled by a block trader.

Block Trader. One who assembles orders on the passive side of block trade and manages the transaction.

Block Trades. Trades in a common stock over 10,000 shares.

Blowing the Whistle. *See* Whistle Blowing.

Blow-out. A new issue which is subscribed on the opening day. It is also called out of the window issue.

Blue Chip Stock. Stock of the largest and best known companies in the United States.

Blue Chips. The ordinary shares of leading companies.

Blue Cross Plans. Typically non-profit, community-oriented pre-payment plans that provide health insurance coverage primarily for hospital services.

Blue Fish Clothing. It refers to enhancing job opportunities in native country by not going for cheap labor from outside.

Blue Shield Plans. Typically non-profit pre-payment plans that provide health insurance coverage mainly for physicians' services.

BM&F. Bolsa Mercandily De Futures.

Board of Directors. A group of persons elected by shareholders votes to be responsible for directing the affairs of a corporation, establishing company objectives and policies, selecting top level managers and reviewing company performances.

Board of Governors. Consists of screen members appointed by the US president and conformed by the US senate responsible for monetary policy and regulation of the banking industry by the federal reserve system.

Boat Owners Package Policy. A special package policy for boat owners that combines physical damage insurance, medical expense insurance, liability insurance, and other coverages in on contract.

Body Language. The way people move their bodies, gesture, position themselves, etc. to convey meaning to others.

Boiler Room. 'High pressure' investments selling from small office rooms by a number of smooth-talking salesmen luring suckers on the telephone. The cacophony of their talk in a congested room creates boiler-room conditions.

Bolton Index. It is by the square root of the difference between the ratio of advances to unchanged and the ratio of declining to unchanged a/u-d/u. The analyst calculates this using the unchanged issues as a basic component. The reason for calculating the square root was that it eliminates a strong downword bias.

BFOQ. Bona Fide Occupational Qualification.

Bond. Long-term debt instrument of corporation.

Bond Anticipation Notes. Short-term securities issued by a state or local government to raise funds to begin a project that eventually will be funded using long-term bonds.

Bond Discount. Bonds which are purchased for less than their face value.

Bond Indenture. The legal contract that specifies the rights and obligations of the bond issuer and the bond holders.

Bond Market. In the context of the US, that is a market in which association broker/dealers and banks in a government and federal agency securities, deal in municipal securities, mortgage backed securities, and money market securities.

Bond Premium. A bond for which the buyers pays more than its face value.

Bond Trust. A public mutual fund investing only in government or corporate fixed interest securities. Although the returns are relatively low, the risk to the investor is minimal.

Bond Value. Present value of the coupons + present value of the face amount.

Bond Washing. It is the practice of buying bonds dividends and selling ex-dividend to reduce the rate of tax payable on the transaction. The dividends on the bond becomes a capital gain on which a lower rate of tax is payable than if the tax were paid on the proceeds as dividend income.

Bonded Warehouse. A building or part of a building used for the storage of imported merchandise under the supervision of US Customs Service and for the purpose of deferring payment of customs duties.

Bonfire Occupational Qualification (BFOQ). It is a legitimate reason why an employer can exclude persons on otherwise illegal bases of consideration.

Bonus Plan. A payment system to provide an incentive for employees to produce more and thus earn more.

Bonus Shares. Sometimes companies capitalize a part of their reserves by the issue of "bonus" shares. Bonus shares are issued free of cost to the existing shareholders in proportion to their existing shareholding. This results in an increase in the paid-up capital of the company. Since bonus shares are issued free of cost, they do not bring-in any additional funds to the company. The issue of bonus shares is essentially a book transfer, thereby a certain sum of money, representing the amount capitalised, is transferred from a company's reserves to the accounting head, share capital. Bonus shares have the effect of increasing the shareholding of each shareholder without any change in the proportionate ownership of the company.

Book. The day-to-day records of a jobber of shares bought and sold.

Book Closure and Record Date. When a company declares a dividend or announces a bonus share or right issue or wants to convey a meeting of the shareholders, it becomes necessary to freeze the list at a point of time to take stock of the shareholders entitled to the benefit. This is known as closure of register of members or just book closure. During the period of book closure, no transfer of share is undertaken by the company.

Book Debt. Debt recorded in an account book.

Book Keeping. Systematic keeping of books of accounts.

Book Loss or Profit. A loss or profit on paper, not realized.

Book Loss. Loss not actually sustained as the investor hasn't sold when the price has fallen. Book loss induces some depression of mind, but does not actually pinch the investor's pocket unless, of course, the book loss keeps mounting and the investor is forced to sell at a consider-able loss, if he can sell at all.

Book Profit. As a noun, unrealised profit when shares which an investor holds have appreciated in price, but the shareholder has not sold any. It induces a sense of well-being without bringing in any tangible profit. It is only in the verbal use of the term, *i.e.* to sell shares when they have appreciated in price. Hence, the stock market adage; unbooked profit is only book profit.

Book Value Method. *See* Accounting rate of return.

Book Value of Equity Shares.

$$*F = \frac{\text{Total value of equity share capital + reserves and surplus}}{\text{Total number of equity shares}}$$

This value indicates the asset coverage that each equity share represents in the company. It represents the net-worth of assets that each share commands.

Book Value. Book value per share indicates the portion of shareholders' funds, that accrue to each equity share. It is an evaluation of shareholders' funds on a per share basis.

$$\frac{\text{Equity share capital + Shareholders' reserves}}{\text{Total no. of equity shares subscribed}}$$

Book-entry Form. The method by which marketable US treasury securities are issued, with the buyer receiving only receipt, rather than engraved certificate, indicating that the purchase is recorded on the Treasury's books or records her approved location.

*F = Female.

Booking Centre. An offshore financial centre whose main function is to act as an accounting centre in order to minimize the payment of taxes.

Booking Profit. Making profit by selling a share which has gone above its purchase price. When shares, which an investor holds, go up in price the investor has made only a notional profit, which is meaningless, except in a DRY RUN PORTFOLIO. He makes some tangible profit only when sold.

Book-strap. It is a cash offer for controlling stake in a company which if accepted, is followed by another (usually at a lower price) for the reminder of the shares.

Boom. In boom condition the frequency and volume of share market transactions reach a very high level. As a result, almost every share listed on the stock exchange becomes an active share.

Boots Trap Acquisition. Term used in connection with a friendly takeover. Threatened with a hostile takeover the target company exchanges some of its assets for shares held by dissident shareholders. Then the target company sells the rest of the company to a friendly acquirer. The friendly acquirer thus gets 100 per cent of the target company for less than he would have paid otherwise. The target company has virtually helped finance part of the takeover.

BOP. Balance of Payments.

Borrowed Capital. The money raised from outsiders is called 'borrowed capital'.

Borrowed Reserves. Reserves that banks borrow from the federal government and other depository institutions without collateral.

Borrowing. The change in liabilities outstanding reported by a sector or unit in the economy over a specified time period.

Bottom Line. Business profits or losses usually reported in figures on the late or bottom line of a company's income statement.

Bottom Out. When shares have hit their lowest and are slowly rising they are said to be on their path of recovery where they are bottomed out.

Bottom-up Approach to Investing. Looking for individual shares with outstanding performances or potential without considering economic trends, on the assumption that individual companies can still do well, even though the industry to which they belong may not be doing well. The companies are often chosen with the help of fundamental analysis, research reports or personal knowledge of their products. Its opposite is TOP-DOWN investing.

Bottom-up Budgeting. Financial planning by those employees more directly engaged in the actual tasks being covered and in which information flows up from the lower levels of an organization for review by top management.

Bottom-up Investing. An investment strategy that considers the fundamental factors driving individual stock performance before considering the economic prospects affecting the industry wish in which that company operates.

Boundaries. *See* Systems, boundaries.

Boundary Agent Role. A work role that links an organization with its environment.

Boundary Condition. The payoff to derivative security at expiration or at an exercise date.

Boundary-spanning Roles. Group behaviors involving interaction with members in other units of the organization or outside the organization.

Bounded Discretion. A condition in which decision makers are limited to a subject of the possible alternatives.

Bounded Rationality. Rational action limited because of lack of information, lack of time, or ability to analyze alternatives in the light of a goal sought, unclear goals, or the human tendency not to take risks in making a decision, to play it safe. *See* also Satisfying.

Boutique. Relatively new form of financial services company, operating in much the same way as a high street shop into which customers walk to seek investment advice and service. It is also known as a financial super-market.

Brainstorming. An approach to improve problem discovery and solving by encouraging unfettered suggestions and ideas, usually from a group of individuals.

Branch (Foreign). A foreign operation of a company that is not a separate entity from the partner that owns it.

Branch Banking. A type of banking organization in which services are sold through multiple offices, all owned and operated by the same corporation.

Branch Office System. Type of life insurance marketing system under which branch offices are established in various areas. Salaried branch managers, employees of the company are responsible for hiring and training new agents.

Branch Store. An extension of a retailing outlet, usually a downtown store opening a new store to compete with other stores in shopping centre and operating under the same policies as the parent store.

Brand. A particular good identified with a company by means of name, logo, or other method, usually protected with a trademark registration.

Brandy Bond. A bond that is swapped for an outstanding loan to a less developed country (LDC).

Bread and Breakfast Deal. Transaction formerly used to minimize the impact of capital gains tax. A shareholder sold his or her holding at loss after the trading closed for the day, and registered the loss for tax purposes. Next morning, the shareholder bought his or her holding back. The tax advantages of the same were withdrawn from the UK in 1998. The US term for bed-and-breakfast deal is swap.

Breadth of the Market. Indicated by the percentage of shares involved in an upward or downward movement of the stock market. If two-thirds of the shares listed in a stock exchange participate during a trading session, the market is said to have a good breadth, *i.e.* the trend it shows is representative, and is not influenced by the price of a few heavily traded shares.

Break Forward. A foreign exchange forward contract where one party has the right, but not the obligation to terminate the contract at one or more predetermined times during the life of the transaction. It is also known as a cancelable forward. The interest rate version of the Break Forward is known as a cancelable swap.

Break Out. When the price breaks out of the range of resistance levels, it moves either up or down beyond the resistance levels. Such level, *i.e.* price level is called break out.

Break Up Value of Shares. The net asset or net-worth of the company, divided by the number of shares issued.

Break Way Gap. They occur as prices break away from an area of congestion. Typically prices will break away from an ascending or descending triangle with a gap. The gap implies that the change in sentiment has been strong and that the ensuing move will be powerful.

Break-even Analysis. Break-even analysis is a specific way of presenting and studying the interrelationships among costs, volume and profits. It provides information to management in a most lucid and precise manner. The break-even point is the point of sales and volume at which total revenue is equal to total cost. It is a no-profit-no-loss point.

Break-even Point Analysis. Charting and analyzing relationships usually between sales and expenses to determine at what size or volume point an operation breaks even between a loss and a profit it can be used in any problems area where marginal effects can be pinpointed.

Bretton Woods Agreement. An agreement among IMF countries to promote exchange rate stability and to facilitate the international flow of currencies.

Bretton Woods. Under this fixed exchange rate system the United States agreed to peg the US dollar to a given amount of gold and other nations pegged their currency to the US dollar.

Bribe. Something of value given to someone in power to influence materially that person's decision.

Broad Money. Money held for spending.

Broadening Formations. They usually have bearish implications. They appear frequently at tops. The theory is that five minor reversals are followed by a substantial decline. Reversals 3 and 5 occur at successively higher points than first top and reversal 4 occurs at a lower point than reversal 2. Broadening Top formation usually suggests a market that is lacking support from the 'smart money' and is beyond control. During the early stages of the formation, well informed selling is completed and in the latter pages less informed will participate. The prices are unpredictable and volume is irregular as to which direction the breakout goes.

Broker. Someone who legally represents the insured, soliciting or accepting applications for insurance that are not in force until the company accepts the business.

Broker (in Foreign Exchange). Specialists who facilitate transactions in the interbank market.

Broker dealers. Firms that assist in the trading of existing securities.

Brokerage Firms. Firms which link buyers and sellers of financial assets.

Brokered Deposits. Wholesale CDs obtained through a brokerage house.

Brownian Motion. A stochastic process the increments of which are normally distributed with zero mean and variance proportional to time

BSE. Bombay Stock Exchange.

Bubble. When stock prices are pushed up to an abnormally high level unsupported by any fundamentals, it is said to have developed a bubble. The market crash on 11 and 12 May 1992 which in two days trading burst the bubble of 4,546 points reached on 2 April 1992 observed on 2 May 1992 that the Indian stock markets had the fun a bubble about to burst.

Bubble Concept. A pollution control plan that determines compliance by measuring combined total emissions from an industrial installation, rather than from each of the plants individual pollution sources.

Bucket Shop. A brokerage firm which is not a member of the recognised stock exchange. The term formerly used to describe a low ginmill where beverages were dispensed in small amounts in buckets.

Budget. A statement of plans and expected results expressed in numerical terms, a "numberized" programme.

Budget Deficit. A government's financial position in which current expenditures exceed current revenues.

Budget Summary. A master summary of operating and capital budgets, usually with a forecast income statement and balance sheet.

Budget Surplus. A government's financial position in which current revenues exceed current expenditures.

Budget Variance. The difference between an actual and a budget amount. Also see control budget variance.

Budget Zero-base. *See* Zero-Base budgeting.

Budget, Programme. *See* Programme budgeting.

Budgeting. The process of establishing formal, written plans to control the availability and cost of financial resources.

Budgets, Variable or Flexible. *See* Variable budgets.

Budliwalla. The member who finances those carry-over transactions is called a 'budliwalla'.

Buffers. Resources or administrative changes that reduce burnout.

Buffer-stock System. A partially managed system that utilizes stocks of commodities to regulate their prices.

Build-operate-transfer (BOT). This is an arrangement in which private entity is responsible for the financing, construction and operation of an infrastructure facility for a specific period after which the facility is transferred to the government.

Bulge Bulge. Sudden, short-lived price rise that may apply to the entire stock market or an individual share.

Bull. A bull is a speculator who takes an optimistic view of the future. He expects the price of a particular share to rise in the immediate future. Therefore, he buys these shares at their current prices with the hope of selling them subsequently at higher prices.

Bull Charge. Bull pushing up share prices vigorously.

Bull Cycle. An extended period during which share prices are generally rising and the stock market indices show an upward trend. *See* Bull & Bear Cycle.

Bull Market Terms. Shoot up, show an uptrend, rise, soar, gain, gain smartly, rally, move up, firm up, flare up, lump, turn, bullish, lookup, upswing, improved sentiments, bears covering short sales, escalate go up, shoot up, boom.

Bull Market. The primary trend usually consists of three phases. In first phase known as 'accumulation' business conditions are poor and the public is generally discouraged with the stock market. The business conditions and corporate earnings begin to improve in second phase. The third phase is characterised by highly publicized 'good news'. Price gains are often spectacular and the public becomes heavily involved.

Bull Speculator. A speculator who purchases shares in expectation of a rise in price is called a bull speculator.

Bull Trap. An erratic movement of share prices upwards, encouraging investors to buy in antici-pation of further rise in prices when the market corrects itself. The prices come down, trapping unwary investors. *See* Bear Trap.

Bullish. The bull is said to "buy long" as opposed to the bear who sells "short" when the stock market is dominated by a lot of bull activity and there is a rising trend in prices, the market is said to be "bullish". And the market is referred to as a "bull market".

Bundesbank. The German Central Bank.

Bureau Exercise Prices or Different Expiry Dates.

Bureau for the protection of industrial property rights.

Bureaucracy. An organizational design that relies on specialization of labor, a specific authority hierarchy, a formal set of rules and procedures, rigid promotion and selection criteria.

Bureaucratic Control. An attempt to control the firm's overall functioning through formal, mechanistic and structural arrangements.

Burglary. Taking of property from within the premises by someone who unlawfully enters or leaves the premises, with marks of forcible entry or exit.

Burn Out Turnaround. Rebuilding the fortunes of a company which would otherwise go in for liquidation.

Burn Rate. The rate at which a new enterprise uses up its venture capital.

Burying the Body. Concealing unpleasant financial facts in a mass of figures and misleading headings on a balance sheet. "Miscellaneous," or "sundries" are such headings which may conceal the fact of bad investments or product failures.

Business and Society. The study of relationship of business with its entire social environment.

Business Credit Institutions. Finance companies specializing in business loans.

Business Cycle. Fluctuations in economic activity, with the economy passing alternately through expansionary (boom) and reversionary (depressed) periods.

Business Cycle Index. An index that indicates the position of the economy on a business cycle.

Business Ethics. The application of general ethical principles to business behaviour.

Business Income Converge Form. Business income form drafted by the Insurance Services Office to cover the loss of business income regardless of whether the income is derived from retail or service operations, manufacturing, or rents.

Business Infrastructure. The basic underlying structure of facilities and services essential to the operation of a market based business system, including a monetary system, standard weights and measures transportation networks, a legal system to make and enforce laws.

Business Level Strategy. The area of responsibility usually assigned to the divisional-level managers.

Business Owners Policy. Package policy specifically designed to meet the basic property and liability insurance needs of smaller business firms in one contract.

Business Plan. A written report that provides an overview and analysis of a proposed business. The plan is the basis of or presentations to prospective investors in the business.

Business Risk. The dispersion in the probability distribution of a firm's earnings before interest and taxes.

Business Units. *See* Strategic business units.

Business. The activity of organizing resources in order to produce and distribute goods and services for society.

Busted Bonds. Certificates of securities issued by famous companies which have gone into liquidation or countries which have repudiated their debts (*e.g.* Russian or Chinese bonds). Bought in hope of eventual repayment, or more commonly as collectors' items.

Butterfly. A term used in options trading. The strategy comprises simultaneous buying and selling call options.

Butterfly Spread. A combination of a vertical bull spread and vertical bear spread with the same expiration date on all options and the same strike price on all short options.

Buy and Hold Strategy. Accumulating shares of a company over the years for long-term growth benefits and foremost capital gains tax on profits. This requires far less of the investor's time, than the buy and sell strategy, which means trading frequently in shares.

Buy and Sell Strategy. Active share trading strategy in which shares are bought at dips and sold at peaks. Since the lowest dip and highest peak are seldom identified, it amounts to buying low and selling high, not holding on to a share or shares for long. As such a strategy results in short term gains, the government claims nearly half the profits in income tax.

Buy Back. Repurchase of convertible or non-convertible debentures or the non-convertible part a partly convertible debentures before the stipulated period, at par or at a discount, by companies or banks. Buy back promises, however, should be lightly taken, as companies devise methods to keep the sellers at bay.

Buy Cheap and Sell Dear. It is one of the most frequently quoted maxims in the share market. Buying a share at cheap or low price and selling at high price seems to be the most obvious way of making money. Share prices are high or low because there is a reason for it.

Buy Local Legislation. Laws that are intended to favour the purchase of domestically sourced goods or services over imported ones, even though the imports may be a better buy.

Buy Order. The buy order executed by the buyer to the broker (stock broker). It contains the name of the company, the number of equity shares intended to be bought and instructions regarding the price at which they are to be bought.

Buy Out. Buying the controlling shareholding of a company to takeover its assets and business. A buy out can be made through negotiations or through accumulation of shares from the stock market or purchase of shares of a major shareholder. When money is borrowed from financial institutions to finance the purchase, it is called a leveraged buy out in which case the loan is repaid from cash generated by the company's business or from the sale of its assets.

Buy Zone. A parallel line equidistant between the basic trend line and return line forming upper channel and lower channel. The lower channel is called 'buy zone'. A return line can also be used to forewarn an impending change in trend. When prices move up to the area of the return line. One can consider the market is weakening.

Buying Climax. If the situation characterises with criteria which are similar to those of the selling climax, *i.e.* Advancing issues account for 70 per cent or more of total issues and declining issues 15 per cent or less. Buying climax takes place generally near intermediate bottoms and is often followed by new high, its significance is not as great as a selling climax.

Buying the Book. Buying up all the shares on a JOBBER'S account book at the current ASKED PRICE, usually under instruction from a financial institution or a stock broker acting on behalf of someone trying to accumulate a particular share.

Buy-sell Decision Rules. The rules are very simple, but it requires careful analysis to arrive at the real value of a share.

Rule 1. If the price of a share is lower than its value, *buy*.

Rule 2. If the price of a share is higher than its value, *sell*.

Rule 3. If the price of a share equals its value, *hold*.

C

C.L. Lot. Carload lot. The rate charges for shipping a full rail car of freight.

C.V. = C.R. × share price.

C-4 Ratio — (Concentration Ratio). In the total market sales, the share of top 4 firms is referred to as C-4 ratio.

CACM. *See* Central American Common Market.

Cafeteria Plan. Generic term for an employee benefit plan that allows employees to select among the various group life, medical expense, disability, dental, and other plans that best meet their specific needs. Also called flexible benefit plans.

Cafeteria Style Benefit Plans. Benefit plans in which employees choose the types and amount of benefits.

Calculated Intangible Value. It is the ability to use tangible assets to outperform other companies in the industry that have similar assets.

Calendar Year Deductibles. Amount payable by an insured during a calendar year before a group or individual health insurance policy begins to pay for medical expenses.

Call. An option to purchase an asset at a set price at some particular time in the future.

Call Feature of Bond or Preferred Stock. Option available to company to repurchase securities at set price over pre-specified period.

Call Money. Instalment in paying for new issues when requested by the company. When all the calls have been paid the share is endorsed as fully paid up. Shareholders then have to send the certificates to the company for endorsement, with proof of payment of call money.

Call Money Market. The inter bank call money market is the cone of the formed money market banks borrow from the call money market in order to meet sudden demand for funds for payments and 1-0 obtain funds to meet any likely short talk in their cash reserve to meet the CRR application or in liquid assets required to be held to meet the SLR stipulation.

Call Option. Gives a buyer the right to buy a financial asset at a specified price up to a specified expiration date. An option giving the buyer the right to purchase the underlying asset at a fixed strike price.

Call Premium. The additional yield purchasers of callable bonds must receive in order to be willing to be exposed to call risk.

Call Privileges. The provision often found in a bond's contract (indenture) that permits the borrower to retire all or a portion of a bond issue by buying back the securities in advance of their maturity.

Call Protected. Bond during period in which it cannot be redeemed by the issuer.

Call Provision. A stipulation in a bond or preferred stock contact enabling the issuing firm to call back (repurchase) the outstanding bond or preferred stock at a predetermined price.

Call Risk. The risk that a bond will be called.

Callable Bonds. Bonds that the issuer may call or redeem after a specified period.

Callable Swap. An interest rate swap where one party has the right to cancel the swap at a certain time without any additional costs.

Called-up Capital. Of the issued share capital, the entire amount may not be called-up. If some Rs. 5/- (say) is called-up for payment out of Rs. 10/- (face value), that portion is known as called-up capital. And the balance which is not yet called for payment is known as uncalled-up capital.

Calls-in-arrear. Out of the called-up capital, on the date of balance sheet, some amount may be outstanding. Such amount not yet paid by the shareholder is known as called-in-arrear amount. The amount that has been received by the company is known as called the paid-up amount. Some shareholders instead of paying the called-up capital they may pay the full amount. This supplies amount which has not yet been called for by the company, but has been paid in advance is known as the calls-in-advance amount.

Cambridge Constant. The reciprocal of velocity.

Cambridge Theory of Money Demand. Asserts that people have two motives for holding money: (a) to make transaction, (b) to create wealth.

Canada-U.S. Free Trade Agreement. An agreement enacted in 1989, establishing a free-trade area involving the United States and Canada.

Cap. A series of European interest rate call options often used by a party that has issued a floating rate note. The cap ensures that the effective interest rate paid on the debt is capped at a fixed rate.

Cap and Collar Mortgage. Mortgage with fixed upper and lower limits of the variable interest rates.

Cap Financing. It is the financing provided by a second lender to borrower when the financing provided by the first lender is insufficient.

Capacity. The maximum load that an organizational unit can carry or operate at a given point in time.

Capacity Utilization. When plant and machinery are installed they have a rated capacity, *i.e.* under optimum utilization they can produce certain quantity of goods working a single shift. The rate of utilization of that plant capacity is expressed in percentage. The nature of demand for the company's product often regulates capacity utilization sometimes, owing to a glut of commodity in the market, *e.g.* fertilizer industry, the government regulates capacity utilization when there are no such controls, a low capacity utilization is generally bad news for the company under conditions of a seller's market, a company may achieve more than 100 per cent capacity utilization by working more than one shift.

Capital. In accounting, this word is too general by itself. In most cases, capital implies owners' equity. Money generated by long-term debt is also often called capital.

Capital Account. That portion of the balance of payments which keeps track of investment by US firms, households, and government, overseas investments by foreigners in the US.

Capital Accumulation. The amount of funds a firm can accumulate to provide for the operation of the business.

Capital Adequacy Ratio (CAR). This is a measure of the amount of bank's capital expressed as a percentage of its risk weighted credit exposures. Two types of capital are measured—tier one capital which can absorb losses without a bank being required to cease trading, *e.g.* ordinary share capital, and tier two capital which can absorb losses in the event of a winding up and so provides a lesser degree of protection to depositors, *e.g.* subordinated debt. The higher the capital adequacy ratio the bank has, the greater the level of unexpected losses it can absorb before becoming insolvent.

Capital Allowance. The amount of depreciation allowed by the income tax to be offset against taxable profits.

Capital Asset. An asset with a life of more than one year that is not bought and sold in the ordinary course of business.

Capital Asset Pricing Model. A model used to estimate the required, and expected, rate of return on an asset. The model presumes that the required rate of return is equal to the risk less rate of interest plus a risk premium dependent on the asset's systematic risk. It is also used to estimate the cost of equity capital of a firm. A theory which shows the relationship between risk and return for efficient and inefficient portfolios.

Capital Budget. A statement showing the forecast of cash receipts, cash disbursements, and net cash balanced over a period of time.

Capital Budgeting. The process of determining the investments a firm should make. The investments normally have a life of more than one year.

Capital Controls. Restrictions on cross-border capital flows that segment different stock markets; limit amount of a firm's stock a foreigner can own, and limit a citizen's ability to invest outside the country.

Capital Costs. An alternate term for fixed costs, emphasizing the fact that fixed costs are needed in order to provide operating facilities and an organization ready to produce and sell at a planned volume of activity.

Capital Distribution. A distribution by a company out of capital profits, or by way of reduction in the nominal value of the capital.

Capital Employed. Net assets used in a business to make profits.

Capital Flight. Movement of large sums of money from one country to another, or within a country from one state to another, to find a more congenial investment climate. The flight may take place because of political uncertainties, high inflation, labour unrest, military *dictatorship* or violence in general.

Capital Gain. The increase in the value of an asset over and above the cost of obtaining that asset. Gains made from capital transactions, *e.g.* buying and selling of financial securities and real estate.

Capital Gains Yield. The dividend growth rate or the rate at which the value of an investment grows.

Capital Gearing or Capital Leverage. *See* Leverage.

Capital Intensity Ratio. A firm's total assets divided by its sales, or the amount of assets needed to generate $ 1 in sales.

Capital Intensive. A project that requires large investments in capital assets especially machinery and equipment is called capital intensive. Automobiles, oil refineries, and steel production are capital intensive and may keep the investor waiting for rewards, unless these make a high profit within a short time or keep the cost of borrowing low. Capital intensive may also mean high proportion of fixed assets to labour or raw materials.

Capital Issue. The issue of shares by a company, whether new issue or premium issue or rights issue.

Capital Lease. A lease in the US is classified and accounted for by a lessee as a capital lease if it meets any of the following criteria: (a) The lease transfers ownership to the lessee at the end of the lease term; (b) The lease contains an option to purchase property at a bargain price; and (c) The lease term is equal to 75 per cent or more of the estimated economic life of the property (exceptions for used property leased towards the end of its useful life).

Capital Loss. Loss incurred when investments are sold at a price lower than the purchase price. If the sale is within a year of the purchase, it is a short-term capital loss. If it is after an year, long-term capital loss is sustained. In income tax returns long-term capital losses can only be set off against long-term capital gains. Whereas short-term capital losses can be set off against short-term capital gains, or against current income from other sources.

Capital Market. Source from which long-term capital is raised for the selling up and sustained growth of companies. The stock exchange is a part of the capital market, not only because it readily provides money for new or existing ventures, but also because it helps investors to trade in their shares and maintain the liquidity of investments. Investment in public and rights issues, convertible and non-convertible debentures, therefore, becomes an attractive propositions and companies are also to raise the resources they need. The capital market is distinct from money market (blanks and leading institutions) which provides short term finance.

Capital Market Instrument. A money market instrument with a maturity of more than one year.

Capital Productivity. The ratio of outputs to capital used in production.

Capital Rationing. Refers to a situation where the firm is constrained for external or self-imposed reasons to obtain necessary funds to invest in all investment projects with positive NPV. Under capital rationing the management has not simply to determine the profitable investment opportunities but it has to decide to obtain that combination of the profitable projects which yield highest NPV within the available funds.

Capital Redemption Reserve Fund. When a company redeems its preference shares, the nominal value of the shares is put in this fund, which becomes part of the paid up capital of the company, with no obligation to pay dividend although the fund can be used towards issuing bonus shares.

Capital Retention Approach. A method used to estimate the amount of life insurance to own. Under this method, the insurance proceeds are retained and are not liquidated.

Capital Structure. The mix of debt and equity maintained by a firm.

Capital Structure of Companies. The capital of a new company consists of issued and subscribed equality shares; redeemable preference shares and secured and unsecured loans. When the company is making profits, that part of profits remaining undistributed among the shareholders is transferred to reserves and becomes part of the capital structure. *See* Financial Structure.

Capital Surplus. The difference between the nominal or face value of shares sold by a company to the public and the sum realized by selling them as a PREMIUM ISSUE.

Capital to Asset Ratio. Ratio of an FI's core capital to its assets.

Capital Transfer Tax. A cumulative tax applied to gifts made during a lifetime and assets left at death.

Capital Turnover. Annual sales divided by paid up equity, studied over a period shows the extent to which a company can grow without additional capital investment.

Capitalism. An economic system wherein the natural laws of supply and demand and free competition within the marketplace will efficiently regulate the flow of resources within a society.

Capitalization. Conversion of FREE RESERVES of a limited company into capital by issuing bonus shares.

Capitalization of Earnings. A business term used to identify the process by which a business is valued on its income-earning potential. Future net income is evaluated by estimating the rate of earning power of a certain investment.

Capped Mortgage. It is a mortgage with a fixed upper limit to its variable interest rate.

Captive Finance Company. Usually a wholly owned subsidiary of a consumer product company to finance purchases from the parent company. Some automobile finance companies belong to this category.

Captive Fund. Fund wholly owned by a larger body than individual entrepreneurs.

Captive Insurer. Insurance company established and owned by a parent firm in order to insure its loss exposures while reducing premium cost, providing easier access to a re-insurer, and perhaps easing tax burdens.

Captive Market. A market waiting for a particular product, its demand, considerably outstripping the supply. Also a product for which there is an assured buyer.

Care Perspective. Involves compassion and an ideal of attention and response to need.

Career. It is the sequence of work-related positions occupied throughout a person's life.

Career Average Formula. Pension plan pays retirement benefits based on the employee's average salary over the entire period of employment.

Career Path. Beginning with a particular job, the sequence of jobs involved in promotion and advancement.

Career Planning. The process of systematically matching an individual's career aspirations with opportunities for achieving them.

Career Plateau. The point or stage of a career at which the individual has no opportunity for further promotion or advancement.

Career Stages. Distinct but interrelated steps or phases of a career including the pre-work stage, the initial work stage, the stable work stage, and the retirement stage.

Cargo Insurance. Type of ocean marine insurance that protects the shipper of the goods against financial loss if the goods are damaged or lost.

Caribbean Community and Common Market (Caricom). A customs union in the Caribbean region.

Carry Forward. A speculator may carry forward the transaction if he feels that the share price will further make bigger profit by holding. In such case he may ask his broker to carry forward his transaction to the next account if he is not willing to pay for the transaction.

Carry Over Margin. The amount which operators must deposit in order to carry over their transaction from one SETTLEMENT period to another. Stock exchange authorities periodically impose such margins in order to curb excessive speculation. The margin varies in amount based on the level of speculative activity and may be imposed either on bulls or bears or both.

Carrying Costs. The costs incurred by carrying an inventory. They include such costs as the taxes and insurance on the goods in inventory, interest on money invested in inventory and storage space, and the costs incurred because of the obsolescence of the inventory.

Cartel. A restrictive trade association of a number of companies bonding a market by carrying it up among themselves, reaching an agreement to peg prices at certain levels, controlling supplies, etc. so as to check unfair profits. OPEC is an example of an oil cartel.

Cascade Tax. Tax imposed at each stage of production. For instance, a company may pass on from one country to another as each stage of production is carried out and attracts taxation at each stage of production.

Case Study. In-depth study of a single person, group, or organization.

Cash Basis. A process of accounting whereby revenue and expense recognition depend solely on the timing of various cash receipts and disbursements.

Cash Break-even Point. When eliminated the non-cash item from revenues and costs the break-even point on cash basis can easily be computed. In most cases depreciation would be the non-cash expense included in fixed costs.

Cash Budget. Cash budget is the most important component of financial budgets. The major objective of the cash budget is to plan cash in such a way that the company always maintains sufficient cash balance to meet its needs and uses the idle cash in the most profitable manner.

Cash Concentration. The practice of and procedure for moving cash from multiple banks into the firm's main accounts.

Cash Coverage Ratio. (EBIT + Depreciation)/Interest.

Cash Cow. A share which yields consistently high rate of dividends. Also a currently profitable business but one which does not have very bright growth prospects and is, therefore, used to fund other enterprises.

Cash Credit. An arrangement whereby the bank allows the borrower to borrow upto a certain limit, the cash credit limit.

Cash Cycle. The time between cash disbursement and cash collection.

Cash Delivery. A relatively new procedure for settling future obligations is cash delivery. This procedure is a substitute for physical delivery. The mechanism of cash delivery is that the price of the relevant contract at the close of trading.

Cash Discount. A reduction from invoice price offered to a customer who pays on or before a designated point in time.

Cash Flow. A general term that must be interpreted carefully. Most strictly, cash flow means inflows or outflows of cash. Frequently, the term is used loosely to represent funds provided by operations.

Cash Flow Equivalent. A stream of cash flows that has the same value as another asset.

Cash Flow from Assets. The total of cash flow to creditors and cash flow to stockholders, consisting of the following: operating cash flow, capital spending, and additions to net working capital.

Cash Flow Process. The process of cash generation and disposition in a typical business setting.

Cash Flow Time Line. Graphical representation of the operating cycle and the cash cycle.

Cash Flow to Creditors. A firm's interest payments to creditors less net new borrowings.

Cash Flow to Stockholders. Dividends paid out by a firm less net new equity raised.

Cash Flow Statement. A financial statement that accounts for actual cash received and spent in the course of doing business. Cash budgets are used to describe money received and spent.

Cash Investment. An investment which can be converted back into the money (originally invested) on demand in short notice.

Cash List. Group B securities, unspecified shares or non-cleared securities.

Cash Management Account. Money market mutual fund sold by investment bank that offer check writing privileges.

Cash Market. It is referred to as the actual or spot market, where the commodities themselves are bought and sold on a negotiated basis. Most of the time, the contract calls for the actual delivery of a commodity.

Cash Offer. A cash offer is a straightforward means of financing a merger. It does not cause any dilution in the E.P.S. and the ownership of the existing shareholders of the acquiring company. It is also unlikely to course wide fluctuations in the share prices of merging companies. The shareholders of the target company get cash for selling their shares to the acquiring company.

Cash Profit. Profit arrived before depreciation and tax are deducted.

Cash Ratio. The ratio of cash and marketable securities to current liabilities. The ratio indicates how soon a company can pay back its creditors.

Cash Refund Annuity. The balance is paid in one lump to the beneficiary after the death of the annuitant, if total payments are not completed.

Cash Reserves. Vault cash and cash deposits held at the Federal Reserve.

Cash Settlement. Settlement for the purchase of an investment which is due.

Cash Shares. *See* Non-cleared securities.

Cash Surrender Value. Field of insurance that covers whatever is not covered by fire, marine, and life insurance. Includes automobile, liability, burglary and theft, workers compensation, and health insurance.

Cash Surrender Value. The accumulated savings element of a life insurance policy that can be recovered on cashing in the policy or borrowed against a specified interest rate.

Cash-and-carry. An investment strategy that duplicates the payoff to a forward contract.

Cash-and-new. When shares bought during the account are sold free of commission at the end of the account and immediately repurchased for the new account.

Casino Society. Investors who put their money into under-valued corporate assets volatile futures contracts or other speculative ventures in an effort to make fast money.

Caste. A social class separated from others by heredity.

Caste System. A system of social stratification in which social position is determined by the family into which a person is born, and change in that position is usually not possible during and individual's lifetime.

Casual Attributions. Suspected or inferred causes of behavior.

Casual Friday. Employees are forced to dress up as they like and the company does not insist upon uniform.

Catastrophic Crop Insurance. Guarantees 50 per cent of the producer's average yield for crop insured, and the indemnity payment is 60 per cent of the expected market price for that crop.

Categorical Imperative. An ethical standard that judges behavior in its consistency with the principle Act as if the maxim of your action were to become a general law binding on everyone.

Cats and Dogs. Shares of small, new, poorly financed or loss making companies infrequently traded are called cats and dogs. They may show appreciation in a bull phase but in bear phase they become practically untradeable.

Cause and Effect Diagram. A method for analyzing process dispersion that relates causes and effects; also known as fishbone analysis.

Causes-of-loss Form. Form added to commercial property insurance policy that indicates the causes of loss that are covered. There are four causes of loss forms: basic, broad, special and earthquake.

Caveat Emptor. Beware of a 'maxim' in Indian market which is still not adequately protected either against unscrupulous brokers or against defaulting companies. Once the Securities and Exchange Board of India gets sufficiently, it is hoped that investor interest will be adequately protected. Beware of brokers who pay very late, show suspiciously low price and delay to execute orders.

CBOE. Chicago Board of Options Exchange. An exchange that has promoted the organized trading of call options.

CBOT. Chicago Board of Trade US based largest futures exchange.

CBT. Chicago Board of Trade.

CD (Cum-dividend Rate). An investor who buys a share at the cum-dividend (cd) rate is entitled to the dividend for which the books are being closed. Stock exchange authorities normally fix the dates on which shares are to be quoted at "cd" or "xd" rates.

Ceding Company. Insurer that writes the policy initially and later shifts part or all of the coverage to a re-insurer.

Cellular Layout. The arrangement of employee and equipment into cells responsible for an entire work process.

CEMA. Council for Mutual Economic Assistance.

Central American Common Market (CACM). A customs union in Central America.

Central Bank. A country's central bank (In India, the Reserve Bank) issues currency, administers monetary policy, regulates the working of its subsidiaries, holds reserves of other banks, regulates foreign exchange policies and is supposed to protect public interest in general.

Central European Free Trade Association (CEFTA). An association which went into effect on July 1, 1992 with an initial membership of the Czech Republic, Slovakia, Hungary and Poland, and whose goal is to establish a free trade area that includes the basic trade structure of the EU by the year 2000.

Central State Control. A socio-economic system in which political social and economic power is concentrated in a central government that makes all fundamental decisions for the society.

Centralization. Decision-making is reserved at central points in the organization. It is the extent to which decision making authority is concentrated.

Centralization of Authority. The tendency to restrict delegation of decision making in an organization structure, usually by holding authority at or near the top of the organization structure.

Centralized Authority. Exists in government ownership economic systems where almost all business decisions are made by a central government level.

Centralized Decision Making. Top managers make all key decisions.

Centralized Depository. The practice of centralizing corporate cash balances in a single depository.

Centrally Planned Economy (CPE). *See* Command economies.

Certainity. The condition that exists when decision makers are fully informed about problem, its alternative solutions and their respective outcomes.

Certainity Decision. A decision in which the manager is certain about the state of nature or competitor's action that will occur. Thus, the probability that a particular event will occur is 1.00.

Certainity Equivalent. A certain cashflow which is equal in desirability to an uncertain cashflow.

Certificate. The document of a title to registered stock or shares.

Certificate of Acceptance. A document whereby the lessee acknowledges that the equipment to be leased has been delivered to him, is acceptable to him, and has been manufactured or constructed in accordance with the specifications.

Certificate of Incorporation. A certificate usually issued by a state government authorizing a group of individuals to establish a business in the legal form of a corporation (*See* Federal chartering).

Certificate of Origin. A shipping document that determines the origin of products and usually validated by an external source, such as a chamber of commerce it helps countries determine the specific tariff schedule for imports.

Certificates of Deposit. Called CDs special redeemable debt obligation issued by banks whose terms usually run from 90 days to 4 years.

Certified Cheque. The cheque that is guaranteed not to bounce as it is issued by a bank with a guarantee of payment. The bank is legally obligated to honour it. The funds to cover it are immediately with drawn from the depositor's account.

Certified Financial Planner (CFP). Professional who has attained a high degree of technical competency in financial planning and has passed a series of professional examinations by the College for Financial Planning.

Certified Insurance Counselor (CIC). Professional in property and liability insurance who has passed a series of examinations sponsored by the Society of Certified Insurance Counselors.

Certified Internal Auditor. An accountant who has a bachelor's degree and two years of experience in internal auditing, and who has passed an examination administered by the Institute of Internal Auditors.

Certified Management Accountant. A professional accountant who has certain educational and experience requirements and been certified by the Institute of Certified Management Accountants.

Certified Public Accountant. An accountant who passes a series of examinations established by the American Institute of Certified Public Accountants.

Certified Transfer. A transfer form or deed certified to the effect that the certificate in respect of the stock or shares transferred is held at the offices of the registrar for the company awaiting the completed document.

CFC. *See* Controlled foreign corporation.

CGAP Effect. The relation between changes in interest rate and changes in net interest income.

Chaebols. Family run conglomerates in South Korea.

Chain Network. Communication network in which information moves up and down through the hierarchy.

Chain of Command. An organizing concept that ensures that all positions are directly linked in some way to top management.

Chain Store. A store under the control of central ownership which stocks and distributes similar lines of goods.

Chairman of the Board. The highest ranking authority in a company. The chairman of the board of directors may be an eminent person or a representative of the controlling group. If he is also the chief executive or managing director of the company, he holds considerable executive authority, otherwise he may be treated simply as a venerable figure head. The chairman presides over the annual general meeting and summarized version (unless it is short) of whose speech is often published in the newspaper along with his photograph.

Chance of Loss. The probability that an event will occur.

Change Agent Role. A work role that promotes different behaviour in others and/ or different conditions in the environment.

Change in Demand. A shift in the entire demand curve caused by a change in income, tastes, expectations, or other determinants of demand.

Change in Quality Demanded. A movement along a given demand curve.

Change in Quantity Supplied. A movement along a given supply curve.

Change in Supply. A shift in the entire supply curve.

Change of Name of Companies. A company may change its name by passing a special resolution at a meeting of shareholders. A recent example is the change of name of IEL to ICI. A change of name, however, does not absolve a company of any of its legal obligations. A change of name may also be occasional by a simple spelling mistake.

Change of Plan Provision. Allow policy owners to exchange their present policies for different contracts, provides flexibility.

Changes Statement. A statement of changes in financial position.

Channel. The medium or method used to transmit the intended information, and meaning, such as by phone or in person.

Channel Length. The number of intermediaries that a product has to go through before it reaches the final consumer.

Channel of Distribution. Marketing intermediaries, such as wholesalers and retailers, who join together to transport and store goods in their path from producers to consumers.

Channel Richness. A channel's ability to transmit information, including the ability to handle multiple cues simultaneously, encourage feedback, and focus personally on the receiver.

Chaotic Theory. A term loosely applied to the notion that entrepreneurs are agents of change, creating chaos by disrupting the status quo in constructive ways to instigate new products, processes or knowledge.

Characteristic Line. A regression line representing the relationship between the return on an individual security and the return on the market portfolio. The slope of the characteristic line is the 'beta' of the security.

Charisma. The ability to inspire admiration, respect, loyalty, and a desire to emulate, based on some intangible set of personality traits; a personal source of power.

Charismatic Leadership. Transforms employees to pursue organizational goals over self interests.

Chart. Visual display of the movement of prices or indices. (*See* also Bar chart, Line chart point and Figure chart.)

Chart Analysis. The use of graphs and charts to analyse prices and trading behaviour and to anticipate future price movements.

Chart of Approval Authorizations. A technique by which the various authority delegations of an enterprise are charted in a matrix from showing the nature of subjects over which authority exists and the organizational positions where decision-making authority rests.

Charted Financial Consultant. An individual who has attained a high degree of technical competency in the fields of financial planning, investments, life and health insurance and has passed professional examinations administered by The American College.

Chartered Life Underwriter. An individual who has attained a high degree of technical competency in the fields of life and health insurance and who is expected to abide by a code of ethics. He must have minimum of three years of experience in life or health insurance sales and have passed professional examinations administered by The American College.

Chartered Property Casualty Underwriter. Professional who has attained a high degree of technical competency in property and liability insurance and has passed professional examinations administered by the American Institute for Chartered Property Casualty Underwriters.

Chastity Bonds. They are the bonds that become redeemable at par value in the event of a takeover.

Chattels. Movable property; opposite of fixtures.

Cheap Money. Easily borrowable money supplied at low rates of interest. Cheap money promotes industrial development and improves the investment climate. When lending is restricted and interest rates are high it is bad for the industry as well as investment.

Cheapest to Deliver. The bond in a futures contract, is least expensive to deliver on the contract.

Check Off. The practice of deducting union dues by the employer.

Checks. Negotiable instruments ordering a bank to pay someone a certain sum of money on demand.

Check-sheets. Data-recording forms that have been designed to allow managers to enter data on the form and simultaneously analyze trends in the data.

Cherry Picking. When a credit rating agency carefully shifts a pool of assets in order to give a very high credit worthiness rating to the one it chooses it is doing 'cherry picking'.

Chicago Mercantile Exchange (CME). The largest commodity exchange in the world, dealing primarily in agriculture products, US treasury bills, coins and some metals.

Child Care. The care of employees' children is a benefit that some firms provide. There are some organizations that provide child care in organizationally sponsored.

Chinese Wall. Watertight compartments in a business house which keeps the information of each department confidential so that those inside the company may not take advantage of such inside information.

Choice Criterion. Often used as a synonym for objective function.

Choice no Fault Plans. Motorists can elect to be covered under the state's no-fault law with lower premiums or can retain the right to sue under the 'tort' liability system with higher premiums.

Chooser Option. An option for which during the life of the option, the option owner can pick either a call option or a put option.

Chronology. It is a structured review of activities during a period of time.

Churning. Overactive trading of customer accounts in order to generate commission or income is called churning.

CIA. The Central Intelligence Agency, a US governmental agency charged with gathering intelligence information abroad.

CIM. Computer-Integrated Manufacturing.

Circle Network. Communication network in which employees communicate only with adjoining members of the organization.

Circuit Brakers. It is a mechanism by which exchanges temporarily suspend the trading in a security when its prices are volatile and tend to breach the price band.

CIS. Commonwealth of Independent States.

CIS. Collective investment schemes.

CISC. UN Convention on Contracts for the International Sale of Goods.

Civil Aeronautics Board. A federal agency which regulates air transportation.

Civil Law. Law that deals with difference between individuals.

Civil Law System. A legal system based on a very detailed set of laws that are organized into a code, countries with a civil law system, also called a codified legal system, include Germany, France and Japan.

Civil Liberties. The freedom to develop one's own views and attitudes.

Civil Rights Act. A Federal Act passed in 1964 that prohibits discrimination in employment as to race, colour, religion, sex and national origin.

Claims Adjuster. Person an agent, company adjuster, independent adjuster, adjustment bureau, or public adjuster, who settles claims.

Claims-made Policy. A liability insurance policy that only covers claims that are first reported during the policy period, provided the event occurred after the retroactive due (if any) stated in the policy.

Class Consciousness. A tendency for individuals to perceive themselves in terms of their class background.

Class Rate. Rates or charges for shipping products grouped into the same class.

Class Rating. Rate making method in which similar insureds are placed in the same underwriting class and each is charged the same rate. Also called manual rating.

Class System. A system of social stratification in which social status is determined by the family into which a person is born and by subsequent socio-economic achievements.

Classical Approach. An approach to management that stresses the manager's role in a formal hierarchy of authority and focuses on the task, machines, and systems needed to accomplish the goals effectively.

Classical Approach to Job Design. The design of jobs based on the principles of division of labor and Job specialization.

Classical Approach to Management. A body of literature that represents the earliest attempts to define and describe the field of management. The approach's main focus is on formally prescribed relationships. Its primary means for acquiring knowledge are personal observation and case studies.

Classical Approach to Organizational Design. Relies on such management principles as unity of command, a balance between authority and responsibility, division of labor, and delegation to establish relationships between managers and subordinates.

Classical Management Motivation Theory. The classical approach to motivation emphasized monetary incentives as prime means for motivating the individual. This approach was undoubtedly strongly influenced by the classical economists, who emphasized man's rational pursuit of economic objectives.

Classical Model of Decision Making. A prescriptive approach, asserting that managers are logical. Rational individuals who make decisions that are in the best interests of the organization, that outlines how managers should make decisions; also known as the rational model.

Classical Theory of Interest Rates. An explanation of the level of and changes in interest rates that relies on the interaction of the supply of savings and the demand for investment capital.

Classical View of Money Demand. Considers income to be the primary determinant of money demand.

Classification. A grouping of objects with the same data structure and behaviour.

Classification of Deposits. Classification of deposits by maturity refers to outstanding amount of term deposits as on the date of the term return. Maturity refers to original period of deposits.

Claw Back. The statutory reduction in life assurance tax relief when a qualifying policy is surrendered within four years.

Clean Balance Sheet. A balance sheet with no debt items, showing that the company has no outstanding.

Clean Describes. The price of a stock after allowing for any accrued interest reflected in the market price.

Clean Desk Policy. It requires everyone to leave their desks neat as a pin at the end of the day.

Clean Float. Controller of Capital Issues may determine the price of a new issue or a rights issue. When there is no such intervention, free market forces determine the price of an issue, it is a clean float.

Clearing House. Transaction in group-A shares can be settled between members by using the facilities of the "Clearing house" attached to the stock exchange.

Clearing House Funds. Money transferred by writing a check and presenting it for collection.

Clearing Member. A member of the clearing house, each clearing member must be a member of an exchange but not all members of an exchange are members of a clearing house. All trades made by a non-clearing member must be registered with and eventually settled through a clearing member.

Clearing Programme. The transactions entered during this period of a week are to be settled either by payment for purchase or by delivery of share certificates sold on notified days which are made known to the members of the exchange through a clearing programme.

Clientele Effect. Agreement that stocks attract particular groups based on dividend yield tax brackets.

Closed Economy Model. A model that does not consider the impact of international trade on the economy.

Closed-end-investment Companies. Specialized investment companies that have fixed supply of outstanding shares but invest in the securities and assets of other firms.

Closed Shop. Requires individuals to join a union before they can be hired.

Closed Shop Agreement. Clause in a labor management agreement that specified that workers had to be members of a union before being hired.

Closed System. An organization that interacts little with its external environment and therefore receives little feedback from or information about its surroundings.

Closed-end-fund. In this type of fund, investors have to commit their money to the fund for a particular period of time as specified by the terms of the offer. The main drawback here is that since an exit is not available from the fund itself; units of such funds are normally traded on stock exchanges at a discount to their existing net asset values (NAVs). However, this discount reduces as funds approach their redemption dates.

Closed-end-mutual Fund. It is an investment company which has a fixed number of shares traded on the stock market after their initial public issue.

Cluster Chain. An exchange in which one person or a selected few share information with only a few others.

CMA. *See* Certified Management Accountant.

Coal Gasification. A process of making a gaseous fuel from solid coal.

Coal Liquifaction. A process of making a liquid fuel from solid coal.

Coalition. Temporary groupings of people who actively pursue a single issue.

COBOL. Common Business Oriented Language, a computer language.

COCOM. *See* Coordinating Committee on Multilateral exports.

Code of Conduct. A set of principles guiding the actions of their contacts with societies.

Codes of Ethics. Formalized rules and standards that describe and delineate what the organization expects of its employees.

Codetermination. A process by which both labour and management participate in the management of a company. Codetermination is a practice whereby union or worker representatives are given positions on a company's board of directors.

Codified Legal System. *See* Civil law system.

Co-efficient of Variation. A measure of depression defined as standard deviation divided by expected value.

Coercive Power. The power of a leader that is derived from fear. The follower perceives the leader as a person who can punish deviant behavior and actions.

Co-generation. An energy conservation process that used steam twice, once for generating electric power or for producing heat and a second time for a supplemental use.

Cognitions. A person's knowledge, opinions, or beliefs.

Cognitive Abilities. The capabilities to think intelligently and to analyze information.

Cognitive Categories. Mental depositories for storing information.

Cognitive Dissonance. A state in which there is a discrepancy between a person's attitude and behavior.

Cognitive Style. The different ways people perceive and process information.

Cohesiveness. The tendency of group members to unite in their pursuit of group goals and to be attracted to the group and each other.

Co-insurance Provision. Common provision in commercial property insurance contracts that requires the insured to maintain insurance on the property at a stated percentage of its actual cash value. Payment for a loss is determined by multiplying the amount of the loss by the fraction derived from the amount of insurance required. If the co-insurance requirement is not met at the time of loss, the insured will be penalized. Co-insurance is also used to refer to the percentage participation clause in health insurance.

Collaborating. Working together to achieve both parties' objectives.

Collaborating Style. A style displaying both high assertiveness and high competition.

Collaborative Arrangement. A formal, long-term contractual agreement among companies.

Collaborative Computing. Using computer software and hardware to help people work better together.

Collar. An interest rate contract that establishes a cap and a floor on a specified rate of interest that is to be paid can also be used in commodity foreign currency, and equity market.

Collateral. Property or assets pledged as a security against default on a loan.

Collateral Source Rule. Under this rule, the defendant can not introduce any evidence that shows the injured party has received compensation from other collateral sources.

Collateral Trust Bonds. Bonds backed by securities (such as stocks) of the company.

Collateralized Mortgage Obligation (CMO). A mortgage-backed bonds issued in multiple classes or trenches.

Collection Policy. Procedures followed by a firm in collecting accounts receivables.

Collective Bargaining. It is the process whereby representatives of management and workers negotiate over wages, hours and conditions of employment. Workers through a spokesman, bargain collectively rather than individually for wages and other issues.

Collectivism. A political system that emphasizes collective goals as opposed to individual goals.

Collectivized Mortgage Obligation. A type of mortgage-backed security offered in more than one maturity class in order to reduce prepayment risk to investors.

Collision Loss. Damages to an automobile caused by the upset of the automobile or its impact with another vehicle or object. Collision losses are paid by the insurer regardless of fault.

Collusion. The act of two or more firms conspiring to act in concert in their pricing or output decisions in order to make both firms better off.

Combined Ratio. A measure of the overall underwriting profitability of a line; equals the loss ratio plus the ratios of loss adjustment expenses to premiums earned as well as commission and other acquisition costs to premiums written minus any dividend paid to policyholders as a proportion of premiums earned.

COMECON. *See* Council for Mutual Economic Assistance.

COMEX. Commodity Exchange, New York.

Command and Control System. A pollution control system based on government regulation, environmental and emission standards and legal penalties for noncompliance.

Command Economies. Economic systems in which the government largely decides what goods and services will be produced?, who will get them?, and how the economy will grow?

Command Group. The group of employees who report to a single manager, as shown on an organization chart.

Commercial and Consumer Finance Companies. Organizations that offer short-term loans to businesses or individuals who either can't meet the credit requirements of regular banks or else have exceeded their credit limit and need more funds.

Commercial Bank. A profit-making organization that receives deposits from individuals and corporations in the form of checking and saving accounts and uses some of these funds to make loans.

Commercial Banking. Banking activity of deposit taking and lending.

Commercial Bill of Exchange. An instrument of payment in international business that instructs the importer to forward payment to the exporter.

Commercial Finance Company. An institution that makes loans on equipment, assets, inventory, and receivables, serving mainly business and agricultural clients.

Commercial General Liability Policy (CGL). Commercial liability policy drafted by the Insurance Service Office containing two converge forms, an occurrence form and a claims made form.

Commercial Invoice. A bill for goods from the seller to the buyer.

Commercial Package Policy (CPP). A commercial policy that can be designed to meet the specific insurance needs of business firms. Property and liability coverage forms are combined to form a single policy.

Commercial Paper. Unsecured promissory notes of $ 25,000 and up that mature (come due) in 270 days or less. Commercial paper is usually sold at a discount from the face amount. Any type of security that promises payment of debt.

Commission Agent. A type of intermediary that sells a manufacturer's agency that deals with multinational enterprises.

Commission Merchants. Do not take title to goods but have physical possession of merchandise and are paid on a commission basis.

Commitment Principle. A group of persons to whom, as a group, some matter is committed for purposes of information, advice, inter-change of ideas, or decision.

Committed Costs. Those field costs arising from the possession of plant and equipment and a basic organization and thus are affected primarily by long-run decisions as to the desired level of capacity.

Committee. A permanent formal group that does some specific task, may be either a functional or cross-functional group.

Commodity. A product or service that has become so common as to have no unique characteristics apart from those of competitors. It is indistinguishable in form or substance, although competitors seek ways to develop unusual brands. Examples include soaps, toothpastes, chewing gums, cereal grains, colas, and light bulbs.

Commodity Agreement. A form of economic cooperation designed to stabilize and raise the price of a commodity.

Commodity Derivative. A derivative written on a commodity.

Commodity Exchange. A securities exchange that specializes in the buying and selling of precious metals and minerals (*e.g.* silver, foreign currencies, gasoline) and agricultural gods (*e.g.* wheat, cattle, sugar).

Commodity Fund. An entity in which funds contributed by a number of people are pooled together to trade futures and option contracts under professional management.

Commodity Futures Trading Commission (CFTC). The Commodity Futures Trading Commission (CFTC) Act of 1974 of the USA established the commission. CFTC has specific powers under the Act. One important area of jurisdiction is the approval of new contracts. CFTC regulates future market trading rules including the daily permitted maximum price fluctuations, certain features of the delivery process and minimum price fluctuation limits.

Commodity Swap. A swap in which counter parties exchange cash flows based on commodity price.

Commodity Futures. A futures contract written on a commodity.

Commodity Money. A physical commodity that is used as money even though it has alternative non-monetary uses.

Commodity Rate. Rates charged for shipping bulky items, such as coal or sand.

Common Agricultural Policy (CAP). An EU policy aimed to form trade, price supports and modernization programmes in agriculture.

Common Carrier. A carrier offering its services to the general public, regulated by various state and federal agencies. The same rates are be charged to all customers.

Common Cost. A cost that is common to all the segments in question and is not clearly or practically allocable except by some questionable allocation base.

Common Law. The body of law that comes from judges' decisions; also referred to as unwritten law.

Common Law Employees. The temporary employees of given job for more than a few months may actually be common law employees. The court argues that they should be treated as permanent employees. They deserve the benefits what permanent employees enjoy. They can sue employers under such laws of value discrimination or sex discrimination.

Common Law System. A legal system based on tradition, precedent, custom and usage, in which the courts interpret the law based on those conventions; found in the United Kingdom and former British colonies.

Common Market. A group of countries committed to: (1) removing all barriers to the free flow of goods, services, and factors of production between each other; and (2) the pursuit of a common external trade policy.

Common Size Statement. An income statement with each entry stated as a percentage of sales, or a balance sheet with each entry stated as a percentage of total assets.

Common Stock. The fundamental ownership claim in a public corporation.

Communication. The transmission of information and understanding through the use of common symbols.

Communication Competence. Ability to effectively use communication behaviors in a given context.

Communication Distortion. Purposely modifying the content of a message.

Communication Skill. Ability of manager to effectively send information to all other individuals in the firm.

Communications Software. Computer programes that take it possible for different brands of computers to transfer data to each other.

Communism. A system in which the state makes all economic decisions and owns all the major forms of production.

Communism. A form of totalitarianism initially theorized by Karl Marx in which the political and economic systems are virtually inseparable.

Communist Totalitarianism. A version of collectivism advocating that socialism can be achieved only through a totalitarian dictatorship.

Communists. Those who believe socialism can be achieved only through revolution and totalitarian dictatorship.

Community Bank. A bank that specializes in retail consumer banking.

Community Employee Owned Firm (CEF). A company owned wholly or in part by a combination of its employees and groups of local community.

Community Reinvestment Act. A federal law passed in 1977 that requires depository institution to designate the market areas they will serve and provide services without discrimination to all neighborhoods within their designated market areas.

Community Relations. The involvement of business with the communities in which it conducts operations.

Commutative Contract. One in which the values exchanged by both parties are theoretically even.

Companies Act. A comprehensive price of legislation regulating the functioning of Joint Stock Companies in India.

Company Adjuster. Claims adjuster who is a salaried employee representing only one company.

Company Objection. An investor sends the certificate along with the transfer deed to the company for transfer. In certain cases the registration is rejected because of signature difference or if the shares are fake, forged or stolen, etc. in such cases the company returns the shares along with the letter which is termed as a company objection.

Comparable Access. A protectionist argument that companies and industries should have the same access to foreign markets as foreign industries and companies have to their markets.

Comparable Worth. It is the concept that jobs requiring comparable knowledge skills and abilities should be paid similarly.

Comparative Advantage Theory. Theory which asserts that a country should produce and sell to other countries those products that it produces most efficiently.

Comparative Management. The study and analysis of management in different environments and in various countries.

Comparative Negligence Laws. Laws enacted by many jurisdictions permitting an injured person to recover damages even though he or she may have contributed to the accident. The financial burden is shared by both parties according to their respective degrees of fault.

Compensating Balance. A proportion of a loan that a borrower is required to hold on deposit at the lending institution.

Compensation Committee. Usually is a sub-group of the board of directors composed of outside directors.

Compensation System. The basis on which an organization gives money, goods, or services to its employees in exchange for their work.

Competent Parties. A requirement of valid contracts which does not include drunkards, insane persons, convicts or individuals under 21 years of age (in some states 18).

Competing Style. A management style involving a stance of high assertiveness with low cooperation.

Competition. A struggle to survive and excel. In business different firms compete with one another for the customers' dollars.

Competition Policy. Regulations designed to promote competition and restrict monopoly practices.

Competitive Benchmarking. Rating an organization's practices, processes, and products against the world's best.

Competitive Markets. A market where all traders act as price takers.

Competitors. Other organizations that produce similar, or in some cases identical, goods or services.

Complements. Goods or services that tend to be used jointly and thus have the property that when the price of one increases the demand for the other decreases.

Complete Crowding Out. Describes a situation in which crowding out is complete. So that the increase in government spending causes a reduction in the sum of investment and consumption spending of an equal but opposite magnitude.

Complete Currency Multiplier. Indicates how much currency holdings will change due to a change in the monetary base.

Complete Money Multiplier. Determines the factor by which the money stock (currency plus deposits) change due to a change in the monetary base.

Completed Operations. Liability arising out of faulty work performed away from the premises after the work or operations are completed; applicable to contractors, plumbers, electricians, repair shops, and similar firms.

Completed Staff Work. Implies presentation of a clear recommendation to a superior based upon full consideration of a problem clearance with persons importantly affected, suggestions about avoiding any difficulties involved and often, the preparation of necessary paperwork for implementing recommendations so that the receiving person can accept or reject the proposal without further study, long conferences, or unnecessary work.

Complexity. The level of differentiation among structural units, including the specialization of jobs, geographical dispersion, and height of the firm.

Compliance Based Ethics Codes. Ethical standards that emphasize preventing unlawful behavior by increasing control and by penalizing wrong doers.

Compliance Costs. The costs incurred by business and other organizations in complying with government regulations such as the cost of pollution control machinery or disposing of toxic chemical wastes.

Component Percentages. Analysis and presentation of financial statement in percentage form to aid comparability.

Composite Strategies. A group of strategies in various related areas that a company or other enterprises may have.

Compounding. The process of accumulating interest in an investment over time in order to earn more interest.

Compound Duty. A tax placed on goods traded internationally based on value plus units.

Compound Growth (Economic Population). Growth in production or population that incorporates periodic increase into the (production or population) base thereby compounding or multiplying the amount of growth experienced.

Compound Interest. The payment of additional interest earnings on previously earned interest income.

Compound Option. An option written on one or more options.

Compound Value. The amount an investment is worth after one or more periods.

Comprehensive Major Medical Insurance. Type of group plan combining basic plan benefits and major medical insurance in one policy.

Comprehensive Model of Planned Change. A step-by-step plan for implementing major change.

Compressed Work Week. A four-day or shorter period in which an employee works 40 hours.

Compromising Style. A style that reflects a moderate concern for both your goals and the other person's goals.

Comptroller of the Currency. An office of the treasury which regulates the formation of national banks from time to time to verify their financial health.

Comptroller. *See* Controller.

Compulsory Insurance Law. Law protecting accident victims against irresponsible motorists by requiring owners and operators of automobiles to carry certain amounts of liability insurance in order to license the vehicle and a drive legally within the state.

Computer Aided Design. The application of computer technology to design products much more quickly than with the traditional paper and pencil approach.

Computer Aided Manufacturing. The application of computer technology to the manufacturing process. The ultimate goal for some companies is "computer-integrated manufacturing" which computerizes the total manufacturing process.

Computer Assisted Design. A computerized approach in the operations function that links the design and manufacturing areas, making information readily available. Also see Computer Aided Design.

Computer Language. The instructions which contain the operations the computer is to perform written in a specific language which the computer can interpret.

Computer Networks. Systems that permit different computers to communicate with each other.

Computer Viruses. Computer programs concealed inside legitimate programs that change or destroy data kept on a computer; can damage or even cripple a system.

Concealment. Deliberate failure of an applicant for insurance to reveal a material fact to the insurer.

Concentration (Corporate Economic Industrial Market). When relatively few companies are responsible for a large proportion of overall economic activity, production, or sales.

Concentration Strategy. A strategy by which an international company builds up operations quickly in one or a few countries before going to another.

Concept Testing. Taking a product idea to consumers to test their reactions.

Conceptual Management Skill. The ability to coordinate and integrate ideas, concepts, and practices. Such skill is most important to top-level managers.

Conceptual Schema (in a Relational Data Base). A design from the perspective of an entire enterprise.

Conceptual Skill. The ability of a manager to see the overall picture.

Conceptual Skills. Skills that involve the ability to picture the organization as a whole and the relationship among its various parts.

Concessionary Bargaining. Economic problems have resulted in givebacks or concessions being made by the union to management. The firm's existence or long-term survival is the theme that management has used to secure concessions.

Conciliation. It is a process in which an outside entity attempts to help two deadlock parties continue negotiation and arrive at a solution. A third party, the conciliator, attempts to get labour and management together to discuss issues involved in their disagreement.

Concurrent Control. The techniques and methods that focus on the actual, ongoing activity of the organizations.

Conditional Sale. A transaction for purchase of an asset in which the user for income tax purpose is treated as the owner of the equipment at the outset of the transaction.

Conditional Sale/Lease. A term for a lease which in substance is a conditional lease.

Conditional Value. The value that will ensure if a particular event occurs.

Conditions. Provisions inserted in an insurance contract that qualify or place limitations on the insurer's promise to perform.

Conditions Precedent. Those conditions specified in the credit agreement or terms sheet for a credit that must be fulfilled before drawings are permitted.

Confidence. A person's faith that his or her decisions are reliable and good.

Confirmed Letter of Credit. A letter of credit to which a bank in the exporter's country adds its guarantee of payment.

Conflict. One party perceives its interests are being opposed or set back by another party.

Conformity. Adherence to the group's norms, values, and goals.

Conglomerate Merger. The joining of firms in completely unrelated industries.

Conglomerates. Firms that pursue unrelated diversification strategies.

Congress of Industrial Organizations. Union organization of unskilled workers; broke away from the AFL in 1935 and rejoined it in 1955.

Congruence Model of Change. An approach that emphasizes the inter-relationships between the parts of an organization and how change in one part will cause reactive change in other parts.

Consensus. Presenting opinions and gaining agreement to support a decision.

Consensus Forecast. A prediction of interest rates or economic conditions based on a variety of projections derived from different forecasting methods.

Consequential Loss. Financial loss occurring as a consequence of some other loss. Often called an indirect loss.

Conservatism. A characteristic of accounting systems which implies that companies are hesitant to disclose high profits that are consistent with their actual operating results; more common in Germanic countries.

Consideration. A requirement of valid contracts which means all parties must contribute some thing of value. It refers to behaviour indicating trust warmth friendship and mutual respect between the leader and the group members.

Consideration Behaviors. Patterns of being friendly and supportive by listening to employees' problems, supporting their actions, 'going to bat' for them, and getting their input on a variety of issues.

Console. A type of perpetuity.

Console Bond. A bond that pays a fixed coupon each year forever.

Consolidated Statements. Statements that combine legally separate companies as though they were a single fused entity.

Consolidated Tax Return. An income tax return that combines the income of two or more affiliated firms.

Consolidation. An accounting process in which financial statements related entities, such as a parent and its subsidiaries are combined to yield a unified set of financial statements; in the process transactions among the related enterprises are eliminated so that the statements reflect transactions with outside parties.

Consortium Lease. A lease in which a number of lessors participate. The usual reason for this is that the cost or the potential risk is too high to be borne by one lessor.

Consortium. A temporary combination of two or more companies for the purpose of bidding for a large project. They are formed to obtain a competitive edge over other bidders, as the pooling of financial and technical resources enable them to offer an attractive package.

Constant Dollars. Those monetary units restated so as to represent the same general purchasing power.

Constant Returns to Specialization. The units of resources required to produce a good are assumed to remain constant no matter where one is on a country's production possibility frontier.

Constant Yield Swap. An interest rate swap in which both parts are floating.

Constraint Index. A quantitative score that reflects the level of a nation's environment for effective business operations.

Constraint Index. A quantitative score that reflects the level of a nation's environment for effective business operations.

Constructive Receipt. In non-qualified benefit plans, a legal doctrine governing the timing of an employer's deduction for compensation paid to an employee and here porting of the compensation as part of taxable income by the employee. The employee is deemed to be in constructive receipt of the compensation when he or she acquires an irrevocable right to receive it.

Consular Invoice. A document that covers all the usual details of the commercial invoice and packing list, prepared in the language of the foreign country for which the goods are destined, on special forms obtainable from the consulate or authorized commercial printers.

Consumer Advocates. Persons who act to protect the interests of the consumer.

Consumer Behaviour. Actions of individuals involved in deciding which goods and services to purchase.

Consumer Goods. Goods purchased and used by the final consumer for his personal or household use.

Consumer Loans. Loans obtained by individuals for intermediate-term purchased such as automobile purchases as well as merchandise purchased with credit card.

Consumer Market. All the individuals or households who want goods and services for personal consumption.

Consumer Movement. The actions of consumer advocates to improve products and business practices.

Consumer Price Index. The consumer price index measures the percentage change in the expenditure of family for buying a fixed "basket" of commodities and services. Since January 1999, the prices of the basket representing the consumption of the urban families in 1997 are measured according to Household Expenditure Survey, 1997-First Findings, and the official index is presented on the base of the period: average 1998 = 100.0 there are in fact several Consumer Price Indices. Each tracks the retail prices of goods and services for different groups of people, because the consumption patterns of different groups differ.

Consumer Responsibilities. The obligations of consumers to act fairly, intelligently, honestly and helpfully towards sellers.

Consumer Rights. The legitimate claims of consumers to safe products and services adequate information free choice, a fair hearing and competitive prices.

Consumer Sovereignty. The freedom of consumers to influence production through the choice they make.

Consumer Sovereignty. The idea that consumers, through their purchases decide what will be produced by business firms.

Consumer-directed Market Economy. An economy in which there is minimal government participation while growth is promoted through the mobility of production factors, including high labour turnover.

Consumerism. The activities undertaken by independent individuals, groups, and organizations to protect their rights as consumers. A social movement that seeks to augment the rights and powers of buyers in relation to sellers.

Consumption Goods. Goods and services demanded by households.

Contemporaneous Reserve Accounting. The method of determining the amount of legal reserves a bank or other depository institution must hold behind its deposits and other reversible liabilities in which other reserve computation and reserve maintenance periods overlap.

Content Theories. A group of theories that assume workers are motivated by the desire to satisfy needs and identify what their needs are.

Continental Terms. *See* European terms.

Contingency Approach to Leadership. A theory that leadership depends upon the group task situation and the degree to which the leader's style, personality, and approach fit the group.

Contingency Approach to Organization Design. A set of ideas, which concludes that there exists an effective organization design for a specific organization depends upon factors in the setting.

Contingency Factors. Variables that influence the appropriateness of a leadership style.

Contingency Management. Management which recognizes differences or contingencies in people, at various times as in actual situations, also referred to as "situational management", an approach that emphasizes that there can be no "one best way" in all situations.

Contingency Model of Leadership Effectiveness. A leadership model developed by Fred Fiedler which postulates that a leader's effectiveness dependents upon three variables: (1) how well a leader accepted by subordinates; (2) the degree to which subordinate's positions are routine and clearly spelled out in contrast to being vague and undefined; and (3) the formal authority in the position occupied by a leader.

Contingency Planning. The process of preparing alternative courses of action that may be used if the primary plans do not achieve the objectives of the organization.

Contingency Strategies. Strategies are developed when unforeseen events or circumstances may make a selected strategy obsolete or unsuitable.

Contingency Theory. The suggestions that successful leadership requires matching leaders with primarily stable leadership styles to the demands of the situation.

Contingent Beneficiary. Beneficiary of a life insurance policy who is entitled to receive the policy proceeds on the insured's death if the primary beneficiary dies before the insured or the beneficiary who receives the remaining payments if the primary beneficiary dies before receiving the guaranteed number of payments.

Contingent Liability. A firm may be liable for the work done by an independent contractor if the activity is illegal, the situation does not permit delegation of authority, or the work is inherently dangerous.

Contingent Premium Option. *See* Paylater option.

Contingent Rentals. Rentals in which the amounts are dependent upon some factors other than passage of time.

Contingent Workers. Workers who do not have the expectation of regular, full time employment.

Continuity Convention. *See* Going concern convention.

Continuous Bargaining. A joint labor management committee meets on a regular basis to explore and solve problems.

Continuous Budgeting. Continuous budgeting provides for a system of revising the budget for the changing conditions continuously.

Continuous Improvement. Constantly improving the way the organization does things so that customer needs can be better satisfied.

Continuous Probability Distribution. A probability distribution, which has an infinite number of possible outcomes or values within any finite range in the distribution.

Continuous Process Production. Producing the same product over an extended period of time using automated equipment.

Continuous Production. A production process that produces a standardized product. Raw materials are continually fed into the production process.

Continuous Reinforcement. A reinforcement schedule that involves administering a reward each time a desired behavior occurs.

Continuous Technology. A method of production in which raw materials flow continuously through a system that transforms them into finished products.

Continuous Trading. A market where trading can take place continuously in time.

Continuously Compounded Interest Rates. Interest rates in which interest is compounded continuously.

Contra Accountant. A separate offsetting account. Examples are allowance for uncollectible accounts and accumulated depreciation.

Contract. A legally enforceable agreement between two or more parties.

Contract Bond. Type of surity bond guaranteeing that the principal will fulfill all contractual obligations.

Contract Carrier. A carrier which offers its services to an individual person or firm. This carrier may charge different rates to customers served.

Contract Concessions. An agreement reached between a labour union and an employer to reduce monetary benefits, change work rules, and/or modify fringe benefits in an existing labour contracts in order to improve the competitive standing of the employer firm.

Contract Hire. Expression for an operating lease, usually for vehicles or handling equipment. Lessor carries the residual value risk, and the fixed rentals may include a maintenance charge.

Contract Law. Laws that specifies what constitutes a legally enforceable agreement.

Contract Manufacturing. The company in concern (in this case UB), enters into a contract with an individual/organization, termed as a 'contractor'. The contractor selected will be responsible for manufacturing a product with the company's (UB's) name on it. The bottom line in contract manufacturing is to assemble a working product and deliver it, on time, and in the specified budget.

Contract Market. A commodity futures market or an exchange that qualifies under the Commodity Futures Trading Commission Act.

Contract of Adhesion. The insured must accept the entire contract, with all of its terms and conditions.

Contracting for Leadership Style. A process whereby employees may not initially agree with a manger's assessment of their development level, thus requiring a leader's skill in thriving at an assessment consensus and an agreed-upon leadership style.

Contractual. An obligation that includes financial obligations like interest, lease, rentals and financial payments which are matters of contract and should not be defaulted.

Contractual Distribution System. A distribution system in which members are bound to cooperate through contractual agreements.

Contractual Institutions. Financial institutions that attract saving from the public by offering contracts that protect the saver against risk in the future, such as insurance policies and pension plans.

Contractual Liability. Legal liability of another party that the business firm agrees to assume by a written or oral contract.

Contractual Obligation. Include those financial obligations like interest lease rentals and financial payments that are matters of contract and should not be defaulted.

Contrast Effect. Perceiving something a larger or smaller than it is because of the size of a reference point.

Contributed Capital. The total amounts invested by owners at the inception of a business or subsequently, usually distinguished from capital arising from retained income.

Contribution Approach. A method of preparing income statements that separates variable costs from fixed costs in order to emphasize the importance of cost behaviour patterns for the purpose of planning and control.

Contribution by Equal Shares. Type of other-insurance provision often found in liability insurance contracts that requires each company to share equally in the loss until the share of each insurer equals the lowest limit of liability under any policy or until the full amount of loss is paid.

Contribution Margin. Excess of sales price over variable expenses. Also called marginal income. It may be expressed as a total, as a ratio, or on a per unit basis.

Contributory Negligence. Common law defense blocking an injured person from recovering damages if he or she has contributed in any way to the accident.

Contributory Plan. Group life, health, or pension plan in which the employees pay part of the premiums.

Control. The planning, implementation, evaluation and correction of performance to ensure that organization objectives are achieved.

Control Factor Unit. A measure of workload. For example, lines per hour and pieces mailed per hour.

Control of Overall Performance. Control designed to measure the total performance of an enterprise, an integrated division of it, or a major programme or project.

Control Process. In managing, the basic process involves: (1) establishing standards; (2) measuring performance against standards; and (3) correcting for undesirable deviations.

Control Strategy. Coping strategy that directly confronts or solves problems.

Control Unit. The computer component which directs and controls the internal flow of information according to instructions contained in the computer programme.

Control-budget Variance. *See* Flexible-budget variance.

Controllable Cost. A cost that may be directly regulated at a given level of managerial authority, either in the short run or in the long run.

Controlled Disbursement Account. A disbursement practice under which the firm transfers an amount to a disbursing account that is sufficient to cover demands for payment.

Controlled Foreign Corporation (CFC). A foreign corporation of which more than 50 per cent of the voting stock is owned by US shareholders (taxable entities that own at least 10 per cent of the voting stock of the corporation).

Controlled Sample. A non-probability sample that includes convenience and judgment samples.

Controller. The chief management accounting executive also spelled as comptroller.

Controlling. A management function that involves determining whether or not an organization is progressing towards its goals and objectives and taking corrective action if it is not.

Controlling Function. All managerial activities undertaken to assure that actual operations go according to plan.

Controlling Interest. A firm has a controlling interest in another business entity when it owns more than 50 per cent of that entity's voting stock.

Convenience Build. The implied or non-pecuniary return from holding a commodity. It is also a measure of the degree backwardation in a market.

Convenience Good. A good sold through many retail outlets sold at a low unit price it is nationally advertised as well as being purchased frequently with little or no thought given to making the purchase. Also, the quality is standardized.

Convenience Goods. Products that the consumer wants to purchase frequently and with a minimum of effort.

Convenience Store. This store is usually located away from major shopping centres, open long hours and sells national brand name merchandise at higher prices.

Convenience Value. The value to storing a commodity for its use in production.

Convenience Yield. The convenience value expressed as a per cent.

Conventional Corporation. A state chartered legal entity with authority to act and have liability separate from its owners.

Conventional Home Mortgage Loan. Credit funds extended to a home buyer by a private lender without a government guarantee behind the loan.

Conventional Investment. Conventional investment can be defined as one whose cash flows take the pattern an initial cash outlay followed by cash inflows.

Conventional Mortgages. Mortgages issued by financial institutions that are not federally insured.

Convergence Theory. A theory that as nations industrialize they are inevitably pulled towards similarity (also known as convergence hypothesis).

Convergence. Refers to the tendency of cash and futures prices to come together (*i.e.* the basis shrinks) as a futures contract approaches expiration.

Convergent Thinking. Seeing similarities between situations.

Conversion Costs. Direct labour plus factory overhead.

Conversion Factor. A pricing factor used to determine the prices of T-bonds or T-notes eligible for delivery on futures contracts. These factors are provided by exchanges.

Conversion Price. The face value of a convertible security divided by its associated conversion ratio.

Conversion Ratio and Conversion Price. The conversion ratio is the number of ordinary shares that on investor-cum-receive when he exchanges his convertible debenture. The conversion price is the price paid for the ordinary share at the time of conversion.

Conversion Value. The conversion value of a convertible debenture is equal to the conversion ratio multiplied by the ordinary shares market price.

Convertibility. The ability to exchange one currency for another currency without restrictions.

Convertible Bond. A bond that can be converted into common stock in the issuing company.

Convertible Security. A bond or preferred stock issue that is exchangeable into another form of security (usually common stock) at the investor's option.

Convexity. A measure of the bonds sensitivity to large changes in the bond's yield.

Cookies. Pieces of information, such as registration data or user preferences, sent by a website over the Internet to a web browser that the browser software is expected to save and to send back to the server whenever the user returns to that website.

Cooling off Period. When workers in a critical industry return to their jobs while the union and management continue negotiations.

Cooling Period. Banks, under collateralized lending could borrow after 4 weeks. An additional period of 2 weeks are allowed.

Cooperative. A business owned and controlled by the people who use it—producers, consumers, or workers with similar needs who pool their resources for mutual gain.

Cooperative Advertising. Advertising made jointly by manufacturing firms and retailers.

Cooperative Chain. Retailers who form their own wholesaling organization in order to compare with cooperative chains.

Cooperative Group Reward. A reward tied to the group's overall performance, with each member receiving the same reward.

Cooperative System. A system, as perceived by Chester I. Barnard, as one whose purpose is cooperation and which comprises physical, biological, social, and psychological elements.

Coopration. Making allies of former adversaries by engaging them in a common effort.

Coordinating Committee on Multilateral Exports (COCOM). An agreement among Western industrial nations to limit militarily useful exports to communist countries disbanded in 1991 after the former Soviet Union broke up.

Coordination-of-benefits Provision. Provision of a group medical expense plan that prevents over-insurance and duplication of benefits when one person is covered under more than one group plan.

Coordination. Achieving harmony of individual and group efforts towards the accomplishment of group purposes and objectives.

Coping. Process of managing stress.

Copyright. Exclusive right conveyed by federal statue to reproduce and sell a book, design, pamphlet, drawing, or other creations, and to forbid the publication of excerpts or other limitations.

Core Competence. Firm's skills that competitors cannot easily match.

Core Deposits. Deposits of the bank that are table over short period of time and thus provide a loan-term funding source to a bank.

Core Job Dimensions. As proposed by Hickman and others, the five core job dimensions that, if present, provide enrichment for jobs. The dimensions are variety, task identify, task significance, autonomy, and feedback.

Core Technology. The dominant technology used for producing goods and services at the lowest level of an organization's hierarchy.

Core Time. In a flextime plan, the period when all employees are expected to be at their job stations.

Corner. A market situation where a trader or group of traders acting in unison own the available supply of an asset.

Corporate Bond. A debt instrument issued by a corporation that states it will make specified interest payments (typically twice each year) and a principal amount or "face value" (usually $ 1000) at maturity (say 30 years from the date of issue).

Corporate Culture. The common values shared by employees in a corporation, which form a control mechanism that is implicit and helps enforce other explicit control mechanisms.

Corporate Distribution System. A distribution system in which all of the organizations in the channel of distribution are owned by one firm.

Corporate Governance. The Cadbury Report, the financial aspects of corporate governance, which was published on December 1992, focused the corporate governance debate in four main areas: (1) The responsibilities of executive and non-executive directors for reviewing and reporting on performance to shareholders. (2) The case of establishing audit committees. (3) The principal responsibilities of auditors. (4) The links between shareholders, board of directors and auditors. The report contained a Code of Best Practice, most elements of which were adopted as part of the London Stock Exchange's Listing Rules for all quoted companies. Beyond the detail, the Cadbury Report states that, "Corporate governance is the system by which companies are directed and controlled".

Corporate Legitimacy. Public acceptance of the corporation as an institution that contributes to society's well-being.

Corporate Note. A debt contract (IOU) of a corporation whose original maturity is five years or less.

Corporate Policy. Dimension of social responsibility that refers to the position a firm takes on social and political issues.

Corporate Responsibility. Dimension of social responsibility that includes everything from minority hiring practices to the making of safe products.

Corporate Social Involvement. The interaction of business corporations with society.

Corporate Social Responsibility. There is no complete agreement about the definition of this term. In a broad context it means that corporation considers seriously the impact of the enterprise's actions on society. A business obligation to seek socially beneficial results along with economically beneficial results in its actions.

Corporate Social Responsiveness. The ability of a corporation to relate its operations and policies to the social environment in ways that are mutually beneficial to the company and to society.

Corporate Stakeholder. A person or group affected by corporations' policies and actions.

Corporate Stock. An equity instrument that represents ownership of a share of the assets and earnings of a corporation.

Corporate Takeover. The acquisition or merger of one corporation by another.

Corporation. A legal entity with authority to act and have liability separate from its owners. Organizations that are 'artificial beings' created by individual state laws.

Corpus. The total funds available with a mutual fund scheme. Corpus is worth the current market values of the instruments into which it is invested.

Correction. A correction means prices had gone too high and had to come down to realistic levels.

Corrective Advertising. Advertising sometimes required by government that is intended to correct misleading claims made by the advertiser in earlier ads.

Correlation. A measure of the cause-and-effect relationship between variables.

Correspondent (Bank). A bank in which funds are kept by another, usually foreign, bank to facilitate check clearing and other business relationships.

Correspondent Banking. A relationship between a small bank and a large bank in which the large bank provides a number of deposits, lending, and other services.

Corridor Deductible. Major medical plan deductible that excludes benefits, provided by a basic plan if both a basic and a supplemental group major medical expense policy are in force.

Corridor Portfolio. An option portfolio a call option and a put option, both equally out of the money write a call option and a put option. Each further out-of-the-money than the call and put options that were purchased. All options have the same time to expiration.

Corridor Principle. The idea that by doing one thing, or following one idea, new opportunities arise from these efforts, and subsequent opportunities may arise from continued efforts. Eventually, the process may result in an exceptional idea that would not have occurred without earlier activities.

Cost Accumulation. Gathering of costs in some organized way via an accounting system.

Cost Application also Called Cost Absorption. The allocation to products rather than to departments.

Cost Approximation. *See* Cost estimation.

Cost Behaviour Pattern. *See* Cost function.

Cost Benefit Analysis. A systematic method of calculating the costs and benefits of a project or activity that is intended to produce benefits.

Cost Benefit Criterion. As a system is changed, its expected additional benefits usually must exceed it expected additional costs.

Cost Effective. Carrying out an activity by prudent and efficient use of resources.

Cost Effectiveness Analysis. Seeking the best ratio of benefits and costs; this means, for example, finding the least costly way of reaching an objective, or getting the greatest value for given expenditures.

Cost Estimation. An attempt to specify some underlying relationship between x and y over a stimulated relevant range of x that may be of interest. An approximation of how a cost truly behaves. The approximation is in linear rather than nonlinear form.

Cost Function. A relationship between a cost and one or more variables such as the total cost of repairs in relation to miles driven.

Cost Leadership Strategy. An overall corporate strategy that involves being the lowest-cost producer in the industry.

Cost Method for Investments. The method whereby the initial investment is recorded at cost and dividends are recorded as income.

Cost Objective. Any activity for which a separate measurement of cost is desired. Examples include departments, products, territories, etc.

Cost of Capital. A term often used broadly to refer to the minimum rate of return that must be earned on an investment in order to leave the market price of the firm's common stock unchanged. More specifically, the term refers to the minimum rate of return on investments that have the same systematic risk as the firm as a whole without the investment.

Cost of Debt. The return that lenders require on the firm's debt.

Cost of Equity. Shareholders' required rate of return which equates the present value of expected dividends with the market value of the share is the cost of equity.

Cost of Goods Sold. A measure of the cost of merchandise sold or cost of raw materials and supplies used for producing items for resale.

Cost of Individual Source of Capital. The explicit cost of a specific form of financing such as debt, preferred stock, convertible securities, retained earnings, or common stock. The effect of using one form of financing on the cost of another form is ignored in this computation.

Cost of Living Rider. Benefit that can be added to a life insurance policy under which the policy owner can purchase one year term insurance equal to the percentage change in the consumer price index with no evidence of insurability.

Cost of Quality (COQ) Accounting System. A system that permits managers to calculate precisely the costs and savings associated with their quality efforts.

Cost of Retained Earnings. The rate of return on dividends foregone by the equity shareholders.

Cost of Sales. *See* Cost of goods sold.

Cost Pool. A group of individual costs that is allocated as a group to cost objectives in some plausible way.

Cost-allocation Base. A common denominator used to trace the cost or costs in question to the cost objectives. Examples are direct-labor-hours and machine-hours.

Cost-of-carry. The costs associated with holding (or carrying) a commodity or an asset. These include financing costs, storage costs and insurance costs.

Cost-of-living Adjustment. An increase in compensation given to an expatriate employee when foreign living costs are more expensive than those in the home country.

Costs. Fixed cost are those that do not vary with production or sales, they are debts or expenses that must be met regardless of operations. Fixed costs include mortgages, lease payments, loan payments, insurance, and operational components of salary overhead. Variable costs are those that are incurred, with production, services, and sales.

Cost-sacrifice. Made for goods or services.

Council for Mutual Economic Assistance (CMEA or COME-CON). A regional form of economic integration that involved essentially those communist countries con-sidered to be within the Soviet bloc; terminated in 1991.

Council of Ministers. One of the five major institutions of the EU; composed of one member from each country in the EU and entrusted with making major policy decisions.

Counter Cyclical Policy. Policy actions aimed at counteracting business cycle influences on the economy.

Counter Party. The opposite party to a financial contract.

Counter Party Risk. The risk that a counter party to a contract might default.

Counter Productive Behavior. Activity that damages the employer, such as drug use and white-collar crime.

Counter Purchase. A reciprocal buying agreement.

Counter Trade. A reciprocal flow of goods or services valued and settled in monetary terms.

Counter Trade Agreements. The bartering of a product for other products instead of currency.

Countervailing Duty. An import duty imposed to protect a home industry against what is regarded as unfair foreign competition.

Country Analysis. A process of examining the economic strategy of a nation-state, taking a holistic approach to understanding how a country and in particular its government has behaved, is behaving and may behave.

Country or Sovereign Risk. The risk that repayment from foreign borrowers may be interrupted because of interference from foreign governments.

Country Risk Analysis. Country risk is a broad concept that refers to the risks emanating from an underlying combination of economics, finance, geopolitics, sociology, and history issues. As the new global economy raises the level of uncertainty and complexity for the international firm's cross-border strategy. Country risk analysis has become today an essential component of strategy decisions regarding export, investment, partner-ship, mergers, as well as takeovers.

Country Similarity Theory. The theory that a producer having developed a new product in response to observed market conditions in the home market, will turn to markets that are most similar to home.

Country Size Theory. The theory that larger countries are generally more self-sufficient than smaller countries.

Coupon. The interest payment made on a bond.

Coupon Bond. A bond that makes coupon payments.

Coupon Effect. The size of a debt security's promised interest rate (coupon) influences how rapidly its price moves with changes in market interest rates.

Coupon Interest Rate. *See* Coupon rate.

Coupon Rate. The percentage of the face value of a bond that will be paid each year as an interest payment.

Court of Justice. One of the five major institutions of the EU composed of one member from each country in the EU and serves as a supreme appeals court for EU law.

Coverage for Damage to Your Auto. That part of the person auto policy insuring payment for damage or theft of the insured automobile. This optional coverage can be used to insure both collision and other-than-collision losses.

Covered Call. A position in a call option with an opposite position in the underlying asset.

Covered Interest Arbitrage. An arbitrage that occurs when two countries have interest rates, a spot exchange rate, and a forward exchange rate that allows an arbitrager to profit.

Covered Option. A written option that is covered by an offsetting cash or futures position in the underlying asset or by an offsetting option position with specific characteristics. As such, it has little or no risk.

CPE (Centrally Planned Economy). *See* Command economies.

CRA. Country Risk Assessment.

Craft Union. A union whose members possess a particular skill or craft, such as carpentry or plumbing.

Cram-down Deal. It is a situation in which the shareholders are forced to accept undesirable terms because of lack of attractive alternatives in the event of a merger or a leveraged buyout.

Crash. A system service failure.

Creativity. The ability to develop new concepts, ideas, and problem solutions.

Credit. In accounting, means one thing and one thing only—"right", as distinguished from "left", It typically refers to an entry in an account or the balance of an account.

Credit Analysis. The process of determining the probability that customers will or will not pay.

Credit Availability View. A view of economic policy that contends that both fiscal policy (government spending and taxation) and monetary policy (activities of the central bank) are needed to achieve nation's economic goals.

Credit Card. An authentic plastic card that allows the holder to borrow cash or to pay for goods and services with credit.

Credit Cost Curve. Graphical representation of the sum of the carrying costs and the opportunity costs of a credit policy.

Credit Crunch. Situation in which loan that must be repaid over a short time-scale (short credit) becomes scarce and thus more expensive than loans that must be repaid over a long period of time (long credit).

Credit Derivatives. Credit derivatives are used generally to describe financial instruments that are specifically designed to allow for the separate trading in, and management of, credit risk. Credit derivatives are designed to transfer credit risk from a party to another. Credit risk is not like other market risks in that it is an event risk and not a price risk. Credit derivatives are designed to transfer credit risk from a party to another. It is done so that one can offload risk that he already has. The person undertaking to accept the risk is paid for it and hopes that the event (default) does not crystallize.

Credit Enhancements. Financial devices, such as letters of credit from a bank, that upgrade the credit rating of a borrower and allow that borrower to obtain credit at lower cost.

Credit Equivalent Amount. The amount of credit risk exposure of an off-balance sheet item calculated by multiplying the face value of an off-balance sheet instrument by a conversion factor.

Credit File. A firm maintains a credit file for each customer. The firm's trade experiences, with the customer and his performance report based on financial statements submitted by him will be recorded in his credit file. A regular examination of the customers credit file will reveal to the firm the credit standing of the customers.

Credit Instrument. The evidence of indebtedness.

Credit Insurance. Protects a firm against abnormal credit losses because of customer insolvency or past due accounts when they are filed for collection within a specified time stated in the polcy.

Credit Investigation. It is a difficult task a firm use numerical credit scoring to appraise credit applications when it is dealing with a large number of small customers. The firm is based on its past experience or empirical study may identify both financial and non-financial attributes which measure the credit standing of a customer.

Credit Period. The length of time that credit is granted.

Credit Risk. The risk that an issuer of debt securities or a borrower may default on its obligations.

Credit Scoring System. A mathematical model that uses observed loan applicant's characteristics to calculate a score that represents the applicant's probability of default.

Credit Scoring. The process of quantifying the probability of default when granting consumer credit.

Credit Spread Call Option. A call option whose payoff increases as a yield spread decreases below a stated spread.

Credit Standards. They are criteria to decide the types of customers to whom goods could be sold on credit.

Credit Terms. It refers to the conditions under which the supplier sells on credit to the buyer, and the buyer is required to repay credit.

Credit Unions. Non-profit, member owned financial cooperatives that offer basic banking services such as accepting deposits and making loans to their members.

Credit Unions. A depository institution that operates as a cooperative, accepting deposits from and lending to only a closed group such as employees of a specific company, members of a specific labour union, or even members of a specific institution, unlike savings and loans. Credit unions typically do not make mortgage loans.

Creeping Acquisition. Gradual increase in the shareholding through open purchase on the stock exchange with the aim of increasing ones holding in the desired company.

Creolization. The process by which elements of an outside culture are introduced.

CRISIL. Credit Rating Information Service of India Limited.

Crisis Stock. Its performance will in lack ("some things check it") times but not all that well in a rising market.

Criterion. A standard by which success in an activity may be measured.

Critical Incident Method. A method by which the appraiser uses a log of positive and negative critical incidents to assess the performance.

Critical Path. The longest path in a PERT network, from the network beginning event to the network ending event.

Cross Border Lease. In case of cross border lease the lessor and the lessee are situated in two different countries. Because the lease transaction takes place between parties of two or more countries. It is called cross-border lease. It involves relationships and tax implications more complex than the domestic lease when the lease transaction takes place between the parties manufacturer/lender, lessor and lessee in three different countries, it is called foreign-to-foreign lease.

Cross Cultural Management. Understanding and teaching behavioral patterns in different cultures.

Cross Cultural Training. Training in recognizing and adapting to cultural differences.

Cross Functional Groups. Groups that cut across the firm's hierarchy and are composed of people from different functional areas and possibly different levels.

Cross Functional Team. A team with members from several functions that is responsible for a project that crosses functional lines.

Cross Hedge. The purchase of futures contract for a different financial instrument than is being traded in the cash market.

Cross Hedging. Hedging a commodity by using a futures contract on a different but related commodity. A cross hedge is based on the premise that the price movements of the two commodities are related.

Cross Licensing Agreement. An agreement in which a company licenses valuable intangible property to a foreign partner and receives a license for the partner's valuable knowledge, reduces risk of licensing.

Cross Rate. An exchange rate between two currencies used in the spot market and computed from the exchange rate of each currency in relation to the US dollar.

Cross Rate Option. A foreign currency option for which the numerate is not dollars but a foreign currency.

Cross-sectional Analysis. Another way of comparison is to compare the ratios of one firm with some selected firms in the same industry at the same point of time. This kind of comparison is known as cross-sectional analysis. In most cases it is more useful to compare the firm's ratios with ratios of a few selected competitors who have similar operations. This kind of comparison indicates the relative financial position and performance of the firm.

Cross-border Leasing. Where the lessor and lessee are in different countries under different legal systems.

Cross-cultural Literacy. Understanding how the culture of a country affects the way business is practiced.

Cross-licensing. The exchange of technology by different companies.

Cross-selling Agreements. Cross-selling means offering related items when a customer places an order. For example when a customer is served a burger, the waiter can inquire whether the customer would like fry with it.

Crowding Out. Describes the effect of increase in government purchases on other private spending government borrowing raises interest rates and hence reduces investment and consumption spending.

Crowding Out in the Open Economy. In the open economy an increased government spending financed by borrowing causes an increase in the interest rate which not only reduces consumption and investment, but also net exports counteracting the increase in government spending. It is most severe when exchange rates are flexible.

Crown Jewels. They are the most desirable entities within a diversified corporation as measured by asset value, earning power and business prospects. The crown jewels usually figure prominently in takeover attempts; they are the main objectives of the acquirer and may be sold by the takeover target to make the rest of the company less attractive.

Crush Speed. The purchase (or sale of soybean futures and the simultaneous sale or purchase) of soybean oil and soy-meal futures.

CSCE. Coffee, Sugar and Cocoa Exchange, New York.

CTN. Cotton Exchange, New York.

Cultural Conflict. The tension or friction between culture groups that stems from a lack of understanding by one group of the values.

Cultural Controls. Achieving control by persuading subordinates to identify with the norms and value systems of the organization (self control).

Cultural Distance. The amount of difference between two social systems.

Cultural Diversity. Differences in age, gender, race, ethnicity, nationality, and ability.

Cultural Relativism. The belief that behaviour has meaning and can be judged only in its specific cultural context.

Cultural Shock. A person's disorientation and insecurity caused by the strangeness of a different culture. (Also known as culture shock.)

Culture. Culture is a very complex environmental influence that includes knowledge, beliefs, law, morals, art, customs, and any other habits and capabilities an individual acquires as a member of society. It is important to be aware that cultures are learned, cultures vary, and cultures influence people's behavior.

Culture Shock. A generalized trauma one experiences in a new and different culture because of having to learn and cope with a vast array on new cues and expectations.

Cum-dividend. A stock trading before a dividend is paid.

Cumulative Preferred Stock. Preferred stock in which missed dividend payments go into arrears and must be made up before any common stock dividends can be paid.

Cumulative Voting. All directors up for election are voted on at the same time. The number of votes assigned to each stockholder equals the number of shares held multiplied by the number of directors to be elected.

Currency. All coin and paper money issued by the federal reserve banks, and all gold coins.

Currency Appreciation. When a country's currency rises in value relative to other currencies, meaning that the country's goods are more expensive for foreign buyers and foreign goods are cheaper (all else constant).

Currency Board. A currency board is an arrangement under which a country fixes its exchange rate and maintains 100 per cent backing of its money supply with foreign exchange. As reserves, it holds high-quality, interest-bearing securities denominated in the reserve asset. The currency board makes profits from the difference between the interest on the securities that it holds and the expense of maintaining its note and coin circulation. It remits to the government all profits beyond what it needs to pay expenses and maintain its reserve ratio.

Currency Crisis. Occurs when a speculative attach on the exchange value of a currency results in a sharp depreciation in the value of the currency or forces authorities to expand large volumes of international currency reserves and sharply increase interest rates to defense the prevailing exchange rate.

Currency Depreciation. When a country's currency falls in value relative to other currencies, meaning the country's goods become cheaper for foreign buyers and foreign goods become more expensive for foreign sellers.

Currency Exchange. Exchange of currency from one country with currency from another country.

Currency Futures and Options Market. Agreements that allow businesses or individuals acquiring or selling foreign currencies to protect themselves against future fluctuations in currency prices by shifting currency risk to someone else willing to bear that risk.

Currency Risk. Possible losses to a borrower or lender in foreign markets or to a holder of assets in foreign markets due to adverse changes in currency prices.

Currency Speculation. Involves short-term movement of funds from one currency to another in hopes of profiting from shifts in exchange rates.

Currency Sterilization. An action taken by a central bank to offset the impact from government purchases or sales of currencies on bank reserves and deposits through the use of central bank policy tools.

Currency Swap. A contract designed to reduce the risk of loss due to changes in currency of another that is of more use to a borrower.

Currency Translation. Converting the financial statements of foreign subsidiaries into the currency of the home country.

Current Account. That portion of the balance of payments that consists of the merchandise account, the services account, and the balance of unilateral transfers. Part of balance of payments which refers to national income and expenditure, including visible and invisible trade.

Current Account Deficit. The current account of the balance of payments is in deficit when a country imports more goods and services than it exports.

Current Account Surplus. The current account of the balance of payments.

Current Assets. Cash plus those assets that are reasonably expected to be converted to cash or sold or consumed during the normal operating cycle.

Current Assumption Whole Life Insurance. Non-participating whole life policy in which the cash values are based on the insurer's current mortality, investment, and expense experience. An accumulation account is credited with a current interest rate that changes over time. Also alled interest-sensitive whole life insurance.

Current Cost Accounting. Method that adjusts all items in a financial statement to factor out the effects of inflation.

Current Cost. Cost stated in terms of current market prices instead of historical cost.

Current Exposure. The cost of replacing a derivative securities contract at today's prices.

Current Liabilities. Liabilities that fall due within the coming year or within the normal operating cycle if longer than a year.

Current Rate Method. Using the exchange rate at the balance sheet date to translate the financial statements of a foreign subsidiary into the home currency.

Current Ratio. The ratio of current assets to current liabilities. (Current ratio = current assets/current liabilities.)

Current Savings. The change in net worth recorded by a sector or unit in the economy over the current time period.

Current Yield. The ratio of the annual coupon payment to the price paid for the bond.

Current-account Balance. Exports minus imports of goods services and unilateral transfers.

Current-cost Method. *See* Current cost.

Currently Attainable Standards. Standards expressing a level of economic efficiency that can be reached with skilled, diligent, superior effort.

Currently Insured. Status of a covered person under the Old Age, Survivors, and Disability Insurance (OASDI) program who has at least six quarters of coverage out of the last thirteen quarters, ending with the quarter of death, disability, or entitlement to retirement benefits.

Current-rate Method. A method of translating foreign currency financial statements that is used when the functional currency is that of the local operating environment.

Custodians. Custodians are connected to exchange. At the end of each day, they receive a report of all trades done on behalf of their clients. The custodians are required to confirm such trades. The last date for confirmation of trades is one day after close of trading period, *i.e.* Wednesday. Any trades, which are not confirmed by the custodians, are reverted back to the trading member. Custodians had to develop software and modify their procedures to meet the exchange schedules.

Customer Departmentalization. The grouping of jobs so that the job holders interact with a specific customer group or clientele.

Customer Division Structure. The organization of division by customer.

Customer Scenario. A profile of the 'typical' customer in a market segment that describes personal characteristics, buying habits, and consumer expectations.

Customers. Those who purchase an organization's goods and/or services.

Customs Duties. Taxes imposed on imported goods.

Customs Union. A form of regional economic integration that eliminates tariffs among member nations and establishes common external tariffs.

Customs Valuation. The value of goods on which customs authorities charge tariffs.

Cutoff Rate. Minimum desired rate of return.

Cycle Time. The time that elapses between a customer's request and the fulfillment of that request.

Cyclical Variation. A measure of the business cycle.

D

D. Definition of the US money supply that includes the total debt of domestic non-financial sectors.

D/A Terms. Documents against Acceptance where the documents to title of the goods are given to the purchaser only after the purchaser accepts, gives his acceptance to the draft Bill of Exchange/*Hundi*.

D'Amato Act. Act passed in 1996, similar to the Helms-Burton Act, aimed at Libya and Iran.

Daily Compounding. Sometimes compounding may be done continuously. For example, banks may pay or charge interest continuously they call it daily compounding.

Daily Margins. Normally payable in respect of every contract outstanding at the end of the day, generally at the rate of 5 to 10 per cent of the contract value which can be hiked to higher levels depending upon the volatility of the market. The higher rates being made applicable to bulls in a rising market and to bears in a falling market.

Daily Price Limits. The maximum and minimum daily price movement allowed on a futures contract.

Damage to Property of Others. Damage covered up to $500 per occurrence for an insured who damages others property. Payment is made despite the lack of legal liability. Coverage is included in Section II of the homeowners policy.

Damages. The monetary settlement awarded to a person who is injured by a branch of contract.

Data. Unorganized facts, statistics, opinions, and predictions gathered from various sources inside and outside the company.

Data Bank. Electronic storage file for data—unorganized information opinions and predictions from various facts, statistics gathered sources inside and outside the company.

Data Base Program. Computer program that allows users to work with information that is normally kept in lists names and addresses schedules inventories and so forth.

Data of Payment. Data that dividend checks are mailed.

Data of Record. Data on which holders of record are designated to receive a dividend.

Data Processing. Technology that supports an existing business; primarily used to improve the flow of financial information.

Database. A collection of related data—past, present, and projected—organized for convenient access.

Day Care Centers. The first day care center opened in New York City in 7. Charged with gathering intelligence information abroad.

Day Traders. Exchange members who take a position within a day and liquidate it before day's end.

Day's sales in receivables = 365 days/ receivable turnover.

Day-order. A day order as the name suggests, is an order which is valid for the day on which it is entered. If the order is not matched during the day, at the end of the training day, the order gets cancelled automatically.

Days sales in inventory = 365 days/ inventory turnover.

DB. Development Bank.

DC. Developed Country.

DDB. *See* Double-declining-balance depreciation.

De Novo Office. A newly established office.

Dealer Brands. Products that don't carry the manufacturer's name but carry a distributor or retailer's name instead.

Dealer in Non-cleared Securities. The dealer in non-cleared securities specialises in buying selling on his own account shares which are not on the active list. He is generally prepared to buy what is on offer and sell what is required but the price at which he deals varies with the activity of the particular stock.

Dealer Paper. Short-term commercial notes sold by borrowing corporations and issued through security dealers who contact interested investors to determine whether they will buy the notes.

Debenture. A bond that is not backed by any specific collateral but is backed by "the full faith and credit" of the selling firm or institution.

Debenture Bonds. Bond that are unsecured.

Debenture Bonds. Bonds backed by financial reputation of a company.

Debit. An entry on the left side of an account.

Debit Card. An authentic plastic card that is used to identify the owner of the card or to make immediate payments for goods or services.

Debt Capital. Funds raised through various forms of borrowing that must be repaid.

Debt Fund. A fund that invents in debt securities, it attempts generates a study income while preserving the investors principal. The returns from such funds are generally better than those from money market mutual funds and gift funds. These funds are generally presented by investors not willing to take on a higher risk.

Debt Instrument. A written promise by a borrower to pay the owner of the instrument a specified amount in the future. Asset requiring payments of fixed amounts, such as a government or corporate bond.

Debt Management Policy. The refunding or refinancing the federal governments debt in a way that contributes broad national goals and minimizes the burden of the debt.

Debt Market. A market where lenders provide funds to borrowers for some specified period of time. The market for trading debt instruments.

Debt Securities. Financial claims against the assets of a business firm, individual, or unit of government, represented in bonds and other contracts evidencing a loan of money.

Debt-equity Ratio. Total debt/total equity.

Debt-equity Ratio. Indicator of financial leverage. Compares assets provided by creditors to assets provided by shareholders. Determined by dividing long-term debt by common stockholder equity.

Debtor Nation. Country that owes more money to other nations than they owe it.

Debtors Turnover. Debtors turnover is found out by dividing credit sales by average debtors. Debtors turnover indicates the No. of Times the debtors turnover each year. Generally the higher the value of debtors turnover the more efficiency is the management of credit.

Debt-service Ratio. The ratio of interest payments plus principal amortization to exports.

Debt-trap. During the periods of low profits a highly debt finance company suffers great strain it cannot even pay the interest charges of creditors. As a result their pressure and control are further tightened to meet their working capital needs the firm finds difficulty in getting credit. It may have borrow on highly unfavourable terms. Thus it gets entangled in a debt-trap.

Decentralization. The relative freedom to make decisions. The lower the level in the organization that decisions are made, the greater the decentralization. It is the extent to which decision making authority/ responsibility is dispersed downward.

Decentralization of Authority. The tendency to disperse decision-making authority in an organization structure.

Decentralization of Performance. The geographic dispersal of operations in an enterprise.

Decentralized Decision Making. Lower level managers are empowered to make important decisions.

Decertification. The process by which workers take away a union's right to represent them.

Decimalization. In preparation for the industry-mandated conversion from fractional pricing to decimal pricing in the US equities and options markets, Instinet is continually planning to ensure that all products and services are decimal complaint by the industry imposed targets. The conversion will result in a new display format and potentially decreases the Minimum Price Variation (MPV) at which securities will be traded. These pricing increments will result in volume and frequency impacts on the securities industry. Clients can also e-mail their decimalization inquiries directly to Instinet at decimal@instinet.com.

Decision. A choice made from alternative courses of action in order to deal with a problem.

Decision Making. The selection from among alternatives courses of action or a rational selection of a course of action.

Decision Model. A formal method for making a choice that often involves quantitative analysis.

Decision Support Systems (DSS). The application of computers to facilitate the decision-making process of semi-structured tasks.

Decision Table. A convenient technique for showing the total expected value of each of a number of contemplated acts in the light of varying probabilities of the events that may take place on the varying values of each act under each of the events.

Decision Trees. An approach towards seeing risks and probabilities in a problem situation involving uncertainty, by sketching in the form of a "tree" decision points, chance events, and the probabilities involved in various courses that might be undertaken.

Decisional Roles. Activities that deal primarily with the allocation of resources in order to reach organizational objectives.

Declaration Date. Date on which the board of directors passes a resolution to pay a dividend.

Decline. The stage marked by decreases in the product's market share.

Declining Firms. Firms that would earn on investment the rate of return less than the minimum required by investors. Investors of such firm would like earnings to be distributed to them so that they may either spend it or invest elsewhere to get a rate higher than earned by the declining firms.

Decoding. The mental procedure that the receiver of a message uses to decipher the message.

Deep Pocket View. It refers to the theory that some subsidiary companies might have access to more funds than an independent firm of a similar size. It further argues that the subsidiary may call upon greater resources of its present to engage in competition with independents in the sector.

Deep-discount Bond (DDB). It is zero interest bond.

Default Risk Premium. The difference between the interest rate charged on safe loans, loans considered default-free, and the interest rate charged on loans that have a higher default risk.

Default Risk. The risk to the holder of debt securities that borrower will not meet all promised payments at the time agreed upon.

Default-free. A payoff to a security that has no possibility of default.

Defensive Behavior. Behavior (*e.g.* aggression, withdrawal, and repression) that is resorted to by an individual who is blocked in attempts to satisfy needs.

Deferral. The postponing of taxation of foreign source income until it is remitted to the parent company.

Deferred Annuity. A retirement annuity that provides benefits at some future date.

Deferred Call. Bond call provision prohibiting the company from redeeming the bond prior to a certain date.

Deferred Charge. An expenditure not recognized as a cost of operations of the period in which incurred but carried forward to be written off in one or more future periods.

Deferred Credit. Often used as a synonym for deferred revenue or as a description for deferred income tax. In its bookkeeping application, the term refers to an amount that is classified as a liability that will eventually be transferred as a credit to revenue or a credit to expense.

Deferred Equity Financing. By issuing convertible debentures, the firm is in turn selling ordinary shares in future. A company would do so when it considers the current market price of its share to below, but wants to issue shares at a higher price.

Deferred Income Tax (Liability). A liability in the balance sheet that represents the additional federal income taxes that would have been due if a company had not been allowed to deduct greater amounts for expenses of income tax-reporting purposes than are recorded for financial-reporting purposes.

Deferred Income. It represents fund required by the firm for goods and services, which it has agreed to supply in future. Also see Deferred revenue.

Deferred Revenue. Income received or recorded before it is earned.

Deferred Swap. A forward swap.

Deficit Budget Unit. An individual, business firm, or unit of government whose current expenditures exceed its current receipts of income, forcing it to become a net borrower in the money and capital markets.

Defined Benefit Plan. A type of pension plan in which the retirement benefit is known in advance but the contributions vary depending on the amount necessary to fund the desired benefit.

Defined Contribution Plan. Type of pension plan in which the contribution rate is fixed but the retirement benefit is variable.

Deflation. A situation where prices are actually declining.

Deflationary Gap. The difference between the actual level of investment and the level necessary to restore full employment.

De-gearing. Reduction of risk or leverage, examples include cutting borrowing and reducing exposures to forces which a company or dealer cannot control.

Degree of Financial Leverage. A measure of the relative percentage change in earnings per share (EPS) in response to a given percentage change in earnings before interest and taxes (EBIT).

Degree of Operating Leverage. A measure of the relative percentage change in operating earnings (EBIT) in response to a given percentage change in sales.

Degree of Total Leverage. A measure of the relative percentage change in earnings per share (EPS) in response to a given percentage change in sales.

Delegated Monitor. An economic agent appointed to act on behalf of smaller investors in collecting information and/or investing funds on their behalf.

Delegating. Assigning authority and accountability to others while retaining responsibility for results.

Delegation. The process by which authority is distributed downward in an organization.

Delegation of Authority, Process of. The determination of results expected from a subordinate, the assignment of tasks, the delegation of authority for accomplishing these tasks, and the holding of people responsible for the accomplishment of such tasks.

Delivery Date. The date on which the underlying asset is exchanged for a cash payment on a forward contract or a futures contract.

Delivery Month. The calendar month during which delivery as a futures contract must be made.

Delivery Period. Whenever a book closure or record date is announced by a company, the exchange sets a no delivery period for that security. During this time, trading is permitted in that security. However, these trades are settled only after the no delivery period is over. This is done to ensure that investor's entitlement for corporate benefits.

Delivery Price. The price used in determining the value of a contract held to maturity.

Delivery Stock. The quality of a commodity that meets exchange specified quality standards and is available for delivery at exchange specified locations (such as approved warehouse).

Delphi Group Technique. A technique employing a written survey to gather expert opinions without holding a group meeting.

Delphi Method. A group decision-making technique in which the group solicits and compares anonymous judgments on an issue through questionnaires and feedback. The technique is normally used for forecasting such future events and conditions as technological developments by obtaining estimates of experts in a field and feeding back summaries of these estimates for additional estimates by those experts, until a reasonable degree of convergence in estimates is obtained.

Delta. A measure of how much an option's premium changes for a given unit change in the underlying asset price must be made.

Delta Neutral. A portfolio position that has a delta of zero.

Demand. The amounts that buyers would be willing to purchase at corresponding schedule of prices.

Demand Curve. The relationship between the price of a good or service and its quality demanded.

Demand Deposit. The technical name for checking account; the money can be withdrawn anytime on demand from the owner.

Demand Deposits. Checking accounts in commercial banks. Deposits in depository institutions which can be withdrawn by depositors upon demand, *i.e.* whenever they choose. Demand deposits are transferable by cheque.

Demand for Net Exports. The demand for exports minus the demand for imports.

Demand Function. Describes the relationship that exists during some period of time between the number of units of a good or service that consumers are willing to buy and a given set of conditions that influence the willingness to purchase, such as price, income level, and advertising.

Demand Loan. A borrowing of funds (usually by a security dealer) subject to recall of those funds on demand by the lender.

Demand Oriented Pricing. A method of pricing in which the seller attempts to set the price at the level that the intended buyers are willing to pay.

Dematerialization. Dematerialization is the process by which shares in the physical/paper form are cancelled and converted in the form of electronic. Balance is maintained in highly secure system at the depository.

Democracy. Political system in which government is run by the people, exercised either directly or through elected representatives. Thus, it is a political system that relies on citizens' participation in the decision-making process.

Democratic Socialism. The belief that economics and politics are so closely connected that the voters should rely on their elected governments to control the economic system.

Demographics. The study of population characteristics such as age, sex, ethnic background, occupation, education, immigration and changes in population statistics or behavior. Demographics are used to describe customer scenarios or market segments.

Demography. The statistical study of human population to learn its size, density, and other characteristics.

Demotion. Downward movement to a job of lesser responsibility and pay.

Denominator Variance. Same as production volume variance.

Department Store. A store which is described as a collection of speciality stores under one roof.

Department. A distinct area, division, or branch of an enterprise over which a manager has authority for the performance of specified activities and results.

Departmentalization. The process of grouping jobs together on the basis of some common characteristics, such as product, client, location, or function.

Departmentation by Customer. The grouping of activities around customers.

Departmentation by Function. The grouping of activities in departments in accordance with this functions of an enterprise undertakes. For example, in a manufacturing company marketing, production, engineering, and finance.

Departmentation by Process or Equipment. The grouping of activities around a process or type of equipment used, such as electronic data-processing or painting departments.

Departmentation by Product. The grouping of activities around a product or product line.

Departmentation by Territory. The grouping of activities by territory segments; geographic departmentation.

Dependence Theory. The theory holding that LDCs have practically no power when dealing with MNEs as host countries.

Dependency Period. Period of tie following the readjustment period during which the surviving spouse's children are under eighteen and therefore dependent on the parent.

Dependency. A state in which a country is too dependent on the sale of one primary commodity and/or too dependent on one country as a customer and supplier.

Deposit Administration Plan. Type of pension plan in which all pension contributions are deposited in an unallocated fund. An annuity is purchased only when the employee retires.

Deposit Float. The amount of cheque sent by a customer which is not yet collected is called collection of deposit float.

Deposit Multiplier. A number that indicates how many dollars of new deposits will result from an injection of one more dollar or excess reserves into the banking system.

Depository Institution De-regulation and Monetary Control Act of 1980 (DIDMCA). Legislation designed to solve problems created in part by disintermediation.

Depository Institutions. Institutions which accept deposits from individuals and use the funds to participate in the debt market.

Depository Transfer Checks. A means for moving funds from local bank accounts to concentration accounts. The depository transfer check itself is an unsigned, non-negotiable instrument. It is payable only to the bank of deposit for credit to the firm's specific account.

Depository Trust Company. It is the principal depository company owned jointly by the New York Stock Exchange (NYSE) and American Stock Exchange (AMEX).

Depreciation. The systematic write-off of the cost of a tangible asset over its estimated useful life. The allocation of the acquisition cost of plant, property, and equipment to the particular periods or products that benefit from the utilization of the assets.

Depreciation Tax Shield. Depreciation is a deductible expense and saves taxes. It is equal to the amount of depreciation multiplied by the tax rate.

Depreciation of US Dollar. Depreciation of the US dollar means the dollar buys fewer units of foreign currency than before.

Depression. A severe recession.

Deregulation. The lifting for liberalization of government rules that restrict what private businesses can do to serve their customers. The removal or scaling down of regulatory authority and regulatory activities of government.

Derivative Security. A financial contract the value of which is derived from some underlying asset.

Derivatives Market. Market in which forward contracts futures, options, and swaps are traded in order to hedge or protect foreign exchange transactions.

Derivatives Securities Market. *See* Derivatives market.

Derived Association. An association that is defined in terms of other association.

Derived Demand. An individual bank's demand for deposits is called a derived demand because it is derived from the demand for loans that bank try to satisfy.

Descriptive Statistics. Quantitative data used to describe a particular characteristic such as the number of births.

Desired Currency to Deposit Ratio. The amount of excess reserves bank's wish to hold as a fraction of demand deposits.

Detachability. A warrant can be either detachable or non-detachable. If a warrant can be sold separately from the debenture to which it was originally attached, it is called a detachable warrant. A debenture holder may sell his warrant when its price increased continues holding the debenture.

Determinants of Demand. Variables that determine the position of demand curve, changes in them shift the curve.

Determinants of Supply. Variables that determine the position of the supply curve, changes in them shift the curve.

Deterministic Interest Rates. Future interest rates that are known with certainty.

Detinue. It is a legal term which means action to recover some thing that has been detained.

Devaluation. Lowering the value of a nation's currency relative to other currencies.

Developing Country. A poor country also known as a Third World country or a less developed country.

Development. The organization's efforts to help employees acquire knowledge, skills, and behavior that improve their ability to meet changes in the job requirements and customer needs.

Development Practices. Focus on preparing diverse employees for greater responsibility and advancement.

Devil's Advocacy. Assigning someone the role of critic.

DFIs. Development Finance Institutions.

Dia Terms. Documents against acceptance where the documents to title of the goods are given to the purchaser only after the purchaser accepts, given his acceptance to the draft bill of exchange/hundi.

Diagnosis. The use of data collected by interviews, surveys, observations, and records to learn and draw conclusions, about people or organizations.

Diagnosis-related Groups. Method for reimbursing hospitals under the Medicare program. Under this system, a flat, uniform amount is paid to each hospital for the same type of medical care or treatment.

Diagonal Communication. The flow of information often in matrix structures.

Dialectic Method. Fostering a debate of opposing viewpoints to better understand an issue.

Dictionary of Occupational Titles. A book listing 25,000 titles and descriptions and published by the department of labour.

Difference in Conditions Insurance (DIC). "All-risks" policy that covers other perils not insured by basic property insurance contracts, supple-mental to and not insured by basic property insurance contracts, supplemental to an excluding the coverage provided by underlying contracts.

Differential Cost. *See* Incremental cost.

Differential Pricing. The pricing strategy of offering a different price to different markets segments, differential threshold—the difference in pricing between alternative choices necessary before a buyer will switch to the other choice.

Differentiation. A characteristic of an open system, and social in particular, by which it tends to become more specialized in its structure and behaviour patterns.

Differentiation Strategy. An overall corporate strategy that involves creating real and perceived differences between the firm's products/services and those of competitors.

Diffusion of Responsibility. Members' view that responsibility for group tasks is divided among the groups, rather than being the burden of any single group or member.

Digital Computer. Computers, which work directly with numbers and alphabetic and special characters.

Digital Option. An option that at maturity pays one dollar if in-the-money, zero otherwise.

Diminishing Returns to Specialization. Applied to international trade theory, the more of a good that a country produces. Greater the units of resources required to produce each additional item.

Direct Bankruptcy Cost. The cost that are directly associated with bankruptcy, such as legal and administrative expenses.

Direct Choice Modeling. This approach allows the measuring of brand-specific price elastic ties as well a brand cross-price elasticity. The modelling involves developing choice sets that show products available in the market, along with their descriptions.

Direct Control. Control techniques designed to identify and correct the deviations in plans.

Direct Costs. Fixed or variable cost incurred by and solely for a particular product, department, program, sales, territory, or customers account.

Direct Finance. Finance that occurs when savers lend funds directly to borrowers.

Direct Financing Lease. Under accounting rules, a non- leveraged lease by a lessor (not a manufacturer or dealer) where the lessee meets criteria definitions of a capital lease (see above) plus the extra requirement that the collection-ability surround the amount of reimbursable costs to be incurred by the lessor under the lease.

Direct Fixed Costs. Costs that are incurred by and solely for a particular product or segment but that do not vary with an activity level.

Direct Identification Drawback. A provision that allows US firms to use imported components in the manufacturing process without having duty paid on the imported goods.

Direct Investment Entry Strategy. The strongest commitment to becoming an MNC, when management decides to begin producing the firm's products abroad. This strategy enables the firm to maintain partial to full control over production, marketing and other key functions.

Direct Labor. All labor that is obviously related to and specifically and conveniently traceable to specific products.

Direct Labor Productivity. The ratio of outputs to the labor used-to produce them.

Direct Loss. Financial loss that results directly from an insured peril.

Direct Marketing. Marketing that allows consumers to buy products by interacting with various advertising media without meeting a sales person face-to-face.

Direct Material. All raw material that is an integral part of the finished good and can be conveniently assigned to specific physical units.

Direct Method. A method that ignores other service departments when any given service department's costs are allocated to revenue-producing or production departments.

Direct Paper. Any financial transaction in which a borrower and a lender of funds communicate directly and mutually agree to the terms of a loan.

Direct Quote. A quote expressed in terms of the number of units of the domestic currency given for one unit of a foreign currency.

Direct-response System. A marketing method where insurance is sold without the services of an agent. Potential customers are solicited by advertising in the mails, news-papers, magazines, television, radio, and other media.

Direct Selling. A sale of goods by an exporter directly to distributors of final consumers rather than to trading companies or other intermediaries in order to achieve greater control over the marketing functions and to earn higher profits.

Direct Transfer. A corporation sells its stock of debt directly to investors without going through a financial institution.

Direct Variable Costs. Costs that vary directly with activity level.

Direct Writer. An insurer that markets its services through its own employees.

Directing. The management function dealing with the face-to-face supervision of employees.

Direction. A method of concurrent control that refers to the manager's acts of communicating orders to subordinates and overseeing their work.

Directive. A proposed form of legislation in the EU.

Directive Counselling. An approach in which the counsellor asks specific questions.

Dirty Float. Situation where the exchange rate is determined by supply and demand, but the government influences supply and demand by buying and selling currency.

Dirty-float System. A system under which a country's currency is nominally allowed to float freely against other currencies, but in which the government will intervene, buying and selling currency.

Disability Insured. Status of an individual who is insured for disability benefits under the Old-age, Survivors, and Disability Insurance (OASDI) Program. The covered person must be disability-insured and have at least twenty quarters of coverage out of the last forty, ending with the quarter in which the disability occurs. Fewer quarters are required for persons under age thirty.

Disbursing Float. Funds available in the company's bank account until its payment check has cleared through the bank system.

Disc Based Advertising. Product information provided on a CD-ROM or computer disk.

DISC. Domestic International Sales Corporation.

Discharge. The action of one party not having to meet his obligation to a contract because other parties to the contract have not fulfilled their obligation.

Discount (in Foreign Exchange). A situation in which the forward rate for a foreign currency is less than the spot rate, assuming that the domestic currency is quoted on a direct basis.

Discount. A reduction in price.

Discount Bond. A zero coupon bond.

Discount Broker. A stockbroker who conducts trades for customers but does not offer investment advice.

Discount Method. A method for calculating the interest charge on a loan that deducts the interest owed from the face amount of the loan, with the borrower receiving only the net proceeds after interest is deducted.

Discount Payback. The number of years required in recovering the costs outlay on the present value basis is the discounted payback period.

Discount Points. Interest payments made when the loan is issued (at closing). One discount point paid up front is equal to 1 per cent of the principal value of the mortgage.

Discount Rate. (1) The interest rate that the Fed charges for loans to member banks. (2) As used in capital budgeting, the minimum desired rate of return.

Discount Store. This store features a wide variety of goods at low prices.

Discount Window. Banks and other depository institutions can "go to the window" to borrow from the federal government. Presentation of assets as collateral is not required, banks merely promise to repay the loan in the future.

Discount Yield. Measure of yield frequently used in the case of treasury bills, but which understates the actual yield to maturity.

Discounted Cash Flow (DCF) Valuation. The process of valuing an investment by discounting its future cash flows.

Discounted Cash Flow. Technique for assessing the present value of future income and payments which takes into account of the time value of money.

Discounted Future Earnings Method. A method of valuation to establish the market value of a business acquisition by using net-present-value techniques to convert future earning potential into current dollar terms.

Discounting. A financial institution lending money to a customer's debt obligation to the business as security of the loan.

Discovery Premium to Nav. The difference between the unit price and the NAV in percentage terms if the price is higher than the NAV, the units are trading at a premium if the price is lower.

Discrete Probability Distribution. A probability distribution that has a finite number of possible outcomes.

Discretely Compounded Interest Rates. Interest rates that include compounding over discrete time periods.

Discretionary Costs. Fixed costs arising from periodic, usually yearly, appropriation decisions that directly reflect top-management policies. Also are called programmed costs or managed costs.

Discretionary Monetary Policy. A situation where the federal government has the flexibility to respond, however, it sees fit. Without any constraint to follow some pre-existing rule.

Discrimination (EEOC Definition). It is the use of any test that adversely affects hiring, promotion, transfer or any other employment or membership opportunity of classes unless the test has been validated and is job related; and/or an employer can demonstrate that alternative hiring, transfer, or promotion procedures are unavailable.

Discrimination (in Jobs or Employment). Unequal treatment of employees based on non-job-related factors such as race, sex, age, national origin, religion, colour, and physical or mental handicap.

Disequilibrium. In economic theory, either a shortage or surplus creating an excess or lessening in demand. Entrepreneurship is concerned with creating disequilibrium, or taking advantage of opportunities that exist because of disequilibrium.

Disinflation. Buying several different investment alternatives to spread the risk of investing.

Dis-intermediation. Describes the phenomenon of depositors withdrawing funds from financial intermediaries in favour of direct finance.

Disjunctive Tasks. Tasks that can be completed through individual efforts of group members.

Displaced Log Normal Distribution. A log normal distribution the mean of which is translated along the horizontal axis.

Distance Effect. It indicates the time required to computer two numbers is an inverse function of the numerical distance between them.

Distinctive Competence. What a firm does well relative to its competitors.

Distortion. A deviation between the sent message and the received message.

Distribution Logistics. An operations research optimizing model that treats the entire materials flow system of an enterprise—from sales fore-casting through purchasing and processing of materials, inventorying them, to shipping of finished goods to sales warehouses—as a single system.

Distribution. The course-physical path or legal title—that goods take between production and consumption.

Distributive Justice. The perceived fairness of how resources and rewards are distributed.

Distributor. A merchant in a foreign country who purchases products from the manufacturer and sells them at profit.

Divergent Thinking. Seeing differences between situations.

Diversification. Buying different investment alternatives to spread the risk of investment.

Diversification Strategy. A strategy by which an international company produces or sells in many countries to avoid relying on one particular market.

Diversified Portfolio. A portfolio which invests among a variety of securities with different risk, reward, and correlation statistics so as to minimize unsystematic risk.

Diversify. *See* Diversification.

Diversion in Transit. A service offered by rail carriers which permits a shipper of goods to re-route his goods to a destination from the original destination while the goods are in transit.

Diversity. The host of individual differences that make people different from and similar to each other.

Divestment. A strategy selling off businesses as the company no longer wishes to maintain, either because they are failing or because the company has changed its corporate strategy and does not wish to be in such businesses any longer.

Dividend. A return-on-investment payment made to the owners of shares of corporate stock at the discretion of the company's board of directors.

Dividend Capitalization. The value of a share today is a function of cash inflows expected by investors and risk associated with those cash inflows. Cash inflows expected from an equity share consists of dividends expected to be received by the owner while holding the share and the price which he expects to obtain when the share is sold.

Dividend Decision. Dividend decision is the major financial decision. The financial manager must decide whether the firm should distribute all profits or retain some of them or distribute a portion of them and retain the balance. The payout ratio is equal to the per cent of dividends to the earning available to the shareholders.

Dividend Growth Model. Model that determines the current price of a stock as its dividend next period divided by the discount rate less the dividend growth rate.

Dividend Pay-out Ratio. The dividend pay-out ratio is DPS (dividend per share) divided by the EPS (earnings per share).

Dividend Per Share. It is the earnings distributed to ordinary shareholders divided by the number of ordinary shares outstanding.

Dividend Policy. A firm's policy regarding the payment of dividends to its owners.

Dividend Yield. The ratio of the annual dividends per share to the price of the stock.

Division of Labor. The idea of breaking down an entire job into its component parts and assigning each specific task to an individual member also called specialization.

Divisional/Departmentation. The process of grouping employees according to market or operation characteristics.

Documents of Title. Instruments that denote ownership or merchandise or goods which can be transferred by endorsement.

Dogs. Businesses that have only minimal profits or even losses due to their low market share in slow growing market.

Dollar Return. One plus the per cent return.

Dolphin. Dolphin is an informed term referring to a person who buys shares in new issues and then sells for high profits as soon as trading opens.

Domestic Insurer. Insurance company domiciled and licensed in the state in which it does business.

Domestic Organization. An organization that operates within a single country.

Dominance. The expectation of: (1) both higher return and lower risk for one asset than the other, (2) higher return for one asset than for others with the same risk, or (3) lower risk for one asset than for another with the same return.

Dominant Strategy. Situation in game theory where one player has an action or strategy that is best, regardless of what the other players do.

Domino Effect. An action being affected by a previous action known as domino effect.

Dormant Partner. A partner who assumes no active role in the business and who is not known as a partner to the public.

Double Coincidence of Wants. A situation that occurs in a barter transition between two individuals the first individual wants, and the second individual has goods or service that the first individual wants.

Double Declining Balance Depreciation (DDB). A form of accelerated depreciation that results in first-year depreciation being twice the amount of straight-line depreciation when zero terminal disposal value is assumed.

Double Dipping. The structuring of leases to draw benefit from the benefits on capital investment in more than one country.

Double Entry Bookkeeping. The concept of writing every transaction in two places.

Double Indemnity Rider. Benefit that can be added to a life insurance policy doubling the face amount of life insurance if death occurs as a result of an accident.

Double Taxation. Under this system, shareowners' earnings are taxed twice. First, the corporate tax is levied on the profits at the level of the company, and then, the profits are distributed as dividends and such dividends are taxed as ordinary income in the hands of shareholders.

Dow Jones Average. Index of stock prices composed of four different averages of stock.

Dow Jones Industrial Average. The average cost of 30 selected industrial stocks; used to give an indication of the direction (up or down) of the stock market over tie.

Down and Dirty. Getting so deeply involved in some thing so that getting dirty and doing it does not matter.

Down Payment. A portion of the purchase price of the property a financial institution requires the mortgage borrower to pay up front.

Down-and-in Option. For down-and-in options, a lower level (barrier) is specified for the asset price on which the option is written. For a down-and-in call (put) option the contract becomes a standard call (put) option if the price of the underlying asset falls below the barrier. If the price of the underlying asset never falls below the barrier during the life of the contract, the contract expires worthless.

Down-and-out Option. For down-and-out options, a lower level (barrier) is specified for the asset price on which the option is written. For a down-and-out call (put) option the contract ceases to exist if the price of the underlying asset falls below the barrier. If the price of the underlying asset falls below the barrier during the life of the contract, the contract expires as an ordinary call (put) option.

Downside Risk. That portion of probability distribution of the returns on an investment to the left of the mean; the probability of earning less than expected.

Downsizing. Elimination of jobs and thereby shirking asset size.

Downward Communication. The traditional flow of information from upper organizational levels to lower levels, such as job directions, assignment of tasks, performance feedback and information concerning the organization's goals.

Draft. Bill of lading.

Draw. It is an amount advanced to an employee and repaid from future commissions earned by the employee.

Drawback. A provision allowing US exporters to apply for refunds of 99 per cent of the duty paid on imported components provided they are used in the manufacture of goods that are exported.

Drawee. The party to whom a bill of lading is presented.

Drip Feed. Funding a new company in a number of stages rather an at once.

Driver Education Credit. Student discount or reduction in premium amount for which young drivers become eligible on completion of a driver education course.

DRR. Debenture Redemption Reserve.

DTB. Deutsche Terminborse, Frankfurt, Germany.

Du pont Identity. Popular expression of breaking ROE into three parts: operating, asset use efficiency, and financial leverage.

Dual Banking. The system of banking in which banks can obtain either a state or a national charter.

Dual Banking System. *See* Dual banking.

Dual Class Firms. Two classes of common stock, are outstanding, with differential voting rights assigned to each class.

Dual Function Discount System. Reduction in price granted distributors or dealers who perform different marketing functions for the manufacturer. For example, one channel of distribution may consist of wholesalers and retailers, while another channel used by the same manufacturer may consist only of retailers. In the latter channel, some of the functions performed by the retailers may be for a wholesaling nature, hence these retailers are performing a 'dual function' for the manufacturer.

Dual Problem. A linear-programming problem that is associated with the primary problem. Solution of the primary problem automatically provides a solution to the dual problem.

Dual Rate of Return. An internal rate of return measure. An arbitrary reinvestment rate applied to periods in which cash surpluses arise under the lease.

The appropriate pre-tax borrowing rate as determined by interactive procedures.

Dual Trading. Floor brokers execute the order at the market place/floor at the exchange to trade future contracts that are accepted by FCMS. Floor traders are individual members at the exchange who act as agents for FCMS they make trading to their own accounts as well as for customer's account. This practice is known as dual trading.

Dual Variable. A variable that measures the objective function (for example, profit or cost) will change if a given constraint is increased by one unit, provided the increase in the resource does not shift the optimal solution to another extreme point of the feasible solution space.

Due Date. It is the date by which the supplier expects payments.

Dumping. Selling goods abroad at a lower price than charged for them in the home market. It is an example of discriminating monopoly. If the monopolist covers all his fixed expenses in the home market he can add to his total profit even if the price he fixes for foreign buyers is little higher than what is sufficient to cover his marginal cost. Dumping gives rise to strong protest from producers of similar goods in the country in which the goods are dumped.

Duopsony. It is a market in which there are only few purchasers of goods and services but a number of competing suppliers.

Durable Goods. Tangible goods which can be expected to last for a relatively long time even though used repeatedly.

Duration. A measure of the average life of a bond.

Duration Gap. A measure of overall interest rate risk exposure for an FI.

Duress. When threat or other action causes a person to perform an act against his will.

Dutch Auction. A form of auction in which the auctioneer (or an electronic device) starts with a high price and successively announces a lower price until a bidder bids and wins the lot for sale.

Duty. A government tax (tariff) levied on goods shipped internationally.

Dwelling Property 1. Property insurance policy that insures dwelling at actual cash value, other structures, personal property, fair rental value, and certain other coverages covers a limited number of perils.

Dwelling Property 2. Property insurance policy that insures the dwelling and other structures at replacement cost. It adds additional coverages and has a greater list of covered perils than the Dwelling Property 1 policy.

Dwelling Property 3. Property insurance policy that covers the dwelling and other structures against direct physical loss from any peril except for those perils otherwise excluded. However, personal property is covered on a named-perils basis.

Dying Intestate. Dying without a will.

Dynamically Complete. A market where any derivative can be synthetically replicated using a dynamic trading strategy.

Dynamism. A condition of constant and rapid change.

Dysfunctional Behaviour. Actions taken in conflict with management goals.

Dysfunctional Conflict. Threatens organization's interests.

E

Earned Surplus. A virtually archaic term for retained income.

Earning Assets. Investment securities plan net loans and leases.

Earnings Cap. Limit of earnings introduced in the 1989 Financial Act for pension purposes. It represents the maximum earnings that can be pensioned. It does not apply to scheme members under approval basis before 1989 or to retirement annuities.

Earnings Per Share. Net income divided by the number of common shares outstanding.

Earnings Test (Retirement Test). Test under the Old-Age, Survivors, and Disability Insurance (OASDI) program that reduces monthly benefits to those persons who have annual income in excess of the maximum allowed.

i. Earnings before interest and taxes/total assets.

ii. Earnings before interest and taxes/ sales.

Earnings Yields. Hypothetical figure that provides a reliable measurement of the worth of an investment. It is reached by relating a company's divisible net earnings to the market price of the investment. Sometimes, with reference to fixed interest securities, the term is used interchangeably with flat yield.

Earnings. The excess of revenues over expenses.

EAT. Earnings After Taxes.

EBIT. The appropriate measure of profit is operating profit. Operating profit is equivalent to earnings before interest and taxes (EBIT). This measure of profit shows earnings arising directly from the commercial operations of business without the effect of financing. On an after tax basis profit to investors is equal to EBIT (I-T) where T is corporate tax.

EBRD. European Bank for Reconstruction and Development.

Eclectic Paradigm. Argument that combines location-specific assets or resource endowments and the firm's own unique assets often requires FDI; it requires the firm to establish production facilities where those foreign assets or resource endowments are located.

Ecological Balance. A natural equilibrium maintained among any group of living things and environment they occupy.

Ecology. The study of how living things plant and animals interact with one another and with their environment.

E-commerce. Conducting business on-line through the internet.

Economic Community of West African States (ECOWAS). A form of economic integration among certain countries in West Africa.

Economic Dimension. The overall condition of the complex economies through-out the world.

Economic Exposure. The foreign exchange risk that international business face in the pricing of products, the source and cost of inputs, and the location of investment.

Economic Forces. The relationship of people to resources.

Economic Goods and Services. Anything of value produced by an economic system includes all products and services.

Economic Growth. An increase in the economy's ability to produce real output of goods and services.

Economic Integration. The abolition of economic discrimination between national economies such as within the EU.

Economic Life of Leased Property. The estimated remaining period during which the property is expected to be economically usable by one or more users, with normal repairs and maintenance, for which it was intended at the inception of the lease.

Economic Lot Size. Synonym for economic order quantity.

Economic Metric Models. The use of systems of equations and statistical estimation methods to explain or forecast changes in interest rates or other variables.

Economic Opportunity Loans. Direct loans and loan guarantees made available through the small business administration to be qualified minority or disadvantaged persons for business operations.

Economic Order Quantity. The optimum order quantity of an inventory item; the order quantity that results in the least total cost for the firm.

Economic Profit. The difference between total revenue and total economic cost. Economic cost includes a normal rate of return on the capital contributions of the firm's owners.

Economic Risk. The likelihood that events, including economic mismanagement, will cause drastic changes in a country's business environment that adversely affects the profit and other goals of a particular business enterprise.

Economic System. The system concerned with allocation of scarce resources.

Economic Union. A group of countries committed to (1) removing all barriers to the free flow of goods services, and of production between each other; (2) the adoption of a common currency; (3) the harmonization of tax rates; and (4) the pursuit of a common external trade policy.

Economic Value Added (EVA). It is the value-added to shareholders by generating operating profit in excess of the cost of capital employed in the business.

Economics. The study of how society chooses to deploy resources to produce goods and services and distribute them for consumption among various competing groups and individuals.

Economies of Scale. The lowering of cost per unit as output increases because of allocation of fixed costs over more units produced.

Economies of Scope. The degree to which an FI can generate cost synergies by producing multiple financial service products.

Ecosystem. All of the plants and animals, together with their natural environment living together in an inter-dependent system.

ECOWAS. *See* Economic Community of West African States.

Ecu. A basket of EU currencies that serves as the unit of account for the EMS.

ECU. *See* European Currency Unit.

Edge Act Corporations. Special subsidiaries of US banking organizations authorized by federal law to offer international banking services.

EEA. European Economic Area.

EEC Patent Convention. An important cross-national patent convention that involves the members of the EU objectives should be, and whether revised plans needed to meet these objectives.

Effective. Accomplishing objectives with a minimum of resources.

Effective Annual Rate (EAR). The interest rate expressed as if it were compounded once per year.

Effective Interest Rate. If compounding is done more than once a year, the actual rate of interest paid (or received) is called the effective interest rate, and it would be higher than the nominal interest rate.

Effective Manual Yield. The promised rate of return on an investment in a bond.

Effective Tariff. The real tariff on the manufactured portion of developing countries exports which is higher than indicated by the published rates because the *ad valorem* tariff is based on the total value of the products include raw materials that would have had duty free entry.

Effectiveness. The achievement of the desired objectives.

Effectiveness Lags Increase. The time between policy action and the result in changes in the economy.

Efficiency. The minimal use of resources.

Efficiency Variance. The standard price for a given resource, multiplied by the difference between the actual quantity of inputs used and the standard quantity of inputs allowed for the number of good outputs achieved.

Efficient Assets (Portfolios). Assets (portfolios) whose risk-return points lie on the efficient frontier.

Efficient Capital Market. One in which market prices 'fully reflect' all information available at a given time.

Efficient Consumer Response. The electronic linking of firms to provide more efficient response to consumer needs.

Efficient Frontier. The investment projects or asset portfolios that dominate all other investment projects or asset portfolios in a given set on the basis of their return and risk characteristics.

Efficient Markets Hypothesis. It states that the current price of an asset such as a share of stock, reflects all available information about the value of the asset.

Efficient Portfolio. The portfolio which has the highest expected returns for a given level of risk is called an efficient portfolio.

Efficiently. Accomplishing objectives with a minimum of resources.

EFTA. *See* European Free Trade Association.

Elaboration. The tendency of an open system, and social system in particular, to enlarge its boundaries or create a new suprasystem with wider boundaries.

Elastic (Product Demand). A condition in which sales are likely to increase or decrease by a percentage that is more than the percentage change in income.

Elastic Currency. A money supply which can be easily converted from demand deposits into currency.

Elasticity. A measure of how responsive one variable is to a change in another variable. For instance, the elasticity of supply of deposits is the percentage change in the quantity supplied of deposits divided by the percentage change in the interest rate paid on deposits.

Electoral Politics. Activities undertaken by business and other interest groups to influence the outcome of elections to public office.

Electronic Data Interchange (EDI). The electronic movement of information via computers and telecommunications equipment.

Electronic Funds Transfer System. A computerized system that electronically performs financial transactions such as making purchases, paying bills, and receiving paychecks.

Electronic Mail. Uses the internet/intranet to send computer-generated text and documents.

Eligibility Period. Brief period of time during which an employee can sign up for group insurance without furnishing evidence of insurability.

Elimination Period. Waiting period in health insurance during which benefits are not paid. Also a period of time that must be met before benefits are actually payable.

Embargo. A complete ban on the import or export of certain products.

Embargoes. Keeps goods from entering a nation may be on a product or nation basis.

EM. Export Management companies.

EMC. *See* Export Management Company.

EMCF. European Monetary Cooperation Fund 889.

Emission Standard. A legally defined specific amount of a pollutant permitted to be discharged from a polluting source in a given period of time (compare with Environmental-quality standard).

Emotional Buying Motive. A decision to buy which involves little or no thought.

Emotional Stability. The extent to which a person's emotions are even.

Emotions. Complex human reactions to personal achievements and setbacks.

Empathy. Viewing an issue as another person would view it.

Empirical Probability. The likelihood of the occurrence of an event cannot be determined without experimentation.

Employee Centered Leader Behavior. An effort to lead employees by developing a cohesive work group and ensuring employee satisfaction.

Employee Centered Leaders. The most effective managers, who engage in both dimensions of leadership behaviors by getting employees involved in the operation of their departments or divisions in a positive and constructive manner, setting general goals, providing fairly loose supervision, and recognizing employees' contributions.

Employee Dishonesty Coverage Form. Commercial crime insurance form drafted by the Insurance Services Office that covers the loss of money, securities, and other covered property because of dishonest act of a covered employee or employees.

Employee Orientation. The activity that introduces new employees to the organization to fellow employees; to their immediate supervisors; and to the policies, practices, and objectives of the firm.

Employee Retirement Income Security Act (ERISA). Legislation passed in 1974 applying to most private pension and welfare plans that requires certain standards to protect participating employees.

Employee Safety. A work environment that provides personal protective equipment control of exposure to air contaminants and clean orderly work areas.

Employee Stock Ownership Plan (ESOP). It is a stock bonus plan whereby employees gain ownership in the firm for which they work.

Employee-assistance Programme. It provides counselling and other help to employees having emotional, physical, or other personal problems.

Employees Association. A union whose membership is made up almost entirely of professional, state and local government workers.

Employer's Association. Joining together of employers of different firms to present united efforts in dealing with labour unions demands.

Employers' Liability Insurance. Covers employers against law suits by employees who are injured in the course of employment, but whose injuries (or disease) are not compensatable under the state's workers compensation law.

Employment Contract. Mutual written and implied expectations between employer and employees.

Empower. Transfer power to others.

Empowerment. The extent of a group's authority and ability to make and implement work decisions.

EMU. Economic and Monetary Union.

Enabling. Giving workers the education and tools needed to assume their new decision-making powers.

Encoding. The process of transforming information into understandable symbols, typically spoken or written words or gestures.

Encounter Group Training. A group training method in which intense personal discussion may threaten the privacy of one or more participants.

End Prices. The prices of the lowest and the highest priced products in a product line.

Ending Rate. The spot exchange rate when budget and performance are being compared.

Endogenous Money Supply. Upward sloping money supply curve that results when the determinants of the money supply—most notably the currency to deposit ratio and the desired excess reserve ratio—are endogenous and depend on economic variables like interest rates.

Endorsement. Written provision that adds to, deletes, or modifies the provisions in the original contract.

Endowment Insurance. Type of life insurance that pays the fee amount of insurance to the beneficiary if the insured dies within a specified period to the policy owner if the insured survives to the end of the period.

Engineered Cost. Any cost that has an explicit, specified physical relationship with a selected measure of activity.

English Auction. A form of auction in which the highest bidder among potential buyers, or the lowest bidder among potential sellers, is the winner.

Enlightened Self Interest Model of Social Involvement. The view that social responsiveness and long run economic return are compatible.

Enter the Market. In the case of an OS sell orders the order gets triggered if the last traded price is less than or equal to the OS sell order price.

Enterprise of the America. A proposed series of bilateral trade relationships between the United States and Latin American countries, based on a "hub and spokes" concept and eventually resulting in one huge multilateral relationship involving the America.

Enterprise Resource Planning. Computer based production and operations system that links multiple firms into one integrated production unit.

Enterprise Self-audit. The making by an enterprise of an audit, or appraisal, of its position, where it is heading under present programmes.

Entire Contract Clause. Provision in life insurance policies stating that the life insurance policy and attached application constitute the entire contract between the parities.

Entity. A specific area of accountability that is the focus of the accounting process. It may be a single corporation, a tax district, a department, a papermaking machine, or a consolidated group of many interrelated corporations.

Entrepreneurship. The process of creating and managing a business to achieve desired objectives.

Entrepreneurial Team. The combined effort by venture founders and key personnel who together provide the talent and inspiration to succeed.

Entrepreneurs. People with the ability to see an opportunity, to obtain the necessary capital, labour, and other inputs, and to know how to put together an operation successfully, and with the willingness to take the personal risk of success or failure.

Entropy. The tendency of systems to deteriorate or break down over time.

Entry and Exit Loads. These are shares to investors to sell (exit) or buy (enter).

Environment. All of those factors that affect the operation of the organization.

Environment—Climate. The external conditions in host countries that could significantly affect the success of a foreign business enterprise.

Environment—Economic. That environment of managers which has to do with such elements as capital, materials, labour availability, quality, and price/price levels, productivity, availability of high-quality entrepreneurs and managers, government fiscal and tax policy, customers, and demands for goods and services.

Environment—Ethical. That environment of managers which has to do with generally accepted sets of standards of personal conduct.

Environment—Political. That environment of managers which has to do with the complex of laws, regulations, and government agencies and their actions.

Environment—Social. That environment of managers which has to do with the attitudes, desires, expectations, degrees of intelligence, beliefs, and customers of people in any people in any given group or society; social forces.

Environment—Technological. That environment of managers which has to do with such laments as knowledge of ways of doing things; inventions; and techniques in the areas of processes, machines and tools.

Environmental Forecasting. Forecasting the future environment—economic, technological, social, ethical, and political—as it may affect the enterprise.

Environmental Impact Statement. A report on the expected environmental effects of a planned development. Such reports are required when federal funding or federal jurisdiction is involved.

Environmental Quality Standard. A legally defined specific amount of a pollutant permitted to be present in areas such as a plant where toxic substances are used in a region where auto traffic is heavy (compare with Emission standard).

Environmental Responsibility. The responsibility of business to help maintain a quality environment by helping to eliminate all forms of pollution.

Environmental Scanning. Examining an organization's environment to discover trends and forces that may have an impact on the organization.

EPO. European Patent Organization.

Equal Credit Opportunity Act. A federal law passed in 1974 forbidding lending institutions from discriminating in the granting credit based on the age, race, ethnic origin, religion, or receipt of public assistance of the borrowing customer.

Equal Employment Opportunity. The principle that all persons otherwise qualified should be treated equally with respect to job opportunities, workplace conditions, pay fringe benefits and retirement provisions.

Equal Opportunity. The chance for all persons and groups in society to compete on the same basis for personal and social goals. Equal opportunity does not guarantee personal or social or economic equality because some persons are more talented or luckier than others.

Equal Results. A goal to insure that all people in a social system actually have equal benefits such as education and income.

Equalization Reserve. Return on capital invested in a unit trust. All investors in a trust receive an equal sum per unit held, although some may only have invested in the period since the last distribution. The distribution paid on the latter's stock therefore comprises the dividend and an equalization that brings the return up to par.

Equation of Exchange. MV = PY; links aggregate spending in an economy and the stock of money.

Equilibrium. Situation where there is no tendency for the price to change any further.

Equipment Trust Bonds. Bonds used to finance the purchase of new equipment (used chiefly by railroads).

Equity. It is the perceived fairness of what the person does (inputs) compared with what the person receives (outcomes).

Equity Alliance. A situation in which a cooperating company takes an equity position (almost always a minority) in the company with which it has a collaborative arrangement.

Equity Capital. Capital of the company that belongs to the owners of the company in many cases holder of ordinary shares. Funds obtained for the business by selling ownership.

Equity Financing. A form of capital in which investors become partners or stockholders in a company. Equity instruments create ownership rights.

Equity Fund. A fund that invests primarily in stocks, the riskiest asset class available in Indian markets. Such funds show volatile performance with equity prices fluctuating daily and can show significant losses well. Baring this risk, these funds can show superior performance to others as equities can yield greater capital appreciation than other asset classes.

Equity in the Unearned Premium Reserve. Amount by which an unearned premium reserve is overstated because it is established on the basis of gross premium rather than net premium.

Equity Instruments. Shares of common stock represent the ownership of a share of a firm.

Equity Kicker. A loan guaranty that the lender will relieve.

Equity Market. A market where ownership shares are bought and sold.

Equity Method. A basis for carrying long-term investments at cost plus a pro-rata share of accumulated retained income since acquisition. Equivalent units—the expression of output in terms of doses or amount of work applied thereto.

Equity Method of Accounting. Where ownership of voting common stock is between 20 to 50 per cent, the accounting profession adopts the view that the holding company has effective control of dividend policy of the subsidiary. The initial cost of the investment in the subsidiary stock is shown separately as a long-term investment under assets on the holding company's balance sheet. As time passes, the investment account is adjusted upward for the holding company's share of subsidiary profits, and downward for its share in subsidiary losses and for dividend received. This is referred to as the equity method of accounting for subsidiaries.

Equity multiplier = Total assets/total equity.

Equity Participation Mortgage. A mortgage that is similar to a SAM except that an outside investor shares in the appreciation of the property rather than the financial institution.

Equity Swap Ratio. When a company merges with another company, recommend Equity swap ratio on the basis of which merging company shares are equated with the shares of merged company.

Equity Theory. A theory stating that the extent to which people are willing to contribute to an organization depends on their assessment of the fairness of the rewards they will receive in exchange.

Equivalent Annual Returns. Rate earned over a 12-month period taking the compounding of interest into account.

Equivalent Martingale Probabilities. The probabilities for computing the risk neutral value.

ERG Theory. Alderfer's theory that people are motivated by a hierarchy of existence, relatedness, and growth needs.

Ergonomics. It is a study of workers and choices that confront them in ordinary working situations. Ergonomics has as its goal, *i.e.* increase in the efficiency of the workforce and therefore the productivity.

Erosion. The cash flows or a new project that come at the expense of a firm's existing projects.

Erratic Fluctuations. Changes of a short-term duration difficult to measure and predict because of their un-expectedness.

Error Free Production. A manufacturing process consisting of maintaining machinery and equipment, quality inspection checks and well trained employees.

Errors and Omissions Insurance. Liability insurance policy that provides protection against loss incurred by a client because of some negligent act, error or omission by the insured.

Escalation of Commitment. The tendency to persist with a failing course of action.

Escape Strategy. Coping strategy that avoids or ignores stressors and problems.

Escheat. The reversion of property to the state when a person having no legal heir dies without making a valid will.

Escrow. Property or money held by a third party until the agreed upon obligations of a contract are met.

Espoused Values. The values of employees to which they consciously refer when making decisions.

Essential Insurance. Includes those coverages required by law or by contract such as workers compensation insurance.

Essential-industry Argument. The argument holding that certain domestic industries need protection for national security purposes.

Establish the Defendant's Negligence. It does not preclude the defendant from establishing a defense.

Estate Planning. Process designed to conserve estate assets before and after death distribute property according to the individual's wishes, minimize federal estate and state inheritance taxes and provide estate liquidity to meet costs of estate settlement and the family's financial needs.

Estimation Risk. The possibility that errors in projected cash flows lead to incorrect decisions.

Estoppel. Legal doctrine that prevents a person from denying the truth of a previous representation of fact especially when such representation has been relied on by the one to whom the statement was made.

ETC. *See* Export trading company.

Ethical Formalism. A philosophy that focuses on human rights or values and on the intentions associated with a particular behavior.

Ethical Issue. An identifiable problem, situation, or opportunity that requires a person or organization to choose among several actions that may be evaluated as ethical or unethical.

Ethical Systems. Cultural beliefs about what is proper behavior and conduct.

Ethics. The rules or principle that define rights and wrong conduct.

Ethics Code. A written statement that describes the general value system and ethical rules of an organization.

Ethnocentric Behavior. Behavior that is based on the belief in the superiority of one's own ethnic group or culture, often shows disregard or contempt for the culture of other countries.

Ethnocentric Business. A company whose business standards are based on its home nation customs, markets and laws.

Ethnocentric Staffing. A staffing approach within the MNE in which all key management positions are filled by parent country nationals work abroad.

Ethnocentricity. The feeling that one's culture is superior to all others.

Ethnocentrism. A belief that one's own group is superior to others and also used to describe a company's belief that what worked at home should work abroad.

E-trade. Selling and buying shares on the internet.

ETUC. European Trade Union Confederation

EU. European Union.

Euro. Legal currency of the eleven participating countries of European Union.

Euro-bonds. A bond placed in countries other than the one in whose currency the bond is denominated.

Euro-commercial Paper. Euro-securities issued by dealers of commercial paper without involving a bank.

Euro-credit. A loan, line of credit, or other form of medium, or long-term credit on the Eurocurrency market that has a maturity of more than one year.

Eurocurrency. Money deposited in a financial center outside the country whose currency is involved.

Eurocurrency Deposits. Deposits of funds in a bank denominated in a currency foreign to the bank's home country.

Eurocurrency Loans. Loans made by a multinational bank in a currency other than that of the bank's home country.

Eurocurrency Market. An international wholesale market that deals in Euro-currencies.

Eurodollar. Dollar banked outside the United States.

Eurodollar Bond. Dollar-denominated bonds issued mainly in London and other European centers such as Luxemburg.

Eurodollar Contracts. Derivative securities written on Eurodollar deposits.

Eurodollar Deposit. Dollar-denominated deposits in non-US banks.

Eurodollar Futures Contract. A futures contract written on a Eurodollar deposit.

Eurodollar Market. The market in which Eurodollars are traded.

Euro-equity Market. The market for shares sold outside the boundaries of the issuing company's home country.

Euro-notes. Short-term notes similar to commercial paper. These instruments are most frequently used by European banks that deal in commercial paper.

Europe 1992. Legislation enacted by the EU and designed to eliminate most key barriers to trade of goods and services by December 31, 1992.

European Commission. One of the five major institutions of the EU; composed of a president, six vice presidents and ten other members whose allegiance to the EU and serving as an executive branch for the EU.

European Community (EC). The predecessor of the European Union.

European Council. One of the five major institutions of the European Union; made up of the heads of state of each of the EU members.

European Currency Unit (ECU). A unit of account based on a currency basket composed of the currencies of the members of the EU.

European Economic Community (EEC). The predecessor of the European community.

European Free Trade Association (EFTA). A free trade association including Norway, Iceland, and Switzerland.

European Free Trade Association (EFTA). A Free-trade area among a group of European countries that are not members of the EU.

European Monetary System (EMS). EU system designed to create a zone of monetary stability in Europe to control inflation and coordinate exchange rate policies of EU countries.

European Option. An option that can be exercised only on the option expiration date.

European Parliament. One of the five major institutions of the EU. Its representatives are elected directly in each member country.

European Union (EU). An economic group of 15 European nations: Austria, Belgium, Denmark, Finland, France, Germany, Great Britain, Greece, Netherlands, Ireland, Italy, Luxembourg, Portugal, Spain, and Sweden. Established as a customs union, it is now moving towards economic union. (Formerly the European community.)

Euro-sclerosis. Popular term for a seizure (breakdown) in the Euro markets caused by illiquidity or some other financial panic.

Event Risk. The probability that changes inside a firm or other security issuing individual or institution or external happenings affecting the value of the securities involved.

Events. Set of relevant occurrences that can happen. Synonym for states of nature.

Ex Ante Real Interest Rate. *See* Real interest rate.

Ex Post Real Interest Rate. The nominal interest rate minus the actual inflation rate.

Excess Insurance. Under an excess insurance plan, the insurer does not participate in the loss until the actual loss exceeds a certain amount.

Excess Material Requisitions. A form to be filled out by the production staff to secure any materials needed in excess of the standard amount allotted for output.

Excess Reserves. Reserves in excess of required reserves.

Excess Returns. The rate of return on an asset above the riskless rate of interest.

Exchange Controls. Restrictions on the amount of a particular currency that may be bought or sold.

Exchange of Futures for Physical (EEP). An alternative delivery procedure for futures contracts where there is an exchange of a specified quantity of the cash instrument for the equivalent quantity of futures contracts at mutually agreed-upon terms and price. Partners to an EEP must notify the clearing-house of such transaction.

Exchange for Physical Order. This order permits the exchange of futures position for a physical position.

Exchange Rate. The rate at which one currency is converted into another.

Exchange Rate Mechanism. Mechanism for aligning the exchange rates of EU currencies against each other.

Exchange Rate Risk. The risk related to have an international operations in a world where relative currency values vary.

Excise Duty. Duty levied on home produced goods either to control consumption and thus influence spending or to raise revenue.

Exclusions. Listing in an insurance contract of the perils, losses and property excluded from coverage.

Exclusive Channels. A distribution channel that outsiders find difficult to access.

Exclusive Distribution. Distribution that sends products to only one retail outlet in a given geographic area.

Exclusive Provider Organization (EPO). A plan that does not cover medical care received outside of a network of preferred providers.

Ex-divided Date. The day on which a common stock makes a dividend payment.

Executive Information System (EIS). An easy to use DSS designed for executives who have limited experience using computers but need access to the firm's database.

Exempt Employees. Those who are not required to be paid overtime under the Fair Standards Act.

Exercise. The action taken by the holder of an option contract either to acquire the underlying asset at the options strike price or to the underlying asset at the option's strike price.

Exercise Date. It is the date on which the option is actually exercised. In the case of European Options, the exercise date is the same as the expiration date while in

American Options; the options contract may be exercised any day between the purchase of the contract and its expiration date (*See* European option).

Exercise Price. The price at which the underlying asset may be purchased or sold when an option is exercised.

Exercise Ratio. It states the number of ordinary shares they can be purchased at the E.P. per warrant. The same as the conversion ratio in the case of convertible securities.

Exit Interview. An interview conducted with personnel leaving the firm to determine the cause of their leaving.

Exogenous Money Supply. Vertical money supply curve that results when changes in interest rates do not alter the currency to deposit ratio or the desired excess reserve ratios of banks.

Exotic Option. A non-standard option.

Expatriate. Anyone living or working in a foreign country.

Expatriate Failure. The premature return of an expatriate manager to the home country.

Expatriate Managers. Managers who work in a country other than their country of origin.

Expectancy. A person's expectation that effort will lead to high performance.

Expectancy Theory. A theory stating that motivation depends not only on how much a person wants something but also on the person's perception of how likely he or she is to get it.

Expectations. What people think they will perceive.

Expectations Hypothesis. The hypothesis that longer-term interest rates are an average of the shorter-term interest rates expected to prevail during the life of the longer-term asset.

Expected Rate of Return. The interest rate an investor would earn on a security if he or she buys the security at its current market price, receives all promised or expected payments on the security and sells the security at the end of his or her investment horizon.

Expected Value. A statistical measure of an alternative value calculated by multiplying each possible outcome by the probability of that outcome occurring, then summing all these products.

Expected Yield. The weighted average return on a risky security composed of all possible yields from the security multiplied by the probability that each possible yield will occur.

Expediting Payment. Gifts to lesser government and private employees primarily to assure that they carry out promptly/ cooperatively and efficiently the duties for the gift giver that their job normally requires them to do.

Expenditure. Cash or other resources paid or to be paid for an asset purchased or service acquired.

Expense. The cost of a earning revenue is called an expense.

Expense Ratio. That proportion of the gross rate available for expenses and profit. Ratio of expenses incurred to premiums written.

Experience Attribute. A product attribute that can be evaluated only after purchase and use.

Experience Curve. The reduction in costs per unit that occurs when production, marketing and distribution increase cumulatively. Typically, these cost reductions occur because of learning effects, economies of scale and improvement in technology.

Experience Curve Pricing. A method of pricing in which the seller sets the price sufficiently low to encourage a large sales volume in anticipation that the large sales volume would lead to a reduction in average unit costs.

Experience Products and Services. These products have attributes that can be evaluated only after purchase and use.

Experience Rating. A rating that indicates the amount of state tax an employer is expected to pay based on the employer's history of laying off a share of its workforce.

Experienced Meaningfulness. Feeling that one's job is important and worthwhile.

Experienced Responsibility. Believing that one is accountable for the outcomes.

Expert Power. Power or influence derived from a person's special knowledge or expertise in a particular area.

Expert System. Decision support programs that minimise human decision-making processes by using a collection of thousands of "if-then" rules to solve complex problems.

Expiration Date. The maturity date of a derivative security.

Expiration of Rights Date. It is the date before which existing shareholders should transfer the shares to be eligible for rights issue.

Expired Costs. Expired costs are the ones that have helped to produce revenues. They are recognized as expenses in the income statement. They are also known as revenue expenditure.

Explicit Transactions. Events such as cash receipts and disbursements that trigger nearly all day-to-day routine entries.

Exploding Warrant. Warrant introduced on order to dilute to the need for an additional capital.

Export Import Bank (Exim Bank). A US government agency that offers direct financial assistance for overseas projects. It also offers loan guarantees and insurance for exports or foreign exchange transactions.

Export Management Company. Export specialists who act as an export marketing department for client firms.

Export Management Company (EMC). A company licensed to act on behalf of domestic companies for exporting products. EMCs specialize in one industry or a range of products, such as chemicals and represent many companies with similarities.

Export of Jobs. A business beginning or expanding a branch in another nation which may cause a loss of jobs in the business of home operations.

Export Trading Company (ETC). Licensed by the US government. ETCs can make direct purchases or facilitate overseas contracts for exporting domestic goods.

Exporting. The sale of goods and services to foreign markets enabling organizations of all sizes to participate in global business.

Exposure Unit. Unit of measurement used in insurance pricing.

Expropriation. *See* Nationalization.

Extended Credit. Represents long-term lending to troubled depository institutions.

Extended Non-owned Coverage. Endorsement that can be added to an automobile liability insurance policy that covers the insured while driving any non-owned automobile on a regular basis.

Extendible Bonds. A bond for which the bondholder has no option to extend the maturity of the bond.

External Data. Data pertaining to activities outside an individual firm.

External Environment. All the factors outside the organization that may affect its manager's actions.

External Factors. Environmental characteristics that cause behavior.

External Forces for Change. Originate outside the organization.

External Locus of Control. Attributing outcomes to circumstances beyond one's control.

Externalities. Knowledge spillovers.

Externally. A positive or negative side effect of production or consumption in a market system.

Externally Convertible Currency. Non-residents can convert their holdings of domestic currency into foreign currency, but the ability of residents to convert the currency is limited in some way.

Extinction. It is the absence of response to a situation.

Extra Expense Coverage Form. A separate form that can be used to cover the extra expenses incurred by a firm to continue operations during a period of restoration.

Extreme Lookback Options. For a call option, the payoff at maturity depends on the maximum value of the price of the underlying asset over the life of the option.

Extrinsic Rewards. Financial, material or social rewards from the environment.

Extroversion. The degree to which a person is social, gregarious, talkative and assertive.

F

Fabrication. One category of the synthetic process of production in which materials are combined to form a product. The materials are not altered.

Face Value. The amount paid when a financial instrument, like a Treasury Bill, matures.

Facilitators. Leaders who help the group overcome internal obstacles or difficulties so that it may achieve desired outcomes.

Facilities. The buildings and equipment used for producing, storing and distributing products.

Factor Endowments. A country's endowment with resources such as land, labor, and capital.

Factoring. It is a method of converting a non-productive and inactive asset into a productive asset by selling receivables to a company that specializes in their collection and administration. Factoring commission is paid for credit evaluation and collection and other services and to cover bad-debt losses.

Factors of Production. Inputs into the productive process of a firm, including labor, management, land, and technological know-how.

Factory Mutual. Mutual insurance company insuring only prosperities that meet high underwriting standards; emphasizes loss prevention.

Facultative Re-insurance. Optional, case-by-case method of resurface used when the 'ceding' company receives an application for insurance that exceeds its retention limit.

Facultative-obligatory Re-insurance. It is a type of treaty agreement whereby the insurer can choose whether or not to reinsure a risk, but once chosen, the reinsurer must accept.

Fair Access to Insurance Requirements (FAIR). Federal property insurance plan that provides basic property insurance to property owners in areas where they are unable to obtain insurance in the normal markets. Each state with such a plan has a central placement facility.

Fair Credit Billing Act. A federal law giving customers the right to question entries on bills sent to them for goods and services purchased on credit and giving them the right to expect that billing errors will be corrected as quickly as possible.

Fair Credit Reporting Act. A federal law that gives credit to customers the right to view their credit record held by a credit bureau and to secure quick correction of any errors in that record.

Fair Rental Value. Amount payable to an insured home-owner for loss of rental income due to damage that makes the premises uninhabitable.

Fair Rental. The expected rental for equivalent property under similar terms and conditions of FASB (Financial Accounting Standard Board).

Fair Use Doctrine. A concept applied to using material protected by copyright in which a person can replicate or copy certain protected materials as long as the use is 'fair' . Consequently, educators are allowed to use materials with few restrictions in the course of education or research.

Fair Value. The theoretical value of an option or futures contract derived from a mathematical evaluation model. It is also referred to as the no arbitrage value.

Fairy Godfather. A prospective supporter or investor in a particular company.

Fallen Angel. The company, or shares in a company, whose rating has recently fallen significantly.

Family Income Policy. Special life insurance policy combining decreasing term and whole life insurance that pays a monthly income of $10 for each $1000 of life insurance if the insured dies within the specified period, at which time the face amount of insurance is paid.

Family Purpose Doctrine. Concept that imputes negligence committed by immediate family members while operating a family car to the owner of the car.

FASB. Financial Accounting Standards Board.

FAS 13. Technical statement of Financial Accounting Standards Board, November 1976.

FASB Statements. Official rules and regulations regarding external financial reporting issued in a numbered series by the Financial Accounting Standard Board.

FDI. Foreign Direct Investment.

FDIC. Federal Deposit Insurance Corporation.

FE. Foreign Exchange.

Feasibility Plan. An initial written plan comprising all the elements of a good business plan with the objective of determining whether a new venture can be expected to succeed.

Feasible Solution Space. The set of all possible combinations of the decision variables that simultaneously satisfies all the constraints of the problem.

Fed Funds Rate. The interest rate on short-term funds transferred between financial institutions, usually for a period of one day.

Federal Agencies. Departments or divisional units of the federal government empowered to borrow funds in the open market in order to make loans to private businesses and individuals or otherwise subsidize private lending or borrowing.

Federal Agency Securities. Debt obligations of corporations and agencies created to carry out the lending programs of the US government.

Federal Chartering. A proposed plan for giving the federal government power to issue certificates of incorporation.

Federal Debt. The total amount the federal government owes its creditors.

Federal Deposit Insurance. Insurance issued by the FDIC that guarantees the full payment to owners of certain deposit accounts at member banks.

Federal Deposit Insurance Corporation. Established in 1934 to insure depositors against loss due to bank failure.

Federal Financing Bank. A unit of the federal government created in 1973 that borrows money through the US treasury department and channels these funds to federal agencies.

Federal Funds. Short-term loans of reserve deposits between banks.

Federal Funds Market. An inter-bank market for short-term borrowing and lending of bank reserves.

Federal Funds Rate. Rate at which banks can borrow funds from another bank to obtain funds on a short-term basis.

Federal Home Loan Mortgage Corporation. A federal agency created in 1970 to improve the resale market for home mortgages.

Federal Housing Administration. An agency of the federal government established in 1934 to guarantee mortgage loans for low-priced and medium-priced homes, thereby reducing the risks of lending by financial institutions making qualified home loans.

Federal National Mortgage Association. A federal agency created in 1938 to buy and sell selected residential mortgages in the secondary market and encourage the development of a resale market for home loans.

Federal Open Market Committee. The policy-making arm of the Federal Reserve System.

Federal Personal Income Taxes. Interest received on municipal bonds is free of federal income taxes and is not included in gross income.

Federal Reserve Bank. One of 12 regional banks chartered by the US congress to provide central banking services to a specific region of the nation.

Federal Reserve Board Trading Desk. Unit of the Federal Reserve Bank of New York through which open market transactions are conducted bills.

Federal Reserve Notes. U.S. paper money, also called dollar bills.

Federal Reserve Statement. A listing of the factors supplying reserves to an absorbing the reserves of depository institutions.

Federal Reserve System. Established as the Central bank for the United States by the Federal Reserve Act of 1913.

Federal Surety Bond. Type of surety bond required by federal agencies that regulates the actions of business firms. It guarantees that the bonded party will comply with federal standards, pay all taxes or duties accrued or pay any penalty if the bondholder fails to pay.

Federal Trade Commission Act (1914). Placed a blanket prohibition against 'unfair methods of competition' and created the federal trade commission to enforce it.

Federally Insured Mortgages. Mortgages originated by financial institutions, with repayment guaranteed by either the Federal Housing Administration (FHA) or the Veterans Administration (VA).

Fee-based Financial Services. Financial services, like insurance and ATM services, for which prices are started in dollars or other currency units.

Feedback. The receiver's response to the sender's communication.

Feed Back Control. Techniques and methods that analyze historical data to correct future events.

Feed-forward Control. A control system that attempts to identify future deviations from plans, early enough to take action before the deviations occur, by developing a model of system or process inputs, monitoring these inputs, and taking action in time to prevent undesired of unplanned system outputs.

Felt Conflict. The third stage of conflict, during which employees have an emotional reaction to the problem.

Fiat Money. Paper money, money does not represent a claim to any physical commodity. Fiat money is money which has a face value (or value as money) that exceeds its value as a commodity. Examples include U.S. federal reserve notes.

Fidelity Bond. Bond that protects an employer against dishonest or fraudulent acts of employees, such as embezzlement, fraud or theft of money.

Field Study. Examination of variables in real life settings.

Field Theory of Motivation. Psychologist Lewin's theory that motivation depends on organizational climate and must be looked upon as an element in a larger field restraining and driving forces.

File-and-use Law. Law for regulating insurance rates under which companies are required only to file the rates with the state insurance department before putting them into effect.

Fill-or-Kill (FOK). Must be executed immediately upon receipt by the broker or be automatically cancelled. It is a combination of two orders entered at the same time, with one contingent or the other. On-the-opening, order is executed during the opening period of the trading session. On-the-closing, order is executed during the closing period.

Filtering. Screening out negative information by the sender of a communication and sending in only favourable information.

Final Pay Formula. Pension plan pays retirement benefit based on a percentage of the average salary during a specified number of years at the end of the employee's career times the number of years of service.

Finance Companies. Financial-service firms that provide both business and consumer credit.

Finance Lease. A financing device whereby a user can acquire use of an asset for most of its useful life. Rentals are net to the lessor and the user is responsible for maintenance, taxes and insurance. Rental payments over the life of the lease are sufficient to enable the lessor to recover the cost of the equipment plus a return on its investment.

Finance Managers. Managers concerned with the value of the organization's assets and various investment strategies that would increase net worth.

Financial Accounting. It is concerned mainly with how accounting can serve external decisions as distinguished from Management Accounting.

Financial Accounting Standard. The primary regulatory body over accounting principles and practices. It is an independent creature of the private sector.

Financial Analysis. Financial Analysis is the process of identifying the strengths and weaknesses of the firm by properly establishing relationships between the items of balance sheet and profit and loss account.

Financial Asset. A claim against the income or wealth of a business firm, household, or unit of government usually represented by a certificate, receipt, other legal document.

Financial Audit. A periodic and comprehensive examination of a firm's financial records.

Financial Budget. That part of the master budget composed of the capital budget, cash budget, budgeted balance sheet, and budgeted statement of changes in financial position.

Financial Capital Maintenance. The quantity of financial resources (usually historical costs) as distinguished from physical resources or operating capability to be recovered before income emerges.

Financial Disclosure. The provision of relevant information to the public to aid individuals and institutions in making sound financial decisions.

Financial Distress. Financial distress occurs when the firm finds it difficult to honour the obligations of creditors. The extreme form of financial distress is insolvency. The firm may have to sell its assets at "distress" price. More important consideration is the inflexibility of raising funds when needed and non-availability of funds on acceptable terms.

Financial Flows. Financial flows include interest, dividends lease rentals, repayments of debt, etc.

Financial Futures Contracts. Contracts that call for the future delivery of sale of designated securities at a price agreed upon the day the contract is made.

Financial Innovation. A trend in the financial system towards developing new services and new service delivery methods.

Financial Institution Reform, Recovery, and Enforcement Act of 1989 (FIRREA). This Act was directed at the problems faced by the loan industry during late 80s. It abolished the federal saving and loan insurance corporation and the federal home loan bank board which had regulated the savings and loan industry.

Financial Institutions. Institutions that perform the essential function of channeling funds from those with surplus funds or those with shortage of funds.

Financial Intermediary. A financial institution that accepts funds from savers, transforms them, and lends them to borrowers.

Financial Investment. The net change in financial assets held by a sector or unit in the economy over a specified time period.

Financial Lease. Long-term, non-cancellable lease contract is known as financial lease. Financial leases are very popular with high cost and high-technology equipment. Financial leases amortize the cost of the asset over the term of lease. They are, therefore, also called capital or full pay-out leases. Most financial leases are direct leases.

Financial Leverage. Financing a portion of the firm's assets with securities bearing a fixed rate of return.

Financial Market. An institution or arrangement that facilitates the purchase and sale of financial instruments such as corporate stocks and bonds, government bonds and more exotic things such as options and futures contracts.

Financial Ratios. Relationships determined from a firm's financial information and used for comparison purposes.

Financial Responsibility Law. Law that requires persons involved in automobile accidents under certain circumstances to furnish proof of financial responsibility up to a minimum dollar limit or face having driving privileges revoked or suspended.

Financial Risk. The combinations of (1) increased variability in earnings per common share, and (2) the higher risk of insolvency induced by the firm's use of financial leverage.

Financial Service Markets. Markets in which individuals and firm purchase services that enhance the working of debt and equity markets.

Financial Structure. Mix of debt and equity used to finance a business.

Financial System. The collection of markets, individuals, institutions, laws, regulations, and techniques through which bonds, stocks, and other securities are traded, financial services produced and delivered and interest rates determined.

Financing. Acquiring of debt or equity through various combinations to fund a venture.

Financing Decision. Financing decision is to decide when, where and how to acquire funds to meet the firm's investment needs. The mix of debt and equity is known as the firm's capital structure.

Financing Gap. The difference between a bank's average loans and average (core) deposits.

FINEX. Financial instruments exchange, New York.

Finished Goods Inventory. Those products that are ready for sale such as a fully assembled automobile ready to ship to a dealer.

Fire Legal Liability. Liability of a firm or person for fire damage caused by the negligence of and damage to property of others.

Fire Sale Price. The price received for an asset that has to be liquidated (sold) immediately.

Firm Commitment Offering. Securities offered from the issuing firm purchased by an underwriter.

Firm Commitment Underwriting. The issue of financial instrument by an investment bank in which the investment bank guarantees the corporation a price for newly issued instruments by buying the whole issue at a fixed price from the corporate issuer. It then seeks to resell these instruments to suppliers of funds (investors) at a higher price.

Firm Risk of a Project. The risk of an investment to the investing firm. It will be less than the project risk if there are any portfolio effects within the firm.

Firm Specific Credit Risk. The risk of default for the borrowing firm associated with the specific types of project risk taken by that firm.

First Lien. The first claim against an asset.

First Mover Advantages. Advantages accounting to the first to enter a market.

First Mover Disadvantages. Disadvantages associated with entering a foreign market before other international market.

First Order Condition. A test to locate one or more maximum or minimum points of an algebraic function.

First-in First-out. The stock of merchandise or material that is acquired earliest is assumed to be used first; the stock acquired latest is assumed to be still on hand.

First-level Management. The lowest level of the hierarchy. A manager at this level coordinates the work of non-managers but reports to a manager.

Fiscal Agent. A role of the Federal Reserve System in which it provides services to the federal government, such as clearing and collecting checks on behalf of the US Treasury and conducting auctions for the sale of new Treasury Securities.

Fiscal Policy. Government spending or tax policy.

Fiscal Termites. The fiscal termites help wealthy people and multinational corporations plan their tax strategies. There are other, less interesting words for these tax consultants: tax minimization, tax defense, tax planning, or tax optimization. In addition, while the termites munch in increasingly complex pattern, they are finding it easier, faster and there are more of them than ever. Eventually, just like the termites in our houses, they bring the whole thin down.

Fisher Effect. The theory of inflation and interest rates that argues that nominal interest rates respond one-for-one to change in the expected rate of inflation over the life of a loan.

Fisher Equation. The equation that sets the nominal interest rate equal to the real interest rate plus the expected inflation rate.

Fit Perspective. Assumes that culture must align with its business or strategic context.

Five Cs of Credit. The five basic factors to be evaluated: character, capacity, capital, collateral, and conditions.

FIX Connectivity. Connectivity makes it easier to trade by reducing keystrokes. FIX stands for Financial Information Exchange (FIX) Protocol. It is a "language" that was developed specially for the communication of securities transactions and is a public domain specification owned and maintained by FIX Protocol Organization.

Fixed Amount Option. Life insurance settlement option in which the policy proceeds are paid out of fixed amounts.

Fixed Annuity. Annuity whose periodic payment is a guaranteed fixed amount.

Fixed Assets. Tangible assets or physical items that can be seen and touched often called property, plant, and equipment of plant assets.

Fixed Cost. A cost that, for a given period of time and range of activity called the relevant range, does not change in total but become progressively smaller on a per-unit basis as volume increases.

Fixed Exchange Rates. Exchange rates in which a country or group of countries pledge to keep the exchange rate within a narrow band of a target level.

Fixed Period Option. Life insurance settlement option in which the policy proceeds are paid out over a fixed period of time.

Fixed Position Layout. Making products in a fixed location with employees and machines moving around as needed.

Fixed Price Purchase Option. A purchase option where the price a lesser would have to pay to become equipment owner or lease termination is established at the start of the lease, and may be nominal. Such options have so far been most common in Continental Europe but will be permissible in US Finance Leases in 1984. All purchase options are forbidden in a UK Lease.

Fixed Rate Bond. Offers a fixed set of cash payoffs each year until maturity. And the investor also receives the face value of the bond in cash.

Fixed Rate Mortgage. Mortgage loan that carries an unchanging loan rate.

Fixed-ratio Schedule. A pattern offering reinforcement after a specified number of desired performance behaviors, regardless of the time elapsed between them.

Flat Benefit Formula. Pension plan that pays a flat amount for every year of employment.

Flat Rate Pricing. A fixed price is charged regardless of levels of volume or other characteristics of service for which costs vary with some measure of usage.

Fleet Insurance. It is a motor insurance policy that covers a group of vehicles from one organization.

Flex Rating Law. Type of rating law in which prior approval of rates is required only if the rates exceed a certain percentage above and below the rates previously filed.

Flexibility. The organization's ability to modify its operations systems with little cost in terms of time, money, or quality.

Flexibility Principal. The more that flexibility (the ability to change direction without undue cost, embarrassment, of friction) can be built into plans, the less the danger of losses incurred by unexpected.

Flexible Budget. A budget, often referring to overhead costs only, that is prepared for a range, rather than for a single level, of activity—that can be automatically geared to changes in the level of volume. Also called variable budget. Direct material and direct labour are sometimes included in the flexible budget.

Flexible Cell Production. A flexible manufacturing system in which groups of workstations (the cells) can be reconfigured and reprogrammed to meet changing needs.

Flexible Exchange Rates. The exchange rate is determined strictly by the intersection of private supply and demand, without any government intervention.

Flexible Machine Cells. Flexible manufacturing technology in which a grouping of various machine types, a common materials handler, and a centralized cell controller produce a family of products.

Flexible Manufacturing. A manufacturing processing which computers can direct machinery to adopt to different versions of similar operations.

Flexible Manufacturing Systems. Production processes that link high-tech machinery and computer systems.

Flexible Manufacturing Technologies. Manufacturing technologies designed to improve job scheduling, reduce set up time, and improve quality control.

Flexible Premium Annuity. An annuity contract that permits the owner to vary the size and frequency of premium payments. The amount of retirement income depends on the accumulated sum in the annuity at retirement.

Flexible Spending Account. An arrangement by which the employee agrees to a salary reduction, which can be used to pay for plan benefits, unreimbursed medical and dental expenses and other expenses permitted by the internal revenue code.

Flexible-budget Variances. Difference between actual amounts and the flexible-budget amounts for the actual output achieved.

Flexible-control-budget Variances. Same as flexible budget variances.

Flex-time. A plan that allows employees limited control over scheduling their own hours of work, usually at the beginning and end of the work day.

Flight Response. To either confront stressors or try to avoid them.

Flimsies. The hand written newsletters delivered by messenger to subscribers in the Wall Street area were known as 'flimsies' in 1882.

Float. The difference between book cash and bank cash, representing the net effect of checks in the process of clearing.

Floating Exchange Rate. A country's decision to allow its currency value to change freely. The currency is not constrained by Central bank intervention and does not have to maintain its relationship with another currency in a narrow band. The currency value is determined by trading in the foreign exchange market.

Floating Policy. It is an insurance policy that covers goods of different values and at different locations in marine insurance, it covers a ship's cargoes for a stated number of voyages.

Floating Rate Note. A debt instrument that pays interest based on a changing (floating) rate of interest.

Floating Rental Rate. Rental which is subject to upward or downward adjustments during the lease term. Floating rents sometimes are adjusted in proportion to prime interest rate or commercial paper rate changes during the term of the lease.

Floating Stock. The amount of securities believed to be available for immediate purchase.

Floor. A put option on interest rate, often with multiple exercise dates.

Floor Broker. Exchange members who place trade from the public.

Floor Let. One of the component interest rate put options in a floor.

Floor Traders. A member of exchange who trades on the floor of the exchange.

Floor. A series of European interest rate put options, often used by a party that has purchased a floating rate note. The floor ensures that the effective interest rate received from the note never falls below a fixed level.

Flow of Funds Statements. A system of social accounts prepared quarterly by the Board of Governors of the Federal Reserve System which reports the amount of saving and borrowing in the US economy by major sectors.

Flow-chart. A tool that diagrams a process from starting to finish, identifying those aspects of the process that need improvement.

FOB Origin Pricing. A method of pricing where the seller quotes prices from the point of shipment.

FOB with Freight Allowed. A form of delivered pricing in which the buyer arranges and pays for the transportation, but deducts these transportation costs from the invoice total and remits the net amount.

Focus. A business strategy in which the business concentrates on one part or segment of the market and rises to meet the demands of that segment.

Focus Strategy. An overall corporate strategy that involves developing either a cost leadership or differentiation strategy in a specific market segment of an industry.

Follow-on Offering. The company will have an under-written public offering in the foreign country, timing of the issue depends on the time taken for getting necessary approvals in India and in the foreign country.

Force-field Analysis. A process for managing the forces that drive and restrain change.

Forecasting. An important element of the planning function that makes two basic determinations: (1) what level of activity can be expected during the planning period, and (2) what level of resources will be available to support the projected activity. In a business organization, the critical forecast is the sales forecast.

Forecasting Risk. The possibility of errors in projected cash flows lead to incorrect decisions.

Fore-closure. The process of taking possession of the mortgaged property in satisfaction of a defaulting borrower's indebtedness and forgoing claim to any deficiency.

Foreign Activities Entry Strategy. As exports increase in importance to the firm, it may decide that it can justify its own foreign activities. This decision usually involves joining with nationals in the foreign country to establish product and/or marketing facilities. It differs from direct investment, in that some type of association is formed with a local firm or individual, usually in the form of licensing or joint venture reagents. Licensing is granting the right to produce and/or market the firm's product in another country to an outside firm. Join venture arrangements involve foreign investors forming a group with local investors to begin a local business with each group sharing ownership.

Foreign Bonds. International bonds issued in a single country, usually denominated in that country's currency.

Foreign Corrupt Practices Act of 1977. A federal law that regulates questionable payments of United States firms operating in other nations.

Foreign Corrupt Practices Act. A federal law that requires adequate internal controls, among other requirements.

Foreign Currency. Active futures trading at foreign currencies dates back to the inception at freely floating exchange rates in the early 1970s. Contracts as US dollars, Canadian dollar, Japanese Yen, British pound, the Swiss franc, German marc, French franc, Dutch guilders, etc.

Foreign Currency Derivative. A derivative security written on foreign currency spots exchange rates.

Foreign Currency Forwards Price. The forward price of a foreign currency.

Foreign Currency Futures. A futures contract written on a foreign currency spot exchange rate.

Foreign Currency Futures Option. An option written on a foreign currency futures.

Foreign Currency Option. An option written on foreign currency spot exchange rate.

Foreign Currency Swap. An exchange of payments converting a series of cash flows in one currency to series of cash flows in another currency.

Foreign Exchange Intervention. Commitments between countries about the institutional aspect of their intervention in the foreign exchange markets.

Foreign Exchange Market. The market where different currencies are bought and sold.

Foreign Exchange Rates. The prices of foreign currencies expressed in terms of other currencies.

Foreign Exchange Risk. Risk that cash flows will vary as the actual amount of US dollars received on a foreign investment change due to a change in foreign exchange rate.

Foreign Insurer. Insurance company chartered by one state but licensed to do business in another.

Foreign Sales Corporation (FSC). A classification given to domestic companies selling exports overseas; FSCs enjoy certain tax-deferred benefits and incentives to export when doing so improves trade relations or foreign exchange balances.

Foreign Service Corporation. An offshore special service corporation which is used by US companies to invest in a equipment which is utilized in foreign service under certain guidelines. Through such it US investors pay less tax on rentals and revenues derived from the assets.

Foreign Trade Zone. A domestic site, usually at an international port of call or at a government-licensed company, where imported product can be received duty-free for domestic use.

Formal Communication. Communication that flows along the organization's lines of authority or task responsibility.

Formal Groups. The established departments, units and teams created by the managers in an organization.

Formal Leader. A leader whose leadership activities are directly related to his other position in the organization.

Formal Organization. The planned structure of a business in which individuals are given authority and responsibility to perform specific tasks assigned to them.

Formalization. The degree to which organization's procedures, rules and personnel requirements are written down and enforced.

Forming Stage. The stage when group members meet for the first time or two, become acquainted and familiarize themselves with the group's task.

For-profit Companies. Companies owned either privately by one or more individuals or stockholders.

Fortran. Formula Translation, a computer language.

Fortuitous Loss. Unforeseen and unexpected loss that occurs as a result of change.

Forward Calendar. The anticipated supply of new bonds or other securities expected to come to market over the next week, month, or other period.

Forward Contract. A deferred contract in which two parties agree to buy and sell an asset at some future time under condition that are mutually agreeable.

Forward Exchange Rate. An exchange rate and quantity of currency contracted for today, but the actual exchange takes place at a specific future date.

Forward Foreign Exchange Transaction. The exchange of currencies at a specified exchange rate (or forward exchange rate) at some specified date in the future.

Forward Market. Forward markets are contracts for deferred delivery.

Forward Option. An option on a forward contract.

Forward Price. The delivery price written in a forward contract such that the initial value of the forward contract is zero.

Forward Rate Agreement. A contract written on LIBOR that requires a cash payment at maturity based on the difference between a spot rate and a forward rate of interest.

Forward Rate. An expected rate (quoted today) on a security that originates at some point in the future.

Forward Swap. An interest rate swap in which the swap rate is set but the swap does not commence until a later date.

Forward Trade. Agreement to exchange currency at some time in the future.

401(k) Plans. Employer-sponsored plans that supplement a firm's basic retirement plan.

Fossil Fuel. Fuel derived from the ancient fossilized remains of plants and animals that were deposited many years ago. Coal, petroleum, and natural gas are examples.

Four-fifths (4/5th) Rule. It states that discrimination generally occurs if the selection rate for a protected group is less than 80 per cent of the selection rate of the majority group.

Fractional Reserve Banking. A banking system in which bank reserves equal only a fraction of outstanding demand deposits.

Frame of Reference. Combination of experiences and expectations giving rise to a particular mind-set.

Framing. The tendency to view positively presented information favorably and negatively presented information unfavorably.

Franchise Deductible. Deductible found in some marine insurance contracts in which the insurer has no liability if the loss is under a certain amount, but once this amount is exceeded, the entire loss is paid in full.

Franchise. It is a licence to manufacture or market a product with an established trade name or to operate a service, the equipment or supplies, which are manufactured by a monopoly producer. Franchises are often given for a particular area. The franchisee (or the holder of the licence) make an initial payment or pays a royalty.

Franchisee. The firm that receives the franchise.

Franchiser. The parent company that franchises firms to sell their products.

Franchising. A form of licensing in which a company (the franchiser) agrees to provide a franchisee element associated with the franchiser's business, in return for a financial commitment and the agreement to conduct business in accordance with the franchiser's standard of operations.

Fraternal Insurer. Mutual insurance company that provides life and health insurance to the orders of a social organization.

Fraud. Intentional mis-representation of the truth to deceive another.

Fraudulent Conveyance. A transaction such as sale of securities or transfer of assets to a particular party that is determined to be illegal.

Free Asset Ratio. In insurance the ratio of an insurer's free assets (at market value) to its liabilities.

Free Banking System. A system begun in Michigan (1837) and New York (1838) to make entry into the banking industry less difficult by simplifying the process of obtaining a state charter and to make bank notes more safe that anyone could open a bank and issue notes so long as that person provides the requisite collateral.

Free Cash Flow. It is the cash flow available to service both creditors and shareholders who have provided funds to financial investments.

Free Enterprise Ideology. A set of beliefs about an ideal way to organize economic life, including freedom, private property, equality of opportunity, competition, natural laws, and a limited government.

Free Enterprise System. An economic system based on the free market, with an accompanying free enterprise ideology that explains why the free market is an ideal way to organize economic life.

Free Market. The ideal form of an economic system based on voluntary and free exchange among buyers and sellers. Competition regulates prices in all market exchanges.

Free Reserves. The difference between total earnings and the total amount of dividends to date is known as reserves and surplus. It represents total undistributed earnings.

Freedom. Ability to make one's own decisions and take responsible actions without restrictions.

Free-Market Economies. An economic system in which the government does not interfere in any way with business activity. There are no price controls, no permits, no kickbacks, no trading restrictions and no foreign exchange controls. India is making hesitant moves towards this economy.

Free-rein Leadership. Emphasizes a leadership style of "the less supervision the better".

Free-riding. The tendency of some individuals to perform at less than their optimum in groups, relying instead on others to carry their share of workload.

Freight Forwarder. *See* Foreign freight forwarder.

Frequency of Loss. The probability that a loss will occur.

Frictional Unemployment. Unemployment which occurs as people quit one job to seek another, or as people are displaced from jobs due to technical change.

Frictionless Markets. Markets where there are no restrictions nor costs to trading assets.

Friendship Group. An informal group that evolves because of some common characteristic such as age, political sentiment or background.

Fringe Benefit. An employee benefit other than salary, wages and cash bonus.

Frivolity Theory. It says that future market trends can be predicted by looking at the amount of money the citizens of a country spend on food. If the amount is above 36 per cent of a household's income, the market will drop.

Frustration. An emotion that occurs when individuals are unable to satisfy their needs. Frustration may result in constructive problem-solving behavior or in defensive behavior.

FSC. *See* Foreign Sales Corporation.

FTAA. Free Trade Agreement of the America.

FTZ. *See* Foreign Trade Zone.

Full Bodied Money. A commodity money in which the commodity itself circulates as money.

Full Cost. It has two commonly used meanings. First, it is often a synonym for absorption cost. Second, it often means absorption cost plus an allocation of non-manufacturing cost.

Full pay-out Lease. *See* Finance lease.

Full-bodied Money. Gold money that is worth its face value as a commodity.

Full-service Wholesaler. Provides full line of services such as taking title to merchandise, maintaining sales force, and extending credit to customers.

Fully Amortized. The equal periodic repayment on a loan that reflects partly interest and partly principal over the life of a loan.

Fully Insured. Insured status of a covered person under the Old Age, Survivors, and Disability Insurance (OASDI) Program. You must have one·quarter of coverage for each year after 1950 (or after the year you attain age twenty-one, if later) up to the year of death, disability or attainment of age sixty-two. A minimum of six quarters and a maximum of forty quarters are required.

Functional Analysis. An analytical approach that helps society match social needs to the organization's most capable of meeting those needs.

Functional Approach. *See* Functional costing.

Functional Authority. Normally it is a limited line-type of authority applicable only to specialized areas and representing a delegation to a specialist by a superior manager with authority over both the position given functional authority and the position subjected to this authority. For example, a company controller is ordinarily given functional authority to prescribe the system of accounting throughout the company but this specialized authority is really a delegation from the chief executive.

Functional Conflict. Serves organization's interests.

Functional Costing. Classifying costs by allocating them to the various functions performed such as manufacturing, warehousing, delivery and billing.

Functional Currency. The currency of the primary economic environment in which an entity operates.

Functional Departmentalization. The (grouping of) jobs that perform similar functional activities such as finance, manufacturing and human resources.

Functional Division. An organization structure in which each function (*e.g.* marketing or production) reports separately to a counterpart functional group at headquarters.

Functional Groups. Groups that perform specific organizational functions with members from several vertical levels of the hierarchy.

Functional Model. Description of aspects of a system that transforms values using functions, mappings, constraints and functional dependencies.

Functional Organization. An organization which uses specialized authority. This type of organization has characteristics of both line and staff.

Functional Regulation. Regulations aimed at a particular function of business such as labor relations.

Functional Social Support. Support sources that buffer stress in specific situations.

Functional Structure. The grouping of similar economic activities, such as finance, production operations and marketing.

Functionalism. The ideal that social functions should be performed by the institutions that can carry them out most efficiently.

Functions of Management. The activities, a manager must perform to do his job. Management functions include planning, organizing, directing, controlling and coordinating.

Fund. A specific amount of cash or securities earmarked for a special purpose.

Fund Manager. A professional investment manager appointed by the AMC to invest money in accordance with the stated objectives of the scheme.

Fundamental Attribution Bias. Ignoring environmental factors that affect behavior.

Fundamental Risk. A risk that affects the entire economy or large number of persons or groups within the economy.

Funded Method. It provides pension benefits over a long period from funds accumulated ahead of time.

Funding Agency. A financial institution or individual that provides for the accumulation or administration of the pension contributions that will be used to pay pension benefits.

Funding Instrument. An insurance contract or trust agreement that states the terms under which the funding agency will accumulate, administer, and disburse the pension funds.

Funds Provided by Operations. The excess of revenue over the expenses requiring working capital.

Funds Statement. A statement of sources and applications of working capital or cash.

Future Cost. The cost that would be incurred if the firm were to raise capital from each source at present or in the near future. The historical costs that were incurred in the past in remaining capital are not relevant in financial decision making.

Future Market. In the future market, standardized contractual agreements are bought and sold, not the actual commodities. A futures contract is very specific as to quantity and date but it does not involve immediate transfer of ownership of the commodity. One can buy and sell commodities in a future market regardless of whether or not one owns the particular commodity.

Future Shock. A human reaction to rapid technological change where individuals experience difficulty in coping with the new conditions of life brought out by new technology.

Future Value. The value at some future date, given the prevailing interest rate of a present amount.

Futures Commission Merchant (FCM). An individual or organization legally authorized to solicit or accept orders to buy or sell futures under the rules of a contract market. An FCM also accepts payments from customers and holds the margin deposits. An FCM must be registered with the Commodity Futures Trading Commission. Futures Commission Merchant does the function similar to a broker in the stock market.

Futures Contract. It is legal commitment between a buyer and a seller in which they agree to exchange something at a specified price, at the end of a designated period of time the buyer agrees to take delivery of something and the sellers agrees to make delivery.

Futures Option. An option on a futures contract.

Futures Price. The delivery price written in futures contract.

G

Gain Sharing. A concept of sharing with employees monetary gains derived from operations a form of profit sharing.

Game Theory. A mathematical theory of group decision making, situations in which a conflict of interest exists between two or more of the participants.

Gamma. The change in the options deal for a unit change in the underlying asset's price.

Gamma Neutral. A portfolio position that has a zero gamma.

Gamma Stocks. Stocks of small, new, poorly financed or loss making companies, which are infrequently traded. They are also referred to as cats and dogs.

Gantt Chart. A technique for planning and controlling developed by Henry L. Gantt showing bars on a chart the time requirements for various tasks or 'events' of a production or other programme.

GAP Management. A technique for protecting a financial institution's earnings from losses due to changes in interest rates by matching the volume of interest-sensitive assets held to the volume of interest-sensitive liabilities taken on.

Garbage Can Model. Holds that decision making is sloppy and haphazard.

Garnishment. It is a court action in which a portion of an employee's wages is set aside for paying a debt owed to a creditor.

Garn-St. Germain Act of 1982. Legislation designed to make depository institutions more competitive with money market mutual funds.

Gender Flex. Temporarily using communication behaviors typical of the other gender.

General Adaptation Syndrome. Describes the way a person tries to adapt to a stressor.

General Agency System. Type of life insurance marketing system in which the general agent, an independent business person who represents only one insurer, is in-charge of a territory and responsible for hiring, training, and motivating new agents.

General Aggregate Limit. The maximum amount the insurer will pay for the damages under coverage A, B and medical expenses under coverage C.

General Agreement on Tariffs and Trade. The General Agreement on Tariffs and Trade (GATT) was drawn up by 23 countries in 1948. Most of the rounds deal with tariff reduction only. The Kennedy Round (1964-67) came to an agreement on anti-dumping. And the Tokyo Round went further in dealing with subsidies and countervailing measures technical arrears to trade, import licensing procedures, government procurement and other non-tariff areas of concern. The most recent round, the Uruguay Round, was the most comprehensive of any, lasting over seven years and creating a legal institution—the World Trade Organization to replace the provisional GATT.

General Average. In ocean marine insurance, a loss incurred for the common good is shared by all parties to the venture.

General Cash Offer. An issue of securities offered for sale to the general public on a cash basis.

General Credit Controls. Monetary policy tools that affect the entire banking and financial system such as open market.

General Environment. The broad complex factors that affect all organizations.

General Obligation Bonds. Debt obligations issued by state and local governments, backed by the full faith and credit of the issuing government.

General Partner. A partner who must maintain an active part in the business with unlimited liability.

General Store. A store which usually sells a wide range of goods but in limited amounts of selections.

Generalized System of Preferences. Preferential import restrictions extended by industrial countries to developing countries.

Generally Accepted Accounting Principles (GAAP). A technical term including both broad concepts or guidelines and detailed practices. The accounting standards accepted by the accounting profession in each country as required for the preparation of financial statements for external users. It includes all conventions, rules, and procedures that together make up accepted accounting practices at a given time.

Generation X. It refers to those who were born between 1965 and 1978. They are hesitant to accept responsibilities.

Generation Y. People born between 1979 and 1994. They are 3 times more than generation Xers. They have more buying power.

Generic. Any of a class of products, rather than the brand of a particular company.

Geo-centric. Operations based on an informed knowledge of both home and host country needs.

Geo-centric Business. A company whose business standards and policies are worldwide in outlook including multinational ownership, management, markets and operations.

Geographic Division. An organizational structure in which a company's operations are separated for reporting purpose into regional area.

Geography. A science dealing with the earth and its life, especially with the description of land, sea, air and the distribution of plant and animal life.

Gilt Fund. Funds that invest only in government securities and treasury bills. They provide investors an opportunity to buy risk-free government securities. These funds generally provide a slightly higher yield than a money market fund. They are good for investors who desire safety or principal.

Gilts. British and Irish government securities.

Glass Ceiling. An invisible barrier that keeps women from attaining the top most positions.

Glass-steagall Act (1933). Also known as the Banking Act of 1933. This legislation made fundamental changes in the structure of the banking industry. Among other things, it created the federal deposit insurance corporation (FDIC).

Global Bond. A combination of domestic bond and Eurobond that is issued simultaneously in several markets and must be registered in each national market according to that market's registration requirements.

Global Business. A strategy in which organizations treat the entire world or major regions of it as the domain for conducting business.

Global Company. A company that integrates operations located in different countries.

Global Dimension. Pertaining to the general environment, those factors in other countries that affect the organization.

Global Organization. An organization that takes a flexible approach to identifying needs and opportunities throughout the global competitive market.

Global Social Support. The total amount of social support available.

Global Sourcing. The acquisition on a worldwide basis of raw materials, parts and sub-assemblies for the manufacturing process.

Globally Integrated Company. *See* Global company.

GNMA. Government National Mortgage Association.

Goal. The final result that a firm wishes to achieve.

Goal Commitment. Amount of commitment to achieving a goal.

Goal Congruence. Sharing of the same goals by top managers and their subordinates.

Goal Difficulty. The amount of effort required meeting a goal.

Goal Setting Theory. A theory which recognizes the importance of goals in improving employee performance.

Goal Specificity. Quantifiability of a goal.

God-father Offer. A takeover offer so attractive that the target company cannot reject.

Go-go-fund. A mutual fund invested in highly speculative shares with investors looking for huge short-term profits.

Going Concern Convention. An entity that is assumed will continue indefinitely or at least will not be liquidated in the near future.

Going Concern Value. It is the amount that a company could realize if it sells its business as an operating business.

Gold Certificates. Paper claims that are redeemable for a specified amount of gold.

Gold Exchange Standard. A system for making international payments in which each national currency is freely convertible into gold bullion at a fixed price and also freely convertible into other currencies at relatively stable prices.

Gold Standard. International fixed exchange rate system in which currencies are pegged to specified amounts of gold. Before World War I, the world economy operated under the gold standard which means that the currency of countries was convertible directly into gold. American dollar, for example, could be turned into the US Treasury and exchanged for approximately 1/20 ounce of gold.

Golden Parachute. A provision in a corporate executive's contract that guarantees all or some portion of the executive's salary and/or benefits if discharged.

Goldi-locks. It is an economic scenario in which both corporate earnings and overall economy stay not too hot and not too cold.

Go-no-go Decision. A decision such as on foreign investments, that is based on minimum threshold criteria and does not compare different opportunities.

Good Accounts. It is financially strong customer.

Good Student Discount. Reduction of automobile premium for a young driver at least sixteen who ranks in the upper 20 per cent of his or her class, has B or 3.0 average or is on the Dean's list. It is based on the premise that good students are better drivers.

Good-bad-delivery. A share certificate together with its transfer form which meets all the requirements of the title transfer from seller to buyer is called a good delivery in the market. Delivery of a share certificate, together with a deed of transfer, which does not meet requirements of title transfer from seller to buyer is called a bad delivery in the market.

Goodwill. The total purchase price of assets acquired in a lump-sum purchase that exceeds the total of the amount that can be justifiably assigned to the individual assets. An intangible asset, the good name and reputation of the business firm that attracts customers.

Gordon Model. A mathematical formula for estimating either the cost or the share price where dividends are presumed to grow at a constant rate.

Gossip Chain. The spreading of information by one person to many others.

Government and Business Partnership. A sub-type of socio-economic system in which government and business work cooperatively to solve social problems.

Government Budget Constraint. The restriction that the government cannot purchase goods and services without having a source of funds to pay for these purchases.

Government National Mortgage Association. A federal government agency created in 1968 to assist the home mortgage market through such activities as purchasing mortgages to finance low-income family housing projects and guaranteeing principal and interest payments on securities issued by private mortgage lenders that are backed by pools of home mortgages.

Government Ownership. Exists when government owns and controls business firms.

Government Paper. Government securities are called government paper, *e.g.* 182 days treasury bills.

Government Purchases. Goods and services demanded by government.

Government Securities. Long-term debt instruments issued by the US Treasury bonds and notes.

Governmental Politics. Activities undertaken by business and other interest groups to influence government policies, forthcoming legislation, and the actions of regulatory agencies.

Grace Period. Period of time during which a policy (insurance) owner may pay an overdue premium without causing the policy to lapse.

Grade. The measured quality of a commodity.

Graduated. Payment mortgages in which borrowers make small payment early in the life of the mortgage. Payments then increase over the first 5 to 10 years and finally payments level off at the end of the mortgage period.

Grandchild Subsidiary. An operation that is under a tax haven subsidiary also called a second tier subsidiary.

Grand-fathered Subsidiaries. Subsidiaries established prior to the passage of a restrictive law and not subject to that law.

Grantback Provisions. Stipulations requiring that licences provide licensors with the use of improvements made on the technology originally licensed.

Grapevine. A kind of informal organization network over which information tends to flow regularly between persons who know and trust each other.

Graphic Rating Scales. A printed form with various job dimensions used by an appraiser to provide a rating for each appraise.

Grass-roots Campaign. A method of influencing government action from the bottom up.

Gravelled. It is the London equivalent to bottoming out. This occurs when a stock's price starts up after it hits a low, which then sparks interest in the security because of its low price.

Greed Index. It is a system of grading portfolio managers. The lower the score the more bearish, thus more preferable. A manager can receive up to 10 points in each of the 10 categories which includes, institutional activity, preference of stocks to bonds, money manager of personal investment, investment for aggressive growth, etc.

Greeks. The options partial derivatives with respect to its input parameters.

Green Baize Door. Also called Chinese wall, it is an artificial barrier erected between the underwriting and brooking departments in a brokerage firm. The purpose of a Chinese wall is to prevent insider trading.

Green Card. It is the International Motor Insurance card which is issued to a holder of motor insurance, certifying that the cover provided is at least the statutory minimum period required by the foreign country or countries named.

Green Shoe Provision. The use of personal borrowing to change the overall amount of financial leverage to which an individual is proposed.

Greenbacks. Fiat currency used during the civil war that was not backed by gold or otherwise redeemable.

Greenhouse Effect. A rise in the average temperature of the earth's atmosphere caused by increased amount of carbon dioxide that is a by-product of the burning of fossil fuels.

Greenmail. It is a procedure whereby a person with sufficient shareholding in a company seeks a sum of money or the repurchase of his shares by the company at a very high price, in order to induce him to refrain from making a takeover bid.

Greshan's Law. The theory states that if a country has two forms of currency, the citizens will hoard the currency with higher intrinsic value, thus forcing the other currency out of circulation.

Grey Knight. In a takeover situation, a third party acting as counter bidder whose intentions towards the target company are not clear. Grey knights are not normally welcome to both the target and the original raider.

Grey Market. Grey market refers to the players who do not belong to the organized sector and sell personal computers that are locally assembled.

Grey Wave. The term is normally used in venture capital circles to describe a company or new industry that shows potential but whose realization is a long way in the future.

Grid OD. A six-phase organizational intervention that comprehensively and systematically attempts to enhance personal management style, team functioning, inter-group organizational functioning and the organization's ability to improve its method of solving problems, resolving conflicts, and making decisions.

Grid Training. A leadership development method proposed by Blake and Mouton that emphasizes the necessary balance between production orientation and personel orientation.

Grievance. It is a specific formal notice of dissatisfaction expressed through an identified procedure.

Grievance Procedure. It is a formal channel of communication used to resolve formal complaints (grievance).

Gross Book Value. Carrying amount of an asset before deducting any related amounts (such as accumulated depreciation).

Gross Debt Service Ratio. Gross debt service ratio calculated as total annual accommodation expenses divided by annual gross income.

Gross Domestic Product (GDP). The total of incomes earned by residents of a country, regardless of where the productive assets are located.

Gross Estate. The value of the property that one owns when one dies. Also includes value of jointly-owned property, life insurance, death proceeds, and certain other items.

Gross Margin. Also called gross profit. Excess of sales over the cost of goods sold, i.e. over the cost of merchandise or inventory that is acquired and resold.

Gross National Product. The total value of all goods and services produced by the nation.

Gross Premium. Amount paid by the insured, consisting of the gross rate multiplied by the number of exposure units.

Gross Proceeds. The price at which the investment bank resells the stock to investors.

Gross Profit. The amount of money received from the sale of products after the costs of the product are deducted. General and selling expenses are not included.

Gross Profit Margin. *See* Gross margin.

Gross Rate. The sum of pure premium and a lading element.

Grossing Up. The practice of adjusting pre-tax profits and tax charge by an amount of national tax benefits on non-taxable Region Development Grants in the UK. This practice is also recommended by the Equipment Leasing Association UK in dealing with the problem of pre-tax losses on leases which are profitable after tax during the transitional period.

Group. Two or more individuals who communicate with one another, share a collective identity, and have a common goal.

Group Building Techniques. Programs for building group identify and teaching inter-personal skills through discussions.

Group Cohesiveness. The attraction of individual members to a group in terms of strength of the forces that impel them to remain active in the group and to resist leaving it.

Group Decision Support Systems. A special set of computer systems designed to aid group decision making.

Group Development. The phases or sequences through which a group passes: mutual acceptance, decision making, motivation, and control.

Group Differed Annuity. Type of allocated pension plan in which a single-premium deferred annuity is purchased each year and is equal to the retirement benefit for that year.

Group Insurers. Two or more insurers operating as a team under common ownership or management.

Group Liabilities. The negative features of groups, such as the group pressure that is expected to bring dissident members into line, the takeover by a dominant member and the reduced creativity that results from the embarrassment of members about expressing themselves.

Group Life Insurance. Life insurance provided on number of persons in a single master contract. Physical examinations are not required, and certificates of insurance are issued to members of the group as evidence of insurance.

Group Maintenance Roles. Behaviors that help the group engage in constructive interpersonal relationships, and help members to fulfil personal needs and derive satisfaction from group participation.

Group Norm. Agreement among group members about how they should behave.

Group of 7 (G-7). A group of developed countries that periodically meets to make economic decisions and this group consists of Canada, France, Germany, Italy, Japan, the United Kingdom and the United States.

Group of Thirty. An international financial policy organization, the members of which include representatives of central banks, international banks, and securities firms.

Group Term Life Insurance. Most common form of group life insurance. Yearly renewable term insurance on employee during their working careers.

Group Think. A phenomenon that occurs when a group believes that it is invincible, turns off criticism, attempts to bring members into line and that everyone is in agreement.

Group Universal Life Products (GULP). Universal Life Insurance Plans sold to members of a group such as individual employees of an employer. There are some differences between GULP plans and Individual Universal Life Plans; for instance, GULP expense charges are generally lower than those assessed against individual policies.

Groupware. Software that enables several users to work on the same file or send and receive messages simultaneously.

Growing Equity Mortgages (GEM). Mortgages in which the initial payment are the same as conventional mortgages, but they increase over a portion or the entire life of the mortgage. The incremental increase in monthly payments on GEMs reduces the principal on the mortgage more quickly. This reduces the actual life of the mortgage.

Growing Work Force. The average age of workforce is increasing as workers would like to work longer years and people's life is also rising.

Growth. The concept of expanding sales, operations, assets, and usually a major strategic objective.

Growth Firm. Growth firms are those which expand rapidly because of investment opportunities yielding returns than the opportunity cost of capital. These firms are able to reinvest earnings at a rate which is higher than the rate expected by the shareholders. They will maximize the value per share if they follow a policy of retaining all earnings for internal investment.

Growth Stock. The stock of a company that reinvests profits back into the firm in order to generate growth in earnings.

GSP. *See* Generalized System of Preferences.

GTC. A good, till cancelled order will remain in the system until it is cancelled by the trading member.

GTD. A good, till day's order allows the trading members to specify the days upto which the order should stay in the system. At the end of this period the order will get flushed out from the system.

Guaranteed Investment Contract. An investment contract with an insurer in which the insurer guarantees both principles and interest on a pension contribution.

Guaranteed Purchase Option. Benefit that can be added to life insurance policy permitting the insured to purchase additional amounts of life insurance at specified times in the future without requiring evidence of insurability.

Guaranteed Renewable. Continuous provision of a health insurance policy under which the company guarantees to renew the policy to a stated age, typically sixty-five and whose renewal is at the insured's option. Premiums can be increased for broad classes of insured.

Guaranteed Replacement Cost. In the event of a total loss, the insurer agrees to replace the home exactly as it was before the loss even though the replacement cost exceeds the amount of insurance stated in the policy.

H

Half-year Convention. A widely used custom, regarding all depreciable assets placed in service during the year as if they had been placed in service at the year's midpoint.

Hallo-error. A bias in perception that occurs when ratings of specific types of behavior reflect the perceiver's overall rating of the person.

Hand Delivery. Delivery and payment within the time or on the date stipulated when entering into the bargain, which item of date shall not be more than fourteen days following the date of the contract.

Hands-on-training. Training in which trainees try new skills during the course of the training session.

Hard Currency. A currency that is freely traded without many restrictions and for which there is usually strong external demand; often called a freely convertible currency.

Hard Rationing. The situation that occurs when a business cannot raise financing a project under any circumstances.

Hardiness. Personality characteristics that neutralizes stress.

Hardship Allowance. A supplement to compensate expatriates for working in adverse conditions.

Hard-to Employ. Individuals who have never worked, who have been unemployed for long periods of time.

Hardware. The mechanical and electronic processing equipment.

Hawthorn Studies. Management studies conducted at the Western Electric Hawthorne plant in a suburb of Chicago. These are the most famous studies ever conducted in the field of management.

Hazard. Condition that creates or increases the chance of loss.

Hazardous Waste. Waste materials from industrial, agricultural, and other activities capable of causing death or serious health problems for those persons exposed for prolonged.

Health. It refers to a general state of physical, mental and emotional well-being.

Health Maintenance Organisation (HMO). It is a form of health care which provides services for a fixed period on a prepaid basis.

Heath-jarrow-morton Model. A model for pricing interest rate derivatives.

Hedge. Attempt to protect foreign currency holdings against an adverse movements of an exchange rate.

Hedge Funds. A hedge fund is an investment vehicle for individuals and institutions. By limiting investment to a select few, these funds are not subject to same regulations as that of a standard mutual fund. They are sometimes referred to as high risk/high return mutual funds. They employ speculative and complex investing strategies.

Hedge Ratio. The number of future or option contracts required to achieve a certain hedging objective.

Hedgers. Those who go to the forward market to buy or sell currency now in order to protect against fluctuations in exchange rates.

Hedging. Buying and selling in the futures commodity market in order to shift the risk to speculators.

Hedonism. The concept that people generally behave in ways intended to maximize pleasure and minimize pain.

Heroes. Role models who embody the attributes of the culture.

Hiterarchy. An organizational structure in which management of an alliance of companies is shared by so-called equals rather than being set up in a superior subordinate relationship.

H-form Organization. An organizational design based on product departmentation with the products being the organization's various businesses.

Hi Tech. A concept that suggests the current state-of-the-art technology or application of knowledge in new processes or products. High tech is relative and in Edison's time, the light bulb was 'high tech', just as the electric typewriter was in the 1930s. Today, high tech connotes microelectronic and bio-technological applications.

Hickenlooper Amendment. A US Act requiring cessation of aid to country that nationalizes assets of U.S. citizens or has moved to abrogate contracts without taking appropriate means of settlement within a reasonable period of time.

Hierarchy of Needs. A well-known motivation theory stating that there is a hierarchy of needs and that people must fulfil the lower order needs sufficiently before they are motivated by the higher order ones.

High-context Culture. A culture in which most people consider that peripheral and hearsay information are necessary for decision making because they bear on the context of the situation.

High Powered Money. Currency in the hands of the public plus commercial bank reserves also called the monetary base.

Highly Leveraged Transactions (HLT) Loan. A loan that finances a merger and acquisition. A leveraged buyout results in a high leverage ratio for the borrower.

High-need Achiever. One who will work very hard to achieve material or career success, sometimes to the detriment of social relationships or spiritual achievements.

High-pay-out Clientele. Investors, who prefer near dividends to future dividends, are high-pay-out clientele. They prefer dividends than capital gains. They wish firms to pay higher dividends than retention of profits.

High-technology. The applications of technology that are new at the time the term is being used.

High-value Activities. Activities that either produce high profits or done by high salaried employees such as managers.

Hire Purchase. Hire purchase contract involves regular payments for acquiring (owning) an asset.

Hired Gun. An expert who is hired by a takeover target to fight off a predator.

Histogram. A graphic summary of data that enables a user to interpret patterns that are difficult to see in a simple table of members.

Historic Volatility. The volatility estimated from using past observations of the underlying asset's price.

Historical Cost. *See* Sunk costs.

Historically Planned Economy (HPE). The World Bank's term used for second world countries in transition to market economies.

History. A branch of knowledge that records and explains past events.

Hold Harmless Clause. Clause written into a contract by which one party agrees to release another party from all legal liability, such as a retailer who agrees to release the manufacturing from legal liability if the product injures someone.

Hold Over. To defer settlement of a deal on the stock exchange until the next settlement day.

Holding Company. An organization composed of several very different kinds of businesses each of which is permitted to operate largely autonomously.

Holding Gains. Increase (or decrease) in the replacement cost (or other appropriate measure of current value) of the assets held during the current period.

Holding Period Yield. The rate of return received or expected from a loan or security over the period the investor actually holds it including the price for which the instrument is sold to another investor.

Holding-of-the-register of Members Date. It is the date which is taken as a basis for sending letters of rights to the existing shareholders of the company when it issues rights.

Holistic Wellness Approach. Advocates personal responsibility in reducing stressors and stress.

Home Equity Loan. Extension of credit to individuals who own their homes in which the borrowers' homes are pledged as collateral to support the loans. The amount of the loan is based on the difference between the market value of home mortgage and debt outstanding.

Homeowners 2 Policy (Broad Form). Homeowners insurance policy that provides coverage on a named-perils basis on the dwelling, other structures and personal property. Personal liability insurance is also provided.

Homeowners 3 Policy (Special Form). Homeowners insurance policy that covers the dwelling and other structures on risk-of-direct-loss basis and personal property on a named perils basis. Personal liability insurance is also provided.

Homeowners 4 Policy (Contents Broad Form). Homeowners insurance policy that applies to tenants renting a home or apartment, covers the tenant's personal property and provides personal liability insurance.

Homeowners 6 Policy (Unit-owners Form). Homeowners insurance policy that covers personal property of insured owners of condominium units and cooperative apartments on a broad form named-perils basis. Personal liability insurance is also provided.

Homeowners 8 Policy (Modified Coverage Form). Homeowner policy that is designed for older homes. Dwelling and other structures are indemnified on the basis of repair cost using common construction materials and methods. Personal liability insurance is also provided.

Home Service Life Insurance. Industrial life insurance and monthly debit ordinary life insurance contracts that are serviced by agents who call on the policy owners at their home to collect the premiums. The amount of life insurance policy generally is larger than $ 1000.

Home-country Nationals. Expatriate employees who are not citizens of the country in which the company is headquartered.

Home-made Leverage. The use of personal borrowings to change the overall amount of financial leverage to which an individual is exposed.

Homeo-statis, Dynamic. The characteristic of a system whereby it is constantly in motion with a tendency to seek equilibrium at various changing levels.

Homogeneous Expectations. All investors have the expectations about the expected return and risk of securities.

Homogeneous Risk Classes. Firms can be grouped into homogeneous risk classes. Firms would be considered to belong to a homogeneous risk class if their expected earnings have identical risk and characteristics. It is generally implied under the M-M hypothesis that firms within the same industry constitute a homogeneous class.

Homogenization. The tendency of different financial institutions to offer the same services.

Horizontal Communication. Occurs when the communi-cator and the receiver are at the same level in the organization.

Horizontal Coordination. The linking of subunits on the same level.

Horizontal Expansion. Any foreign direct investments by which a company produces the same product that is produced at home.

Horizontal Integration. Mergers with or acquisitions of competitors organizations in related industries.

Horizontal Option Spread. Buying and selling call or put options with the same strike price but different expiration dates.

Horizontal Specialization. The division of labor at the same level of the organization into simple, repetitive tasks.

Horse and Penny Insurance. A specialist form of insurance cover which can be an extension to a household policy or stand-alone. Compensation is provided in the event of death, injury, and loss by theft. Extensions to the basic coverage can be provided to cover equipment and third party liability.

Hospital Expense Insurance. Individual health insurance that pays for medical expenses incurred while in a hospital—both a daily hospital benefit for room and board and benefits for miscellaneous expenses.

Host Country. Any foreign country in which an international company operates.

Host Country National. Someone from a host country hired by organization to work in its facility.

Hourly Rate. Payments to workers on an hourly basis.

Hull Insurance. C class of ocean marine insurance that covers physical damage to the shop or vessel insured, typically written on an 'all-risks' basis.

Human Asset Accounting. Programmes attempting to measure the value and its changes of investment in human assets of an enterprise.

Human Capital. The skills and training an individual acquires that makes her a productive employee or entrepreneur.

Human Capital Resources. An organization's employees are described in terms of their training, experience, judgment, intelligence, relationships and insight.

Human Life Value. For purposes of life insurance, the present value of the family's share of the deceased breadwinner's future earnings.

Human Management Skill. The ability to work with, motivate and counsel people who need help and guidance, most importantly to first-level managers.

Human Relations Approach. An approach to management that emphasizes the important role individuals play in determining the success of an organization. It embarked on the critical task of compensating some of the deficiencies in classical theory. Basically, it took the premises of the classical approaches given but showed how these premises were modified as a result of individual behavior and the influence of the work group.

Human Relations Movement. A practice whereby employees came to be viewed as informal groups of their own with their own leadership and codes of behavior, instead of unrelated individual workers assigned to perform individual basis.

Human Relations School. School of management based on the view that satisfied employee will work harder.

Human Relations Skill. The ability of a manager to deal effectively with people.

Human Resource Accounting. It is a specialized personnel audit that attempts to quantify the value of organizational human resources.

Human Resource Development. It focuses on increasing the capabilities of employees for growth and advancement in the organization.

Human Resource Information System (HRIS). It is an integrated computerized system designed to provide information to be used in making decisions.

Human Resource Managers. Managers concerned with developing and carrying out programs used to make decisions about employees, such as selection, training and compensation.

Human Resource Planning. It consists of analyzing and identifying the need for and the availability of the human resources required for an organization to meet its objectives

Human Resources Management. The process of accomplishing organizational objectives by acquiring, retaining, terminating, developing and properly using the human resources in an organization.

Hurdle Rate. Minimum desired rate of return also called required rate of return.

Hybrid Funds. Funds consisting of stock and bond securities.

Hybrid Structure. A combination of different structures, the most common form of organizational structure.

Hygiene Factors in Motivation. Hezberg's theory startes that certain human needs that motivate merely cause dissatisfaction if they are not met. In other words, the meeting of this latter class of needs is a 'maintenance' or 'hygiene' factor. They are such factors in a work situation as salary, company policy and administration, quality of supervision, working conditions, interpersonal relations, status, and job security.

Hygiene Factors. Job characteristics associated with job dissatisfaction.

Hyperinflation. An extended period in which inflation exceeds 100 per cent per year.

I

IAC. International Anti-counterfeiting Coalition, 1348.

IAS 17 Interest Rate Implicit in a Lease. The discount rate which, when applied to minimum lease payments (excluding executor costs paid by the lessor) and unguaranteed residual value, causes the aggregate present value at the beginning of the lease term to be equal to the gain value at the beginning of the lease term to be equal to the fair value of the leased property at the inception of the lease minus any investment tax credit retained by the lessor and expected to be realized by him. The international accounting standard on treatment of losses, published by the International Accounting Standard Committee in London, September 1982. The Standard is not binding on individual lease transactions but is expected to serve as a model for mandatory rules adopted by national organizations in future.

IC. International Company.

ICC. International Clearing Corporation.

ICCH. International Commodities Clearing House Limited.

IDA. International Development Association.

IDB. Inter-American Development Bank.

Ideal Capacity. The absolute maximum number of units that could be produced in a given operating situation with no allowance for work stoppages or repairs, also called theoretical capacity.

Idealism. Trying to determine principles before settling small issues.

Ideology. A set of basic beliefs that define an ideal way of living for an individual, an organization, or a society.

Idle Time. A classification of indirect labour that constitutes wages paid for unproductive time due to circumstances beyond the workers control.

IEC. International Electro-technical Commission.

IFC. International Finance Corporation.

IFE. *See* International Fisher Effect.

IFS Alliance (Interactive Financial Services Alliance). This is an alliance formed between members of leading financial institutions and IBM in the Asia Pacific Region. The mission of this alliance is to promote the usage of the IFS platform for e-business within the Asia Pacific Region. The alliance will also work to providing inputs and direction to IBM on the functionality and content of its platform. It will work with regulatory bodies and provide input to national and international agencies concerning e-commerce.

Illiquid. The description of a bank that lacks enough liquid assets to meet the immediate demands of its creditors and depositors.

ILO. *See* International Labour Organization.

Image Advertising. Advertising designed to influence perceptions of the organization or its brands.

IME. International Monetary Exchange.

IMF. *See* International Monetary Fund.

Imitation Lag. A strategy for exploiting temporary monopoly advantages by moving first to those countries most likely to develop local production.

Immediate-participation Guarantee (IPG) Plan. Type of pension plan in which all pension contributions are deposited in an unallotted fund and used directly to pay benefits to retirees.

Immediate Confirmation. It indicates that people learn best if reinforcement is given as soon as possible after training.

Immediate or Cancel Order (IOC). It allows a trading member to buy or sell a security as soon as the order is released into the market failing which the order will be removed.

Immediate Recognition. According to this principle, the costs which will not provide any future benefits should be recognized immediately. The examples of such costs are selling, administration expenses and losses.

Immunized. Describes an FI that is fully hedged or protected against adverse movements in interest rates (or asset prices).

Imperfect Information. In the loan market, when banks do not know for certain which borrowers will and will not repay loans, but only that some borrowers are more likely to repay than others.

Implementation Lags. The time between when a policy action is needed and the time when the action occurs.

Implicit Premiums. Deposit insurance premiums or costs imposed on a bank through activity constraints rather than direct monetary charges.

Implicit Transactions. Events (like the passage of time) that are temporarily ignored in day-to-day recording procedures and that are recognized via end-of-period adjustments.

Implicit Volatility. The volatility implied from option prices.

Implied Rate of Interest. The market's expectation about future interest rates as indicated by the shape of the yield curve or by financial futures prices.

Implied Repo Rate. The interest rate implicit in a forward contract.

Implied Volatility. The future price volatility of an asset that the market currently expects based on the current price of a particular option contract.

Import. A good or service made overseas but purchased by a U.S. resident. A product that is brought in from another nation for sale in the nation.

Import Broker. An individual who obtains various government permissions and other clearances before forwarding necessary paperwork to the carrier that will deliver the goods from the dock to the importer.

Import Deposit Requirement. Government requirement of a deposit price to the release of foreign exchange.

Import Licensing. A method of government control of the exchange rate whereby all recipients exporters and others who receive foreign exchange are required to sell to the Central bank at the official buying rate.

Import Specie Point. Point in the variation of exchange rates at which it becomes cheaper for a nation on the gold standard to import gold rather than buy foreign currency.

Import Substitution. An industrialization policy whereby new industrial development emphasizes products that would otherwise be imported.

Import Tariff. A tax placed on goods entering a country.

Importing. The purchase of goods and services from foreign service.

Impression Management. Getting others to see us in a certain manner.

Impulse Buying. A purchase made without preplanning.

Imputed Negligence. Case in which responsibility for damage can be transferred from the negligent party to another person such as an employer.

In the Money Option. An option is in-the-money if it has intrinsic value. A call option is in the money if the current asset price is above the option strike price; a put option is the money if the current asset price is below the option price.

Incentives. They are rewards designed to encourage and reimburse employees for efforts beyond normal performance.

Inception of a Lease. The date on which the lease commitment or agreement is signed, provided the property to be leased has been constructed or has been acquired by the lessor. Otherwise, the property is acquired by the lessor.

Income. A flow of earnings over some given time interval.

Income and Growth Plans. An income plan pays annual or other such periodic income in the form of dividends to the investors, while a growth plan reinvests the earnings. Investors who want an income prefer the former, while growth plans are suited for those who prefer capital appreciation.

Income Bond. A bond which has characteristics of both non-cumulative preferred stock and bonds.

Income Effect. The fact that a higher return on assets leaves a person with more income which normally leads to the purchase of more assets.

Income Percentage of Revenue. Income divided by revenue.

Income Statement. A statement that evaluates the operating performance of the corporation by matching its accomplishments (revenue from customers, which usually is called sales) and efforts (cost of goods sold and other expenses). It is a measure of income, expenses and profit over a specific period of time.

Income Stock. The stocks of companies that have a low level of retained earnings and thus pay most of their earnings to shareholders as dividends.

Incontestable Clause. Contractual provision in a life insurance policy stating that the insurer cannot contest the policy after it has been in force two years during the insured's lifetime.

Incorporate Stock Holding. It exists when a corporation holds stock in other corporations and is unlawful when it injures competition.

Incremental. The change in total results (such as revenue, expense, or income) under a new condition comparison with some given or known condition.

Incremental Approach. A method of determining which of the two alternative courses of action is preferable by calculating the present value of the difference in net cash inflows between one alternative and the other.

Incremental Borrowing Rate. The interest rate which a person would expect to pay for a certain loan at a certain time.

Incremental Cash Flows. Cash flows from an investment when compared to a hypothetical zero-cash-flow project.

Incremental Change. A relatively small change in processes and behaviors within just one or a few systems or levels of the organization.

Incremental Cost. The difference in total cost between two alternatives. It is also called differential cost.

Incremental Influence. This concept refers to the influence of a leader over and above the influence base best owned by a position in the organization.

Indemnification. Compensation to the victim of a loss, in whole or in part, by payment, repair, or replacement.

Indemnity Agreement. In a leveraged lease, an agreement whereby the owner participates and the lease indemnify the trustees from liability as a result of ownership of the leased equipment. In a leveraged lease, an agreement whereby the owner participants and the lessee indemnity the trustees from liability as a result of ownership of the leased equipment.

Indemnity Clause. Although lease documentation contains various indemnities, the indemnity clause actually refers to the tax indemnity clauses whereby the lessee indemnifies the lessor from loss of tax benefits.

Indenture Trustee. In a leveraged lease, the indenture trustee holds the security interest in the leased equipment for the benefit of the lenders. In the event of default, the indenture trustee exercises the rights of a mortgagee. The indenture trustee is also responsible for receiving rent payments from the lessee and using such funds to pay the amounts due the lenders with the balance being paid to the owner trustee. The indenture trustee verifies that correct filings are made to protect the security interest of the lenders. The bond register is maintained by the indenture trustee, who also acts as transfer agent.

Indenture. An indenture is a legal agreement between the company issuing debentures and the debenture trustee, who represents the debenture holders. It is the responsibility of the trustee to protect the interests of debenture holders by ensuring that the company fulfils the contractual obligations.

Independence. An extreme situation in which a country would not rely on other countries at all.

Independent Adjuster. Claims adjuster who offers his or her services to insurance companies and is compensated by a fee.

Independent Agency Insurer. An insurer that market its services through independent agents who may represent many insurers.

Independent Agency System. Type of property and liability insurance marketing system, sometimes called the American agency system in which the agent is an independent business person representing several insurers. The agency owns the expirations or renewal rights to the business and the agent is compensated by commissions that vary by line of insurance.

Independent Events. The occurrence of one event has no effect on the occurrence of the other event.

Independent Insurer. An insurer that sets its own prices and does not subscribe to a rating organization.

Independent Lessor. Any leasing company investing in leases, also brokers without funds to invest in leases sometimes prefer to call themselves "independent lessors" rather than "brokers". Any leasing company investing in lease without funds to invest in leases sometimes prefer to be called themselves "independent lessors" rather than brokers.

Independent Monetary Policy. A policy conducted through open market operations with the goal of changing the money supply without changing taxes or spending.

Indeterminate-premium Whole Life Insurance. Non-participating whole life policy that permits the insurer to adjust premiums based on anticipated future experience. Initial premiums are guaranteed for a certain period. After the initial guaranteed period expires, the insurer can increase premiums up to some maximum limit.

Index Amortized Swap. An interest rate swap for which the notional principal is amortized over the life of the swap. The rate of amortizations is related to the level of interest rates.

Index Arbitrage. Process of selling stocks at the same time as buying stock index futures, or *vice versa*. It is a form of programme trading.

Index Number. A ratio of two numbers expressed as a percentage.

Index Options. Optional contracts written on a stock index.

Indigenization. The process of introducing elements of an outside culture.

Indirect Bankruptcy Cost. The cost of avoiding a bankruptcy filing incurred by a financially distressed firm.

Indirect Finance. Finance that involves a middleman, viz. a third party linking the borrower and lender.

Indirect Labour. All factory labour that is not direct labour.

Indirect Manufacturing Costs. All manufacturing costs other than direct material and direct labour.

Indirect Quote. An exchange rate given in terms of the number of units of the foreign currency for one unit of the domestic currency.

Indirect Selling. A sale of goods by an exporter through another domestic company as an intermediary.

Indirect Transfer. A transfer of fund between suppliers and users of funds through a financial intermediary.

Individual Brand. A manufacturer's policy of distributing each of his products under different brand names.

Individual Deductible. Amount that an insured and each person of his or her family covered by the policy must pay before the group or individual medical insurance policy begins to pay for medical expenses.

Individual Differences. Characteristics that vary from one person to another.

Individual Retirement Account (IRA). Individual retirement plan that can be established by a person with earned income. An IRA plan enjoys favorable income tax advantages. It allows an employee to set aside in a special account the funds which are tax-deferred until the employee retires.

Individualism. A belief that each individual person has an inherent worth and possess basic human rights that should be by society. Each person is presumed to be a free agent capable of knowing and promoting his or her own self-interest.

Individualism vs Collectivism. The degree to which people act as individuals rather than members of a group.

Individually Validated Licence (IVL). A special export licence under which certain restricted products need to be shipped.

Inductive Statistics. The making of predictions, forecasts, and generalizations about a larger set of data based on information derived from a smaller set of data.

Industrial Development Bonds (IDBs). Tax-exempt bonds issued by municipalities or non-profit intermediaries to encourage local economic development or projects of social or economic interest.

Industrial Engineering. A field that seeks to maximize the efficiency of the methods and resources used to produce commercial products.

Industrial Goods. Goods which are used in producing another product or expended in connection with carrying on business operations.

Industrial Life Insurance. A type of life insurance in which policies are sold in small amounts and the premiums are collected weekly or monthly by a debit agent at the policy owner's home.

Industrial Products. Products or services sold to and used by other businesses as value-added elements of their business ventures including automobile windshields, wheels, ball bearings, pipes and steel or industrial products. The act of selling industrial products is called institutional sales and it can include supplies, maintenance materials, equipment and services.

Industrial Robot. A machine designed to move materials, parts, tools, or specialized devices through variable programmed motions for the performance of a variety of tasks.

Industrial Society. A society in which the building and mechanical processing of material goods dominates work and employs the largest proportion of the labour force.

Industrial Source Base. The minerals, energy sources, water supplies, skilled labour force, and human knowledge necessary for industrial production.

Industrial Union. A union whose members, regardless of their skills or craft work in a particular industry such as automobile manufacturing or the chemical industry.

Industrialization Argument. A rationale for protectionism which argues that the development of industrial output should come about even though domestic prices may not become competitive on the world market.

Industry Analysis. To determine the financial condition and performance of a firm, its ratios may be compared with the average ratios of the industry of which the firm is a member. This sort of analysis is known as the industry analysis. It helps to ascertain the financial standing and capability of the firm *vis-à-vis* other firm in the industry.

Industry-specific Regulation. Regulations aimed at specific industries such as telephone service or railroad transportation involving control of rates charged, customers served and entry into the industry.

Inelastic (Product) Demand. A condition in which sales are likely to increase or decrease by a percentage that is less than the percentage change in income.

Infant-industry Argument. The position which argues that an emerging industry should be guaranteed a large share of the domestic market until it becomes efficient enough to compete against imports.

Inflation. A persistent, general rise in the average price of all goods.

Inflation Caused Depreciation Effect. Changes in the expected inflation rate may not lead to equivalent increase in nominal interest rates due to the tendency of depreciation charges on existing plant and equipment discouraging business investment and credit demand.

Inflation Caused Income Tax Effect. The presence of a progressive income tax structure tends to cause nominal interest rates to increase by more than the expected increase in inflation.

Inflation Caused Wealth Effect. Changes in inflation may alter the value of wealth held in financial assets by individuals and institutions causing a change in their savings plans and leading to offsetting movements in real and nominal interest rates.

Inflation Premium. The part of the nominal interest rate that is over and above the real interest rate. This compensates for the decline in purchasing power due to inflation.

Inflation Rate. The rate of change in the price level stated as a percentage change on an annual basis.

Inflation Risk. Risk that the actual inflation rate will differ from that expected by borrowers and lenders.

Inflationary Expectations. Expectations or educated estimate of the inflation rate.

Inflation-guard Endorsement. Endorsement added at the insured's request to a homeowners policy to increase periodically the face amount of insurance on the dwelling and other policy converges by a specified percentage.

Info-preneure. He is a person who makes out a living by collecting and selling information to interested parties.

Informal Communication. Communication outside the organization's authorized channels.

Informal Groups. Natural groupings of people in response to some need.

Informal Leader. A leader whose leadership activities are unrelated to his or her position in the organization.

Informal Organization. Generally, patterns of human behaviour and relationships coexisting with, or lying outside, the formal organization structure. According to professor Keith Davis, it is a network of personal and social relations not established or required by the formal organization but arising spontaneously as people associate with one another, structured around people and based on the interpersonal relationships of workers which exists within the framework of the formal organization.

Informal Risk Capital. Investments by people who seek equity positions in new ventures with potential for unusually high returns.

Information. Data that are relevant for a specific purpose.

Information Lags. Lags in the availability of information about the state of the economy.

Information Overload. The conditions of having too much information to process.

Information Power. Power that is a result of having access to important information that is not common knowledge or of having the ability to control the flow of information to and from others.

Information Retrieval. The furnishing of information rapidly to the place where it is needed.

Information Richness. Information-carrying capacity of data.

Information System. A set of resources and procedures dedicated to gathering and organizing data and disseminating information.

Information Technology. Electronic hardware and software used for communication and information processing.

Informational Roles. Activities, such as reports or briefings, that focus on obtaining data important for the decisions the manager needs to make.

Infrastructure. The underlying foundation of a society such as roads, schools, and so forth, that allows it to function effectively.

Ingratiation. The use of praise and compliments to gain another person's favor or acceptance.

In-group Exchange. A partnership characterized by mutual trust, respect, and liking.

Initial Direct Costs. Direct costs incurred by a lessor in negotiating and consummating a lease such as commissions and legal fees.

Initial Investment Outlay. The immediate cash commitment required to undertake an investment.

Initial Margin. Initial margin is the amount a trader must deposit before trading futures. This margin is approximately equal to the maximum daily price fluctuations permitted for the contract being traded. The amount of money that customers must put up while establishing a futures or options position to guarantee their contract obligations.

Initial Public Offerings (IPOs). The first public issue of financial instrument by a firm.

Initial Reserve. In life insurance, the reserve at the beginning of any policy year.

Initiating a Position. This implies knowing that the types of orders and types of markets in the futures industry is all good and fine but knowing how to apply that knowledge is usually best left to the professionals.

Initiating Structure Behavior. Defining and structuring leader-employee roles through activities such as scheduling, defining work tasks, setting deadlines, criticizing poor work, getting employees to accept work standards and resolving problems.

Initiating Structure. It refers to task-oriented efforts on the part of the leader to get the job done.

Injunction. A court order obtained by management to prohibit the union from performing some act.

Injury Tax. A tax levied against an organization, based on the number and severity of job-related injuries suffered by its employees. Institutional investor—a financial institution, insurance company, pension fund endowment fund or similar organization that invests its accumulated funds in the securities offered for sale on stock exchanges.

Inland Marine Insurance. Transportation insurance that provides protection for goods shipped on land including imports, exports, domestic shipments, means of transportation, personal property floater risks and commercial property floater risks.

Innovation. The transformation of creative ideas into useful applications by combining resources in new or unusual ways to provide value to society for new or improved products, technology or services.

Input. Putting data into the computer which are to be processed.

Input-output Table. A tool used widely in national economic planning to show that resources utilized by different industries for a given output as well as the inter-dependence of economic sectors.

Inquiry Window. It is this window that the inquiries such as market by order, market by price, previous trade, order log, outstanding order and the shape quote as regarding the various orders available in the system can be viewed.

Inside Money. That part of money supply produced by the private banking system.

Insolvency Risk. The risk that an FI may not have enough capital to offset a sudden decline in the value of its assets relative to its liabilities.

Insolvent. The description of a bank with total liabilities that exceed the value of its assets.

Inspection. Checking for defective products in the quality control process.

Installment Credit. All liabilities of a borrowing customer other than home mortgages that are retired in two or more consecutive loan payments.

Installment Refund Annuity. Pays the annuitant a lifetime income, but if death occurs before receiving payments equal to the purchase price, the income payment is continued to the beneficiary.

Installment Sales Contracts. Contracts in which a customer agrees to pay for a purchase by paying a certain amount of money each month for specific number of months.

Instant Crossing. Instant crossing is an after-hours equity trading product designed to lower transaction costs by providing a passive trading environment. In this environment, instant customers reap the benefits of anonymity, neutrality and confidentiality while relying on benchmark prices. These benchmark prices are the last sale on the primary exchange and the midpoint of the closing inside bid and offer for OTC securities.

Institutional Advertising. Advertising with the purpose of building a positive image for the company.

Instrument. In terms of monetary policy variables the policy maker can control.

Instrument Instability. It rises when a change in the instrument affects the targeted variable over a number of future periods. Leading to ever widening swings in the instrument in order to stabilize the targeted variable.

Instrumental Values. Beliefs about what kinds of behavior are appropriate for reaching goals.

Instrumentality. A person's expectation that performing a task will lead to a desired outcome.

Insufficient-reason Criterion. Assumes that if a manager is operating under conditions of uncertainty, there is an actual probability that each of the possible states of nature or competitive actions may occur.

Insurable Risk. A loss exposure that is insurable by a private or public insurer. Few, if any, such risks meet the requirements of an ideally insurable risk.

Insurance. Pooling of fortuitous losses by transfer of risks to insurers who agree to indemnify insured for such losses, to provide other pecuniary benefits on their occurrence or to render services connected with the risks.

Insurance Companies. Business that calculates the risk of any loss and insure against that loss for the payment of premiums. Financial institutions that help protect individuals against certain risks. Such as risks to health, disability and life.

Insurance Exchange. Term used to describe a facility that existed in a few states to provide a market for reinsurance and for the insurance of large and unusual domestic and foreign risks that are difficult to insure in the normal markets.

Insurance Guaranteed Fund. A fund of required contributions from within the state insurance companies to compensate insurance company policyholders in the event of a failure.

Insurance Ombudsman. Official in-charge of service set up by insurance companies in 1981 to arbitrate the disputes between insurance companies and policy holders.

Insurance Services Office. Major rating organization in property and liability insurance that drafts policy forms for personal and commercial lines of insurance and provides rate data on loss costs for property and liability insurance lines.

Insured Pension Plan. A pension fund administered by a life insurance company.

Insured Plan. It is one administered through insurance companies or similar institutions which buy retirement annuity policies.

Insured Value. A schedule included in a lease which states the agreed value of equipment of various times during the term of the lease and establishes the liability of the lessee to the lessor the event the leased equipment is lost or rendered unusable the lease term due to a casualty.

Insuring Agreement. That part of an insurance contract which states the promises of the insurer.

Intangible Assets. Assets that have no form but do have value such as goodwill and patents, etc.

Intangible Fixed Assets. Represents the firm's rights and they include patents, copyrights, franchises, trademarks, trade names and goodwill. Patents are the exclusive rights granted by the government enabling the holder to control the use of an invention. Copyrights are the exclusive rights to produce and sell literary, musical and artistic works.

Intangible Property. *See* Intellectual property rights.

Intangible Reward. Exists in the form of recognition and it has little or no money value.

Integrated System. A system for taxation of the corporate income aimed at preventing double taxation through the use of the split rates or tax credits.

Integrating Manager. A manager who has formal authority to coordinate the work of interdependent groups.

Integration. Cooperation among specialists to achieve common goal.

Integrative Bargaining. The union and management work at resolving a number of issues. There is a give and take atmosphere in the negotiation.

Integrity Tests. Tests that measure an application designed to facilitate functioning between two or more groups by helping the groups, understand and deal with areas of conflict.

Intellectual Property Rights. Ownership rights to intangible assets such as patents, trademarks, copyrights and know-how.

Intelligence. Capacity for constructive thinking, reasoning and problem solving.

Intelligence Information. Data on elements of the organization's operating environment (*e.g.* clients, competitors, suppliers, creditors and government) for use in short-run planning, and data on developments in the economic environment (*e.g.* consumer income trends and spending patterns) in the social and cultural environment for use in long-run strategic planning.

Intensive Technology. A service technology in which employees adjust the work process in response to feedback from their customer.

Inter Commodity Spread. A spread between two future contracts written on different but related commodities.

Interactive Model of Business. The combined primary and secondary interactions that business has with society.

Interactive System. The closely intertwined relationships between business and society.

Inter-bank Market. The market for foreign-exchange transactions among commercial banks.

Inter-bank Transactions. Foreign-exchange transactions that take place between commercial banks.

Inter-corporate Deposits. Inter-corporate lending/borrowing of deposits (CDs) is a popular short-term investment alternative for companies. Generally, cash surplus companies will deposit their funds in sister or associate companies or outside companies with high credit standing. In practice, companies can negotiate inter-corporate borrowing or lending for very short periods. The risks of default are high, but returns are quite attractive.

Inter-corporate Funds Market. Inter-corporate loans have been a traditional feature of corporate financing in India. These loans are generally made by corporate units with seasonal surplus funds to other companies whether directly or through brokers. The loans are generally for short periods and may be secured.

Interdependence. The existence of mutually necessary economic relations among countries.

Interest Aggregation. The collection of interests in the political system.

Interest Arbitrage. Investing in debt instruments in different countries and earning a profit due to interestrate and exchangerate differentials.

Interest Articulation. The process by which politicians, individuals, business and interest groups make their desires known in the political process.

Interest Coverage Ratio. Interest coverage ratio or the times-interest-earned is used to test the firm's debt servicing capacity. The interest coverage ratio is computed by dividing earnings before interest and taxes (EBIT) by interest charges. The interest coverage ratio shows the number of times the interest charges are covered by funds that are ordinarily available for their payments.

Interest Earning Assets. Futures trading, an interest bearing assets started in 1975, but the growth at this market has been phenomenal. Contracts are traded on treasury bills, euro-dollars, deposits, municipal bonds, etc.

Interest Elasticity of Demand for Loans. The percentage change in the quantity demanded of loans divided by the percentage change in the interest rate.

Interest Group. A group formed to achieve some job related objective.

Interest on Interest. Interest earned on the reinvestment of previous interest payments.

Interest Option. Life insurance settlement option in which the principal is retained by the insurer and interest is paid periodically.

Interest Rate. The price of credit, or ratio of the fees charged to secure credit from a lender to the amount borrowed usually expressed on an annual percentage basis.

Interest Rate Adjustment Act (1961). Extended the glass-steagall interest rate limits to thrifts.

Interest Rate Ceiling. A specified amount above which the interest rate is not permitted to rise.

Interest Rate Derivative. A derivative security the value of which depends on the evolution of the term structure of interest rates.

Interest Rate Differential. An indicator of future changes in the spot exchange rate.

Interest Rate Floor. A feature of many financial instruments that prevent the interest from falling below some specified amount.

Interest Rate Implicit in a Lease. The discount rate which, when applied to minimum lease payments (excluding execution costs paid by the lessor) and unguaranteed residual value, causes the aggregated present value at the beginning of the lease term to be equal to the the fair value of the leased property at the inception of the lease, minus any investment tax credit retained by the lessor and expected to be realized by him.

Interest Rate Insurance. An insurer agreeing to reimburse a borrower for additional interest expenses if the borrower's loan rate climbs above some specified maximum loan rate.

Interest Rate Parities. A theory stating that the forward premium or discount on one currency in terms of another currency is directly related to the short-term interest rate difference between the two countries.

Interest Rate Parity Theorem. The theory that the domestic interest rate should equal the foreign interest rate minus the expected appreciation of the domestic currency.

Interest Rate Parity. An arbitrage relations that holds between foreign currency spot prices and interest rates.

Interest Rate Risk. The risk of a change in the overall level of interest rates, and the resulting change in the bond prices.

Interest Rate Spread. The difference between lending and deposit rates.

Interest Rate Structure. The concept that the interest rate or yield attached to any loan or security consists of the risk-free (or pure) rate of interest plus risk premiums for the security holder's exposure to various forms of risk.

Interest Rate Swap. A swap based on interest rates.

Interest Tax Shield. The profit after tax figure excludes interest on borrowing. Interest is tax deductible and therefore a firm which pays more interest pays less taxes. Tax saved on account of payment of interest is called interest tax shield.

Interest-adjusted Method. Method of determining cost to an insured of a life insurance policy that considers the time cost of one by applying an interest factor to each element of cost.

Interfaces. They are areas of contact between the personnel unit and other managers in an organization that occur in personnel activities.

Inter-firm Analysis. The analysis of the financial performance of all firms in an industry and their comparison at a given point of time is referred to as the cross-sectional analysis or the inter-firm analysis.

Inter-group Conflict. The disagreements, hostile emotions, and problems that exist among groups. These conflicts emerge because of limited resources, communication problems, differences in perceptions and attitudes, and lack of clarity.

Inter-group Team Building. An exercise designed to facilitate functioning between two or more groups by helping the groups understand and deal with areas of conflict.

Interim Rent. Daily rental accruing from delivery, acceptance and/or funding until a later starting debate for a basic lease term, often used when equipment delivered over a period of time.

Interlocking Directorates. Exists when a person is a member of the board of directors of more than one corporation. It is unlawful when the firms are in competition.

Intermediate Target. This target is a value for a variable that the policy maker tries to achieve not because it is desirable in its own right, but becaus it helps achieve the final target.

Intermediate-term Assets. Assets in the debt market which mature between one and ten years from the date of issue.

Intermittent Production. Also called job lot production. Orders are produced to each customer's specifications.

Intermittent Reinforcement. Reinforcing some but not all instances of behavior.

Intermittent Reinforcement. A reinforcement schedule that involves rewarding desired behavior only periodically.

Internal Accounting Control. Methods and procedures that are mainly concerned with the authorization of transactions, safeguarding of assets and accuracy of the financial records.

Internal Change Forces. Forces for change that occur within the organization, such as communication problems, morale problems, and decision-making breakdowns.

Internal Data. Data collected by a firm from its own records and reports.

Internal Debt. Government borrowing within the country.

Internal Environment. All elements that made up the organization, such as owners, management, employees, and board of directors.

Internal Forces for Change. Originate inside the organization.

Internal Growth Rate. The maximum growth rate a firm can achieve without external financing of any kind.

Internal Locus of Control. Attributing outcomes to one's own actions.

Internal Measure. Ratio assesses a firm's ability to meet its regular cash expenses, is the internal measure. It relates liquid assets to average daily operating cash outflows.

Internal Motivation. Motivation caused by positive internal feelings.

Internal Rate of Return. The rate of return on an investment, determined by finding the discount rate that will equate the present value of all future cash flows from the investment with the initial investment outlay, also called time adjusted rate.

Internalization. Control through self-handling of foreign operations, primarily because it is less expensive to deal within the same corporate family than to contract with an external organization.

International Accounting Standards Committee (IASC). The international private sector organization that sets financial accounting standards for worldwide use.

International Balance of Payments. The net effect or balance of all payments made by a nation, all payments received by that nation in its trading and investments relationships with other nations. A favourable balance exists when net payments received are greater than net payments made. An unfavourable balance occurs when net payments made exceed net payments received.

International Banking Act. A US law passed in 1978 to bring foreign banks operating in the US under regulation.

International Banking Facilities. A domestically based set of computerized accounts recording trans-actions of a US with its foreign customers.

International Bureau for the Protection of Industrial Property Rights (BIRPI). A multilateral agreement to protect patents, trademarks and other property rights.

International Business. The buying, selling and trading of goods and services across national boundaries.

International Division. An organizational structure in which virtually all foreign operations are handled within the same division.

International Fisher Effect (IFE). The theory that the relationship between interest rates and exchange rates implies that the currency of the country with the lower interest rate will strengthen in the future.

International Labour Organization (ILO). A multilateral organization promoting the adoption of humane labour conditions.

International Lending Supervisory Act of 1983. Legislation which addressed the issue of bank capitalization and authorized the federal reserve system, the FDIC, and the comptroller of the currency to set and enforce minimum capital requirements.

International Monetary Fund (IMF). A multi-governmental association organized in 1945 to promote exchange rate stability and to facilitate the international flow of currencies.

International Monetary Market (IMM). A specialized market located in Chicago and dealing in select foreign currency futures.

International Organization of Securities Commissions (IOSC). An international organization of securities regulators that wants the IASC to establish more comprehensive accounting standards.

International Standard of Fair Dealing. The concept that investors should receive prompt, adequate, and effective compensation in cases of expropriation.

International Trade Administration (ITA). A branch of the U.S. Department of Commerce offering a variety of services to U.S. exporting companies.

International Trade. Buying and selling products between nations.

International Union. An affiliation of local unions and membership in Canada, Mexico and Central America as well as United States.

Internet. A global network of computer networks.

Interperiod Tax Allocation. Accounting procedures that account for timing differences between revenues and expenses reported to income tax authorities and to others.

Interpersonal Conflicts. Conflicts between two or more individuals with differing values, goals or needs.

Interpersonal Roles. Activities that involve interacting with others who may be external or internal to the organization and at the same time, at a higher or lower level than the manager.

Interpersonal Skills. Those management skills such as communication, conflict resolution, and leading that are necessary to work with others.

Interpretation. Stage of perception that consists of looking for explanations for the stimuli observed.

Interstate Commerce Commission. A federal agency which regulates common carriers engaged in interstate transportation by rail and pipelines which move oil or other commodities (except water and gas) in interstate commerce.

Intervention Currencies. The currencies in which a particular country trades the most.

Interview Method. Information gathering technique mainly using personal interview, telephone and questionnaire.

Interview. The face-to-face contact between the company representative and the applicant.

In-the-money. A term referring to a call (put) option when the market value of the asset on which the option is written is greater (less) than the strike price.

Intra-commodity Spread. A spread between two futures contracts written on the same commodity but with different delivery months.

Intranet. An organization's private internet.

Intra-personal Conflicts. Conflicts between an individual's values, goals, and needs.

Intrapreneur. A contrived word from the term 'intra-corporate-entrepreneur' meaning a person who pursues an innovation, becoming a champion for its development, but does so from within the security of his or her organizational position.

Intra-zonal Trade. Trade among countries that are part of a trade agreement such as the E.U.

Intrinsic Rewards. Rewards that are part of the behavior.

Intrinsic Rewards. Self-granted, psychic rewards.

Intrinsic Value of an Option. The difference between an option's exercise price and the underlying asset's price.

Intrinsic Value. For a call option the difference of the asset price less the strike price if positive zero otherwise. For a put option, the difference of the strike price less the asset price if positive zero otherwise.

Intuition. The immediate comprehension that something is the case, seemingly without the use of any reasoning process or conscious analysis.

Invention. The creation of new products, processes, and technologies not previously known to exist.

Inventory. All the material a firm holds in storage for future use.

Inventory Loan. A secured short-term loan to purchase inventory.

Inventory Models. A type of production control model that answers two questions relating to inventory management. "how much?" and "when?". An inventory model tells the manager when goods should be recorded? and what quantity should be purchased?

Inventory Approach to Money Demand. Pioneered by William Baumol and James Tobia in the 1950s, provides a micro-economic justification for including interest rates a determinant of money demand.

Inventory Control. The process that strives to maintain adequate materials while minimizing inventory carrying costs.

Inventory Management. Management of stocks of raw materials, stocks available for sale or in the process of being made ready for sale.

Inventory Period. The time it takes to acquire and sell inventory.

Inventory Turnover. Cost of goods sold divided by average inventory for a specific period.

Investing. Purchasing stock with the intent of holding it rather long period of time with the anticipation of appreciation in value.

Investment. Expenditures on capital goods or on inventories of goods, or raw materials that are used to produce other goods and services.

Investment Banks. Financial institutions that purchase large blocks of stock from issuing companies and resell them in the market in small lots.

Investment Canada. A Canadian act whose intent is to persuade foreign companies to invest in Canada.

Investment Centre. An area of responsibility for costs, revenues and related investments.

Investment Companies. Financial intermediaries that sell shares to the public to raise funds and invest the proceeds in stocks, bonds, and other securities.

Investment Decision. It involves the decision of allocation of capital or commitment of funds to long term assets that would yield benefits in the future.

Investment Goods. Goods and services demanded by businesses for use as capital inputs into production.

Investment Institutions. Financial intermediaries selling their customers securities and other financial assets in order to build up savings for retirement or for other customer uses. (Also see Investment Comparies.)

Investment Performance. This has been calculated using the internal rate of return method. The return calculated have been adjusted for rights, bonuses and dividends for the period of existence of the scheme. It takes the face value of the scheme as the initial outflow and the latest net asset value as the inflow. The formula takes into account rights, bonus, or dividends during the period under consideration and makes suitable adjustments for the same. All returns have been annualized.

Investment Period Method. Lessor accounting method, which apportions profit earned on a lease to those periods where lessor has an after tax, net investment in the lease.

Investment Tax Credit. Direct reductions of income taxes arising from the acquisition of depreciable assets.

Investments in Affiliates. Often used to describe investments in voting stock that represents 20% to 50% ownership.

Investments in Associates. Often used as synonym for investment affiliates.

Invisible Hand. A phrase derived from Adam Smith to describe market competition as the regulator of a free-market economy.

Invisible. *See* Services.

Invitee. Someone who is invited onto the premises for the benefit of the occupant.

Invoice. Bill for goods or services provided by the seller to the purchaser.

Invoice Price. The actual price that a long pays to a short at delivery after all adjustments.

IO Strips. The owner of an IO strip has a claim to the present value of interest payments by the mortgages in the GNMA.

IPE. International Petroleum Exchange.

IPLC. International Product Life Cycle.

IPO. Initial Public Offering of equity shares.

IRC. International Revenue Code.

IRDA Act. An Act to provide for the establishment of an Authority to protect the interests of holders of insurance policies, to regulate, promote and ensure orderly growth of the insurance industry and for matters connected therewith or incident thereto and further to amend the Insurance

Act, 1938, the Life Insurance Corporation Act, 1956 and the General Insurance Business (Nationalization) Act, 1972.

Iron Law of Responsibility. The iron law of responsibility states that in the long run those who do not use power in a way that society considers responsible will tend to lose it.

Irrevocable Beneficiary. Beneficiary designation allowing no change to be made in the beneficiary of an insurance policy without the beneficiary's consent.

Irrevocable Letter of Credit. A letter of credit that cannot be cancelled or changed without the consent of all parties involved.

ISA. International Seabed Authority.

ISDA. International Swaps and Derivatives Association.

Islamic Laws. A system of theocratic law based on the religious teachings of Islam; also called Muslim law.

ISO. International Organization for Standards.

ISO 9000. A quality standard developed by the International Standards Organization in Geneva that requires companies to document their commitment to quality at all levels of the organization.

Issues Management. Identifying, analyzing, developing recommendations and implementing policies concerning issues that have special meaning and importance for a company.

IVL. *See* Individually validated licence.

J

JAJO. It represents January, April, July and October which are expiration months of successively offered option contracts. It also represents payments that are due quarterly.

Jamaica Agreement. A 1976 agreement among countries that permitted greater flexibility of exchange rates, basically formalizing the break from fixed exchange rates.

James Bond. It is the nickname for a US Treasury bond, that matures in the year 2007, so named because the maturity date is James Bond's agent number in the popular series of movies.

Jargon. Terms that have a precise meaning among specialists but are unfamiliar to non-specialists.

Jeffersonian Ideal. The preferences, usually attributed to Thomas Jefferson for a society composed of many small-scale procedures, a representative political system, widespread dispersal of power, and individual freedom and responsibility for all citizens.

Jelly Roll Spread. A long and short position in the same index option with different classes a put and a call, which have different expiration dates.

Jeopardy Clause. It is a situation in the Euro-currency agreement that guarantees certain actions to protect the market if some events curtail the lender's activities or Euro market operations.

Job. It is a grouping of similar positions.

Job Analysis. A systematic collection of all information about a job to determine its requirements.

Job Centered Leaders. Less effective managers, who are mostly directive in their approaches and more concerned with closely supervising employees, explaining work procedures, and monitoring progress in task accomplishment.

Job Depth. It is the amount of planning and control responsibilities in a job.

Job Description. The description of requirements of the job.

Job Design. The structuring of a job in terms of content, function and relationships. It may focus on individual positions or on work groups.

Job Diagnostic Survey. A questionnaire that made employed perceptions of the core job characteristics, critical psychological states, and moderators.

Job Enlargement. It is the concept of broadening the scope of a job by expanding the number of different tasks to be performed.

Job Enrichment. Programmes of building into jobs a high sense of meaning, challenge, and potential for accomplishment.

Job Evaluation. It is the systematic determination of the relative worth of jobs within an organization.

Job Evaluation Methods. Techniques that determine the value of an organization's jobs and arrange these jobs in the order of pay according to their value.

Job Extension. Combing several relatively simple jobs to form a job with a wider range of tasks.

Job Involvement. Attitude of caring about one's job so much that the employer routinely exceeds the normal expectations for job performance.

Job Lot. Collection of stocks or goods sold together perhaps to somebody who wants only some of them.

Job Order. A document that shows the costs allocated to a specific batch of product.

Job Order Costing. The method of allocating costs of products that receive varying attention and effort.

Job Performance. Behaviors that are relevant to the organization's goals and can be measured in terms of each individual's proficiency or level of contribution.

Job Posting. Notices of the vacancy displayed on bulletin boards in company newsletters and memos.

Job Redesign. Restructuring the work of employees to allow a more direct connection between an employee's personal effort and the tangible results of that work effort.

Job Rotation. A plan that allows employees to move periodically from one job to another within an office or plant, as one way to reduce boredom or monotony and improve the quality of work life.

Job Satisfaction. An affective or emotional response to one's job.

Job Scope. It refers to the number and variety of tasks performed by a job holder.

Job Sharing. A work option in which two part-time employees carry out the tasks associated with a single job.

Job Specialization. Making jobs simpler and more routine to improve efficiency. Also a detailed list of the personal qualifications needed for each job.

Johari Windo. A grid that describes tendencies for facilitating or hindering interpersonal communication.

Joint and Several Liability Rule. Slightly responsible may be required to pay the full amount of damages.

Joint and Survivor Annuity. Annuity based on the lives of two or more annuitants. The annuity income (either the full amount of the original income or only two-thirds or one-half of the original income when the first annuitant dies) is paid until the death of the last annuitant.

Joint Product Costs. Costs of two or more manufactured goods, of significant sales values, that are produced by a single process and that are not identifiable as individual products up to a certain stage of production, known as the split-off point.

Joint Stock Companies. Now called limited company. Although a limited company has quite a few characteristics, the 'limited' refers to the liability of the members, which is confined to the face value of shares they have bought. A limited company is a legal entity, *i.e.* it can enter into contracts as a person, independent of its members. Most of the companies public or private, are limited by shares, the number of which is stated in its memorandum of association. A public limited company needs a certificate of incorporation from the Registrar of Companies.

Joint Underwriting Association (JUA). Organization of automobile insurers operating in a sate that makes automobile insurance available to high-risk drivers. All underwriting losses are proportionately shared by insurers on the basis of premiums written in the state.

Joint Venture. Two or more people joining together in co-ownership for a specific limited purpose. A specialized form of a partnership.

Jones Town Defense. Any form of defensive tactics against a hostile take over bid that is so extreme as to appear suicidal.

Judge. A third party with low control over the processes and high control over the outcome of conflict resolution.

Judgment Rating. Rate-making, method for which each exposure is individually evaluated and the rate is determined largely by the underwriter's judgment.

Judicial Bond. Type of surety bond used for court proceedings and guaranteeing that the party bonded will fulfil certain obligations specified by law.

Jumbo Certificate. A jumbo certificate is a single composite share certificate issued by consolidating/aggregating a large number of market lots.

Junior Stocks. Stocks offered to executives of companies at below market price. Initially they have a low dividend rate.

Junk Bonds. Bonds that have a relatively high risk of default.

Junk Mail. Unselected mail not wanted by the receiver.

Junk Telephone Call. An unsolicited telephone call not wanted by the receiver.

Just in Time. A system of inventory control that concentrates on the final manufacturing process and then looks backward throughout the preceding processes. The earlier processes produce only enough quantities to replace those withdrawn by the subsequent processes.

Justice. A concept used in ethical reasoning that refers to the fair distribution of benefits and burdens among the people in a society, according to some agreed-upon rule.

Justice Perspective. Based on the ideal of reciprocal rights and driven by rules and regulations.

Just-in-time (JIT) Inventory System. A system that decreases inventory costs by having components and parts delivered as they are needed in production. The supplier delivers the components and parts to the production line 'just in time' to be assembled. Other names for this or similar methods are 'zero inventory' and 'stockless production'.

Juvenile Insurance. Life insurance purchased by parents for children under a specified age. Provides permanent life insurance that increases in face value five times at age twenty one with no increase in premium.

K

Kangaroo. Stock exchange's nickname for shares in Australian companies, especially those dealing in tobacco, property and mining.

Kappa. *See* Vega.

KCBOT. Kansas City Board of Trade.

Keiretsu. A corporate relationship linking certain Japanese companies, usually involving a non-controlling interest in each other, strong high level personal relationship among managers in different companies and interlocking directorship.

Keogh Plan (H.R. 10 Plan). It·allows self-employed individuals to establish an individualized pension plan.

Keogh Plan for the Self-employed (HR-10 plan). Retirement plan individually adopted by self-employed persons that allows a tax-deductible contribution to a deferred-contribution or defined-benefit plan.

Key Industry. Any industry that might affect a very large segment of a country's economy or population by virtue of its size or influence on other sectors.

Keyman Insurance. In order to see that any loss of personnel due to unforeseen incidents like ill-health or accidents does not adversely influence the profitability, venture capitalists ensure that management writes a 'keyman insurance policy'. Under this, the core employees of the organization are insured.

Keynesians. Followers of John Maenad Keenness who view the economy as unstable and in need of government intervention and control. They tend to argue that the interest elasticity of money demand can be high.

Knowledge of Results. Feedback about work outcomes.

Knowledge Society. A society in which the use and electronic manipulation of knowledge and information dominate. Work and employ the largest proportion of the labor force.

Known Dividend Model. An extension of the Black-Scholes model for pricing European options which the underlying asset pays dividends.

L

L Monetary Aggregate. M3 + short-term Treasury securities + commercial paper + saving bonds + banker's acceptances.

L.C.L. Lot. Less than carload lot. The rate charges for shipping less than a full rail car of freight.

Labor Relations. Managing the human resource issues concerning the relationship between union and management.

Laboratory Study. Manipulation and measurement of variables in contrived situations.

Labour Market. The mix of available workers and labour costs available to companies.

Labour Union. An association of workers intended to promote and protect the welfare interests and rights of its members primarily by collective bargaining.

Lag Effect. A functional relationship between one variable in the current time period and another variable in the previous time periods. Thus it might be postulated that the increase in current consumer spending is the effect of a bull run in the stock markets in the previous year.

Lag Strategy. An operational strategy that involves delaying collections of foreign currency receivables if the currency is expected to strengthen. Delaying payment if foreign-currency is expected to weaken. The opposite of a lead strategy.

Lagged Reserve Accounting System. An accounting system in which the reserve computation and reserve maintenance period do not overlap.

Laissez Faire. A French phrase meaning to let alone used to describe an economic system where government intervention is minimal.

Lambda. A measure of the change in an option premium with respect to a unit change in the price volatility of the options underlying asset.

Land. In the economic terms, it represents a natural resource.

Lapsed Policy. One that is not in force because premiums have not been paid.

Last Clear Chance Rule. Statutory modification of the contributory negligence law allowing the claimant endangered by his or her own negligence to recover damages from a defendant if the defendant has a last clear chance to avoid the accident but fails to do so.

Last in First Out. A cost-flow assumption that the stock acquired earliest is still on hand; the stock of merchandise or material acquired latest is used first.

Latent Conflict. The first stage of conflict, during which employees' differences in goals or opinions lead to an awareness of conflict.

Lateral Communication. Message directed to someone at the same level in the hierarchy.

Latin American Free Trade Association (LAFTA). A free-trade area formed by Mexico and the South America countries in 1960; it was replaced by ALADI in 1980.

Lattice. A tree describing the evolution of an asset price or interest rate over time. The branches in the lattice recombine. If the branches do not recombine, the lattice is usually called a bushy lattice.

Launder. Transfer of funds to conceal their origin.

Laundering. It is a method of disguising the origin of funds by moving them rapidly from one account or country to another, making it difficult to trace their origin, movements and the ultimate destination.

Law of Demand. A law of economics which states that as the price of a good or service rises, consumers will purchase less of it.

Law of Diminishing Marginal Returns. Economic principle states that as the amount of one input increases and all other inputs remain constant, the marginal product of the input eventually begins to decline.

Law of Effect. Behavior with favorable consequences is repeated; behavior with unfavorable consequences disappears.

Law of Large Numbers. Concept that the greater the number of exposures, the more closely will actual results approach the probable results expected from an infinite number of exposures.

Law of Persistent Under Development. Severe environmental constraints tend to perpetuate low development in a nation.

Law of Supply. More goods or services are provided when the price is high.

LDC Loan. Loans made to a less developed country.

Lead Country Strategy. A strategy of introducing a product on a test basis in a small-country/market that is considered as representation of a region before investing to serve larger country/markets.

Lead Strategy. An operational strategy that involves collecting foreign currency receivables early when the currency is expected to weaken expected to strengthen; the opposite of lag strategy.

Lead Subsidiary Organization. A foreign subsidiary that has global responsibility (serves as corporate headquarters) for one of a company's products.

Lead Time. The length of time between ordering and receiving an item of inventory. Inventory on hand must be sufficient to meet demand during the lead-time period.

Leader Member Exchange Theory. A description of how leaders develop "unique" working relationships with each of their employees, based on the nature of their social exchanges.

Leader Member Exchange Theory. A theory that describes leadership in terms of exchange, relationships established by the leader with individual employee.

Leader Member Relations. Situational model of leadership, refers to the degree of confidence, trust, and respect that followers have in the leader.

Leader Trait. Personal characteristics that differentiate leaders from followers.

Leadership. In the context of management theory, the ability of a person to influence the activities of followers in an organizational setting.

Leadership Continuum. The concept advanced by Tannenbaum and Schmidt in which leadership is seen as involving a variety of styles ranging from highly boss-centred to highly subordinate-centred, depending on situations.

Leadership Enhancers. Aspects of the task, subordinates, or organization that amplify a leader's impact on employees.

Leadership Grid. Represents four leadership styles found by crossing concern for production and concern for people.

Leadership Neutralizers. Aspects of the task, subordinates, or organization that have the effect of paralyzing, destroying, or counteracting the effect of a leadership behavior.

Leadership Prototype. Mental representation of the traits and behaviors possessed by leaders.

Leadership Substitutes. Aspects of the task, subordinates, or organization that act in place of leader behavior.

Leading. The function of managers involving the process of influencing people so that they will contribute to organization and group goals.

LEAPS. Long Term Equity Anticipation Securities (long term options on the S&P 500 index).

Learned Helplessness. Lack of motivation to improve or remove oneself from undesirable situations.

Learning. The process of acquiring knowledge or skills.

Learning Capabilities. The set of core competencies and internal processes that enable an organization to adapt to its environment.

Learning Curve. A concept used to support the infant industry argument for protection it assumed that costs will decrease as workers and managers gain more experience.

Learning Modes. The various ways in which organizations attempt to create and maximize their learning.

Learning Organizations. Proactively creates, acquires, and transfers knowledge throughout the organization.

Lease. A contract between a lessor and a lessee for the hire of a specific asset. The ownership of the asset is retained by the lessor but the right to use the asset is given to the lessee for an agreed period of time in return for a series of rentals paid by the lessee to the lessor.

Lease Line. A lease line of credit similar to a bank line of credit which allows a lessee to add equipment, as needed, under the same basic terms and conditions without negotiating a new lease contract.

Lease Purchase. As an alternative to outright purchase where the company regards eventual ownership as desirable. Legally hire purchase but with a different rental stream.

Lease Rate. The equivalent simple annual interest rate implicit in minimum lease rentals, not the same as interest rate implicit in a lease.

Lease Rental. Lessee pays lease rentals to the lessor periodically for the use of the asset.

Lease Term. The fixed non-cancellable term of the lease, includes for accounting purposes, all period covered by fixed-rate renewal options which for economic reasons appear lively to be exercised at the inception of the lease and for tax purposes, all periods covered by fixed-rate renewal options.

Lease Underwriting. An agreement whereby a packager commits firmly to enter into a lease on certain terms and assumes the risk of arranging any financing.

Leasing. The process of contracting for equipment or facilities whereby the owner does not take title to assets.

Least Preferred Co-worker Scale (LPC). A measurement of leader's style consisting of a series of adjective continuums.

Ledger. A group of accounts.

Legal Form. A contract may be written or verbal depending upon its nature and provisions and the state in which it is enacted.

Legal Purpose. A requirement of valid contracts which means that the contract must call for action that is legal under law.

Legal Reserve. Liability item on a life insurer's balance sheet representing the redundant or excessive premiums paid under the level-premium method during the early years. Assets must be accumulated to offset the legal reserve liability. Purpose of the legal reserve is to provide lifetime protection.

Legal Value. Par or stated value that is always far below the actual cash invested by a stockholder.

Legislative Lags. Lags in the enactment of the appropriate legislation needed for a policy action to occur.

Legitimacy of Organizational Influence. Acceptance by others of an organization's authority to require a specific standard of performance from them.

Legitimate Power. The power that gives to a leader in the managerial hierarchy. For example, the department manager possesses more legitimate power than the supervisor because the department manager is ranked higher than the supervisor.

Lender. He makes money available to the firm on a lending basis and retains title to the funds lent.

Lenient Credit Policy. Credit once granted for longer periods even to those customers whose credit worthiness is not fully known or whose financial position is doubtful.

Leontief Paradox. A finding by Wassily Leontief that over all U.S. exports were less capital intensive and more labour intensive than U.S. imports.

Less Developed Country (LDC). *See* Third World countries.

Lessee. A person who pays rent for an asset or property another person for an agreed period of time. The user of the equipment being leased.

Lessee's Incremental Borrowing Rate. The interest rate which the lessee, at the inception of the lease, would have incurred to borrow over a similar term the funds necessary to purchase the leased assets. In a leveraged lease, the rate of bonds is normally used.

Lessor. The owner of the equipment which is being leased to a lessee or user.

Letter of Credit. A precise document by which the import's bank extends credit to the importer and agrees to pay the exporter.

Level Payments. Equal payments over the term of the lease.

Leverage. Applied to financing, leverage means the use of more debt than to underwrite income-generating operations. This translates to a higher use of fixed-capital assets (machinery or new technology) in place of variable cost assets (people) to accomplish tasks.

Leverage Lease. A lease which meets the criteria for a direct financing lease or a capital lease plus all of the following characteristics: (a) At least three parties are involved; a lessee, a lessor, and a long-term creditor; (b) The financing provided by the creditor is substantial to the transaction and without recourse to the lessor; (c) The lessor's net investment typically declines during the early years of the lease and rises during the late years of the lease.

Leverage Ratios. Financial ratios designed to measure the extent to which a firm has financed its assets with non-owner sources of funds.

Leveraged Buyouts. The use of debt to purchase a company by pledging future earnings and assets to obtain cash for consideration.

Liabilities. Liabilities are debts payable in future by the firm to its creditors. They represent economic obligations to pay cash or to provide goods or services in some future period. Liabilities are two types: (1) current liabilities and (2) long-term liabilities.

Liability Coverage. That part of personal auto policy which protects a covered person against a suit or claim for bodily injury or property damage arising out of negligent ownership or operation of an automobile.

Liability of Foreignness. Foreign companies lower survival rate than local companies for many years after they begin operations.

Liability Without Fault. Principle on which workers compensation is based holding the employer absolutely liable for occupational injuries or disease suffered by workers, regardless of who is at fault.

Liaison Individuals. Consistently pass along grapevine information to others.

Liaison Position. A job that builds communication through bargaining, persuasion, and negotiation.

LIBID. London Interbank Bid Rate. The rate at which a bank is willing to lend Eurodollars.

LIBOR. London Interbank Offer Rate. The rate at which a bank is willing to lend Eurodollars.

Licence. Formal or legal permission to do some specified action a governmental method of fixing the exchange rate by requiring all exporters and others that receive foreign exchange to sell it to the Central bank at the official buying rate.

License. Sometimes who enters or remains on the premise with the occupant's expressed or implied permission.

License and Permit Bond. Type of surety bond guaranteeing that the person bonded will comply with all laws and regulations that govern his or her activities.

Licensing. A contract to gain access to the rights of a proprietary product, process, name brand, trademark, copyright, or technology for commercial purposes. A business owner can also use licensing to expand, such as licensing a foreign agent to sell his or her products overseas.

Licensing Agreement. A procedure that requires potential importers or exporters to secure permission from governmental authorities before they conduct trade transactions.

Lie Detector. *See* Polygraph.

Lien. A public record attached to the title of the property that gives a financial institution the right to sell the property if the mortgage borrower defaults.

Life and Career Planning. The use of structures counseling and group discussions to assist employees in planning career paths and integrating life and career goals.

Life Annuity with Guaranteed Payments. Pays a life income to the annuitant with a certain number of guaranteed payments.

Life Cycle Costs. The cost of a durable good over its entire operating or useful life.

Life Cycle Model. Theory that leaders should choose, a ledership style that matches the readiness of the followers.

Life Income Option. Life insurance settlement option in which the policy proceeds are paid during the lifetime of the beneficiary. A certain number of guaranteed payments may also be payable.

Life Insurance Planning. Systematic method of determining the insured's financial goals, which are translated into specific amounts of life insurance, then periodically reviewed for possible changes.

Lifetime Employment. The Japanese custom that workers are effectively guaranteed lifetime employment with the company and that workers seldom leave for employment opportunities with other companies.

LIFFE. London International Financial Futures Exchange.

LIFO. *See* last-in first-out.

LIFO Increment. *See* LIFO layer.

LIFO Layer. A separately identifiable additional segment of LIFO inventory.

LIFO Pool. *See* LIFO layer.

LIFO Reserve. The amount of "cushion" or "under-statement" of current inventory values that the LIFO method produces in relation to FIFO.

Limit Order. An order to transact at a specified price.

Limited Branching. Restrictions that limit the ability of banks to open offices within the state's boundary.

Limited Liability. Corporate creditors ordinarily have claims against the corporate assets only. Therefore the stock-holders as individuals have no liability beyond their original investment in the corporation.

Limited Partner. A partner who may or may not be active in the business, but who has limited liability. May be silent, secret, dormant or nominal partner.

Limited Partnership. A person or legal entity who is party to, and invests in, a limited partnership. Limited partners contract to invest, and they enjoy limited liability to the extent of their contract obligations. They are exempt from managing or actively participating in operational decisions.

Limited Payment Policy. Type of whole life insurance providing protection throughout the insured's lifetime and for which relatively high premiums are paid only for a limited period.

Limited Purpose. A specialized form of partnership.

Limited Self Discretion. The establishment, at some sites, of work teams whose members have multiple skills are responsible for managing their efforts to carry out a well-defined segment of work.

Limited-function Wholesaler. Specializes in one or only a few lines of trade and serves particular customers' needs.

Limiting Factor. The item that restricts or constrains the production or sale of a product or services.

Line. An authority relationship in organizational positions where one person (a manager) has responsibility for the activities of another person (the subordinate). It is commonly, but erroneously, though of as a department or a person, and not a relationship; it is also commonly, but inaccurately, thought of as the major departments of an enterprise believed to be most closely contributing to the achieving of enterprise objectives, such as marketing and production in a manufacturing company.

Line and Staff Conflict. Conflict arising from the role and perceptual differences between line and staff employees.

Line and Staff Organization. An organization plan which adds specialists or staff personnel who give advice and make recommendations to the line managers.

Line Authority. Authority that is exerted downward over subordinates.

Line Chart. A chart useful in presenting data covering longer periods of time.

Line Function. Activities that contribute directly to the creation of the organization's output. In manufacturing, the line functions are production, marketing and finance.

Line Managers. Have authority to make organizational decisions.

Line of Credit. An amount of credit a bank determines to without security being pledged.

Line Organization. The oldest and simplest form of organization plan which is especially suitable for small organizations. Line managers have total and direct authority, and subordinates report to a single supervisor.

Linear Programming. A technique for determining the optimum combination of limited resources to obtain a desired goal, it is based on assumption that a linear relationship existing between variables and that the limits of variables can be determined.

Linguistic Style. A person's typical speaking pattern.

Liquid Asset. An asset is liquid if it can be converted into cash immediately or reasonably soon without loss of value.

Liquidation Strategy. A strategy in which the firm dismantles an operation and/or sells off parts that may be more valuable as separate entities than as pat of the business as a whole.

Liquidation. Termination of the firm as a going concern.

Liquidation Value. It is the amount that a company could realize if it has sold its assets, after having terminated its business.

Liquidity (Settling) of Futures Position. Under the futures contract, the traders have an obligation to take delivery (a long position) or to make delivery (a short position) the underlying commodity. Three ways at liquidating a futures position are: Physical delivery, by making an off setting futures transaction (called offsetting) and by engaging in an exchange for physicals (called an EEP) settlement by cash delivery. The relative ease with which an asset may be converted into the medium of exchange without sub-stantially losing value.

Liquidity Preference. A theory that helps explain capital budgeting and when applied to international operations means that investors are willing to take less return in order to be able to shift the resources to alternative users.

Liquidity Premium. The additional interest rate lenders must receive to compensate them for liquidity risk.

Liquidity Ratios. Financial ratios designed to measure the ability of the firm to pay its bills on time.

Liquidity Risk. Risk due to the possibility that it will be necessary to liquidate a bond or other debt instrument prior to maturity, with some probability that the price received in such a situation will be less than favourable.

List Price. The selling price of an item before any discounts or reductions in price.

Listening. Actively decoding and interpreting verbal messages.

LLCs. Limited Liability Companies.

LLPs. Limited Liability Partnerships.

LME. London Metals Exchange.

Load Fund. A mutual fund for which the investor pays a commission.

Load. A charge by fund when an investor buys (entry load) or sells (exit load) units in the fund. The charge is used to discourage investors from taking short-term positions in the fund's units. A fund has to sell holdings to pay investors, if too many of them cash this can eat into the fund's overall returns. Most short-term funds, like guilt funds and Monday funds, charge no loads. Loads are limited by SEBI regulations to 7%. A fund cannot quote a difference of more than 7% between the sale and repurchase price of its units.

Loading. The amount that must be added to the pure premium for expenses, profit, and margin for contingencies.

Loan Commitment Agreement. Contractual commitment to loan of a firm, certain maximum amount at given interest rate terms.

Loan Guarantee. An agreement usually by the federal government, to repay a bank loan if a borrower cannot repay it. The borrower pays a fee to the government for this guarantee.

Loan Participant. A lender in a leveraged lease, a holder of debt in a leveraged lease.

Loan Sharks. Sub-prime lenders who charge unfairly exhorbitant rates to desperate, sub-prime borrowers.

Loan Value. The amount of cash that can be borrowed on a life insurance policy.

Loan-able Funds. Funds supplied by lenders as demanded by borrowers. The prices of these financial services are stated as an interest rate.

Loan-able Funds Theory. A theory of interest rate determination that views equilibrium interest rates in financial markets as a result of the supply and demand for loan-able funds.

Loans Sold. Loans originated by FI and then sold to other investors that can be returned to the originating institution.

Lobbying. Attempts to influence government policies, laws, and regulations.

Lobbyist. An individual who participates in advancing or otherwise securing passage of legislation by influencing public officials before and during the legislation process.

Local Content Requirement. A requirement that some specific fraction of a good be produced doestically.

Local Content. Costs incurred within a given country, usually as a percentage of total costs.

Local Rationality. When subsystems have their own goals not in concurrence with overall organization, it is called local rationality. If the local rationality is strong the system becomes dysfunctional.

Local Union. The primary organizational unit for labour groups.

Locally Responsive Company. Synonym for multi-domestic company.

Locals. Citizens of the country in which they are working.

Location Advantage. The competetive advantage that accrues to a firm when customers value the convenience of utilizing a firm located in close proximity to where they live.

Location Economies. Cost advantage for performing a value creation activity at the optional location for that activity.

Location-specific Advantages. Advantages that arise for using resource endowments or assets that are tied to a particular foreign location and that a firm finds valuable to combine with its own unique assets (such as the firm's technological, marketing, or management know-how).

Lock Boxes. Special post office boxes set up to intercept and speed up accounts receivable payments.

Lock-in-period. The period between the grant of options and vesting of option (at least one year). The company has the freedom to specify the lock-in-period for the shares issued pursuant to exercise the option. The employee does not have right to receive any dividend to vote or in any manner.

Lockout. Employees are locked out of the firm until a settlement of the labour dispute is reached.

Logistics. The procurement and physical transmission of material through the supply chain, from suppliers to customers.

Log-normal Distribution. A probability distribution for a random variable x such that the natural logarithm of x follows a normal distribution.

London International Financial Futures and Options Exchange (LIFFOE). It specializes in futures on financial instrument.

London Stock Exchange (LSE). A stock exchange located in London and dealing in Euro-equities.

Long Hedge. A future or option position to protect against a possible increase in prices.

Long Lived Assets. Resources that held for an extended time, such as land, buildings, equipment, natural resources, and patents.

Long Position. A position in an asset that has been purchased.

Long Tail Loss. A loss for which a claim is made some time after a policy was written.

Long-term Assets. Assets in the debt market which mature more than ten years from the date of issue.

Long-term Care Insurance. A form of health insurance that pays a daily or monthly benefit for medical or custodial care received in a nursing facility or hospital.

Long-term Investments. Represents the firm's investments in debentures, shares, bonds of other firms or government bodies for profits and control. These investments are held for a period of time greater than the accounting period. Usually long-term investments are shown at the original cost but the current market price may also be indicated.

Long-linked Technology. A service technology in which employees perform a standard series of simple tasks, with the job moving from one employee to the next until the process is complete.

Long-run Aggregate Supply Curve (I.R.A.S.C.). Characterizes the supply side of the macro-economy in the long run, *i.e.* summarizes the total quantity of goods and services that an economy will produce at various price levels, after allowing the prices of inputs and prices expected to adjust to any changes in the price level.

Long-term Liabilities. Liabilities (debts) that are not payable for one year or less.

Long-term-short-term Orientation. The degree of which a culture focuses on the future rather than the past and present.

Loss Adjustment. The functional process of an insurer that involves the investigation and resolution of claims in accordance with the insurer's claims resolution philosophy.

Loss Aversion Bias. A preference for choices that do not involve risk of losing.

Loss Control. Risk management activities that reduce both the frequency and severity of losses for a firm or organization.

Loss Leader Pricing. Featuring items priced below cost or at relatively low prices to attract customers to the seller's place of business.

Loss Ratio. A measure of pure looses incurred to premiums earned.

Loss Reserve. Amount set aside by property and liability insurers for claims reported and adjusted but not yet paid, claims reported and filed but no yet adjusted and not yet paid, claims reported and filed but not yet adjusted, and claims incurred but not yet reported to the insurer.

Loss Severity. The probable size of the losses that may occur.

Losses. Losses (or other appropriately descriptive terms) are decreases in owners' equity (net assets) from peripheral or incidental transactions of an enterprise and from all other transactions and other events and circumstances affecting the enterprise during the period excepts those that result from expenses or distributions by the enterprise to owners.

LOST. Law of the Sea Treaty.

Low Ball Bid. A bid to perform a lease transaction purposely priced below market or with terms not acceptable from a tax or accounting stand point, with a view to renegotiating of a higher price and/or more expensive terms at a later date once the bid is awarded the low ball bidder and the other interested lessor are no longer available. Typically, the low ball bidder raises the price when it is too late for the lessee to seek other leasing sources.

Low Context Cultures. Primary meaning derived from written and spoken words.

Low Load Fund. Mutual fund that charges a low initial fees.

Low Pay-out Clientele. Investors in high-tax brackets desire the company to declare low dividends and retain more, as to avoid personal taxes.

Low Tech. Products or services that require little or no skill, no unusual combinations of resources, and complicated techniques.

Low-context Culture. A culture in which most people consider relevant only information that they receive firsthand and that bears very directly on the decision they need to make.

Lower First Line Managers. Those concerned with the direct production of items or delivery of service.

Lower of Cost or Market. The super-imposition of a market-price test on an inventory cost method.

Luddities. Groups of early nineteenth century English workers who believe that machines took away jobs from workers destroyed factory machinery.

Lump-sum Payment. A single cash flow occurs at the beginning and end of the investment horizon with no other cash flows exchanged.

Luxury Tax. It is the tax assessed against non-essential items, such as built-in swimming pools, etc.

M

M&M Proposition I. The value of the firm is independent of its capital structure.

M&M Proposition II. A firm's cost of equity capital is a positive linear function of its capital structure.

M-form Organization. An organizational design based on specialization in particular industries.

M1. This is a symbol used to represent the money supply. M1 represents the narrow version of money, comprising the total value of bank notes and coins in circulation together with national currency and bank deposits on current account.

M1 Money Aggregate. Currency + demand deposits + traveller's cheques + other checkable deposits.

M2 Money Aggregate. M1 + savings deposits + small time deposits + money market deposit accounts + money market mutual shares (not owned by institutions) + overnight repurchase agreement + overnight Eurodollars.

M2 Money Supply. It is defined as notes and coins in circulation plus non-interest bearing bank deposits, building society deposits and National Savings accounts.

M3 Money Aggregate. M2 + large denomination time deposits + money market mutual shares (institutional) + term repurchases agreements + term Eurodollars. This represents a broader version of money supply comprising in addition to M1, interest bearing deposit accounts (including deposits in any currency held by the citizens of the concerned country) and certificates of deposits.

Maastricht [Treaty of]. The treaty approved in December 1991 that was designed to bring the EU to a higher level of integration and is divided into Economic and Monetary Union (EMU) and political union.

Maastricht Treaty. The leaders of the 12 European Community (EC) nations—Great Britain, France, Germany, Italy, Belgium, Denmark, Netherlands, Spain, Portugal, Greece and Luxembourg—reached an agreement in December, 1991 on a former plan to create a closure economic and political Union. The treaty on European Union was finalized at a summit at Maastricht, Netherlands, and it came to be known informally as the Maastricht Treaty. The treaty and its provisions were binding on the existing EC members as well as post-communist nations in Eastern Europe that sought to join the Union. The Maastricht Pact created a new common European entity, the European Union (EU), which would have greater powers than the old EC over matters that had previously been the jurisdiction of national governments. The EU was intended to pursue a common foreign policy and defence policy and coordinated economic agenda. The treaty took effect on November 1, 1993.

Machine Bureaucracy. A highly structural, formal organization that emphasizes procedures and rules, has a functional formal structure, and contains an informal structure.

Macro Political Risk. Negative political actions affecting a broad spectrum of foreign investors.

Macro-hedging. Hedging the entire duration gap of an FI.

Macro-prudential Indicators. Indicators of the health and stability of the financial system.

Magnetizing the Deficit. Paying for government spending by printing money.

Magnitude Effect. Indicates that, for equal numerical distance, it is easier to discriminate small numbers (for example, 1 versus 2) than larger numbers (for example, 8 versus 9).

Mail-float. Funds tied up during the time that elapses from the moment a customer mails his remittance checks until the firm begins to process it.

Mail Order House. Selling by means of catalogue orders.

Main Frame Computer. A full-scale computer that is capable of handling huge amounts of data. Some of these "supercomputers" are used for engineering, simulation, and the manipulation of large.

Maintenance Factor. Distinguished by Hertzberg in his "two-factor" theory of motivation, those conditions of the job that operate primarily to dissatisfy employees when they are not present. However, their presence does not build strong motivation among employees. Hertzberg distinguished 16 of these factors (*e.g.* salary, job security, work conditions, etc.).

Maintenance Margin. Maintenance margin is an additional margin required by the broker from the client. When there has been a price decline or advance on the loss in the margin account, the client should deposit just enough money to bring the amount of margin back to the original margin then the client can continue trading. The call for then maintenance margin is a variation call because a change in the market price required the additional margin.

Maintenance Roles. Relationship building group behavior.

Major Medical Insurance. Health insurance designed to pay a large proportion of the covered expenses of a catastrophic illness or injury.

Maker. Person or business initiating a bill of lading (draft).

Maloney Act. Provides for setting up the National Association of securities dealers, a self-regulating agency or over the counter dealers.

Malpractice Liability Insurance. Covers acts of malpractice resulting in harm or injury of patients.

Managed Care. A generic name for medical expense plans that provide covered services to the members in a cost-effective manner.

Managed Costs. *See* Discretionary costs.

Managed-float System. System under which some currencies are allowed to float freely, but the majority are either managed by government intervention or pegged to another currency.

Management. The process of designing and maintaining environment in which individuals work together in groups to accomplish efficiently the selected aims.

Management Accounting. Concerned mainly with how accounting can serve internal decision makers. Defined as the process of identification, measurement, accumulation, analysis, preparation, interpretation, and communication of information that assists executives in fulfilling organizational objectives.

Management as a Science. Organized knowledge—concepts, theory, principles, and techniques—underlying the practice of managing science systematically explains phenomena in managing as it does in any field.

Management as an Art. The use of underlying knowledge and application of it to realities in a situation, usually with blend or compromise, to obtain practical results: managing is an art but management is more properly used to refer to the body of knowledge—science—underlying this art.

Management Auditing. Auditing the quality of managers through appraising them as individual managers and appraising the quality of the total system of managing in an enterprise.

Management by Exception. The practice by the executive of focusing his or her attention mainly on significant deviations from expected results. It might also be called management by variance.

Management by Objectives (MBO). Joint formulation, by a manager and his or her superior, of goals and plans for achieving the goals for a forthcoming period. A performance appraisal plan in which each subordinate sets his own goals as the basis for improving his own performance.

Management Contract. An arrangement whereby one company provides management personnel to perform general or specialized management functions to another company for a fee.

Management Development. Programmes designed to provide managers with opportunity to improve their managerial skills and also to provide training for potential managers.

Management Information System. A formal system to gather, integrate, compare analyze, and disperse information internal and external to the enterprise in a timely, effective, and efficient manner.

Management Inventory. A technique by the use of chart, whereby managers in an enterprise are designated as promotable now. Promotable in one year. Have potential for future promotion are satisfactory but not promotable or should be terminated. Another term for "inventory chart" is "management replacement chart".

Management Networks. A network of informal contacts between individual managers.

Management Science Approach. A body of literature characterized by its use of mathematical and statistical techniques to build models for the solution of production and operations problems. The approach's primary means for acquiring knowledge is mathematical deduction.

Management Science School. The school of management that involved applying the scientific method, using statistics and quantitative techniques to solve management problems.

Management Techniques. Ways of doing things in managing.

Management Theory Jungle. The term applied by Harold Koontz in 1961 identify the existence of a variety of schools or approaches to management theory and knowledge. He found just six such schools or approaches in 1961, but in 1979 identified are eleven. He found that the school or approach tended to vary in their semantics and their view of management.

Management Training. The provision of opportunities through various approaches and programmes to improve a person's knowledge and proficiency in the managerial task.

Manager. One who gets things done through others. He oversees the works.

Manager Development. The progress a person makes in learning how to manage effectively.

Managerial Appraisal. Evaluating the performance of managers in their positions, ideally evaluating performance in setting and achieving verifiable objectives and performance as a manager.

Managerial Effort. Exertion towards a goal includes all actions (such as watching or thinking) that result in more efficiency and effectiveness.

Managerial Grid. A way of analyzing leadership styles, developed by Blake and Mouton whereby leaders are classified on a grid with the two dimensions of concern for people and concern for production.

Managerial Know-how. Managerial knowledge applied effectively in practice. It includes both knowledge of the science underlying managing and the artful ability to apply it to realities.

Managerial Options. Opportunities that manager can exploit if certain things happen in the future.

Managerial Roles. The organized sets of behavior that belong to the manger's job. The three main types of managerial roles discovered by such researchers as Mint berg are interpersonal, informational, and decisional roles.

Managers. Those who undertake the tasks and functions of managing, at any level in any end of enterprise.

Managers, Function of. To do planning, organizing, staffing, leading, and controlling.

Managers, Goal of. To establish and maintain an environment for performance that individuals will contribute to group objectives with the least cost—whether money, time, effort, materials, discomfort, or dissatisfaction—to create a surplus value, or 'profit'.

Managers, Task of. The design and maintenance of an environment for the effective and efficient performance of individuals working together in groups towards the accomplishment of reselected missions and objectives.

Managing by Objectives. Programmes, basing much of managerial planning, operation, and appraisal on having each manager set objectives in verifiable terms (with the superior's approval) and assessing his or her performance against the achievement of these objectives, sometimes called as management by objectives or 'MBO'. More recently, MBO is seen as a system of managing that includes key managerial activities in planning, organizing, staffing, leading, and controlling.

Managing Diversity. Creating organizational changes that enable all people to perform up to their maximum potential.

Manifest Conflict. The fourth stage of conflict during which employees act out conflict by intentionally frustrating their opponents.

Manufacture Resource Planning (MRP). A system that creates a financial model for use in production scheduling, human resource planning, materials purchasing, control of cash flow, inventory and distribution.

Manufacturer's Agent. Represents more than one manufacturer simultaneously and sells only a part of the manufacturer's goods in a limited geographical area.

Manufacturer-owned Store. A retailing outlet owned by the manufacturing company.

Manufacturing Automation Protocol (MAP). A network of machines and various office devices looked together. General motors, for example, has been very active in linking robots with numerically controlled machine tools.

Manufacturing Interchange. A process by which various plants produce a range of components and exchange them so that all plants assemble the finished product for the local market.

Manuscript Policy. Policy designed for a firm's specific needs and requirements.

Maquiladora. An individual operation developed by the Mexican and U.S. governments in which U.S. sourced components are shipped to Mexico duty free assembled into final products and re-exported to the United States.

Mareva Injunction. Injunction that prevents the transfer of funds overseas until a case concerning them has been heard in the UK courts.

Margin. The Dollar amount of cash or securities used as collateral to purchase some derivative security or asset.

Margin Call. A demand made by clearing house to a clearing member, or by a brokerage firm to a customer for additional funds.

Margin Cash Flows. The members at an exchange are classified as clearing members and non-clearing members. Non-clearing member must clear his/her trades through a clearing member. The clearing house demands margin deposits for clearing member to cover all future positions that are carried out by that clearing member.

Margin Requirement. The percentage of down payment required by the federal reserve on stock and other securities.

Marginal Account. The customer with moderate financial health and risk.

Marginal Analysis. A basis for making various economic decisions which analyzes the additional (marginal) benefits derived from a particular decision and compares them with the additional (marginal) costs incurred.

Marginal Cost. The change in total cost caused by a one dollar change in the amounts of loans.

Marginal Cost of Capital. The weighted average cost of new or incremental capital is termed as the marginal cost of capital.

Marginal Costing. *See* Contribution margin.

Marginal Product. The change in total product (or total output) that results from a one-unit change in the usage of a variable input, holding the quantities of other inputs constant.

Marginal Propensity to Import. The tendency to purchase imports with incremental income.

Marginal Resource Cost of Deposits. The change in a bank's cost of deposits arising from a one dollar change in its deposits.

Marginal Revenue Product of Deposits. The marginal product of deposits multiplied by the marginal revenue of a loan indicates the additional revenue earned by a bank if it attracts another $1 in deposits.

Marginal Revenue. The change in total revenue caused by a one dollar increase in the amount of loans.

Marginal Social Cost. The cost of an additional unit of production to society as a whole, taking into account external economies and dis-economies so that optimal conditions can be formulated by a programme of taxes and subsidies. An attempt can be made to alter the marginal costs of individual firms until they equal the marginal social cost causing an increase in welfare for society as a whole.

Marginal Tax Rate. Amount of tax payable on the next dollar earned.

Marginal Utility of Money. It indicates that an investor always prefers a higher return to a lower return and that each successive identical increment of money is worth less to him than the preceding one.

Markdown. The amount of reduction from the selling price.

Marked to Market. Describes the prices on outstanding assets and liabilities that are adjusted each day to reflect current market conditions, for example, asset and balance sheet values are marked to market and their values are adjusted to reflect current market prices.

Market by Order. The purpose of market by order is to enable the trading member participant to view outstanding orders in the trading books in the order of price/time.

Market by Price. The purpose of market by price is to enable the trading members or participants to view aggregate outstanding orders in the trading book at different prices.

Market Capitalization. A common measure of the size of a stock market which is computed by multiplying the total number of shares of stock listed on the exchange by the market price per share.

Market Economy. An economic system in which the interaction of supply and demand determines the quantity in which goods and services are produced.

Market Efficiency. Measured as the speed with which financial security prices adjust to unexpected news pertaining to interest rates or a stock specific characteristic.

Market Environment. The environment that involves the interactions between households (or individuals) and companies to allocate resources free from governmental ownership or control.

Market Frictions. Conditions in the market that make trading costly or restrict trading.

Market Imperfections. Imperfections in the operation of the market mechanism.

Market Lot. Market lot is the minimum number of shares of a particular security that must be transacted on the exchange. Multiples of the market lot are also transacted. In demat scrips the market lost is 'I' share.

Market Makers. Financial service companies that connect investors and borrowers either directly or indirectly.

Market Order. An order to transact at the best price available when the order reaches.

Market Portfolio. The portfolio of all assets in the economy. The stocks in the Standard & Poor's Index of 500 stocks is often used as a proxy for the market portfolio.

Market Power. Ability of a firm to exercise control over industry prices or output.

Market Research. The process of analyzing market information, gathering data on products or services, studying competitors, and evaluating sales potential.

Market Return. The average return on all risky assets in the economy. The Standards & Poor's Index of 500 stock prices is often used as an indicator of the market return.

Market Risk. The risk incurred in trading assets and liabilities due to changes in interest rates, exchange rates, and other asset prices.

Market Risk Premium. Slope of the security market line, the difference between the expected return on a market portfolio and the risk-free rate.

Market Segmentation. The process of focusing on specific customer groups and separating business activities according to well-defined target groups.

Market to Book Ratio. Market price of a share divided by book value per share.

Market to Market Value. *See* Market value.

Market Value. (1) A method of business valuation based on recent sales of comparable assets or entire business ventures. (2) The price of an asset or service in the market, often estimated by determining the present value of the expected cash flows applicable to the asset or service. (3) A bond/debenture may be traded in a stock exchange (sold or bought) is called the market value of the bond/debenture.

Market Value Added (MVA). It is the excess of the market value of the company over the value of investor's capital. In other words, current market value of debt plus equity, minus economic book value (the sum of share capital, free reserves and debt).

Market Value to Book Value (MV/BV Ratio). It is the ratio of market price of share to the book value per share. Note, the book value per share is the net worth divided by the number of shares outstanding. (*See* Market to Book Ratio.)

Market Value Weights. Weighted cost of capital computed using market value weights is known as market value weights.

Market Watch Window. Market watch window is the main focus for a trading member. The purpose of market watch is to view market information at pre-selected securities that are of interest to the trading member.

Marketable Securities. Any notes, bonds, or stocks that can readily be sold via public markets. The term is often used as a synonym for short-term investment.

Marketing. The performance of business activities that direct the flow of goods and services from producer to consumer or user.

Marketing Concept. The philosophy of a consumer-oriented venture in which managers make decisions to assure customer satisfaction as their first priority.

Marketing Functions. Activities that must be performed for goods and services to move from producer to consumer. Marketing functions include selling, buying, transportation, storage, risk bearing, standardization and grading, financing, and market programme.

Marketing Manager. Makes the management decision about the firm's marketing programme.

Marketing Mix. Choices about product attributes, distribution strategy, communication strategy, and price strategy that a firm offers its targeted markets.

Marketing Plan. The strategic plan that focusses on marketing activities to include product development, pricing policies, promotions, and means of distribution.

Marketing Profitability Analysis. A study of the organization's entire marketing and distribution function to determine the profitability of different markets or sales segments, such as products, customers, territories, and sales order sizes.

Marketing Strategy. Identifying the customers to whom the firm will appeal and deciding upon the activities needed to satisfy the customers in the market segment.

Marketing Variance. Synonym for sales volume variance.

Markov Expectations Hypothesis. Asserts that individuals expect the future to be like the most recent past.

Mark-to-market. The process to record daily price changes in the futures markets and to debit or credit accounts.

Markup. The amount of an increase in price over total unit costs.

Martingale. A stochastic processes the expected value of which equals the current value.

Martingale Pricing. A pricing method that used martingale probabilities to compute present values.

Martingale Probabilities. The probabilities used in the risk neutral valuation techniques.

Marxist Theory. This theory is about political and economic system largely based on theories developed by Karl Marx, in which the State makes major economic decisions, owning the capital assets being responsible for production and distribution.

Masculinity-femininity. The extent to which a culture values behavior traditionally considered masculine (competitiveness) or feminine (helpfulness).

Maslow's Hierarchy of Needs. The order in which people strive to satisfy the five basic needs as theorized by Maslow-physiological, security, social, esteem, and self-actualization.

Mass Customization. The production of a variety of end products at a unit cost that could once be achieved only through mass production of a standardized output.

Mass Merchandising. Plan for insuring individual members of a group, such as employees of firms or members of labor unions, under a single program of insurance at reduced premiums. Property and liability insurance is sold to individual members using group insurance marketing methods.

Mass Production. Large scale production employing standardized parts.

Mass Technology. The production of large numbers of the same product.

Master Budget. The budget that consolidates the organization's overall plans.

Master Budgeted Sales. The expected sales employed in formulating the master budget for the period.

Master Contract. Formed between the insurer and group policy owner for the benefit of the individual members.

Master Lease. A lease line of credit which allows a lessee to add equipment under the same basic terms and conditions without negotiating a new lease contract.

Master Production Schedule. A document that details the planned production of all finished goods for a particular time period. The master production schedule is based on the strategic plan and the production plan.

Mastricht Treaty. Treaty agreed to in 1991, but not ratified until, January 1, 1994, that committed the 12 member states of the European Community to a closer economic and political union.

Matching and Cost Recovery. The procedure of accrual accounting whereby expenses are either directly attributed to related revenues (matching) of a given period or otherwise regarded as costs that will not be recovered from revenue in future periods. In short, cost recovery is the justification for carrying unexpired costs as assets rather than writing them off expenses.

Matching Principle. It requires the expenses be reflected in the same period as the revenues to which they are related.

Matching. Establishing a relationship between efforts (expenses) and accomplishments (revenues).

Material Requirement Plan. An inventory planning and controlling technique that involves identifying each component and subassemblies of a complete product and then coordinating the ordering and delivering of those components and subassemblies. The technique usually requires a computer to deal with the mass of required information.

Materiality. The accounting convenient that justifies the exclusion of insignificant information from financial reports. Whether an item is material (significant) is a matter of professional judgment.

Materials Management. The activity that controls the transmission of physical materials through the value chain, from procurement through production and into distribution.

Mathematical Models. A simplified representation of the relevant aspects of an actual system or process.

Mathematical Programming. A term used to describe a wide range of quantitative techniques or algorithms for allocating limited resources.

MATIF. Marche a Terme International deFrance.

Matrix. A method of plotting data on a set of vertical and horizontal axes, in order to compare countries in terms of risk and opportunity.

Matrix Organization. A form of organization in which two or more basic types of departmentations are combined; engineering and marketing. This is likely to be a combination of project (or product) and functional departments with one overlapping the other; often referred to as 'grid' organization structures, 'project' or 'product' management.

Matrix Organizational Design. A design in which a project-type structure is superimposed on a functional structure.

Matrix Organization Structure. *See* Matrix structure.

Matrix Structure. An organizational structure in which foreign units report (by product, function, or area) to more than one group each of which shares responsibility over the foreign unit.

Maturity. It refers to the time period over which the interest and principal are to be made.

Maturity Date. The date on which a derivative security contract matures.

Maturity Factoring. Implies that payment will be made to the client on maturity.

Maturity Value. The dollar amount received by a bondholder when the bond contract has been fulfilled. This is also referred to as the face value or par value of the bond.

Maxi-max Criterion. Criterion used by the optimistic manager, who believes that only the most favorable result will occur and decides to maximize the maximum.

Maximum Acceptable Price. The highest price a buyer is willing to pay for a product or service.

Maximum Possible Loss. Worst loss that is likely to happen to a firm during its lifetime.

May Take. The form of an outlay cost or an opportunity cost.

MBO. Symbol for management by objectives.

Mccarran-Feruson Act of 1945. Regulation confirming the privacy of state over federal regulation of insurance companies.

MCE. Mid America Commodity Exchange.

McFadden Act [1927]. Legislation introduced to allow states to write laws regulating branch banking within their boundaries, and gave states the power to impose these rules on national banks and banks chartered in other states.

ME. Montreal Exchange, Canada.

Mean Reserve. In life insurance, the average of the terminal and initial reserves.

Mechanistic Organization. Structures that are highly formal, complex, and centralized.

Mechanistic Systems. An organizational design in which there is differentiation of job tasks, rigid rules, and a reliance on top-management objectives.

Media. The means by which advertising messages are conveyed.

Median. The value which divides an arrayed list of figures in half.

Mediating Technology. A service technology in which the organization links together clients with complementary needs.

Mediation. The third party the mediator can make specific recommendations for the settlement of a labour management dispute.

Medical Information Bureau. Bureau whose purpose is to supply underwriting infor-mation in life insurance to member companies, which report any health impairments of an applicant for insurance.

Medical Payment to Others. Pays for medical expenses of others under the homeowners policy in the event that a person (not an insured) is accidentally injured on the premises, or by the activities of an insured, resident employee, or animal owned by or in the care of an insured.

Medical Payments Coverage. That part of the personal auto policy that pays all reasonable medical and funeral expenses incurred by a covered person within three years from the date of an accident.

Medium of Exchange. Whatever is commonly accepted as payment for goods and services, or to repay debts. The distinguishing feature of money.

Mega-corporation. One of the very largest business corporations.

Mega-growth. A company that has the ability to offer more services than any similar firm that has capital totalling at least $25 bn.

Megalopolis. A continuous and very extensive city development that occurs when urban and suburban populations expand and merge geographically.

Mega-merger. The merger of banks with assets of $1 billion or more.

Membership Group. A group to which a person belongs, sharing its benefits and responsibilities.

Memory. The computer's storage bank.

Mental Ability Test. A test of general verbal ability reasoning ability, visualizing ability, and social perceptions.

Mentor. A person at headquarters who looks after the interests of an expatriate employee.

Mentoring. Process of forming and maintaining developmental relationships between a mentor and a junior person.

Mercantilism. An economic philosophy advocating that countries should simult-aneously encourage exports and discourage imports.

Merchandise Account. A part of the current account that consists of exports and imports of goods and services, or to repay debts. The distinguishing feature of money.

Merchandise Imports. Goods brought into a country.

Merchandise Trade Account. The part of a country's current account that measures the trade deficit or surplus, its balance is the net of merchandise imports and exports.

Merchandise Trade Balance. The difference between merchandise exports and merchandise imports.

MERCOSUR. A major subregional groups composed of Argentina, Brazil, Paraguay and Uruguay, which spun off from ALADI in 1991 with the goal of setting up a customs union and common market.

Merger. The acquisition of one company by another.

Merit Rating. Rating method in which class rates are adjusted upward or downward based on individual loss experience.

Met Expectations. The extent to which one receives what he or she expects from a job.

Meta Analysis. Pools the results of many studies through statistical procedure.

Mezzanine Bracket. An underwriter, who is next to the major underwriters, subscribes to the next largest portion of the issue.

Mezzanine Finance. Money lent to a small and growing, but financially viable company. It is so-called because the risk of making the loan falls between that of advancing venture capital and the safer course of putting the finance into established debt markets.

MFA. *See* Multifibre arrangement.

MFN. *See* Most-favoured nation clause.

MGE. Minneapolis Grain Exchange.

Micro Political Risk. Negative political actions aimed at specific rather than most foreign investors.

Microcomputer. Smaller than the minicomputer; may be a desk computer, home computer, personal computer, portable computer, or a computer for a small business system.

Micro-hedge. A hedge that reduces the risk involved in owning a security or an asset.

Micro-hedging. Using a futures (forward) contract to hedge a specific asset or liability.

Microprocessor. A small silicon chip capable of a very large number of computational operations (*see* Semiconductor silicon chips).

Mid Tech. Products that require some skill and combination of existing resources without unusual sophistication.

Middle East. The countries on the Arabian peninsula plus those bordering the eastern end of the Mediterranean; also including other adjacent countries, particularly Jordan, Iraq, Iran and Kuwait.

Middle Management. The middle level of an administrative hierarchy. Managers at this level coordinate the work of managers who report them.

Milestone Budgeting. Budgeting by breaking down a programme or project into identifiable and controllable pieces, or 'milestones'.

Minicomputer. Small than the mainframe computer but more powerful than the microcomputer. This kind of computer is often connected with peripheral equipment.

Mini-max Criterion. Criterion used by the manager who believe that once a decision is made and an outcome occurs there will be some regret and who selects the strategy that results in the least regret.

Minimum Coverage Requirement. A test that must be met to prevent employers from establishing a qualified pension plan that covers only the highly compensated.

Minimum Efficient Scale. The level of output at which most plant-level scale economies are exhausted.

Minimum Fill. Minimum fill order allows the trading member to specify the minimum amount by which an order should be filled for example an order of 1000 with minimum fill of 200 will require that each trade be for at least 200.

Minimum Lease Payments for the Lessor. The payments considered minimum lease payments for the lease plus any guarantee by a third party of the residual value payments beyond the lease term.

Minimum Risk Portfolio. A portfolio for which a combination of assets reduces the variance of portfolio returns to the lowest feasible level.

Minimum-risk Hedge Ratio. The number of futures or option contracts that results in the maximum possible reduction in the variability of the value of the total hedged position.

Ministry of International Trade and Industry (MITI). The Japanese government agency responsible for coordinating overall business direction and helping individual companies take advantage of global business opportunities.

Minority. A racial or religious group that is different from the majority group.

Minority Enterprise Programme. A programme to provide assistance in making business opportunities available to minority group members.

Minority Enterprise Small Business Investment Company. A company chartered by the federal government specifically to underwrite a special category of business for those small business owners considered socially or economically disadvantaged.

Minority-interest. The portion of the equity that is not owned by the consolidator or holding company is shown as a 'minority-interest' liability on the balance sheet. Net income on the statement of income is reduced by the portion accruing to minority interests.

Mirror Principle. A human relations concept which contends that people react in the same manner as they receive action.

Mission Statement. Summarizes 'why' an organization exists.

Mission Statement. A long range strategic intent.

Mission, or Purpose. The basic function or task of an enterprise or agency or any department of it.

Missionary Salesperson. Works with middlemen and their customers and assists in setting up promotional displays or training sales force.

Mis-statement of Age or Sex Clause. Contractual provision in an insurance policy stating that if the insured's age or sex is stated, the amount payable is the amount that the premium would have purchased at the correct age.

MIST Favored Customer Pricing. The practice that guarantees a customer the lowest prices the seller offers to anyone.

MITI. Japan's Ministry of International Trade and Industy.

Mixed Bundling. The practice of offering for sale two or more products or services either at individual prices or for one single price.

Mixed Cost. A cost that has both fixed and variable elements.

Mixed Economy. Certain sectors of the economy are left to private ownership and free market mechanisms, while other sectors have significant government ownership and government planning.

Mixed Joint Bundling. A single price is set for combined group of products or services.

Mixed Leader Bundling. The price of a second product is discounted if the first product is purchased at full price.

Mixed State and Private Enterprise. A socio-economic system in which government owns the key industrial and financial enterprises but most business are owned and operated by private individuals and corporations.

Mixed Venture. A special type of joint venture in which a government is in partnership with a private company.

MNE. Multinational Enterprise.

Mobile-home Insurance. A package policy that provides property insurance and personal liability insurance to the owners of mobile homes. A special endorsement is added to HO-2 or HO-3.

Mode. The point of greatest concentration.

Model Mis-specification. The error in a given mode.

Model. A depiction of inter-relationships of recognized factors in a real situation.

Modern Quantity Theory of Money Demand. Model of money demand developed by Milton Friedman that builds on the simple quantity theory by phasing the unique property of money as the medium of exchange.

Modifications. A form of synthetic process in which materials are altered to form a product.

Modified Duration. Duration divided by one plus the bond's yield.

Modified Life Policy. Whole life policy for which premiums are reduced for the first three to five years and are higher thereafter.

Modified No Fault Plan. An injured person has the right to sue a negligent driver only if the bodily injury claim exceeds the dollar or verbal threshold.

Monetary Aggregates. Ways of adding up the quantity of different assets in the economy into a measure of the money stock.

Monetary Base. Currency in the hands of the public plus commercial bank reserves, also called high powered money.

Monetary Economy. An economy in which money is used in most transactions, such as buying or selling goods and services.

Monetary Policy. A tool of general macro-economic policy under the control of monetary authorities that seeks to attain government's economic objectives by influencing money supply and/or rate of interest and therefore credit. The use of interest rates and controls on the money supply by the government or Central Bank to influence the methods of monetary policy include setting of interest rates changed by the Central Bank, sales or purchases of securities to control the money supply and changes in the required reserve ratios of banks and other financial institutions.

Monetary Policy Actions. Government actions directed at the money supply.

Monetary Policy Game. A situation where strategic interactions between the federal and the private sector make the payoffs resulting from their actions interdependent.

Monetary Threshold. An injured motorist would not be permitted to sue but would collect from his or her insurer, unless the claim exceeded the threshold amount.

Monetary Union. A group of nations that have agreed on exchange rates so as to make their currencies inter-changeable.

Monetary-items. A claim receivable or payable in a specified number of dollars; the claim remains fixed regardless of changes in either specific or general price levels.

Monetization. Financing the national debt by printing new money, which causes inflation as a result of a larger money supply.

Money. Anything that is widely and generally accepted as a medium of exchange.

Money Center Bank. A bank that relies heavily on non-deposit or borrowed sources of funds.

Money Management. Managing a firm's global cash resources efficiently.

Money Market. The financial market in which the most liquid, short-term debt obligations are traded. Typically this term refers to the market for financial instruments that mature in one year or less.

Money Market Account. An investment that earns interest at the spot rate of interest.

Money Market Instruments. Money markets are for borrowing and lending money for one year or less. The securities in a money market can be Government Bonds, Treasury bills and commercial paper from banks and companies.

Money Market Mutual Fund (MMMF). A fund that invests in short-term debt, such as treasury bills, or short-term commercial paper. Their goal is to preserve principal while yielding a modest return. They are favoured by investors looking for low risk of investment avenues and who prefer instant liquidity. Mutual funds that sell shares of the fund to savers and invests in short term. Safe assets such as treasury bills, large bank certificates of deposits, commercial paper, and banker's acceptance.

Money Order. A check purchased at a post office or express office which is payable at another post office or express office.

Money Stock. The total amount of money in the economy.

Money Supply Curve. The amount of money that suppliers are willing and able to supply at various interest rates.

Money Supply Equation. A relation that indicates how much money is created in the economy for a given monetary base.

Money Supply. The total amount of currency and demand deposits in circulation in the United States at any time.

Monism. A social system with one centralized power structure that governs all human affairs.

Monochromic Time. Preference for doing one thing at a time because time is limited, precisely segmented, and schedule driven.

Monochronic Culture. A culture in which most of the people prefer to deal with situations sequentially (especially those involving other people) such as finishing with one customer before dealing with another.

Monopoly. An industry or market with one producer or seller.

Monopoly Advantage. The perceived supremacy of foreign investors in relation to local companies which is necessary to overcome the perceived risk of operating in a different environment.

Moore's Law. The power of micro-processor technology doubles and its cost of production falls in half every 18 months.

Moral Hazard. Dishonesty or character defects in an individual that increases the chance of loss.

Moral Philosophy. A set of principles that describe what a person believes is the right way to behave.

Moral Suasion. The Fed's ability to persuade depository institutions and other financial institutions to behave in what it regards as the publics best interest.

Morale. The mental attitude of employees concerning their work environment.

Morality. A situation in which the most fundamental human values are preserved and allowed to shape human thought and action.

Morbidity. The term refers to the probability or the risk of disability.

Mores. Norms seen as central to the functioning of a society and to its social life.

Mortgage. A debt instrument used to finance the purchase of homes and other forms of real estate when the underlying real estate serves as collatoral for the loan.

Mortgage (Asset)-Backed Bonds. Bonds collateralized by a pool of assets.

Mortgage Bond. A bond secured by the real property of the firm (plant, equipment).

Mortgage Sale. Sale of mortgage originated by a bank with or without recourse to an outside buyer.

Most-favoured-nation (MFN) Clause. A GATT requirement that a trade concession given to one country must be given to all other countries.

Motion Study. The process of analyzing work to determine the most efficient motions for performing tasks. Motion study, a major contribution of scientific management, was developed principally through the efforts of Frederick Taylor and Frank and Lillian Gilbreth.

Motivating Potential Score (MPS). The amount of internal work motivation associated with a specific job.

Motivation. It is derived from the word "motive" and is an emotion or desire operating on a person's will and causing that person to act.

Motivational Factors. Distinguished by Herzberg in his "two-factor" theory of motivation, those job conditions that, if present, operate to build high levels of motivation and job satisfaction. However, their absence does not prove highly dissatisfying.

Motivations Research. A technique designed to discover the underlying motives of behaviour.

Motivators. Forces that induce individuals to act or perform.

Motives. The drives, desires, needs, wishes, and similar forces that channel human behaviour toward goals.

Motor Carrier Act. Regulates motor and water carriers engaged in interstate or foreign transportation of passengers or property.

Moving. The transition period (state B) during which the behaviors of the organization or department are shifted to a new level (desired state C).

Moving Average. A moving average is an average of the current and a given number of lagged values of a variable. Each time when we add another observation we delete the observation in the past to calculate the moving average.

Moving Budget. A form of budgeting that involves periodic updating; for example, a 12-month budget will be updated each month and projected for the following 12 months.

MPLS. Minneapolis Grain Exchange.

Multi-bank Holding Company (MBHC). A parent banking organization that owns a number of individual bank subsidiaries.

Multi-car Discount. Reduction in automobile insurance premium for insured who owns two or more automobiles, on the assumption that two such autos owned by the same person will not be driven as frequently as only one.

Multi-cultural Organization. Companies that value their culturally diverse employees as assets, and implement policies designed to promote cultural diversity and equality.

Multi-divisional Structure. The organization of departments together into larger groups called divisions.

Multi-domestic Company. A company with international operations that allows operations in one country to be relatively independent of those in other countries.

Multi-domestic Strategy. Emphasizing the need to be responsive to the unique conditions prevailing in different national markets.

Multi-fiber Arrangement (MFA). *See* Arrangement regarding international trade in textiles.

Multilateral Agreement on Investment (MAI). An agreement that would make it illegal for signatory states to discriminate against foreign investors; would have liberalized rules governing FDI between OECD states.

Multilateral Agreement. An agreement involving more than two governments.

Multilateral Investment Guarantee Agency (MIGA). A member of the World Bank Group that encourages equity investment and other direct investment flows to developing countries by offering investors a variety of different services.

Multi-national Corporation. A company that conducts business in two or more nations, usually employing citizens of various nationalities.

Multi-national Enterprise (MNE). A company that has an integrated global philosophy encompassing both domestic and overseas operations; sometimes used synonymously with multi-national corporation or transnational corporations.

Multi-national Organizations. Organizations with facilities in several countries and a substantial portion of sales in foreign countries.

Multiple Basing-Point Pricing System. A method of pricing in which several locations are designated as basing points and the price is determined by the point that yields the lowest delivered cost of the buyer.

Multiple Deposit Expansion. The process whereby depository institutions create money in the form of checkable deposits that are multiple of the monetary base.

Multiple Exchange-rate System. A means of foreign exchange control whereby the government sets different exchange rates for different transactions.

Multiple Line Insurance. Type of insurance that combines several lines of insurance into one contract, for example, property insurance and casualty insurance.

Multiple of Earnings Method. A business valuation method that consists of multiplying earnings be a predetermined risk-adjusted factor. The SBA uses a multiplier between 3 and 6 and net income before taxes to value a business.

Multiple Peril Crop Insurance. Offers producers a choice of a 65 per cent or 75 per cent yield guarantee, and producers can elect to be paid up to 100 per cent of the expected market price.

Multiple Rates of Return. The possibility that more than one discount rate will make the net preset value of an investment zero.

Multiple Zone Pricing System. A pricing system in which prices are uniform within two or more delivery zones.

Multiplier Effect. A situation in which one event leads to more than one other related event.

Multipoint Competition. Arises when two or more enterprises encounter each other in different regional markets, national markets, or industries.

Multipoint Pricing. Occurs when a pricing strategy in one market may have an impact on a rival's pricing strategy in another market.

Multi-step Profit and Loss Account. This gives more useful information. It makes a distinction between operating revenue and the non-operating revenue.

Municipal Bonds. A bond issued by state or local governments in finance building highways, schools, etc.

Munificence. The degree to which the environment supports and makes resources available to an organization.

Munificent Environment. An environment in which the organization has a large market for its product and has fund needed to continue operations readily available, and other stakeholder groups are satisfied or pleased with the organization's performance.

Musahi Lease. A Japanese leasing structure using foreign currencies.

Muslim Law. *See* Islamic laws.

Muster Lease. Muster Lease provides for a period longer than the asset's life and holds the lessor responsible for providing equipment in good operating condition during the lease period.

Muster Roll. Register of the holders of the security.

Mutual Assets. Requirements of a valid contract specify all parties must agree to the contract of their own free will.

Mutual Funds. Companies that sell their own stock to obtain money which they invest in the securities market.

Mutual Insurer. Insurance corporation owned by the policy owners, who elect the board of directors. The board appoints managing executives, and the company may apply a dividend or give a rate reduction in advance to insured.

Mutual Organization. An institution in which the liability holders are also the owners—for example, in a mutual savings bank, depositors also own the bank.

Mutual Savings Banks. A depository institution designed to promote mortgage lending, much like savings and loans, but owned cooperatively by members with a common interest such as employees of a company, union members, or members of a church.

Mutuality of Interest. Balancing individual and organizational interests through win-win cooperation.

Mutually Exclusive Investment Decisions. A situation where taking one investment prevents the taking of another.

Myths. Anecdotes that are widely recounted within the organization, tell of leaders' behavior, and reinforce underlying assumptions.

N

NAA. *See* National Association of Accountants.

NAFTA (North American Free Trade Agreement). A trade agreement among Canada, the United States, and Mexico in which the three countries are phasing out tariffs and other trade barriers.

Naïve Hedge. A hedge of a cash asset on a direct dollar-for-dollar basis with a forward or futures contacts.

Naked Option Position. An option position with no associated position in the underlying asset.

Named Insured. The person or persons named in the declarations section of the policy as opposed to someone who may have an interest in the policy but is not named as an insured.

Named Perils Policy. Coverage by an insurance contract that promises to apply only for those losses caused by perils specifically listed in the policy.

NASD. National Association of Securities Dealers, a self-regulating agency of over the counter dealers.

NASDAQ (National Association of Securities Dealers Automated Quotations). The automated system which reports over the counter trading activity.

NAT. Net asset value of a mutual fund—equal to the market value of the assets in the mutual fund portfolio divided by the number of shares outstanding.

National Advantage. Some factors that gives one nation an advantage in producing a cheaper product than other nations.

National Association of Accounts. The largest US processional organization of accounts whose major interest is management accounting.

National Association of Insurance Commissioners (NAIC). Group founded in 1871 that meets periodically to discuss industry problems and draft model laws in various areas and recommends adoption of these proposals by state legislatures.

National association of securities dealers automated quotations (NASDAQ).

National Banking Act of 1863. Created a new banking system with charters issued by the federal government.

National Banks. Banks with charters issued by the comptroller of the currency.

National Brand. A brand owned by a manufacturer and advertised and sold in all or nearly all sections of the country.

National Futures Association. National futures association (NFA) is established at the law in USA contemplated for institution of more than a single self-regulatory body. The NFA is responsible for screening futures.

National Responsiveness. Readiness to implement operating adjustments in foreign countries in order to reach a satisfactory level of performance.

National Securities Clearing Corporation Limited. Settlement is on a physical basis requiring the delivery and receipt of documents. NSE has set up a clearing house, *i.e.* National Securities Clearing Corporation Limited (NSCCL) is for managing settlement of securities. There are no sub-groups or sections and all securities are handled by the NSCCL.

National Treatment. Regulation of foreign banks in the same fashion as domestic banks, or the creation of a level playing field.

Nationalism. The feeling of pride and/or ethno-centrism focussed on an individual home country or nation.

Nationalization. Government taking ownership and control of private property with or without pay.

NATO. North Atlantic Treaty Organization.

Natural Advantage. Climatic conditions, access to certain natural resources or availability of labour which gives a country an advantage in producing some product.

Natural Law. A belief, originating in ancient greece, the human affairs are governed by laws of nature. Some eighteenth century philosophers, including Adam Smith, applied the idea to the economic system and developed the "natural laws of supply and demand".

Natural Monopolies. High-fixed-cost industries where duplication is a waste or increases costs, such as utilities, railroads, telephone companies, etc.

Natural Rate of Employment. The level of employment that occurs when there is only frictional unemployment.

Natural Rate of Output. The level of output that corresponds to the long-run supply curve, *i.e.* the amount of goods that can be produced with available technology and the full employment of an economy's capital and labour resources.

Natural Rewards. Normal social interactions such as praise or recognition.

NAV Date. Gives the date for which the NAV figures have been published.

Navigational Change, Principle of. The more planning decision commit for the future, a person can look back with certainty and determines whether or not it has been accomplished; goals or objectives may be verifiable either expressed quantitatively (*i.e.* in numbers) or qualitatively (a programme with certain specific characteristics to be put into effect by a certain date).

NCCL. National Clearing Corporation of India Limited.

Nearby Contract. A futures contract calling for delivery in a month that is nearby in time.

Nearby Future. Futures contracts that are closest to maturity date.

Need for Achievement. Desire to accomplish something difficult.

Need for Affiliation. Desire to spend time in social relationships and activities.

Need for Power. Desire to influence, coach, teach, or encourage others to achieve.

Need Hierarchy. Need hierarchy in the view that human needs exist in some order of priority.

Needs. Physiological or psychological deficiencies that arouse behavior.

Needs Approach. Method for estimating amount of life insurance appropriate for a family by analyzing various family needs that must be met if the family head dies and converting them into specific amounts of life insurance. Financial assets are considered in determining the amount of life insurance needed.

Negative Affectivity. A mood or state characterized by anger, fear, and depression.

Negative Inequity. Comparison in which another person receives greater outcomes for similar inputs.

Negative Reinforcement. It is action taken to repel the person from the undesired action.

Negligence. Failure to exercise the standard of care required by law to protect others from harm.

Negotiable Certificates of Deposits. Marketable receipts for funds deposited in a bank for a fixed period of time. The deposited funds earn a fixed rate of interest.

Negotiable Instruments. Stocks, bonds, promissory notes, etc. that may have their ownership transferred from one party to another party.

Negotiated Budgeting. The give and take between both upper and lower levels of management in developing the most appropriate form of budgetary control for a given situation.

Negotiated Market Price. A transfer price negotiated by the buying and selling segments when there is no market mechanism to fix a price clearly relevant to the situation.

Negotiation. Give and take process between conflicting interdependent parties.

Neighbourhood Shopping Centre. A small shopping centre which form several to a dozen stores.

Neo-mercantilism. The ap-proach of countries that apparently try to run favourable balance of trade in an attempt to achieve some social or political objective.

Net Advantage of Leasing. It denotes the incremental advantage over the NPV of buying the assets through normal financing channels.

Net Amount at Risk. Concept associated with a level-premium life insurance policy. Calculated as the difference between the face value of the policy and the legal reserve.

Net Annual Level Premium. Annual level premium for a life insurance policy with no expense of loading, mathematically equivalent to the net single premium.

Net Asset Value. It is the sum total of the market value of all investments plus accrued income minus the liabilities and expenses for a given scheme.

Net Book Value. Carrying amount of an asset, net of any related accounts (such as accumulated depreciation).

Net Capital Flow. Capital inflow minus capital outflow for other than import and export payment.

Net Cash Benefits (NCBs). The net operating cash flows of an asset, adjusted for taxes; the cash flows of an asset resulting from sales minus cost of goods sold, operating expenses, and income taxes.

Net Cash Flows. In addition to the initial cash outlay, a project may require some reinvestment of cash flows for maintaining its revenue generating ability during its life. As a consequence, net cash flows will be reduced by cash outflows for additional cash expenditure, thus net cash flows will be equal to after tax operating income plus depreciation minus increase in networking capital minus capital expenditure.

Net Charge Offs. Actual losses on loans and leases.

Net Convenience Yield. The convenience yield less the spot rate of interest.

Net Deposit Drain. The amount by which cash withdrawals exceed additions; a net cash outflow.

Net Earnings. The payment to the entrepreneur for under-taking the risk of business. It is also referred to as pure profit. It is the amount that is left to the producer's income after all the payments have been made.

Net Export Effect. Export stimulus minus export reduction.

Net Exports. The net foreign demand for U.S. goods and services, calculated as exports minus imports.

Net Exposure. A financial institution's overall foreign exchange exposure in any given currency.

Net Import Change. Import displacement minus import stimulus.

Net Income. The excess of all revenues and gains for a period over all expenses and losses.

Net Income on Investments. The net flow of investment income such as dividends, interest income and royalties.

Net Interest. Any interest paid on deposit or investment after deduction of income tax at source.

Net Interest Margin. Interest income minus interest expense divided by earning assets.

Net Lease. In a net lease, the net rentals are payable to the lessor. All costs in connection with the use of the equipment are not a part of the rental. For example, taxes, insurance, and maintenance are paid directly by the lessee. Most capital leases and direct financing leases are not leases.

Net Long in a Currency. A position of holding more assets than liabilities in a given currency.

Net Monetary Position. Total monetary assets minus total monetary liabilities.

Net Operating Income. Income before taxes and extra-ordinary items.

Net Payment Cost Index. Method of measuring the cost of an insurance policy to an insured if death occurs at the end of some specified time period. The time value of money is taken into consideration.

Net Premiums Written. The entire amount of premiums on insurance contracts written.

Net Present Value. Present value of the net cash benefits of an investment minus the initial investment outlay, plus the present value of non-operating cash flows of the investment subsequent to the initial outlay.

Net Present Value Method. A method of calculating the expected utility of a given project by discounting all expected future cash flows to the present using some predetermined minimum desired rate of return.

Net Present Value Profile. A graphical representation of the relationship between an investment's net present values and various discount rates.

Net Profit. The amount that remains after all income and expenses are computed.

Net Realizable Value. Esti-mated selling price of a product in the ordinary course of business, less reasonably predictable cost of completion and disposal.

Net Regulatory Burden. Difference between the private costs of regulations and the private benefits for the producers of financial services.

Net Single Premium. Present value of the future death benefit of a life insurance policy.

Net Working Capital. Current assets less current liabilities.

Net Working Capital Gap. The difference between current assets and current liabilities is called networking capital gap.

Networks. Used in the connotation of business relationships and networks are the associations made by entrepreneurs. Personal networks include family, friends, business associates and co-workers. Social networks include professions such as attorneys, bankers, accountants, and potential investors.

Net Worth. A synonym for owner's equity; no longer widely used.

Net Write-offs. Actual loan losses less loan recoveries.

Netting. A contractual agreement to aggregate all payments between two counter parties. The transfer of funds from subsidiaries in a net payable position to a central clearing account and from there to the accounts of the net receiver subsidiaries.

Netting by Novation. A single agreement to combine the obligations of multiple contracts with a single counter party all of which are denominated in the same currency.

Network Advertising. Messages beamed to a large audience covering a wide territory simultaneously.

Network Organization. A situation in which a group of companies is interrelated and in which the management of the interrelation is shared among so-called equals.

New Deal. The popular name given to President Franklin D. Roosevelt's economic programs to combat the Great Depression of the 1930s.

New Trade Theory. The observed pattern of trade in the world economy may be due in part to the ability of firms in a given market to capture first mover advantages.

New Venture Unit. Term applied to 'intra-corporate' efforts to develop commercial innovations through separate operating units or subsidiaries.

Newly Industrializing Country. A Third World country in which the cultural and economic climate has led to a rapid rate of industrialization and growth since the 1960s.

NFA. National Futures Association.

Niche. The notion of market segment with consumers having similar buying behavior, geographic location, or demographic characteristics.

No Fault Insurance. A tort reform proposal in which the injured person would collect benefits from his or her insurer and would not have to sue a negligent third party who caused the accident and establish legal liability.

No-brainer. Fund that tracks the performance of a stock index. Its manager buys all the stock listed on a major index and hence no discretionary management is required.

No-competition Agreement. This agreement is undertaken to protect the venture capitalist and the promoter, under this agreement, certain key employees are bound not to start parallel business in the event of their leaving the organization.

Noise. Any interference with the flow of a message from a sender to a receiver.

Noise Pollution. High levels of sound that are harmful to humans and nature.

No-load Fund. Mutual fund which employ no sales persons and charge no commission.

Nomadic Society. A society in which food gathering, hunting and fishering, dominate work and where human groups move as necessary to find such food.

Nominal Dollars. Those total are not restated for fluctuations in the general purchasing power of the monetary unit.

Nominal Group Technique. A process that involves the use of a highly structured meeting agenda and restricts discussion or interpersonal communication during the decision-making process.

Nominal Interest Rate. The interest rate started in the loan contract.

Nominal Lease. Earlier, parlance for a tax benefit transfer.

Nominal Output. The current dollar value of the final goods and services produced in the economy in one year.

Nominal Partner. A person who lends his name to business firm but who is not actually a partner.

Nominal Return. Return on an investment not adjusted for inflation.

Nominal Wage Rigidity. Nominal wages that are slow to adjust to changes in demand or supply of labour.

Non-analytic. Using pre-formulated rules to make decisions.

Non Assertive Style. Timid and self-denying behavior.

Non Cancelable. Continuance provision of a health insurance policy stipulating that the policy cannot be cancelled, that the renewal is guaranteed to a stated age and that the premium rates cannot be increased.

Non Contributory Plan. It is one in which the employer provides all the funds.

Non Cumulative Preferred Stock. Preferred stock in which dividend payment do not fall into arrear and are never paid.

Non Cumulative Quantitative Discount. A discount granted for volume purchased (measured either in units or dollars).

Non Insurance Transfers. Various methods other than insurance by which a pure risk and its financial consequences can be transferred to another party, for example, contracts, leases, and hold harmless agreements.

Non Insured Pension Plan. A pension fund administered by a financial institution other than a life insurance company.

Non Linear Pricing. Situation when a price structure leads to a change in average per unit price as volume sold.

Non Occupational Disability. The accident or illness must occur of the job.

Non Participating Policy. Term used to describe a life insurance policy that does not pay dividends.

Non Participating Preferred Stock. Preferred stock in which the dividend is fixed regardless of any increase or decrease in the issuing firm's profits.

Non Price Competition. The competition among firms on the basis of variables other than price, such as quantity, brand, assortment or services.

Non Profit Organizations. Institutions such as government, churches, and universities that cannot retain earnings over expenses do not have equity interests and cannot be bought or sold.

Non-blank Bank. A bank divested of its commercial loans and/or its demand deposit.

Non-callable Bonds. This refers to a bond which cannot be redeemed before its maturity.

Non-cash Items. Expenses charged against revenue that do not directly affect cash flow.

Non-clearing Member. He should clear his trades through a clearing member.

Non-conventional Investment. Non-conventional investments one whose cash outflows are not restricted to the initial period, but are interspersed with cash in-flows throughout the life of the project.

Non-convertible Currency. A currency is not convertible when both residents and non-residents are prohibited from converting their holdings of their currency into another currency.

Non-depository Financial Institutions. Financial institutions that do not accept deposits but serve various functions ranging from financial intermediation to selling insurance.

Non-directive Counselling. An approach in which the counsellor uses broad, open-end questions.

Non-durable Goods. Tangible goods which are expected to last only a short time.

Non-forfeiture Law. State law requiring insurance companies to provide atleast a minimum non-forfeiture value to policy-owners who surrender their cash value life insurance policies.

Non-linear Programming. A group of optimization techniques that enable the user to consider non-linear objective functions.

Non-operating Revenues. Revenues which are incidental or indirect to the main operations of the firm, called non-operating revenues, example—dividend and interest income from tem-porary investments.

Non-performing Assets. That part of a bank's assets, currently yielding no return, and on which nothing is expected.

Non-programmed Decisions. Decisions for novel and unstructured problems or for complex or extremely important problems. Non-programmed decisions deserve special attention of top management.

Non-signer's Clause. Exists when one retailer agrees to sell an item above an agreed price and the manufacturer and all other retailers in the state are bound by that agreement.

Non-verbal Communication. A form of communication that takes place without the use of words. Typical nonverbal communications include body language and gestures.

Normal Activity. The rate of activity needed to meet average sales over a period long enough to encompass seasonal and cyclical fluctuations.

Normal Costing. The method of allocating costs to products using actual direct materials, actual direct labour, and pre-determined overhead rates.

Normal Probability Distribution. A probability distribution that forms a symmetrical, bell-shaped curve with specifically defined properties. The relationship between the dispersion and the proportion of the distribution is the same for all normal distributions.

Normative Objectives. Objectives that prescribe how a firm should act given some set of values such as the desirability of making the most efficient use of a set of economic resources.

Norms. Norms are expected standards of behaviour usually unwritten and often unspoken that are generally understood by all members of a group.

North American Free Trade Agreement. Free trade area between Canada , Mexico and the United States.

Not Held Order. This order gives the broker additional discretion and the customer relies on the floor broker market judgment in determining when to buy or sell.

Notation. Discharge of one contract in favour of another. Example: A builder may contract to start work on a certain day and later notifies the client that he or she will be unable to do so. In this case the client may discharge the contract and sign another on the same terms with a second builder.

Note. Unsecured debt, usually with a maturity of under 10 years.

Notes Payable. Promissory notes that are evidence of a debt and state the terms of payment.

Notional Principal. The principal amount involved in a swap.

NRF. It is a performance indicator, *i.e.* BSE, National Index Relative Factor. It is a measure of percentage change in the NAV of a particular scheme over a specific period of time *vis-à-vis* the percentage change in the 100 shares BSE national index over the period. The NRF factor considers only the BSE sensex. Theoretically, it is not applicable to income schemes as these schemes invest their corpus in debt instruments. Same is applicable to income-cum-growth schemes where the corpus is split into debt and equity markets.

NSDL. National Securities Depository Limited.

NSE. National Stock Exchange.

NTB. Non-tariff barriers.

NYCE. New York Cotton Exchange.

NYFE. New York Futures Exchange subsidiary of New York Cotton Exchange.

NYMEX. New York Mercantile Exchange.

NYSE. New York Stock Exchange.

O

Object of Costing. *See* Cost objective.

Objective. The goals of the firm such as profit and sales.

Objective Function. Goal that can be quantified, often expressed as a maximization (or minimization) of some form of profit.

Objective Risk. Relative variation of actual loss from expected loss, which varies inversely with the square root of the number of cases under observation.

Objectives of Future Contracts. The main objectives of the futures contracts are pledging or speculation, price, discovery allocation of resources, etc.

Objectivity. Accuracy supported by convincing evidence that can be verified by independent accounts.

Obligee. The party to a surety bond who is reimbursed for damages if the principal to the bond fails to perform.

Observation Method. Direct observation technique used to gather statistical data such as counting auto traffic on a certain street.

OCC. Options Clearing Corporation.

Occupational Safety and Health Act. An act to protect the health and safety of employees. Employers must furnish workplaces free from recognized hazards to life and health.

Occurrence. An accident, including continuous or repeated exposure to substantially the same general, harmful conditions which results in bodily injury or property damage during the policy period.

Occurrence Policy. A liability insurance policy that covers claims arising out of the occurrences that take place during the policy period, regardless of when the claim is made.

Odd Lot. Number of shares less than the market lot is known as odd lot. Under the scrip based delivery system, these shares are normally traded at a discount to the prevailing price for the marketable lot. Trading in shares of stocks in lots of less than one hundred.

Odd-even Pricing. A form of psychological pricing suggests that buyers are more sensitive to certain final digits. In odd pricing, the price ends in an odd number (*e.g.* 1, 3, 5, 7, 9), of just under a round number (*e.g.* 99, 98). In even pricing the price ends in a whole number or in tens (*e.g.* \$5.00, \$5.10, \$5.90).

Off Balance Sheet Asset. When an even occurs, this item moves onto the asset side of the balance sheet or income is realized on the income statement.

Off Balance Sheet Liability. When an event occurs, this item moves onto the liability side of the balance sheet or an expense is realized on the income statement.

Off Balance Sheet Risk. The risk incurred by an FI as a result of activities related to contingent assets and liabilities.

Off-at-a-specific-time-order. This is a day order with a time contingency. It remains in effect only until the time indicated, when cancelled if not executed.

Offer. The price at which a person is willing to sell a security.

Offer for Sale. Principal method whereby new issues of equities are marketed.

Offer of Rights Date. It is the date on which letter of rights is sent.

Office Manager. Plans, organizes, directs, controls and coordinates all activities of the office to carry out its purpose of service.

Official List. The list, issued by stock exchange authorities, containing the name of securities which are permitted to be traded in the stock exchanges.

Official Settlements Balance. That part of balance of payments which measures the change in official U.S. reserves.

Offset. The liquidation of a futures or option contract through the purchase or sale of an identical contract.

Offset Policy. A pollution control plan that permits excess pollution from one source if another polluting source reduces its emissions by an equal or greater amount.

Offset Trade. A form of counter trade in which an exporter sells goods for cash but then helps businesses in the importing country find opportunities to earn hard currency.

Offsetting. The most common way of liquidation in open futures position is to effect an offsetting futures transaction, in effect, to reverse the initial transaction which established the futures position. In the process, initial buyer of future contract liquidates his position by selling an identical future contract. Similarly, the initial seller liquidates his position by buying an identical contract.

Offshore Financial Centres. Offshore finance centre is, at its simplest, the provision of financial services by banks and other agents to non-residents. These services include the borrowing of money from non-residents and lending to non-residents. This can take the form of lending to corporates and other financial institutions, funded by liabilities to offices of the lending bank elsewhere or to market participants. It can also take the form of taking of deposits from individuals, and investing the proceeds in financial markets or elsewhere.

Offshore Fund. Generally used to refer to a fund in the channel islands.

Offshore Manufacturing. Manufacturing outside the borders of a particular country.

Old Boy Net-work. An exclusive group that wields power through sharing information.

Oligopoly. The market structure in which a few firms compete for customers with each other.

On Bank Holding Company. A parent banking organization that owns one bank subsidiary and non-bank subsidiaries.

On the Job Training. A technique in which the employee learns the job tasks while actually performing the job.

132 annuity present value

$= c \times (1 - \text{present value factor})/r.$

One-man-business. It is the business where a single owner bears the full responsibility for running the business.

One-way Option Stock. Stock with no firm date for redemption, redeemable at the option for the borrower only.

On-stop (or Stop-loss) Order. It allows the trading member to place an order, which gets activated only when the market place of the relevant security crosses a threshold price. Until then the order does not.

On-the-job Training. This type of training occurs while the worker is actually performing the job.

OPEC. Organization of Petroleum Exporting Countries.

Open Account. Buying or selling on credit usually by just an 'authorized signature' of the buyer.

Open Auction. A form of auction in which prices are publicly announced and bidders are able to indicate their willingness to transact at specific prices.

Open Competition Law. Law for regulating insurance rates under which insurers are not required to file rates at all with the state insurance department but may be required to furnish rate schedules and supporting data to state officials.

Open Contract. Contract that has been bought or sold on the financial futures market, but has not been closed by making an offsetting transaction or taking delivery of the financial instrument involved.

Open Economy Model. Model of an economy that is open to international trade.

Open General Licence. In general, the import and export of goods into and out of a country, requires licences. For goods on which there are no restrictions, open general licences are available.

Open Interest. The total number of options contracts outstanding in the market at any given point of time.

Open Market Operations. Buying and selling of banks securities by the Federal Reserve to control the money supply.

Open Market Purchase. The purchase of U.S. government securities by the federal government.

Open Market Sale. The sale of U.S. government securities by the fed.

Open Mutual Fund. A fund for which the supply of shares is not fixed but can increase or decrease daily with purchases and redemption of shares.

Open Order. An order to purchase or sell a security at a specified price. Such order is valid till it is executed or cancelled.

Open Outcry Auction. Method of future trading where traders face each other and 'cry out' their offer to buy or sell a stated number of futures contracts at a stated price.

Open Outcry. Buyers and sellers begin a trade by contacting their FCM which in turn directs the customers order to a floor broker on the exchange floor who executes the trade. The orders are executed on the floor of the exchange. The rules of the exchange requires all bids and offers be exposed to other traders in the pit in order to assure execution of orders at competitive prices. This is called open outcry system.

Open Position. An un-hedged position in a particular currency.

Open Shop. Workers have the right to decide if they desire to become members of the union.

Open System. It is a living entity which takes energy from its environment, processes it, and returns output to the environment.

Open Systems School. School of management that describes organizations as systems that interact with their outside environment.

Open-ended Fund. In such funds, investors are free to enter or exit the scheme at any point of time. The investor can purchase or sell units of mutual funds from/through the mutual fund trust. The price at which the units are purchased/sold depends on the NAV of the fund at that point of time, as specified by the fund.

Open-ended Lease. A lease which contains a provision for the extension of lease of predetermined terms at the end of the fixed period.

Openness to Experience. A person's interest and willingness to consider new ideas and experiences.

Operant Behavior. Skinner's term for learned, consequence-shaped behavior.

Operant Conditioning. An approach to behavior modification which involves manipulating the consequences of behavior to change behavior.

Operating Budget. Budget of the income statement together with supporting schedules.

Operating Budgeting. Budgeting that deals with relatively short-term financial control concerns, such as having sufficient cash on hand to cover daily financial obligations including routine purchases and payroll.

Operating Cash Flow. Cash generated from a firm's normal business activities. Measures the cash generated from operations not counting capital expenditure or working capital requirements.

Operating Cycle. The time span during which cash is used to acquire goods and services.

Operating House. The lead bank in the syndicate negotiates with the issuing company on behalf of the syndicate.

Operating Income Rate of Return. A measure of profits in relation to investment.

Operating Lease. For financial accounting purposes a lease which does not meet the criteria of a capital lease or direct financing lease. Also, used generally to describe a short-term lease whereby a fraction of the useful life of the asset, the lessor may provide services in connection with the lease such as maintenance insurance and payment of personal property taxes. Short-term cancellable lease agreements are called operating lease, convenience and instant services are the hallmarks of operating lease.

Operating Leverage. The responsiveness of changes in EBIT to changes in sales.

Operating Management. Manages the implementation of programs and projects in each area of performance, measures and evaluates results and compares results with objectives.

Operating Margins. Operating profit expressed as a proportion of price.

Operating Procedure. A combination of intermediate targets and procedures for using the policy instruments to achieve the intermediate targets.

Operating Profit Margin. A measure of profits in relation to sales.

Operating Ratio. A measure of the overall profitability of a P&C insurer equals the combined ratio minus the investment yield.

Operating Risk. Operating risk can be defined as the variability of EBIT or return on total assets.

Operating Target. An immediate target of policy, a target for a variable that the federal government can definitely control on a daily or weekly basis such as reserves or a short run interest rate.

Operation Costing. A system where distinctions are made between batches of product. Materials and conversion costs are computed for each operation undergone during production.

Operational Audit. The regular and independent appraisal by a staff in internal auditors of the accounting, financial and other operations of an enterprise.

Operational Centres. Offshore financial centres that perform specific functions such as the sale and servicing of goods.

Operational Goals. Those short-term goals that address activities be performed before tactical goals are fulfilled.

Operational Planning. Planning conducted by managers and employees to determine what they must do and what resources they will need over the next month, week, or day.

Operational Plans. Plans that are intended to achieve operational goals.

Operational Synergies. Operational synergies occur when companies combine their strength. In the process they could shed down over-lapping operations, cut down the manpower, integrate procurement, etc. This leads to cutting down the costs of the company. Complementary operations could also result in obtaining operational synergies.

Operations. A broad term used to describe the activities and flow of work, resources, and materials in goods or service.

Operations Control. The regulation of one or more individual operating systems within an organization.

Operations Management. The development and administration of the activities involved in transforming resources into goods and services.

Operations Research. The use of mathematical models to reflect the variables and constraints in a situation and their effect on a selected goal. Ordinarily thought of using optimizing models; the application of scientific method in a problem situation with a view to providing a quantitative basis for arriving at an optimum solution in terms of goals sought.

Operations System. The system that transforms inputs into outputs.

OPIC. Overseas Private Investment Corporation.

Opinion Leader. One whose acceptance of some concept is apt to be emulated by others.

Opportunity Cost. The maximum alternative earning that might have been obtained if the productive good, service, or capacity had been applied to some alternative use.

Opportunity Costs. The various opportunities that cannot be realized because money is spent for one purpose rather than others.

Optimal Financial Structure. The particular mix of sources of financing that minimizes the firm's cost of capital and maximizes the value of the firm.

Optimal Solution. A feasible solution that maximizes the value of the objective function.

Optimism. A characteristic of an accounting system that implies that companies are more liberal in recognition of income.

Optimize. To maximize or minimize the value of some objective function, such as maximize profits or minimize costs.

Optimizing. Choosing the best possible solution.

Optimum Capital Budget. Means the availability of funds to invest in all profitable projects so that the NPV is maximized.

Optimum-tariff Theory. The argument that foreign producers will lower its prices if an import tax is placed on its products.

Option. A foreign exchange instrument that gives the purchaser the right, but not the obligation, to buy or sell a certain amount of foreign currency at a set exchange rate within a specified time.

Option Class. All listed options of a particular type (call or put) on a particular underlying instrument—all sensex call options (or) all sensex put options.

Option Contract. An instrument that gives the owner a right—but not obligation—to sell or buy an item at a prespecified price within a prespecified period of time.

Option Holder. One who buys an option, which can be a call, or put option. He enjoys the right to buy or sell the underlying asset at a specified price on or before specified time. His upside potential is unlimited while losses are limited to the premium paid by him to the option writer.

Option Markets. Markets where options are traded.

Option Premium. In an option agreement, writer of the option grants the right (to purchase from or sell) to the buyer for a certain sum of money called the option premium. Thus, it is the price paid by the buyer to the seller to acquire the 'right' to buy or sell.

Option Seller/Writer. One who is obligated to buy (in case of put option) or to sell (in case of call option) the underlying asset in case the buyer of the option decides to exercise his option. His profits are limited to the premium received from the buyer while his downside is unlimited.

Option Writer. The person who sells or grants an option in return for a premium, and who is obligated to perform if the option holder exercises his right under the option contract.

Option's Agreement. An option agreement is a contract in which the seller of the option grants the buyer of the option the right to purchase or sell a designated instrument at a specified price or receive a cash settlement within a specified time.

Optionally Renewable Policy. The insurer has the right to terminate a policy on any anniversary date, or in some cases, on a premium date.

Oral Communication. Communication in which the sender's voice is used as the channel.

Order-driven-trading. It is a trading initiated by buy or sell orders from investors or brokers.

Order Entry Window. Order entry mechanism enables the trading member to place orders in the market. The system accepts orders from all trading members and provides equal access to all trading members.

Order Log. The order log shows the activities which have been performed whether the order has been traded fully or partially or it has been modified or cancelled. It displays information only those orders in which some activity has taken place. It does not display orders which have entered the books but have been matched (fully or partially) or modified or cancelled.

Order-driven Trading. It is a trading initiated by buy or sell orders from investors or brokers.

Order-filling Cost. A marketing cost incurred in the storing, packing, shipping billing, credit and collection, and in other similar aspects of selling merchandise.

Order-getting Cost. A marketing cost incurred in the effort to attain a desired sales volume and mix.

Ordering Cost. An element in inventory control models that comprises clerical, administrative, and labor costs. A major cost component that is considered in inventory control decisions. Each time, a firm orders inventory, some clerical and administrative work is usually required to place the order, and some labor is required to put the items in inventory.

Ordinary Incremental Budget. Budget that usually considers the previous period's budget and actual results as a given. The budget amount is then altered in accordance with experience during the previous period and expectations for the next period.

Ordinary Life Insurance. Type of whole life insurance providing protection throughout the insured's lifetime for which premiums are paid.

Organic Organizations. Structures that are less formal, fairly simple, and decentralized.

Organization. A concept used in a variety of ways such as: (1) a system or pattern of any set of relationships in any kind of undertaking, (2) an enterprise itself, (3) co-operation of two or more persons, (4) all behaviour of participants in a group, and (5) the international structure of roles in a formally organized enterprise.

Organization Based Self Esteem. An organization member's self perceived value.

Organization Culture. The general pattern of behaviour, shared beliefs, and values that members of an organization have in common.

Organization Development (OD). A systematic and planned approach to improving the effectiveness of groups of people and of the whole organization. OD uses various techniques for identifying and solving problems.

Organization for Economic Cooperation and Development (OECD). A parisbased inter-governmental organization of 'wealthy' nations whose purpose is to provide its 29 member states with a forum in which governments can compare their experiences, discus the problems they share and seek solutions that can then be applied within their own national contexts.

Organization for Economic Cooperation and Development (OECD). A multilateral organization of industrialized and semi-industrialized countries that helps formulate social and economic policies.

Organization for European Economic Cooperation (OEEC). A sixteen nation organization established in 1948 to facilitate the aid from the Marshall Plan it evolved into the EU and EFTA.

Organization Manual. A handbook given to employees containing essential information on company policies and procedures.

Organization of African Unity (OAU). An organization of African nations that is more concerned with political than economic objectives.

Organization of Petroleum Exporting Countries (OPEC). A producer's alliance among twelve petroleum-exporting countries that attempt to agree oil production and pricing policies.

Organization Structure. The framework which shows the authority and responsibility relationships among people, the formal communication channels, and the relationship of each part of the company to others.

Organizational Authority. Conferring discretion on persons occupying organizational positions the right to use their judgment in decision making.

Organizational Behavior. Interdisciplinary field dedicated to better understanding and managing people at work.

Organizational Change. The intentional attempt by management to improve the overall performance of individuals, groups, and the organization as a whole by altering the organization's structure, behavior, and technology.

Organizational Chart. The formal, structural outline of the company.

Organizational Citizenship. Behavior that contributes to the well-being of the organization.

Organizational Climate. It is a composite view of the characteristics of an organization as seen by employees.

Organizational Commitment. A stage in the development of social responsiveness within a company when social responses have become a normal part of doing business. Therefore, the entire organization is committed to socially responsible actions and politics.

Organizational Communications. Information that flows outward from the organization to the various components of its external operating environment. Whatever the type of organization, the content of this information flow is controlled by the organization.

Organizational Control. A broad-based form of control that guides all organizational activities and oversees the overall functioning of the whole firm.

Organizational Culture. The values, beliefs, traditions, philosophies and rules that are shared by members of the organization.

Organizational Design. The process by which an organization's strategy, culture, human resource management practices, size, technology, and structure fit together.

Organizational Ecologists. Those who study the impact of environmental factors on organizational success/failure and interrelationships among populations and communities of organizations.

Organizational Life Cycle. The pattern of development and transition to encompass a venture's existence. Stages include start-up, expansion, consolidation, revival, and decline.

Organizational Moles. Use the grapevine to enhance their power and status.

Organizational Ombudsman. Person whose formal role involves resolving conflicts.

Organizational Politics. Intentional enhancement of self interest.

Organizational Power. A person's ability to satisfy or deny satisfaction of another's need, based on a formal contractual relationship between an organization and the individual.

Organizational Psychology. The study of behavior and attitudes within an organization including the effect of the organization upon the individual and the individual's effect on the organization.

Organizational Resources. Formal and informal systems for planning, controlling and coordinating; relations among groups in the organization and organization and members of its environment.

Organizational Role. An organizational position designed for individuals to be meaningful to people, it should incorporate: (1) verifiable objectives, (2) a clear concept of the major duties or activities involved, (3) the availability of information and resources necessary to accomplish a task.

Organizational Socialization. Process by which employees learn organization's values, norms, and required behaviors.

Organizational Society. A society often technologically advanced where most areas of life are organized and largely controlled by big organizations such as labour unions, corporations, government agencies, universities, military units, churches and others.

Organizational Strategies. The general approaches that are utilized by the organization to achieve its objectives. These approaches include market penetration, market development, product development, and diversification.

Organizational Structure. The formally defined framework of task and authority relationships. The organization structure is analogous to the biological concept of the skeleton. The way managers group jobs into departments and departments into divisions.

Organizing. The activities involved in designing jobs for employees, grouping these jobs together into departments, and developing working relationships among organizational units and employees to carry out the plans, developing working relationships employees to carry out the plans.

Orientation. The process of familiarizing newly hired employees with fellow workers, company procedures and the physical properties of the organization.

Original Margin. The clearing house guards against the possibility of financial loss to any member. It must obtain some form of guarantee from its member firms. Each member deposit money for each contract that is cleared. The performance money deposited by the member firms is called original margin.

OSE. Osaka Securities Exchange.

Ostracism. Rejection by other group members.

OTC Derivatives. Derivative securities traded in the over-the-counter market.

Other Insurance Provisions. Provisions whose purpose is to prevent profiting from insurance and violation of the principle of indemnity.

Other than Collision Loss. Part of the coverage available under part D: Coverge for damage in the personal auto policy. All physical damage losses to an insured vehicle recovered except collision losses and those losses specifically excluded.

Out Group Exchange. A partnership characterized by a lack of mutual trust, respect, and liking.

Out of the Money. The call option is said to be 'out of the money' if the actual market price is below the exercise price.

Outcomes. Consequences of the various possible combinations of actions and events.

Outdated Transfer Deeds. The transferee who holds outdated transfer deeds has to fill in the prescribed form (form TC) and seek extension of time either from the registrar of companies (ROC) of the state in which the registered office of the company is situated or from the registrar of companies of the state in which he ordinarily resides.

Outflows of FDI. Flow of foreign direct investment out of a country.

Out-Goer. A farmer who accepts financial inducements to turn his or her agricultural profession to another function.

Outlay Cost. A cash disbursement, as distinguished from an opportunity cost.

Out-of-the-Money Option. An option that has no intrinsic value; a call option with a strike price above the current asset price, or a put option with a strike price below the current asset price.

Out-of-the-money. A term referring to call option when the market value of the asset on which the option is written is less than the strike price.

Output Controls. Achieving control by setting goals for subordinates, expressing these goals in terms of objective criteria, and then judging performance by a subordinate's ability to meet these goals.

Output. Data that have been processed.

Outright Forward. A forward contract that is not connected to a spot transaction.

Outside Money. That part of money supply directly produced by the government or central bank, such as notes and coins.

Outside Stockholders' Interest in Subsidiaries. Synonym for minority interest.

Outsourcing. The use by a domestic company of foreign suppliers of components or finished products.

Outstanding Expenses. They are also considered as current liabilities. The firm may owe payments to its employees at the end of the accounting period for the services received in the current year. These payments are payable within very short period, examples are wages payable, rent payable and commission payable.

Outstanding Order. The purpose of outstanding order is to enable trading member to view his or her own outstanding buy or sell orders for a security descriptor. An outstanding order will be an order that was submitted by the trading member but which is not yet completely matched or cancelled.

Out-trade. Floor brokers execute orders on the floor of the exchange. The rules of the exchange requires all bids and offers to be exposed to other traders in the pit in order to assure the execution of orders at open prices. The floor brokers then report all trades to the clearing house. If there is any disagreement as to exactly who executed which order at which price, the errors are corrected by an exchange committee.

Over Absorbed Overhead. *See* over applied factory overhead.

Over Applied Factory Overhead. The excess of overhead applied to products over actual overheads incurred.

Over Funded. A pension plan that has more than enough funds to meet the required future payments.

Over Head Efficiency. A bank's ability to generate non-interest income to cover non-interest expense.

Over Loading. Sending too much information so that receiving messages cannot separate important and unimportant information.

Overseas Private Investment Corporation (OPIC). A U.S. government agency that provides insurance for companies involved in international business.

Overall Cash-flow Coverage Ratio. A leverage ratio.

Overall vs. Specific Cost of Capital. The component costs are combined according to the weight of each component capital to obtain the average cost of capital. Thus, the overall cost is also called the weighted average cost of capital.

Over-allotment Option. Contract provision giving the underwriter the option to purchase additional shares from the issuer at the offering price.

Over-draft. Under the over-draft facility, the borrower is allowed to withdraw funds in excess of the balance in his current account upto a certain specified limit during a stipulated period.

Overhead Costs. The expenses of a business that are not attributable directly to the production or sale of goods.

Over-the-counter Market. (1) An off-exchange market between commercial and investment banks for trading an asset.

(2) A market for trading securities which does not have a centralized location and dealers are spread throughout the country and transact their business by telephone.

Over-the-counter-trading. Trading in those stocks which are not listed on a stock exchange.

Overtime Premium. Classification of indirect labour costs consisting of the wages paid to all factory workers in excess of their straight-time wage rates.

Owner Participant. The lessor or a group of lessors in a leveraged lease holding trust certificates evidencing their beneficial interest as owners under the trust. An owner participant is the same as an equity participant trustee.

Owner's Equity. It is residual in nature reflecting the excess of the firm's assets over its liabilities. The interest of stockholders or other owners in the assets of an enterprise.

Ownership Clause. Profession in life insurance policies under which the policy owner possesses all contractual rights in the policy while the insured is living. These rights can generally be exercised without the beneficiary's consent.

P

P/V Chart. A graph showing volume on the horizontal axis and net income on the vertical axis.

Package Policy. Policy that combines two or more separate contracts of insurance in one policy, for example, home owners insurance.

Packager. A name used to describe the leasing company, investment banker or broker who arranges a leveraged lease.

Pac-man Defence. It is a method of defending against a hostile take over whereby the target company makes a tender offer for the shares of the aggressor.

Pact for Stability and Growth. The stability and growth pact accompanied the introduction of a single currency in the European Union as part of the third stage of economic and monetary union. It will govern the economic policies of the member countries which have joined the single currency, and strongly constrain the policies of those who do not join.

Paid-in Capital. The owner's equity, measured by the total amounts invested at the inception of a business.

Painting the Tape. Method of creating any impression of activity around a share, by reporting fictitious transactions. Painting the tape is illegal.

Pandora's Box. In Greek mythology, a box when opened let loose all kinds of misfortunes on society.

Paper Company. Company established, usually with little capital, merely for financial purposes.

Par Bond Yield. The coupon that makes the price equal to its face value. The yield to maturity equals the coupon rate, given that the bond is selling at par.

Par Bond Yield Curve. The graph of the paranoid yields for bonds of different maturities.

Par Swap Rate. The fixed rate on a plain vanilla interest rate swap that sets the value of the swap to zero.

Par Value. The state value on stock. It is an arbitrary amount assigned to stock and has no relationship to either market value or book value. Exists for accounting purpose. The value printed on the face of the security certificate.

Paradigm. A generally accepted way of viewing the world.

Parallel Importation. Gray marketer buys the product in the country where the product is made and sells it in another country.

Parallel Pricing. Following the pricing practices of other organization, particularly competitors.

Parameter. A constant, such as a, or a coefficient, such as b, in a model or system of equations, such as $y = a + bx$.

Parent Country National. A manager or other employee whose country of origin is the country where the organization has its headquarters.

Pareto Chart. A diagram that graphically illustrates the frequencies of key factors that contribute to poor quality.

Paris Convention for the Protection of Industrial Property. International agreement to protect intellectual property; signed by 96 countries.

Parity of Authority and Responsibility. *See* Authority, parity with responsibility.

Parliamentary Government. A form of government that involves election of representatives to form the executive branch.

Partial Controls. Controls designed to measure performance in a specific activity, such as quality, cash, production, or sales.

Partial Crowding Out. Describes a situation in which crowding out is not complete, so the increase in government spending is greater than the resulting reduction in investment and consumption spending.

Partial Derivative. Measures the marginal effect of a change in one variable on the value of a multivariate function, while holding constant all other variable.

Partial Disability. Inability of the insured to perform one or more important duties of his or her occupation.

Partial Productivity. Output relative to a single input or some combination of inputs.

Participant Agreement. An agreement between the owner trustee, the lenders, the equity participants, the manufacturers, and the lessee which spells out the obligations of the parties under the leveraged lease, also called financing agreement.

Participate Leader. This leader attempts to get people actively involved in decisions affecting them.

Participating Insurer. An insurer whose policyholders participate in the experience of the insurers through dividends, assessments, or both.

Participating Policy. Life insurance policy that pays dividends to the policy owners.

Participating Preferred Stock. Preferred stock in which actual dividends paid in any year may be greater than the promised dividends.

Participation Agreement. An agreement between the owner trustee, the lenders, the equity participants, the manufacturers, and the lessee which spells out the obligations of the parties under the leveraged lease. Also called financing agreement.

Participation in a Loan. The act of buying a share in a loan syndication with limited contractual control and rights over the borrower.

Participation Rate. The percentage of eligible workers in a specific category of age group, who are employed.

Participative Management. Involving employees in various forms of decision making.

Particular Average. An ocean marine loss that falls entirely on a particular interest as contrasted with a general average loss that falls on all parties to the voyage.

Particular Risk. A risk that affects only individuals and not the entire community.

Part-load. Portion or a part of the share capital of open-ended investment companies not covered by the underlying assets.

Partnership. A business ownership comprised of two or more owners who operate under an agreement of the owners. It is not a legal entity form of ownership.

Party-at-interest. A person or persons having a vested interest in a business firm.

Pass through Mortgage Securities. Mortgage-backed securities that 'pass through' promised payments of principal and interest on pools of mortgages created by financial institutions to secondary market participants holding interests in the pools.

Passive Income. Income from investments is tax haven countries or sales and services income that involves buyers and sellers in other than the tax heaven country, where either the buyer or the seller must be part of the same organization as the corporation that earns the income also known as subpart income.

Passive Monetary Policy. Situation where the Reserve Bank does not increase the money supply in an attempt to bring down interest rates in times of economic up-heave.

Passive Rule. A monetary policy that does not depend on the state of the economy. Such as keeping growth in the money supply.

Past Ratio. Ratios calculated from the past financial statements of the same firm.

Past Service Credits. Pension benefits awarded to employees based on service with the employer prior to the inception of the plan.

Patent. Grants the inventor of a new product or process exclusive rights to manufacture, use, or sale of that invention. A right of sole production of a product for 17 years.

Patent Cooperation Treaty. A multilateral agreement to protect patents.

Path Dependent Option. An option the value of which depends on the path of the price of the underlying asset over the life of the option.

Path Goal Theory. A model concerned with how a leader affects employees' perceptions of their personal and work goals and the paths to goal attainment.

Path-goal Approach to Leadership Effectiveness. An approach that sees as the main function of the leader clarifying and setting goals with subordinates, helping them to find the best path for achieving the goals, and removing obstacles.

Patronage Discount. Offering a price reduction based on previous customer relationship or preferred customer standing.

Patronage Motives. The motives which influence a person to return repeatedly to a store to make additional purchases.

Paul V. Virginia. Landmark legal decision of 1869 establishing the right of the states, and not the federal government, to regulate insurance rules that insurance was not inter-state commerce.

Pay. It is the basic compensation employees receive usually as a wage or salary.

Pay Grades. Pay grades are used to group individual jobs having approximately the same job worth together.

Pay Structure. The combination of pay level (average pay for the jobs in an organization) and job structure (relative pay among the jobs in an organization).

Payable through Draft. A financial instrument that has the physical appearance of an ordinary check, but is not drawn on a bank. A payable draft is drawn on and paid by the issuing firm. The bank serves as a collection point and passes the draft on to the firm.

Payback Period. The length of time required for the cash inflows from an investment to cover the initial investment outlay.

Pay-back. The measure of the time needed to recover, in the form of cash inflow from operations, the initial dollars invested. Also called payout and payoff.

Paylater Option. An option in which the premium is paid at expiration contingent on the option being in-the-money.

Payoff Table. *See* Decision table.

Payoffs. Synonym for outcomes.

Pay-order. A Pay-order, as the name suggests, is an order which is valid for the day on which it is entered. If the order is not matched during the day, at the end of the trading day, the order gets cancelled automatically.

Payout. *See* Pay-back.

Pay SOP. It is a payroll-based stock ownership plan.

Pay-to Performance. Monetary incentives tied to one's results of accomplishments.

Peer Rating. Appraisal of managers by other managers at the same or similar organizational level.

Peer Relationship. A relationship between peers that provides support, feedback, information, and/or friendship.

Peg. To fix a currency's exchange rate to some bench-mark such as another currency.

Penetration Pricing. The strategy of setting a product's price relatively low in order to generate a high sales volume.

Penetration Strategy. A strategy of introducing a product at a low price to induce a maximum number of consumers to try it.

Pension Accrual Benefit. A plan makes a pension contribution so that the disabled employee's pension benefit remains intact.

Pension Fund. Fund set up by company and employee contributions to provide retirement benefits. Fund that gathers regular contributions from employees, usually by payroll deduction, to provide retirement income to employees covered by the pension plan.

Pension Plan. Document that governs the operations of a pension fund.

Peppercorn Rental. The nominal rental paid during the secondary period of a finance lease.

Per Bond. A bond in which the present value of the bond is equal to its face value.

Per Capita Income. Total income of the nation divided by the total population which produces the average income per person.

Per See Rules. Rules that define clear-cut business violations.

Perceived Acquisition Value. The buyer's perceptions of the relative worth of a product or service. It is formally defined as the difference between the most a buyer would be willing to pay for the item less the actual price of the item.

Perceived Conflict. The second stage of conflict during which, employees either act on or ignore the problem.

Perceived Quality. The amount of quality buyers believe a product or service has. Perceived quality is based on some information about the product, for example, its price or brand name.

Perceived Transaction Value. The perceived benefits or gains from taking advantage of an offer or deal.

Perceived Value Pricing. A method of pricing in which the seller sets price at the level that the intended buyers value the product.

Percentage Lease. Percentage lease provides fixed returns or some per cent of the previous year's gross revenue to be paid to the lessor. This ensures protection against inflation.

Percentage Participation Clause. Provision a health insurance policy that requires the insured to pay a certain percentage of eligible medical expenses in excess of the deductible.

Perception. The cognitive impression that is formed of reality which influences the individual's actions and behavior.

Perceptual Approach. The approach to job design that seeks to limit each job's information-processing requirements.

Perceptual Organization. The natural and essential process of organizing, interpreting, and attaching value to the selected stimuli.

Perceptual Selection. Choosing a stimuli from the environment for further processing is also known as filtering or screening.

Perfecting Collateral. The process of ensuring that collateral used to secure a loan is free and clear to the lender and the borrower default on the loan.

Performance Ambiguity. Occurs when the causes of good or bad performance are not clearly identifiable.

Performance Appraisal. It is the process of determining how well employees do their jobs compared to a set of standards and communicating that information to the employees.

Performance Evaluation. A feedback control technique that focuses on the extent to which employees have achieved expected levels of work during a specified time period.

Performance Feedback. Sharing the performance information with employees.

Performance Gap. The difference between an organization's desired and actual performance levels.

Performance Management. Defining what performance is desired, measuring actual performance and providing feedback.

Performance Programs. Detailed procedures as how to handle a particular situation.

Performance Report. Comparison of actual results with the budget.

Performance Standards. The level of output expected of workers.

Performance Tests. Examinations that verify an applicant's ability to perform actual job behaviors identified from a job analysis.

Performing Stage. The stage in which members have reached a level of maturity that facilitates total task involvement.

Period Costs. Those costs being deducted as expenses during the current period without having been previously classified as product costs.

Periodic Budgeting. It involves the preparation of budget for the forthcoming year without providing for a comprehensive revision as the budget period passes.

Periods. (Compare with toxic substances.)

Peripheral Norms. Norms that are accepted by some, but are not important for organizational success.

Perpendicular Spread. It is an investment strategy that includes using options with the same expiration dates with different strike prices. And this spread can be bullish or bearish.

Perpetual Inventory. An inventory control system which maintains a running account of materials on hand.

Perpetual Model of Communication. Consecutively linked elements within the communication process.

Perpetuity. A loan that never matures; it consists of an infinite number of periodic interest payments, but no final payment of face value or principal.

Perquisites ("Perks"). Perquisites are special benefits for executives that are usually non-cash terms.

Persistence. Extent to which effort is expended on a task over time.

Person Hob Fit. The degree to which employer and employee each contributes what the other party is seeking from the employment relationship.

Personal Behavioral Leadership Theories. A group of theories based primarily on the personal and behavioral characteristics of leaders. These theories focus on what leaders do and/or how leaders behave in carrying out the leadership function.

Personal Controls. Achieving control by personal contact with subordinates.

Personal Credit Institutions. Finance companies specializing in installment and other loans to consumers.

Personal Injury. Injury for which legal liability arises (such as false arrest, detention or imprisonment, malicious prosecution, slander, defamation of character, violation of the right of privacy, and unlawful entry or eviction) and which may be covered by an endorsement to the homeowners policy.

Personal Liability Insurance. Liability insurance that protects the insured for an amount upto policy limits against a claim or suit for damages because of injury of body or property damage caused by the insured's negligence. This coverage is provided by section II of the homeowners policy.

Personal Policies. Decisions affecting vacancies for which people are recruited.

Personal Power. A person's ability to satisfy or deny satisfaction of another's need, based on an interpersonal relationship between individuals or on his or her personal chrematistics.

Personal Producing General Agent. Term used to describe an above-average salesperson with a proven sales record who is hired primarily to sell life insurance under a contract that provides both direct and overriding commission.

Personal Selling. A form of promotion that relies on individual sales efforts between a buyer and a seller.

Personal Service Firm. A definition ascribed by the Internal Revenue Service to certain businesses that perform individualized services to clients and that are not organized as professional corporations. Examples include computer software consultants, and rehabilitation counselors.

Personal Space. The area around a person that the person feels a right to control.

Personal Umbrella Policy. Policy designed to provide protection against a catastrophic lawsuit or judgment whose coverage ranges generally from $1 million to $10 million and extends to the entire family anywhere in the world. Insurance is excess over underlying coverages.

Personality. The sum of an individual's traits or characteristics. These traits create personality patterns.

Personality Inventories. Programs that measure the thoughts, feelings and behaviors that define an individual and determine the person's pattern of interaction with the environment and events.

Personality Test. A test designed to aid in selecting managers or other personnel whose jobs require skills in interpersonal relations.

Personnel Audit. It is a formal research effort to evaluate the current state of personnel management in an organization.

Personnel Generalist. It is someone who has responsibility for performing a varied range of personnel activities.

Personnel Management. It is a set of activities focusing on the effective use of human resources in an organization.

Personnel Research. Analyzes past and present personnel practices through the use of collected data and records.

Personnel Specialist is someone who has in-depth knowledge and expertise in a limited area of personnel.

Persons Acting in Concert (PAC). PAC are individual(s) or company(ies)/any other legal entity(ies) who are acting in concert for a common objective or for the purpose of substantial acquisition of shares or voting rights or gaining control over the target company either directly or indirectly. Inherent element in this action is an element of cooperation between the entities. This cooperation may either be direct or indirect, formal or informal. The concept of PAC assumes significance in the context of takeovers since it is possible that an acquirer can acquire shares or voting rights in a company "in concert" with any other person in a manner that the acquisitions made by him remain below the threshold limit though taken together with the voting rights of persons acting in concert, the threshold may exceed. In the regulations, certain entities are presumed to be acting in concert, unless the contrary is established like companies with its holding company or subsidiary company or mutual funds with its sponsor/trustee/asset management company, etc.

PERT (Programme Evaluation and Review Technique). A time-event network analysis system in which the various events in a programme or project are identified with the planned time for each and are placed in a network showing the relationships of each event to other events. From the sequence of interrelated events, the path of those events in which there is zero (or the least) slack time in terms of planned completion is the 'critical path'.

Peter Principle. Principle enunciated by Laurence J. Peter and Raymond Hall that managers are to be promoted until they reach the level of their incompetence.

Petro-dollars. They are the large dollar balances that oil-producing countries earned through oil sales and have deposited in financial institutions worldwide.

Phantom Freight. In base point pricing, when the seller quotes a delivered price that includes a freight charge greater than the actual transportation costs.

Phantom Share. An incentive concept whereby an executive receives a bonus based on the market appreciation of the company's stock over a fixed period of time.

Philadelphia Stock Exchange. A specialized market dealing in select foreign-currency options.

Philanthropy (Corporate). Gifts and contributions made by corporations, usually from pretax profits to benefit various types of non-profit community organizations.

Philosophy of Management. Establishes the primary, long-range objectives of a firm and provides the principles, practices and ethical standards of a firm in its relationship with employees.

PHLX. Philadelphia Stock Exchange.

Physical Attributes. Strength, flexibility, coordination, and endurance.

Physical Capital Maintenance. The capacity to maintain previous levels of output of goods and services.

Physical Capital. Economist's terminology for man made inputs into the production process.

Physical Delivery. Liquidating a future position by making or taking physical delivery is usually the most cumbersome process to fulfil contractual obligation. But traders normally do not favour the settlement through physical delivery. However, commercial firms settle through physical delivery and sometimes, it might be financially desirable to settle by physical delivery.

Physical Examinations. Tests that qualify an individual's placement in manually and physically demanding jobs.

Physical Hazard. Physical condition that increases the chance of loss.

Physical Resources. The technology an organization uses, its plant and equipment, its geographic location and its access to raw materials.

Physical Withdrawal. Removing oneself from the workplace through such means as absenteeism and turnover.

Pl/I. Programming language I, a computer language.

Picketing. The practice of workers marching at the entrance to a firm to protest some management practice.

Pie Chart. A chart in a circle divided into wedges frequently used to present data relating to percentages or dollar values.

Piece Chart. Payment to workers on the basis of the number of acceptable units of output produced.

Piggy Back Marketing. The process of contracting with another company to include products in that company's merchandise line.

Piggyback. Combining motor and rail transportation services.

Piggyback Exporting. Use by an exporter of another exporter as an intermediary.

Pink Mood. When the price of a scrip is likely to shoot up, the scrip is said to be in pink mood.

Pioneering Costs. Costs an early entrant bears that later entrants avoid, such as the time and effort in learning the rules, failure due to ignorance and the liability of being a foreigner.

Piracy. The unauthorized use of property rights that are protected by patents, trademarks or copyrights.

Pivotal Norms. Standards that are critical for group success.

Place Utility. Goods or services must be available at the place it is demanded to satisfy a want.

Placing. The sale of a line of stock or shares by arrangement, direct to institution and others by the selling brokers without going through the market.

Plain Vanilla. A standard agreement without any special features.

Plan. A set of activities intended to achieve goals, whether for an entire organization, department or an individual.

Planned Change. The deliberate structuring of operations and behaviors, often in anticipation of environmental forces.

Planning. Selecting missions and objectives strategies, policies, programmes and procedures for achieving them. Decision making involves the selection of a course of action from among alternatives. Thus the management function of formulating in advance the direction a firm to follow to reach its designed objectives.

Planning Function. All managerial activities that lead to the definition of objectives and to the determination of appropriate means to achieve those objectives.

Planning Paradigm. The concept of having a model to follow when developing a new venture, such as creating a feasibility plan based on a good planning model.

Planning Premises. The planning assumptions—the expected environment in which plans will operate. They may be forecasts of the planning environment in which plans will operate. They are forecasts of the planning environment or basic policies and existing plans which will influence any given plan.

Planning Premises, Types of. Premises may be external or internal to an enterprise, quantitative or qualitative or controllable, uncontrollable or semi-controllable.

Planning Process. A rational approach to setting and accomplishing an objective and evaluating alternatives in the light of goals sought and against the environment of planning premises.

Plans, Types of. Purpose or missions, objectives, strategies, policies, procedures, rules, programmes, and budgets.

Plant Assets. Assets, that are not easily converted into cash and have a long life such as building plant and land.

PLC. *See* Product Life Cycle theory.

Pledge. Under this agreement, the borrower is required to transfer the physical possession of the property offered as a security to the bank to obtain credit. The bank has a right of lien and can retain possession of the goods pledged unless payment of the principal interest and any other expenses is made. In case of default, the bank may either (a) sue the borrower for the amount due or (b) sue for the sale of goods pledged.

Plural Executive. A committee or group, which has the authority to execute, as a group, managerial functions.

Pluralistic Society. A society in which many organized groups present various interests. Each group has an impact on other groups, but no one group has an inordinate amount of power.

Pluralism. A society in which numerous economic, political, educational, social, artistic and other groups are organized by people to promote their own interests.

Pluralistic Societies. Societies in which difficult ideologies are held by various segments rather than one ideology being adhered to by all.

PO Strips. Represent the mortgage principal components in each monthly payment by the mortgage.

Point of Service Plan. Establishes a network of preferred providers. If patients see a preferred provider, they pay little or nothing. Outside provider care is covered, but at a substantially higher deductible and co-payment.

Point. On stock market price quotations, a point is one dollar.

Policies. General statements or understandings which guide thinking in decision making; the essence of policies is the existence of discretion; within certain limits, in guiding decision making.

Policy Decision. A stage in the public policy process when government authorizes a course of action. For example, by passing a law issuing a court opinion, or adopting a new regulation.

Policy Evaluation. The final stage in the public policy process when the results of a public policy are judged by those who have an interest in the outcomes.

Policy Formulation. A stage in the public policy process when interested groups take a position and try to persuade others to adopt that position.

Policy Implementation. A stage in the public policy process when action is taken to enforce a public policy decision.

Policy Instrument. Variable that the policy maker can control.

Policy Loans. Loans made by an insurance company to its policyholders using their policies as collateral.

Policy Owner's Surplus. Difference between an insurance company's assets and its liabilities.

Policy Reserves. A liability item for insurers that reflects their expected payment commitments on existing policy contracts.

Policy Targets. Variable that the policy maker tries to influence.

Political Action Committee. A committee organized according to election law by any group for the purpose of accepting voluntary contributions from individual donors and then making contributions to candidates for election to public office.

Political Economy. The political, economical, and legal systems of a country.

Political Forces. The relationship of individuals, their rights, and their property to the state.

Political Freedom. The right to participate freely in the political process.

Political-legal Dimension. Within the general environment, the nature of relationship between various areas of government and the organization.

Political Risk. The likelihood that political forces will cause drastic changes in a country's business environment that will adversely affect the profit and other goals of a particular business enterprise.

Political Science. A discipline that helps explain the patterns of governments and their actions.

Political System. System of government in a nation. The system designed to integrate a society into a viable functioning unit.

Politics. The maneuvering by an individual to try to gain an advantage in the distribution of organizational rewards or resources.

Pollution Charge. A fee levied on a polluting source based on the amount of pollution released into the environment.

Pollution Trade-off. Accepting one form of pollution rather than another when it is not possible to eliminate both.

Polycentric Business. A company whose business standards are based on the customs, markets, and laws of two or few different nations.

Polycentric Staffing. A staffing policy in an MNE in which host country nationals are recruited to manage subsidiaries in their own county, while parent country nationals occupy key positions at corporate head-quarters.

Polycentrism. Characteristics of an individual or organization that in a foreign country real and imaginary, great and small need to accounted for in management decisions.

Polychronic Culture. A culture in which most people are more comfortable and dealing simultaneously all the situations.

Poly-chronic Time. Preference for doing more than one thing at a time because time is flexible and multi-dimensional.

Polygraphs. An operator administered instrument that is used to judge the truth or falsity of a person's statements by measuring physiological changes that tend to be caused by a person's conscience when lying.

Pooled Interdependence. The interdependence that exists when groups operate interdependently but together contribute to the organization's overall success.

Pooling. Spreading of losses incurred by the few over the entire group, so that in the process, average loss is substituted for actual loss.

Populism. The preference for a democratic political system, family-operated farms, small-size business firms and small town life.

Portfolio Effect. The tendency of the variability in the returns from one asset or group of assets to be offset by variations in the returns from other assets owned by the firm.

Portability. Allows employees to move their pension benefits from one employer to another.

Porter Diamond. A diagram that shows four conditions of demand, factor endowments related and supporting industries, firm strategy or structure and rivalry that usually must be favourable for an industry in a country to develop and sustain a global competitive advantage.

Porter-Lawler Expectancy Model. An extension of the expectancy theory stating that satisfaction is the result rather than the cause of performance and that different levels of performance lead to different rewards, which in turn, produce different levels of job satisfaction.

Portfolio Analysis. A technique allowing for managers to visualize their businesses as a set of portfolios using certain common criteria such as profitability or growth potential.

Portfolio Approach to Money Demand. (Also called the asset approach) Developed in the 1950s by James Tobin which provides an alternative justification for Keynes' view that interest rates affect money demand.

Portfolio Investment. An investment in the form of either debt or equity that does not give the investor a controlling interest.

Position. It is a collective of tasks performed by one person.

Position Power. A factor in the Fiedler theory of leadership that refers to the power inherent in the leadership position.

Position Traders. Exchange members who take a position in the futures market based on their expectations about the future direction of the prices of the underlying assets.

Positive Inequity. Comparison in which another person receives lesser outcomes for similar inputs.

Positive Reinforcement. Psychologist Skinner's theory that people are best motivated by properly designing their work environment, giving them prompt feedback on performance, and including ways to help them and praise them for the good things they do.

Positive Sum Game. A situation in which all countries can benefit even if some benefit more than others.

Positive Volume Issues Traded Index (PVITI). It is summation of advances minus declines only on days when total volume of trading increases over that of the previous day.

Possession Utility. A good or service must be in the possession of an individual if it is to satisfy a want.

Post-Implementation Audit. Evaluation of the impact of the information system and compared with expectations; reviews the design, development, and implementation. process to understand what did and did not work.

Post-modern organizations. Flexible organizations that are decentralized, computer linked and less hierarchical than bureaucracies.

Post-industrial Society. A society combining the features of a service society and a knowledge society.

Potential Exposure. The risk that a counter-party to a derivative securities contract will default in the future.

Potential New Competitors. Companies not currently operating in a business but have a high potential for entering the industry.

Power. The ability of individuals or groups to induce or influence the beliefs or actions of other persons or groups. Several kinds of power may be identified such as legitimate power, expertness, reward power and coercive power.

Power Distance. Theory of how a society deals with the fact that people are unequal in physical and intellectual capabilities. High power distance cultures are found in countries that let inequalities. A measurement of preference for consultative or autocratic styles of management.

Power of Sale. The process of taking the proceedings of the forced sale of a mortgaged property in satisfaction of the indebtedness and returning to the mortgage or excess over the indebtedness or claiming any shortfall as an unsecured creditor.

PPP. *See* Purchasing-power parity.

Practical Capacity. The maximum level at which plant or department can realistically operate most efficiently, *i.e.* ideal capacity less allowances for unavoidable operating interruptions. Also called practical attainable capacity.

Pragmatism. Settling small issues before deciding on principles.

PRC. People's Republic of China.

Precautionary Motive. The desire to hold money to meet unexpected expenditure for emergencies or the proverbial rainy day.

Predatory Pricing. Reducing prices below fare market value as competitive weapon to drive weaker competitors out of the market ("fare" being cost plus some reasonable profit margin).

Preemptive Rights. A right of existing stockholders in which new shares must be offered to the existing shareholders first in such a way that they can maintain their proportional ownership in the corporation.

Pre-existing Condition. Physical or mental condition of an insured that existed prior to issuance of a policy.

Pre-existing Conditions Clause. Contractual provision in a health insurance policy stating that pre-existing conditions are not covered or are covered only after the policy has been in force for a specified period.

Preference Capital. Capital referring to preferred shares which give investors a fixed dividend from the company's earnings and entitle them to be paid before common shareholders are paid.

Preference or Utility Theory. The theory that individual attitudes towards risk will vary from statistical probabilities, with some individuals willing only to take lower risks than indicated by probabilities ('risk averters') and others taking greater risks ('gamblers').

Preferential Allotment. Allotment entitled to payment before other debts and liabilities are met.

Preferential Form. Special application forms are usually given to existing shareholders and employees when companies offer shares for public subscription and they are easily identifiable by their pink colour hence they are also known as "Pink forms".

Preferential Hiring. An employment plan that gives preference to minorities, women and other groups that may be under-represented in an organization's workforce.

Preferential Issue. Preferential issue offers the shareholders preferential claims to the dividends, usually at a fixed rate and a prior claim to ordinary shareholders on the company's assets in the event of liquidation. The market price for the preferential shares tends to be more stable than that of the ordinary shares.

Preferred Habitat Hypothesis. Combines key features of both the expectation hypothesis and the segmented markets hypothesis. It says that while investors do have a preference for loanable funds of a given term, they are willing to substitute away from their preferred term—if they are compensated for doing so.

Preferred Provider Organization. It is a health care provider that contracts with an employer or an employer group to provide health care services to employees at competitive rates.

Preferred Risks. Individuals whose mortality experience is expected to be lower than average.

Preferred Stock. A certificate of ownership in a corporation which usually receives preferred payment but does not have voting rights. Stock that has some priority over ordinary shares regarding dividends or the distribution of assets upon liquidation.

Prejudice. Negative attitudes and feelings towards others because of their membership in different cultural group.

Preliminary (or Fed Forward or Steering) Control. A form of operations control that monitors deviations in the quality and quantity of the firm's resources to try to prevent deviations before they enter the system.

Premises Burglary Coverage Form. Commercial crime insurance by the insurance services office that provides converage for premises burglary and rubbery of a guard.

Premium (in Foreign Exchange). The difference between the spot and forward exchange rates in the forward market; a foreign currency sells at a premium when the forward rate exceeds the spot rate and when the domestic currency is quoted on a direct basis.

Premium/Discount to NAV. Gives the premium or discount to the NAV at which the funds are traded on the bourses. A negative value indicates a discount while positive values indicates the extent to the premium.

Premiums Earned. Premiums received and earned on insurance contract because time has passed with no claim filed.

Prepaid Expenses. These are the expenses of future period paid in advance. Accrued incomes are the benefits which the firm has earned. But they have not been received in cash yet. They include items such as accrued dividend, accrued commission or accrued interest.

Prepay. To pay back a loan before its maturity to the FI that originated the loan.

Present Value. The current equivalent value of cash available immediately for a future payment or a stream of payments to be received at various times in the future. The present value will vary with the discount (interest) factor applied to the future payments.

Present Value Annuity Factor. The present value of a series of cash flows of Re 1. per period for a specified number of periods time-adjusted at a given discount rate.

Present Value Interest Factor. The present value of Re. 1 received at the end of a given future period time-adjusted at a given discount rate.

Presentation Methods. Training methods in which the trainer tells or shows trainee the information they are to learn.

Pressure Group. A group that tries to influence legislation or practices to foster its objectives.

Previous Trades. This screen allows the trading members to view all previous trades that have taken place in the market.

Previous-department Costs. *See* Transferred-in costs.

Price Bank. The daily or weekly price limits within which price of a security is allowed to rise or fall.

Price Discrimination. The practice of charging different prices for the same product in different markets.

Price-Earnings Ratio. The market price of a common stock divided by the earnings per share for one year.

Price Elasticity of Demand. A measure of how responsive demand for a product is to changes in price.

Price Escalation. The process by which the lengthening of distribution channels increases a product's price by more than the direct added costs such as transportation, insurance and tariffs.

Price Index. A single number that measures the average percentage change in price, volume or value of a set or 'basket' of related items during the time between some elected base period and current period. In other words a price index measures the average percentage change in the prices of a given physical volume of commodities.

Price Level. A measure of the average prices of goods and services in the economy.

Price Limit. The maximum price advance or decline permitted as a contract during one day or trading session under the rules of exchange.

Price Performance. The price performance indicates net gain to the investor from a scheme on the basis of the latest market price. The price performance has also been calculated using the internal rate of return method and has been suitably adjusted for rights, bonus and dividends. Returns are on an annualized basis.

Price Range. That is not below the level where the business owner can sell at a profit.

Price Rigging. When a person or persons acting in concert with each other collude to artificially increase or decrease the price of a security that process is called price rigging.

Price Risk. The risk that an asset's sale price will be lower than its purchase price.

Price Sensitivity. The percentage change in a bond's present value for a given change in interest rates.

Price Spread. If a trade involves purchase of option and sale option both on the same stock and expiring in the same month but exercise price of one is higher than the other, it is called price spread.

Price Stability. Measured by the stability of the inflation rate and the amount by which inflation exceeds a target level.

Price Stabilization Rule. A money policy rule that prescribes changes to the money supply in response to changes in aggregated supply or demand to keep the price level constant.

Price to Earnings Ratio. Shows the multiple of earnings per share (adjusted for stock splits). Earnings per share for the P/E ratio are determined by dividing earnings for the past 12 months by the number of common shares outstanding. Higher multiple means investors have higher expectations for future growth and have bid up the stock's price.

Price Variance. The term price variance is usually linked with direct material, the item rate variance which is conceptually similar to the price variance usually linked with direct labour.

Pricing Policies. The planned process of determining prices and how prices can be changed in the field or for unusual circumstances such as volume discounting.

Primary Problem. The original formulation of the linear-programming problem.

Primary and Excess Insurance. Type of other insurance provisions that requires the primary insurer to pay first in the case of a loss; when the policy limits under the primary policy are exhausted the excess insurer pays.

Primary Beneficiary. Beneficiary of a life insurance policy who is first entitled to receive the policy proceeds on the insured's death.

Primary Buying Motives. The motives which influence the initial recognition of the need for a piece of merchandise.

Primary Characteristics of Diversity. The born characteristics such as age, gender, ethnicity, abilities and sexual orientation that cannot be changed.

Primary Deficit. The amount, the federal government spends on transfer payments and purchases over and above its current tax collections.

Primary Dimensions of Diversity. Personal characteristics that exert an important and sustained impact throughout our lives.

Primary Insurance Amount. Monthly cash benefit paid to a retired worker at the normal retirement age currently age 65 or to a disabled worker eligible for benefits under the Old Age, Survivors, and Disability Insurance (OASDI) program.

Primary Interactions or Involvement. The direct relationship a company has with those groups that enable it to produce goods and services.

Primary Market. The market where newly issued securities are first offered.

Primary Memory. The volatile semi-conductor memory that the microprocessor uses to temporarily store data and instructions needed by the software programs being used; also called random access memory (RAM).

Primary Needs. Basic physiological needs of human such as food, shelter, clothing, etc.

Primary Period. The period in a finance lease during which the lessor expects to recover the full capital cost of the asset, his money, costs and his profits.

Primary Source of Data. An agency which collects and publishes data.

Primary Spending. Transfer payments and purchases of goods and services. Does not include interest payments on the debt.

Primary Stakeholders. Those who have a formal and/or contractual relationship with the firm such as customers, suppliers, and employees.

Prime Costs. Direct material plus direct labour.

Prime Interest Rate. The rate of interest banks charge their best customers usually large corporation.

Prime Lending Rate. The base lending rate periodically set by banks.

Principal. The bonded party in the purchase of a surety bond who agrees to perform certain acts or fulfil certain obligations.

Principle of Delegation of Authority. Decisions should be made at the lowest competent level in the company.

Principle of Flexibility. The company must be able to adjust to a changing environment both internally and externally.

Principle of Functional Homogeneity. Activities within the company should be grouped on the basis of similarity.

Principle of Indemnity. States that the insured should not profit from a covered loss but should be restored to approximately the same financial position that existed prior to the loss.

Principle of Levels of Management. The number of levels of management within a company should be kept to a minimum.

Principle of Span of Control. There is a limit to the number of people a worker can effectively supervise.

Principle of Unity of Command. A worker should receive orders from and report to a single supervisor.

Principle of Unity of Objectives. Each part of the company must contribute to the accomplishment of overall objectives of the firm.

Principle of Value of Additivity. Value added to capital as a result of incremental cash flows with the investment made in a project.

Principles. Fundamental truths or what are believed to be truths at a given time explaining relationships between two or more sets of variables, usually an independent variable and a dependent variable; may be descriptive, explaining what will happen, indicating what a person should do in the latter case. Principles reflect some scale of values, such as efficiency and therefore imply value judgments.

Prior Approval Law. Law for regulating insurance rates under which the rates must be filed and approved by the state insurance department before they can be used.

Prior Informed Consent. The concept of requiring each exporter of a banned or restricted chemical to obtain through home country government the expressed consent of the importing country to receive the banned or restricted substance.

Priority Incremental Budget. Similar to ordinary incremental budget. However, the budget request must be accompanied by a statement of what incremental activities or changes would occur if the budget were increased or decreased by a given amount or percentage.

Priority of Human Needs. The concept that needs have a definite order of levels and each level must be satisfied before the person advances to the next one.

Privacy. *See* Right of privacy.

Private Brand. A brand owned by a middleman (wholesaler or retailer) and usually advertised and sold in a smaller geographical area such as state or region.

Private Carrier. A carrier which moves its own goods by using its own transportation system.

Private Enterprise. Exists when private citizens rather than the government own business.

Private Goods. Goods that are divisible into finite units for consumption and for which it is easy to keep non-buyers from receiving the benefits of consumption.

Private Mortgage Insurance. Insurance contract purchased by a mortgage borrower guaranteeing to pay the financial institution the difference between the value of the property and the balance remaining on the mortgage.

Private Pension Funds. Fund administered by a private corporation.

Private Placement. Selling equity in a corporation to private parties through various rules established in the Uniform Commercial Code and by the Securities and Exchange Commission that permits stock ownership without having to register 'publicly traded' new securities.

Private Property. A group of rights that gives control over physical and intangible assets to private owners, private ownership is the basic institution of capitalism.

Private Sector Organizations. Profit-making organizations in the US economy.

Privatization. The sale of state owned inter prices to private investors.

Privatizing. Selling of government owned assets to private individuals or companies.

Pro Cyclical Policy. A policy that stimulates the economy during an expansion and restrains an economy during recession.

Probabilities. Likelihood of occurrence of events.

Probationary Period. (1) Waiting period of one to six months required of an employee before he or she is allowed to participate in a group insurance plan. (2) Specified number of days after a health insurance policy is issued during which time sickness is not covered.

Problem. The difference between a desired situation and the actual situation.

Problem Solving. That function of the accountant's information-supplying task which expresses in concise, quantified terms the relative advantages and disadvantages to the firm of pursuing a possible future course of action or the relative advantages of any one of several alternative methods of operation.

Procedural Justice. The perceived fairness of the process and procedures used to make allocation decisions.

Procedures. Plans that establish a required method of handling future activities. They are guides to action; they detail the exact manner in which certain activities must be accomplished.

Process. A series of actions or operations leading to a definite end.

Process Consultation. A technique in which consultant focuses in the dynamic task-related processes and assists the client organization.

Process Costing. The method of allocating costs to the products resulting from the mass production of like units.

Process Layout. Facility layout in which firms organize the transformation process into departments that group related procedures.

Process Style. Likes to discuss issues in detail.

Process Technology. The combination of equipment, techniques and knowledge used in the manufacturing process. Biogenetic engineering is a process technology for making new chemicals and medicines.

Process Theories. A set of theories that try to determine 'how' and 'why' employees are motivated to perform.

Processing Float. Funds tied up during the time required for the firm to process remittance checks before they can be deposited in the bank.

Processing Unit. The computer component in which the computer's arithmetic operations are performed.

Product Costs. Costs that are identified with goods produced or purchased for resale.

Product Development Teams. A special type of project team formed to devise, design, and implement a new product.

Product Division. An organizational structure in which different foreign operations report to different product groups at headquarters.

Product Division Structure. The organization of divisions by product.

Product Lay-out. Facility layout in which production is broken down into relatively simple tasks assigned to workers positioned along the line, and the product moves from worker to worker.

Product Liability. A legal responsibility of a person or firm for the harmful consequences to others stemming from the use of a product manufactured, sold, managed, or employed by the person or firm.

Product Life Cycle Theory. The theory that certain kinds of products go through a cycle consisting of four stages (introduction, growth, maturity, and decline) and that the location of production will shift internationally depending on the stage of the cycle.

Product Recall. An effort by a business firm to remove a defective or sometimes dangerous product from consumer use and from all distribution channels.

Product Safety. Products that are safe in use, free from contamination and safe for health.

Production. A term used to address manufacturing technology and the flow of materials in a manufacturing facility. Activities involved in creating a product.

Production and Operations Managers. Managers who schedule and monitor the work process that turns out the firm's goods and services.

Production Control. A function which ensures the orderly flow of work in manufacturing operations. It determines when, where and how production of a job will occur.

Production Management. Those activities necessary to manufacture products or create services. It includes activities such as purchasing, warehousing, transportation, and other operations to procure raw materials until the product or service is bought by the customer.

Production Switching. The movement of production from one country to another in response to changes in cost.

Production Volume Variance. Difference between budgeted fixed factory overhead and the fixed factory overhead applied to products.

Productivity. The relationship between total inputs and total outputs. Productivity increases when the outputs of an organization increase faster than the inputs necessary for production.

Productivity Agent Role. A role performed by management and others that seeks to use resources in ways that produce the most output (economic and social benefits) for each unit of input (economic and social costs).

Products Completed Operations Hazard. Liability losses that occur away from the premises and arise out of the insured's product or work after the insured has relinquished possession of the product or the work has been completed.

Products Liability. The legal liability of manufacturers, wholesalers; and retailers to persons who are injured or who incur property damage from defective products.

Professional Bureaucracy. An organization that has a functional structure, medium sized and works best in stable environments, but has primarily professional employees and a decentralized informal structure.

Professional Corporation. A form of incorporation available to practicing professionals including for example, physicians, attorneys and accountants.

Professional Traders. Exchange members who trade for their own account.

Professionalism. The use of professionals with extensive work-related knowledge and skills.

Profit. The amount of money left over after the business records all its revenues and subtracts all its expense (total revenues minus total expense). The prime motivator in a private enterprise economic system.

Profit and Loss Control. A control technique designed to measure a division or other part of a business enterprise by calculating the total profit (or loss) of that entity.

Profit Before Depreciation Interest and Taxes. It is equal to revenue minus all operating expenses except depreciation, interest and taxes.

Profit Centre. A segment of a business that is responsible for both revenue and expense.

Profit Maximization. Profit maximization is an economic philosophy that business produces a public good of improved efficiency and reduced prices when it seeks to maximize its profits through competitive activity.

Profit Planning. The term profit planning refers to the operating decisions in the areas of pricing, costs, volume of output and the firm's selection of product lines.

Profit Sharing. Portion of bottom-line economic profits given to employees.

Profitability Accounting. *See* Responsibility accounting.

Profitability Index. It is the ratio of the present value of cash inflows at the required rate of return to the initial cash outflow of the investment.

Profitability Ratios. Financial ratios designed to measure how effectively the firm's management controls expenses and turns sales into profits.

Profits. Gross profits are determined by subtracting cost of goods sold from the net sales. Net profit before tax, which is a commonly used measure, subtracts all expenses except taxes from gross profits. Net profit after tax is the 'bottom line'.

Pro-forma Balance Sheet. A planned or projected statement of financial condition at a future date.

Pro-forma Income Statement. A planned or projected statement of income for a future period.

Pro-forma Statements. Forecasted financial statements.

Program Evaluation and Review Technique. A production planning technique with widespread applicability in organizations that produce large-scale, non-routine products. The technique enables management to make the optimal allocation of resources to the activities that lead to completion of the product.

Programme. The detailed instructions which transmit the calculations. The computer is to make on a set of data.

Programme Analysis. Future ratios are used as standards of comparison. Future ratios can be developed from the projected financial statements. The comparison of current and past ratios with future ratios shows the firms relative strengths and weaknesses in the past and future. The future ratios indicate financial position and an indicator of corrective actions to be initiated.

Programme Budgeting. A budgeting approach used primarily by government agencies, emphasizing goals, the programmes to be achieved by them and budgetary allocations designed to support such programmes.

Programmed Conflict. Encourages different opinions without protecting management's personal feelings.

Programmed Costs. *See* Discretionary costs.

Programmed Decisions. Responses to repetitive and routine problems, which are handled by a standard procedure that has been developed by management.

Programmer. The person who writes the instructions for the computer.

Programmes. A complex of goals, policies, procedures, rules, task assignments, steps to be taken, resources to be employed and other elements necessary to carry out a given course of action, normally supported by capital and operating budgets.

Project Organization. A structural approach that uses teams.

Project Risk. The total risk of an investment in an asset; includes both the systematic and the diversifiable risk of the project.

Project/development Teams. Groups similar to task forces, but usually responsible for running an operation and in control of specific work or project.

Projected Rate. The spot exchange rate for the end of the budget period.

Projection. Assigning (often unconsciously) your own thoughts and feelings to the people or objects.

Promissory Note. A contract in which one party promises payment of funds borrowed plus interest to another party at some specific time.

Promotion. A change within the organization to a higher position with greater responsibilities and usually requiring more advanced skills and knowledge than the previous position. Thus an upward movement to a position of more authority, responsibility and salary. Normally promotion brings greater status and increase in pay.

Promotion Based on Open Competition. The policy of filling positions or making promotions from the most qualified people available whether from inside or outside a given enterprise.

Promotion from Within. The practice of making all promotions in an enterprise from people within, it if it is possible to do so.

Prompt Corrective Action. Mandatory action that regulators must take as a bank's capital ratio falls.

Propensity to Trust. A personality trait involving one's general willingness to trust others.

Property Rights. Bundle of legal rights over the use to which a resource is put and over the use made of any income that may be derived from the resource.

Proprietorship. A separate entity with a single owner.

Prorate Liability Clause. Clause in a property insurance policy that makes each company insuring the same interest in a property liable according to the proportion that insurance bears to the total amount of insurance on the property.

Proration. It is a division of taxes, interest, insurance and similar charges that the seller and the buyer each pay the portion representing the period of his/her ownership.

Prospective Reserve. In life insurance, the difference between the present value of future benefits and the present value of future net premiums.

Prospectus. A booklet containing all information about a company that would affect the value of new securities it wants to issue.

Protected Group Member. It is an individual falls within a group identified for protection under equal employment laws.

Protecting a Position. Once an investor has initiated position and determines that the fundamental and technical factors for a particular commodity are inside and places an order with his broker, he should at the same time determine how far he is willing to let the market go against him before he abandons the position.

Protection and Indemnity Insurance (P&U). Coverage that can be added to an ocean marine insurance policy to provide broad, comprehensive liability insurance on an indemnity basis for property damage and bodily injury to third parties.

Protectionism. It is a policy that favours the use of tariffs, quotas or other import restrictions designed to make domestic products competitive with foreign imports.

Protestant Ethic. A theory that there is more economic growth when work is viewed as a means of salvation and when people prefer to transform productivity gains into additional output rather than additional leisure.

Prototype. A working model of an innovation used to test or demonstrate its practical capabilities.

Provider of Impetus. A role that involves delegating a conflict to the parties—with a threat attached.

Provision Loan Losses. Bank management's recognition of expected bad loans for the period.

Provisions. These are other types of current liabilities. They include provision for taxes or provision for dividends. Every business has to pay taxes on its income. Usually it takes some time to finalize the amount of tax with the tax authorities. Therefore, the amount of tax is estimated and shown as provision for taxes or tax liability in the balance sheet. Similarly, provision for paying dividends.

Proxemics. Hall's term for the study of cultural expectations about interpersonal space.

Proximate Cause. Factor causing damage to property for which there is an unbroken chain of events between the occurrence of an insured peril and damage or destruction of the property.

Proxy. A legal instrument giving another person the right to vote the shares of stock of an absentee stockholder.

Proxy Statement. A statement sent by a board of directors to a corporation's stockholders announcing the company's annual meeting, containing information about the business to be considered at the meeting and enclosing a proxy form for stockholders not attending the meeting.

Psychology. The behavioral science that studies human behavior. It seeks general laws which explain individual and interpersonal behavior.

Psychological Contract. The exchange that underlies a person's working relationship with an employer.

Psychological Needs. Needs of the human body, such as food, water, and sex.

Psychological Withdrawal. Detachment from the work setting.

PTA. Preferential Trade Area for Eastern and Southern Africa.

Public (or Social) Service Leave. A type of corporate gift consisting of a leave of absence granted to an employee to engage in community service work, usually with full or partial pay provided by the employee's business firm.

Public Adjuster. Claims adjustor who represents the insured rather than the insurance company and is paid a fee based on the amount of the claim settlement. A public adjustor may be employed in those cases where the insured and insurer cannot resolve a dispute over a claim or if the insured needs technical assistance in a complex loss situation.

Public Affairs Function. An organization's activities intended to perceive, monitor, understand, communicate with and influence the external environment including local and national communities, government relations, and public opinion.

Public Corporation. A corporation with securities traded publicly through one of the organized exchanges and regulated through the Securities and Exchange Commission.

Public Goods. Goods that may be consumed by more than on person at the same time with little or no extra cost such as services of a lighthouse beacon. For most public goods, it is relatively expensive or even impossible to keep potential consumers from receiving the benefits of the good as in the case of national defense.

Public Investment. Govern-ment investment occurs when the government purchases physical capital.

Public Offering. The process of raising equity capital through an exchange authorized by the Securities and Exchange Commission. A new venture that 'goes public' does so through an initial public offering (IPO) which is its first authorized sale of public securities.

Public Official Bond. Type of surety bond guaranteeing that public officials will faithfully perform their duties for the protection of the public.

Public Pension Funds. Funds administered by a federal, state, or local government.

Public Policy. A plan of action by government to achieve some broad purpose affecting a large segment of the public.

Public Policy Agenda. All public problems of issues that receive the active and serious attention of government officials.

Public Policy Process. All the activities and stages involved in development carrying out, and evaluating public policies.

Public Responsibility Committee. A committee of a corporation's board of directors with the function of identifying social and political issues that may have an influence on the company and making recommendations to the directors about appropriate actions.

Public Trustee. A concept that a business owner or manager should base company decisions on the interests of a wide range of corporate stakeholders or members of the general public. In doing so the business executive acts as a trustee of the public interest.

Publicity. Any type of information about a company or a product which has apparent news value and is reported in the indifferent media and is not paid for by the firm.

Publicly Held Corporation. A corporation whose stock is available for purchase by the general investing public.

Puisne Mortgage. Mortgage issued despite the failure of the lender to take possession of the title deeds to the property offered as security for the loan. The lender may register the property with the Land Registrar, this ensures that any transaction concerning the property must have the approval of the lender.

Pull. A promotion strategy that sells consumers before they reach the point of purchase, usually by relying on mass media.

Pull Strategy. A marketing strategy emphasizing personal selling rather than mass media advertising as opposed to personal selling.

Punched Card. A method of recording instructions to computers by punching holes in the cards and feeding them into the input unit of the computer.

Punishment. Presenting an unpleasant stimulus after a particular behavior leading to a decrease in the behavior. It is action taken to repel the person from undesired action.

Purchase Discount. A reduction in the purchase price of a product because of ordering a relatively large quantity.

Purchase Option. An option to purchase leased property at the end of the lease term. In some jurisdictions (mainly UK) purchase options are impossible if the transaction is to quality as a lease in others (*e.g.* the French system and its derivative), a purchase option is mandatory. In US, if the tax characteristics of a true lease are to be protected, the purchase option may not be at a price less than the assets fair market value at the time when the right is exercised (*See* also Fixed price purchase option).

Purchased Funds. Rate-sensitive funding sources of the firm.

Purchasing. The buying of all materials needed by the organization also known as procurement. Thus, it is the process of acquiring materials and supplies.

Purchasing Power. What a sum of money actually can buy.

Purchasing Power Parity (PPP). An adjustment in gross domestic product per capita to reflect differences in the cost of living. Theory states that the equilibrium exchange rate makes the dollar cost of foreign and domestic goods identical.

Pure Competition. The market structure in which a large number of well-informed buyers. No individual seller or buyer thinks that they can influence the market price.

Pure no-fault Plan. The injured person cannot sue at all, regardless of the seriousness of the claim and no payments are made for suffering.

Pure Premium. That portion of the insurance rate needed to pay losses and loss-adjustment expenses.

Pure Risk. Situation in which there are only the possibilities of loss or no loss.

Purely Competitive Deposit Market. Situation where individual banks are small relative to the entire market for deposits and should pay the market rate on deposits.

Push. A promotion strategy that involves direct selling techniques.

Push Strategy. A marketing strategy of personal selling rather than mass media advertising.

Put Option. Gives a buyer the option to sell a financial asset at a specified price upto the expiration date of the option.

Q

QTL Test. Qualified thrift Lender Test that sets a floor on the mortgage-related assets that thrifts can hold.

Qualitative Factor. A factor that is of consequence but cannot be measured precisely and easily in dollars.

Quality. The degree to which goods or services meet the demands and requirements of the marketplace.

Quality Approach. A viewpoint of management that emphasizes the application of mathematical models, statistics, and structured information systems to support rational management decision making.

Quality Assurance Teams. Generally small groups formed to recommend changes that will positively affect the quality of the organization's products.

Quality Circle. A small group of supervision and workers who meet to discuss ways to improve the overall quality of work done in their unit.

Quality Circles. They are small groups of employees that meet on a regular basis to discuss ways to improve productivity and to cut costs.

Quality Control Circles (or Quality Circles). Participation of workers in solving work-related problems. Often several people, usually rank and file workers are involved in solving the problems.

Quality Control. Inspecting and testing products to ensure only good products are sold to customers.

Quality Function Department. A set of planning and communication routines that focus and coordinate skills within an organization first through design then through the manufacturing and marketing of products.

Quality Loss Function. The idea that a product that fails to meet consumer expectations results in a measurable loss to society.

Quality of Work Life. The favourableness or unforget-ableness of a job environment for an organization's employee.

Quality of Working Life. Programmes representing a systems approach to job design and job enrichment which will make jobs more interesting and challenging. Programmes are closely associated with the socio-technical systems approach.

Quantity Controls. Government limitations on the amount of foreign currency that can be used for specific purposes.

Quantity Variance. Efficiency variance pertaining to materials or direct labour.

Quantum Change. A large-scale planned change in how the firm operates.

Query Operation. An operation that returns a computer a value without modifying any objects.

Question Marks. Those businesses, that are viewed positively in the sense that they are located in attractive fast-growing markets but for which there is a question as to their ability to compete given their low market share.

Questionable Payments. Something of value given to a person or firm which raises significant ethical questions of right or wrong in the host nation or other nations.

Quota. A limit on the quantitative amount of a product allowed to be imported into or exported out of a country in a year.

Quotas (Job, Hiring Employment). An employment plan based on hiring a specific number or proportion of minority's women or other groups who may be under-represented in an organization's workforce.

Quota System. A commodity agreement whereby producing and/or consuming countries divide total output and sales in order to stabilize the price of a particular product.

Quotas. A restriction on the number of goods that can enter a nation.

Quote Sheet. An analysis of costs used as a basis for determining selling prices.

Quote-driven Trading. Trading where brokers/market makers give buy or sell quote for a scrip simultaneously.

R

R Squared. Square of the correlation co-efficiency the proportion of the variability in the series that can be explained by the variability of one or more other series.

Rabbi Trust. A trust agreement applying to funds held to finance a non-qualified retirement benefit to a favored employee. The employer owns a rabbi trust.

Raider. Having positive effect on sensex.

Random Walk Hypothesis. The theory that historical prices on a financial claim cannot help in predicting future prices.

Rate. Price per unit insurance.

Rate Making. Process by which insurance pricing or premium rates are determined for an insurance company.

Rate of Return on Assets. Total profit divided by total assets.

Rate of Return on Equity. A ratio that indicates how well management is performing with the resources available. It is computed by dividing net income by owners' (common stockholders') equity.

Rate of Return on Total Assets. It is computed by dividing operating income by average assets.

Rate Sensitivity. The time to re-pricing of an asset or liability.

Rate Variance. The difference between actual wages paid and the standard wage rate, multiplied by the total actual hours of direct labour used.

Ratification. Occurs when union members vote to accept the terms of a negotiated labour agreement.

Rating Bureau. An organization that collects insurance data from member companies and uses these data to develop insurance rates for the member companies. In other industries this action would be considered a violation of antitrust laws. But it is allowed in insurance.

Ratio. A ratio is defined as the quotient of two mathematical expressions and as the relationship between two or more things.

Ratio Analysis. A method used by managers to take information from balance sheet and income statements in order to measure a company's efficiency, profitability and sources of finances relative to those of other organizations.

Ratio Percentage Test. A test that a qualified pension plan must meet to receive favorable income tax treatment. The pension plan must benefit a percentage of employees that is at least 70 per cent of the highly compensated employees covered by the plan.

Rational Buying Motive. A decision to buy which involves conscious thought and deliberation.

Rationale Decision Making. A logical, consistent process for identifying the alternative with the greatest utility or usefulness for a purpose.

Rationale Model. Logical four-step approach to decision making.

Rational Persuasion. Convincing others that a course of action is logically the best.

Rationality. Analysis enquiring a clear goal, a clear understanding of alternatives by which a goal can be reached, an analysis and evaluation of alternatives in terms of the goal sought, needed information and a desire to optimize.

Rationalized Production. The specialized production by-product or process in different parts of the world to take advantage of varying costs of labour, capital and raw material.

Rationalization. *See* Rationalized production.

Raw Materials Inventory. Materials that have been purchased to be used as inputs for making other products.

Reactive Change. A situation in which organizational members react spontaneously to external and internal forces.

Readiness. Follower's ability and willingness to complete a task.

Readjustment Period. One to two year period immediately following the breadwinner's death during which time the family should receive approximately the same amount of income it received while the breadwinner was alive.

Real Asset. A firm requires real assets to carry on its business. Real asset can be tangible or intangible. Plant, machinery, office, factory, furniture and building are examples of tangible real assets while technical know-how, technological collaborations, patents and copyrights are intangible real assets.

Real Bills Doctrine. The view that loans made by the banking system that are ultimately used to fund the production of goods and services are not inflationary.

Real Exchange Rate. Exchange rate adjusted for inflation.

Real Interest Rate. The nominal interest rate (the interest rate stated in the loan contract) minus the expected rate of inflation.

Real Money Balances. The nominal money stock divided by the price level. It provides a measure of the purchasing power of money.

Real Output. The physical quantity of goods and services produced in the economy in one year.

Real Property. Land and anything permanently attached to the land.

Real Rate of Interest. The rate the borrower actually paid minus the rate of inflation.

Real Return. Return adjusted for the effects of inflation.

Realistic Job Preview (RJP). It is the process of providing a job applicant with an accurate picture of a job.

Realistic Job Preview. Presents both positive and negative aspects of a job.

Reality Shock. A newcomer's feelings of surprise after experiencing unexpected situations or events.

Realization. The recognition of revenue. Generally three tests must be met. First, the earning process must be virtually complete in that the goods or services must be fully rendered. Second, exchange of resources evidenced by a market transaction must occur. Third, the asset received must be cash or convertible into cash with reasonable certainty.

Realized Rate of Return. The interest rate that would exist on a default free security if no inflation were expected.

Reallocation. Allocation of the costs of operating the service departments to the various production departments in proportion to the relative benefits or services received by each production department.

Real-time Information. Information on events as they occur.

Reapportionment. *See* Reallocation.

Rear-end Loading. The practice of constructing a rental schedule where the larger payments are made towards the end of the lease.

Reasonable Person. A legal standard applied in negligence cases, allowing the court to evaluate the facts in particular cases.

Reasons Style. Interested in hearing the rationale behind a message.

Rebate. Return of a portion of the purchase price in the form of cash by the seller to the buyer.

Rebating. A practice—illegal in virtually all states—of giving a premium reduction or some other financial advantage to an individual as an inducement to purchase the policy.

Recaptured Apart from Future Earnings. Store renovations, for example, are sunk costs that have no loan value or market value apart from business operations.

Receivables Turnover. The number of times receivables are turned over during a specified period of time.

Receiver. The person to whom information and meaning are sent.

Receiving. Registration of a message by one or more of the receiver's senses.

Reciprocal Exchange. A type of insurer that an incorporated operates on a nonprofit basis.

Reciprocal Interdependence. The interdependence that exists when each group's output serves as input to other groups.

Reciprocal Quote. The reciprocal of the direct quote; also known as the indirect quote.

Reciprocity. Widespread belief that people should be paid back for their positive and negative acts.

Recognition Lags. Lags in the recognition of the monetary policy maker that a policy action is needed. Based on the information available to it.

Records. Memory of the company.

Recourse. Actions available to a party to a contract when the other parties have not fulfilled their obligations.

Recruiting. It is the process of generating a pool of qualified applicants for organizational jobs.

Recruitment of Managers. Attracting candidates for managerial positions in order to meet the objectives of the enterprise.

Recruitment Practices. Attempts to attract qualified, diverse employees at all levels.

Recycling. The process by which waste products are remanufactured to produce new products. Re-melting old bottles to produce new bottles is an example.

Red Circle Rate. It is a job whose current occupant's pay is out of grade or range.

Red Herring. Preliminary prospectus distributed to prospective investors in a new issue of securities.

Red Herring Proxy. A preliminary version of the prospectus describing a new security issue distributed to potential buyers prior to the security's registration.

Redemption. When a closed-end fund completes its tenure, it is said to be due for redemption. Units are then redeemed at the existing NAV, and investors are refunded their money. As the redemption date nears the discount to the NAV generally tends to reduce.

Redemption Value. The value which a bondholder/ debenture holder will get on maturity is called redemption value. A bond/debenture may be redeemed at par or at premium (more than par value) or at discount (less than par value).

Rediscount Rate. The rate at which the Federal Reserve will discount paper for commercial banks who are member banks.

Redlining. It is the improper practice of some financial institutions to refuse to make home-improvement loans or mortgages in a financially stressed area. The practice is called redlining.

Re-engineering. It aims to root-out needless work and get every process in the company pointed in the direction of customer satisfaction reduced cycle time and total quality.

Reference Group. A group used as a basis for comparison in making decisions or forming opinions.

Reference Price. The price that buyers use to compare the offered price of a product or service. The reference price may be a price in a buyer's memory or the price of an alternative product.

Referent Power. Personal power that results when one person identifies with and admires another.

Reflex Rally. It is a price correction from an oversold position. The Security's price moves up, but does not change the price's established trend.

Refreezing. (1) Stage in Lewin's change model in which change is reinforced as part of a new system. (2) The phase in which the organization is stabilized at a new state of behavioral equilibrium.

Refugee. A person who becomes an entrepreneur to escape an undesirable situation.

Refund. A return of the amount paid for an item.

Regional Economic Integration. Agreements among countries in a geographic region to reduce and ultimately remove tariff and no tariff barriers to the free flow of goods, services and factors of production between each other.

Regional or Super Regional Bank. A bank that engage in a complete array of wholesale commercial banking activities.

Regional Shopping Center. A large shopping center with from 50 to 100 or more stores.

Registered Bond. A bond that is registered to the owner.

Registered Form. The registrar of company records who owns each bond and bond payments are made directly to the owner of record.

Registration Statement. Statement filed with SEC that discloses all material information concerning the corporation making a public offering.

Regression. A statistical method showing relationships among variables.

Regression Analysis. The measurement of the average amount of change in one variable that is associated with unit increase in the mount of one or more other variables.

Regression Method of Forecasting. A forecast method involving the use of a regression equation; usually determined by the method of least squares.

Regression Toward the Mean. The tendency of an extraordinary event to be followed by a more ordinary event.

Regular Cash Dividend. Cash payment made by a firm to its owners in the normal course of business, usually four times a year.

Regular Forbearance. A policy not to close economically insolvent FIs, allowing them to continue in operation.

Regulation. Restricted the maximum interest rate that banks could pay on savings and time deposits.

Regulation A. SEC regulation that exempts public issues less than $ 1.5 million from most registration requirements.

Regulation Q Ceils. An interest ceiling imposed on small savings and time deposits at banks and thrifts until 1986.

Rehabilitative Care, Ordered by a Physician. This level of care is performed under the supervision of skilled medical personnel.

Re-importation. Gray marketer buys the product in a country where the product is sold but not manufactured and sells it back to the country where the product is manufactured.

Reinforcement Theory. A process which assumes that behavior may be reinforced by relating it to its consequences.

Reinstatement. The right of a life insurance policyholder to return a lapsed contract (*see* Lapse) to its original terms. Reinstatement must occur with in the specified time limits provided in the policy. Reinstatement requires evidence of insurability and payment of all policy financial obligations, such as outstanding loan balances and missed premiums payment.

Reinstatement Clause. Contractual provision in a life insurance policy that permits the owner to reinstate a lapsed policy within five years if certain requirements are fulfilled. For example, evidence of insurability is required and overdue premiums plus interest must be paid.

Reinsurance. The shifting of part or all of the insurance originally written by one insurer to another insurer.

Reinsurance Facility. Pool for placing high-risk automobile drivers that arranges an insurer to accept all applicants for insurance. Underwriting losses are shared by all automobile insurers in the state.

Reinvested Earnings. *See* Retained income.

Reinvestment. The use of retained earnings to replace depreciated assets or to add to the existing stock of capital.

Reinvestment Assumption. The cash flows generated by the project can be reinvested at its internal rate of return or at the opportunity cost of capital.

Reinvestment Rate. The interest rate a lessor earns on lease during the period following the investment period of a lease.

REIT. A Real Estate Investment Trust, a closed-end investment company that specializes in investing in mortgages, property, or real estate company shares.

Related Diversification. A firm's acquisition of a business that has some connection with the company's existing business.

Related Parties. In leasing transactions under FAS 13, a parent and its subsidiaries, an owner and its joint ventures, provided the parent or investor has the ability to exercise significant influence over the financial and operating policies of the related party. Under the internal revenue code, 50 per cent ownership is a general test of related party.

Relationship Enterprises. Networks of strategic alliances among big companies, spanning different industries and countries.

Relationship Oriented Behaviors. Behaviors such as considerate, supportive, and helpful to employees by showing trust and confidence, listening to employees problems and suggestions, showing appreciation for contribution and supporting employees' concern.

Relative-value Schedule. Variation of the schedule approach in which units or points are assigned to each surgical operation on the basis of degree of difficulty and a conversion factor is used to convert the relative value into a dollar amount paid to the surgeon.

Relative Cash Flows. The incremental cash-flows found out by comparison between two real alternatives can be called relative cash-flows.

Relaxation Response. State of peacefulness.

Relevant Data for Decision Making. Expected future data that will differ among alternatives.

Relevant Information. *See* Relevant data for decision-making.

Relevant Norms. Norms that are important but not as critical as the pivotal norms.

Relevant Price Range. The price that is neither above what current customers will pay nor bellow these levels; also, the price range that is not bellow the level where the business owner can sale at a profit.

Relevant Range. The band of activity in which budgeted sales and expense relationships will be valid.

Reliability. The consistency of a test in measuring job performance ability.

Religion. A system of shared beliefs and rituals concerned with the realm of the sacred.

Renegotiations. A process by which international companies and government decide on a change in terms for operations.

Renewable Term Life Insurance. A policy that the insured can renew without presenting evidence of insurability.

Re-order Point. The re-order point is that inventory level at which an order should be placed to replenish the inventory.

Reorganization. Financial restructuring of a failing firm to attempt to continue operations as a going concern.

Repatriation. An expatriate's return to his or her home country.

Repetitive Manufacturing. A type of manufacturing operation in which long production runs are used to produce a large quantity of a standardized product.

Replacement Cost. Cost to replenish a given amount of an asset.

Replacement Ratio. The ratio of retirement to preretirement income.

Replacement Value Technique. Determination of the value of a business based on the cost of replacing the firm's assets.

Replacement Value. Replacement value is the amount that a company would be required to spend if it were to replace its existing assets in the current condition.

Replacement-cost Insurance. A property insurance policy in which the insured provides payment for the replacement cost of the insured property rather than the actual cash value. Typical requirement causes the insured to actually replace the damaged property to receive this amount.

Report of Board of Directors. Directors' report provides a summary of profits made and appointed by the company and other relevant information such as industrial relations, investments, financing, reorganization and appointment of auditors and directors, etc.

Report of Condition. Balance sheet of a commercial bank reporting information at a single point in time.

Report of Income. Income statement of a commercial bank reporting revenues, expenses, net profit or loss, and cash dividends over a period of time.

Reporting for. Coverage for commercial property insurance that requires the insured to report monthly or quarterly the value of the insured inventory with automatic adjustment of insurance amount to cover the accurately reported inventory.

Representation. A statement made by an applicant in an insurance application. The insurer relies on the truth of the applicant's representations in underwriting the policy. A material misrepresentation generally allows the insurer to avoid the contract.

Representative Democracy. A type of government in which individual citizen elect representative to make decisions governing the society.

Representative Full-bodied Money. Gold certificates, money that is backed 100% by a commodity.

Representative Group. A group consisting of members from each of the interdependent units who meet to coordinate their activities.

Repurchase Agreement. An agreement between two parties under which one party agrees to sell a security and to buy it back on an agreed-upon date and at an agreed-upon price. The difference between the original sale price and the subsequent repurchase price is in effect the interest on a loan which when expressed as an interest rate, is commonly known as the 'repo' rate.

Repurchase of Stock. Device to pay cash to firm's shareholders that provides more preferable tax treatment for shareholders than dividends. Treasury stock to the name given to previously issued stock that has been repurchased by the firm. A repurchase is achieved through either a Dutch auction open market, or tender offer.

Repurchase. *See* Repurchase of stock.

Required Rate of Return. Minimum desired rate of return.

Required Reserves. The dollar amounts based on reserve ratios that banks are required to keep on deposit at a Federal Reserve Bank.

Required Return. The minimum expected return one would require to be willing to purchase the asset that is to make the investment.

Required Yield. Generally referring to bonds, the yield required by the market place to match the available returns for financial instruments with comparable risk.

Res Ipsa Loquitur. Literally, the thing speaks for itself. Under this doctrine, the very fact that the event occurred establishes a presumption of negligence on behalf of the defendant.

Research and Development Limited Partnership. A partnership allowed through legislation to be created by contract among unusual companies and organizations, such as private and public corporations, individuals, universities and government agencies to pursue research and development activities.

Research Development and Design. Developmental research leading to the design of the product. Also it is a part of business plan.

Reservation of Rights. Notice from the insurer to the insured that the insurer is not certain of coverage that exists, but plans to proceed with the loss adjustment and perhaps the legal defense as if the coverage exists. When certain events occur in the future causing the insurer to reevaluate its position.

Reservation Price. The highest price a buyer is willing to pay for a product manufactured.

Reserve. It has one of three meanings: (1) a restriction of dividend-declaring power as denoted by a specific subdivision of retained income; (2) an offset to an asset and (3) an estimate of a definite liability of indefinite or uncertain amount.

Reserve Agent. It is trust company designated by a State bank department or a national bank located in a central reserve city, which with the approval of the comptroller of the currency, could act as a reserve depository for a portion of the legal reserve requirements of bank.

Reserve Annuity Mortgage. A mortgage for which borrower receives regular monthly payments from a financial withdrawals. Measured as the sum of non-interest-bearing demand deposits and interest-bearing checking accounts.

Reserve Computation Period. Period over which required reserves are calculated.

Reserve Culture Shock. The encountering of culture shock when returning to one's own country having accepted what was encountered abroad.

Reserve Currency. A foreign currency held by Central bank for the purpose of exchange, intervention and settlement of inter-governmental claims.

Reserve Maintenance Period. Period over which deposits at the Federal Reserve Bank should meet or exceed the required reserve target.

Reserve Ratios. Specified percentages of deposits, established by the Federal Reserve Bank, that banks must keep in a non-interest bearing account at one of the 12 Federal Reserve Banks.

Reserve Requirements. The percentage of different types of deposits that member banks are required to hold on deposit.

Reserves and Surplus. *See* Reserve.

Residuals. Parts of stock returns not explained by the explanatory variable (the market index return). They measure the impact of firm-specific events during a particular period.

Residual Assets. Assets that remain after sufficient assets are dedicated to meet all senior debt holders' claims in full.

Residual Claim. Related to equity claim.

Residual Disability. Residual disability means that a proportionate disability-income benefit is paid to the insured whose earned income is reduced because of an accident or illness.

Residual Dividend Approach. An approach that suggests a firm to pay dividends if and only if acceptable investment opportunities for those funds which are currently not available.

Residual Dividend Policy. A dividend policy involving the payment of cash dividends equal to those earnings which the firm cannot reinvest at or above the required rate of return.

Residual Income (RI). The net income of a profit centre, less the imputed interest on the net assets used by the centre.

Residual Insurance. An insurance policy guaranteeing a certain residual value at the end of lease term.

Residual Interest. The owners' equity in the entity's assets after deducting liabilities and any other claims with a higher priority.

Residual Level. A price level above which it is supposedly difficult for a security or market to rise.

Residual Losses. Lost wealth of the shareholders due to divergent behaviour of the managers.

Residual Market. The residual market refers to plans in which automobile insurers participate to make insurance available to high-risk drivers who are unable to obtain coverage in the standard markets. Examples include an automobile insurance plan, joint underwriting association and reinsurance facility. Also called the shared market.

Residual Method. A method allocating the purchase price for the acquisition of another firm among the acquired assets.

Residual Option. An option to renew the lease at the end of the initial lease term. Here, care must be taken in granting a renewal option for a fair rental value. If this is not done properly, it may later be ruled that the lease is not a true lease—indemnity clauses activated.

Residual Value. The predicted disposal value of a long-lived asset.

Resistance to Change. Emotional/behavioral response to real or imagined work changes.

Resources. Anything a nation uses to produce economic goods and services, minerals, labour, etc.

Resource Allocation. The division of authorized resources among the various units under one's command.

Resource Scarcity. A condition in which too little of the desired resources are available to meet everyone's objectives.

Resource-based View of the Firm. A perspective that holds where each company has a unique combination of competencies.

Respondent Behavior. Skinner's term for fun learned stimulus-response reflexes.

Responsibility. The obligation owed by subordinates to their superiors for exercising authority delegated to them in a way to accomplish results expected.

Responsibility Accounting. A system of accounting that recognizes various responsibility centers through-out the organization and reflects the plans and actions of each of these by allocating particular revenues and costs to those having the pertinent responsibilities. Also called profitability accounting and activity accounting.

Responsibility Budget. The responsibility budget specifies plan in terms of individual responsibilities.

Rest. A title given to the surplus account that appears in the published statement of the Bank of England elsewhere in the English bank accounting, this account is called 'Reserve fund'.

Rest Frequency. The frequency with which the floating rate changes.

Restraint of Trade. Actions by business firms that tend to lessen or eliminate competition.

Restrictive Covenants. Provisions that place constraints on the operations of borrowers, such as restrictions on working capital, fixed assets, future borrowings and payment of dividend.

Results Style. Interested in hearing the bottom line or result of a message.

Retail. Individual and institutional customers as opposed to dealers and brokers.

Retail CDs. Time deposits with a face value below $100,000.

Retail Credit. Credit granted by a firm to consumers for the purchase of goods or services.

Retail Inventory Valuation Method. An inventory valuation method approved by the internal revenue service for income tax purpose.

Retailer. A store that sells directly to consumer.

Retained Earnings. That part of a company's post-tax earnings not distributed to the shareholders and thus retained by the firm to finance the day-to-day running of the company and any future expansion. Retained earnings are added to reserves and hence appear on the firm's balance sheet.

Retained Income. Additional owners' equity generated by profits.

Retained Limit. Term found in an umbrella policy (also known as self-insured retention). If the loss is covered by the umbrella policy but not by any underlying contract, the insured must retain or pay a certain amount of the loss.

Retention. The amount of insurance kept by the primary insurer in a reinsurance arrangement.

Retention Rate. Addition to retained earnings divided by the net income.

Retrieval. Stage of the perception process that consists of recalling information about past events.

Retroactive Date. In a claims-made liability policy, the retroactive date determines the first point in time where a covered loss may occur. The retroactive date is subject to change or negotiation.

Retrocession. The purchase of reinsurance by a reinsure.

Retrospective Rating. Type of merit-rating method in which the insured's loss experience during the current policy period determines the actual premium paid for that period.

Retrospective Reserve. In life insurance the net premiums collected by the insurer for a particular block of policies, plus interest earnings at an assumed rate less the amounts paid out as death claims.

Return on Capital. Measure of how well a company's capital is used, equal to 100 times the trading profit (before tax and interest) divided by the average capital used.

Return on Capital Employed. The ratio of accounting profit to capital employed.

Return on Equity (ROE). The amount of profit a firm makes for each dollar it invests. It is an indicator of profitability determined by dividing net income for the past 12 months by common stockholders' equity (adjusted for stock splits). Result is shown as a percentage. Investors use ROE as a measure of how a company is using its money. ROE may be decomposed into return on assets (ROA) multiplied by financial leverage (total assets/total equity).

Return on Investment (ROI). The amount of profit, sometimes measured before and sometimes after the payment of taxes divided by the amount of investment. The yield, the interest rate earned by the lessor in a lease which is measured by the rate which the excess cashflows permit recovery of investment. The rate at which the cashflows not needed for debt service or payment of taxes amortize the investment of the equity participant.

Return on Stockholders' Equity. The rate of return on the invested capital of the shareholders.

Return on Total Assets. A measure of profits in relation to total investment.

Return-on-investment Control. A control technique designed to measure a division or other part of a business enterprise by looking at the profit made as a percentage of the investment in assets in that entity.

Revaluation. A formal change in an exchange rate by which the foreign-currency value of the reference currency rises resulting in strengthening of the reference currency.

Revaluation Equity. The portion of stockholders' equity that shows all accumulated gains not otherwise shown in retained income.

Revenue Conversion. Trading strategy that locks in arbitrage profit by selling short an asset, writing a put and buying a call on the asset with the same terms.

Revenues. Generally, a gross increase in net assets from delivering goods or services. More specifically, revenues are inflows or other enhancements of assets of an enterprise or settlements of its liabilities (or a combination of both) during a period from delivering or producing goods, rendering services or other activities that constitute the enterprise's ongoing major or central operations.

Reverse Discrimination. It may exist when a person is denied an opportunity because of preferences given to protected-group individuals who may be less qualified.

Reverse Split. Stock split under which a firm's number of shares outstanding is reduced.

Revocable Beneficiary. Beneficiary designation allowing the policy owner the right to change the beneficiary without consent of the beneficiary.

Revocable Letter of Credit. A letter of credit that can be changed by any of the parties involved.

Revolving Charge. A charge the customer must make monthly minimum payment on but does not have to pay the bill (unless the amount is less than the minimum payment).

Revolving Charge Account. A loan of credit on which the customer may charge purchases at any time, up to a pre-established limit.

Revolving Credit Agreement. A legal commitment by a bank to lend up to a maximum amount.

Reward Equality Norm. Rewards should be tied to the contributions.

Reward Power. Organizational power that stems from a person's ability to bestow rewards.

Reward System. Mechanisms for defining desired behaviors, evaluating performance and rewarding good performance.

RHO. A measure of the change in an option premium with respect to a percentage-point change in the interest rate.

RI. Symbol for residual income.

Rider. Extra insurance protection not provided by the standard policy.

Right (Human). A concept used in ethical reasoning which means that a person or group is entitled to something or is entitled to be treated in a certain way.

Right of Privacy. A person's expectation of protection from organizational invasion of one's private life and unauthorized release of confidential information about the person.

Right of Rescission. The right of the customer to cancel an installment contract.

It must be exercised within three business days following the sale date or buy date required for such disclosures to be made, whichever is later.

Right to Work. Laws passed by individual states to permit workers the right to work without having to join a union.

Rights Issue. Rights issues are the shares issued to existing shareholders of a company at a subscription price that may be different from the current share price.

Rights Offer. *See* Rights issue.

Right-wing Totalitarianism. A political system in which political power is monopolized by a party, group or individual that generally permits individual economic freedom but restricts individual political freedom, including free speech, often on the grounds that it would lead to the rise of communism.

Rio Declaration. The result of the Rio Earth summit which sets out fundamental principles of environmentally responsive behaviour.

Rio Earth Summit. A meeting held in Rio de Janeiro in June 1992 that brought together people from around the world to discuss major environmental issues.

Risk. The condition of not knowing the outcome of an activity or decision. Nevertheless, risk is capable of being evaluated for relative probabilities. Uncertainty concerning the occurrence of a loss.

Risk Adjusted Discount Rate. The discount rate used to time-adjust a stream of risky cash flows to determine the present value of the stream. The risk rate of interest plus the risk premium appropriate to the level of risk associated with the investment.

Risk Analysis. An approach to problem analysis which weighs risk in a situation by introducing probabilities to give a more accurate assessment of the risks involved.

Risk Averse. Having a dislike of risk. Investors who are risk-averse will value a probability distribution of the return on an investment at less than the expected value of the distribution.

Risk Aversion Bias. A preference for sure outcomes over risky ones.

Risk Avoidance. Preventing risk by choosing not to engage in hazardous activities.

Risk Based Capital. Under new NAIC standards, life and health issuers are graded basing on capital they have to support the friskiness of their investments and operations.

Risk Control. Minimizing potential losses by avoiding or reducing risk.

Risk Financing. Making funds available to cover loss that could not be managed by risk control.

Risk Free Security. It is one which has a zero variance or standard deviation. It will have the same return under all possible economic scenarios.

Risk Management. The process of identifying, evaluating risk, selecting and managing techniques to adapt to risk exposures.

Risk Premium. The portion of the required rate of return on an investment necessary to compensate the investor for the risk assumed in making the investment.

Risk Propensity. A person's willingness to take risks while making decisions.

Risk Reduction. Lessening the frequency, severity or unpredictability of losses.

Risk Retention. Choosing—whether consciously or unconsciously, voluntarily or involuntarily—to manage risk internally.

Risk Taking. The willingness to undertake action without knowing what the result will be.

Risk Transfer. Buying insurance or making contractual arrangements with others in order to transfer risk.

Risk-adjusted Return. Return earned on an asset normalized for the amount of risk associated with the asset.

Risk-free Asset. An asset whose future return is known today with certainity.

Risk-free Rate. The rate earned on riskless asset.

Risky Asset. An asset whose future return is uncertain.

Rites and Rituals. The ceremonies incorporating forms of cultural expression such as recounting legends.

Robbery. The stealing or taking of any thing by force or violence or use of fear.

Robinson-Pitman Act (1936). An amendment to the Clayton Act that prohibits price discrimination where the effect 'may be substantially to lessen competition or create a monopoly'. It prohibits payments of broker's commission where an independent broker is not employed; forbids sellers to provide allowances or services to buyers unless these are available to all buyers on 'equally proportional terms'; and also prohibits a buyer from inducing or receiving a prohibited discrimination in price.

Robot. Any automatic machine that performs work without the direct intervention of a human being.

ROI. *See* Return on investment.

Role. A description of the expected behavior of a specific group member.

Role Ambiguity. Others expectations are unknown.

Role Negotiation. The structuring of interactions between interdependent persons or groups to clarify and negotiate role behaviors and expectations.

Role Overload. Others' expectations exceed one's ability.

Roles. Expected behaviors for a given position.

Roll Over. Most term loans in the Euro-market are made on a roll over basis, which means that the loan is periodically re-priced at an agreed spread over the appropriate, currently prevailing LIBOR rate. Reinvest funds received from a maturing security in a new issue of the same or a similar security.

Rolling Settlement. Prior to July 18, 1994, purchases and sales of securities were combined during an accounting period (normally ten working days) to arrive at a net settlement figure which was due for payment on the second Monday following that account period. After July 18, 1994, rolling settlement was introduced which initially commenced on a ten-day basis (known as T + 10) whereby settlement was due ten days after the deal so as to reduce the settlement periods and generally speed up transactions. Thus rolling settlement is one in which trades outstanding at the end of the day have to be settled (payments made for purchases or deliveries in the case of sale of securities) at the end of the settlement period.

Roll-up Fund. Offshore investments that reinvest interest so that it becomes a part of the capital thus conferring tax advantages.

Room Trader. A stock exchange member who does not maintain a commission house for the execution of customers orders, but who trades solely for his own account. He is a speculator who takes out an exchange membership in order to save the commission charges on his voluminous transactions and to have the privilege of trading on the floor of the exchange to take advantage of the price fluctuations as they occur.

Round Lot. A trading order typically of 100 shares of a stock or some multiple of 100 related odd lot.

Round Turn. It is a complete trading transaction, *i.e.* the sale of a security or a commodity previously purchased. Thus it is a procedure by which the long or short position of an individual to offset by an opposite transaction or by accepting or making delivery of the actual financial instrument or physical commodity.

Rounds. Conference held by GATT to establish multilateral agreements to liberalize trade.

Round-trip Transactions Costs. Costs of completing a transaction, including commissions, market impact costs and taxes.

Routing. The sequence of operations through which a product should pass.

Royalties. Payments for the use of intangible assets abroad.

Rubber Cheque. A cheque that has bounced for insufficient balance in the issuer's account.

Rule of Cost. The idea that all human actions generate costs.

Rule of Reason. A basis for determining the legality of business practices using relevant evidence.

Rules. They are specific guidelines that regulate and restrict the behaviour of individuals.

Running Margins. Difference in the rates of interest on money borrowed and on the same money invested.

S

S Corporation. A corporation where by the tax code allows earnings to be taxed as partnership income to stockholders for avoiding the double taxation on dividends.

Sacrifice. The sum of all costs that customers incur to acquire and use a product or service.

SADC. *See* Southern African Development Community.

Safe Driver Plan. Plan in which the automobile premiums paid are based on the insured's driving record and on the records of those living with the insured.

Safe Harbour Lease. A lease to transfer tax benefits of ownership (depreciation and debt tax shield) from the lessee, if the lessee could not use them, to lessor who could use them.

Safe Harbour Provisions. The provisions in the U.S. Economic Recovery Tax Act (1981) defining the basic criteria under which a financing transaction could meet the definition of a lease for which purpose the rules represent a considerable liberalization of former IRS guidelines on true and allowed pure tax benefits transfer.

Safe Keep. For a fee, bankers will hold in their vault dip coupons on and present for payment at maturity bonds and money market instruments.

Safety. Refers to protection of the physical health of people.

Safety Cushion. In a contingent immunization strategy, difference between the initially available immunization level and safety-net return.

Safety Stock. A minimum inventory that provides a cushion against variations in lead time.

Salary. Payments made to workers on a weekly, bi-weekly or monthly basis.

Sale and Lease Back. Sale of an existing asset to a financial institution which then leases it back to the user. Sometimes, a user may sell an asset earned by him to the lessor (leasing company) and takes it back for lease from him. Thus it is a transaction which involves the sale of the property by the owner and a lease of the property back to the seller.

Sale-lease Back. A transaction which involves sale of property by the owner and lease of the property back to the seller.

Sale-repurchase Spread. Difference between the sale and repurchase price expressed as a percentage of the net asset value. The spread indicates the load that the investor has to bear for investing in an open-ended scheme.

Sales and Cash Receipts Journal. A record of the daily income to the business.

Sales and Purchase Load. It indicates the premium discount to the NAV at which the investor can enter or exit the scheme.

Sales Budget. The primary budget for small business. It serves as the basis for all other budgets.

Sales Charge. The fee charged by a mutual fund when purchasing shares, usually payable as a commission to marketing agent, such as financial advisor, who is thus compensated for his assistance to a purchaser. It represents the difference, if any between the share purchase price and the share net asset value.

Sales Discount. A discount given to induce prompt payment.

Sales Finance Companies. Financial companies that purchase instalment contracts from retailers.

Sales Forecast. A prediction of how a product or service will be purchased within a market during a specified time period. Perhaps the most critical element in business plan, it is the prediction of future sales expressed by units (or measurable volume) and by dollars value of revenue. A key input to a firm's financial planning process. External sales forecasts are based on historical experience, statistical analysis and consideration of various macro economic factors. Thus it is an estimation of future period's sales.

Sales Mix. Relative combination of the quantities of a variety of company products that compose total sales.

Sales Promotion. Marketing activities other than personal selling, advertising and publicity that stimulate consumer purchasing and dealer effectiveness, such as displays, shows, exhibits and other non-recurring selling efforts.

Sales Representative (Foreign). A representative that usually operates either exclusively or nonexclusively within an assigned market and on a commission basis, without assuming risk or responsibility.

Sales Response Function. The amount of sales created at different levels of marketing expenditure.

Sales Volume Variance. Difference between the flexible budget amount and the static budget amount.

Sales-aid Lease. A form of lease to encourage business by offering the customer a package deal including lease facilities known in the US as a vendor lease.

Sales-type Lease. An arrangement whereby a firm leases its own equipment (such as IBM leasing its own computers) thereby competing an independent leasing company.

Salvage. The amount recovered from the sale of damaged property by force or threat of force.

Salvage Value. The minimum value for a depreciable asset. After sufficient depreciation is taken such that the cost minus accumulated depreciation equals salvage value and no more depreciation is taken. Not the same as residual value.

Sample. A small part of a whole intended to show the quality or style of the whole.

Sample Survey. Questionnaire responses from a sample of people.

Samurai Bond. A yen denominated bond issued in Tokyo by a non-Japanese borrower related, bull-dog bond and Yankee bond.

Samurai Lease. Japanese source lease design of fund foreign assets in order to reduce the Japanese balance of payments.

Samurai Market. The foreign market in Japan.

Satisfying. A term used by Herbert A. Simon to denote the tendencies of managers, normally instances of bounded rationality, in making decisions to pick a course of action that is deemed 'good enough' under the circumstances. *See* Bounded rationality.

Saving and Loan Association. A depository institution originally designed as a mutual association of depositors designed to convert funds from savings accounts into mortgage loans.

Savings Bank Life Insurance. Life insurance sold over the counter in mutual savings banks to residents of Massachusetts, New York and Connecticut.

SBC. Strategic Business Center.

SBIC. Small Business Investment Company.

Scalar Chain. The principle of organizing whereby authority should flow through the organization from the top down, one level at a time.

Scalar Relationships. Authority relationships are said to be scalar when subordinates report to their immediate superiors and when their superiors report directly (as subordinates) to their superiors. In other words, the chain of command that runs from the top of an organization to its lowest ranks.

Scale. A bank that offers to pay different rates of interest on CDs of varying rates is said to be 'post a scale'. Order to buy or sell one or more lots in future at designated price intervals and contingent grouped orders entered.

Scale Enhancing. Describes a project that is in the same risk class as the whole firm.

Scale In. When a trader or investor gradually takes position in a security or market overtime.

Scalp. To trade for small gains, it normally involves establishing and liquidating a position quickly, usually within the same day.

Scarce Environment. An environment wherein money is tight, the market is stagnant or declining or stakeholder groups are making conflicting or difficult demands.

Scatter Diagram Method of Forecasting. A technique of financial forecasting that involves plotting the variable to be forecasted against the predicted variable, visually fitting a line to the scatter of points and then extrapolating the relationship to make predictions.

Scatter Diagrams. Illustrations allowing management to valuate the relationship between two variables using one variable to make a prediction about another variable or characteristic.

Scenario Analysis. The use of horizontal analysis to project bond total return under different reinvestment rates and future market yields.

Scenario Technique. Speculative forecasting method.

Schedule Rating. An approach to property insurance rate making in which the specific characteristics of the covered property are compared to standard and charges are applied for above or below standard features when developing a final rate.

Scheduled Cash Flows. The mortgage, principal and interest payments due to be paid under the terms of the mortgage not including possible pre-payments.

Scheduled Personal Property Endorsement. Special coverage added at the insured's request to a homeowners policy to insure items specifically listed. Used to insure valuable property such as jewelry, furs and paintings.

Scheduled Property. The specifically identified property (such as cameras or jewelry) in an inland marine personal property floater or other policy requiring a listing of property.

Scheduling. The assigning of work to be done to departments or to specific machines or persons.

Schema. Mental picture of an event or object.

Science. Organized knowledge of pertinence to an area, usually an area of practice.

Scientific Management. A theory within the classical approach that focuses on improvement of operational efficiencies through the systematic and scientific study of work methods, tools and (performance) standards. A term originally used as denoting the work and approach of F.W. Taylor and his associates in analyzing management. It implies that the methods of scientific inquiry, analysis and summary can be applied to the activities of managers. It implied time study and similar methods used by Taylor and his followers to analyze activities of people in organizations. Basically, it sought to develop: (1) ways of increasing productivity by making work easier to perform and (2) methods for motivating people to take advantage of labour-saving techniques it developed. It may be summarized as: (1) replacing rules of thumb with rules of science, (2) achieving cooperation rather than chaotic individualism, (3) obtaining harmony rather than discord, (4) working for maximum rather than restricted output and (5) developing workers to the fullest extent possible.

Scientific Method. A logical approach to problem solving. It involves the following franchisers to make full presales disclosure nationwide.

Scorched Earth. The term refers to the defensive tactics for a hostile takeover bid in which the target company sells its most attractive assets or initiates adverse publicity about itself in an effort to make it less than desirable acquisition.

Scorekeeping. A data accumulation function of the accountant's information-supplying task which enables both internal and external parties to evaluate the financial performance of the firm.

S-Corporation. Also called Subchapter S: A form of incorporation that allows income and expenses to flow through to stockholders in a fashion similar to general partnership. However, it is limited to certain private placement rules for stockholders and can have no more than 35 individuals.

SCRA (Securities Contract Regulation Act).

Scrap Value. *See* Residual value.

Screen Based Trading. When buying or selling of securities is done using computers and matching of trade is done by a stock exchange computer.

Screening Control. A form of control that regulates operations to ensure that they are consistent with objectives, also called yes/no or concurrent control.

SDRs. *See* Special drawing rights.

Search Attributes. Product attributes that can be readily evaluated before purchase.

Search Costs. Costs associated with locating a counter party to a trade, including explicit costs (such as advertising) and implicit costs (such as the value of time) related, information costs.

Search Products and Services. Products with purchase-determining attributes that buyers can readily evaluate before purchase.

Seasonal Credit. Loans made to depository institutions facing strong seasonal variations in deposits and loans such as banks in agricultural areas.

Seasonal Dating. Tailoring the credit period offered to customers, whose business is seasonal, to fit their ability to pay.

Seasonal Variation. Regular, recurring fluctuations confined to a one-year time period.

Seasoned Dating. Extended credit for customers who order goods in periods other than peak seasons.

Seasoned Issue. Issue of a security for which there is market.

Seasoned New Issue. A new equity issue of securities by a company that has previously issued securities to the public.

Seat. The membership on a stock exchange.

SEC. Securities and Exchange Commission, the primary federal regulatory agency of the securities industry.

Second Level Communication. It is a measure of customer sensitivity. Customer goes to higher level with his complaint when lower level person rejects it. This is called second level communication. The more the company is customer sensitive the less such complaints at higher level.

Second-order Condition. A test to determine whether a point that has been determined from the first-order condition is either a maximum point or a minimum point.

Second Pass Regression. A cross-sectional regression of portfolio returns on betas. The estimated slope is the measurement of the reward for bearing systematic risk during the period analyzed.

Secondary Boycott. The boycotting of a company that does business with a company being boycotted.

Secondary Characteristics of Diversity. Characteristics, such as work background, material status, and education, that can be changed.

Secondary Data. Market information that has been previously compiled.

Secondary Dimensions of Diversity. Personal characteristics that people acquire, discard and/or modify throughout their lives.

Secondary Interactions or Involvement. The relationship a company has with those social and political groups that feel the impact of the company's main activities and take steps to do something about it. These relationships are derived from the firm's primary interactions.

Secondary Issue. Procedure for selling blocks of seasoned issues of stocks. More generally, sale of already issued stock.

Secondary Market. The market where existing financial assets are bought and sold.

Secondary Needs. Human needs that are behaviour based, such as ego and recognition needs.

Secondary Period. Frequently optional, the period in a finance lease which follows the full pay-out of the lessor's investment plus profit.

Secondary Source of Data. Data republished by an agency other than the original collector and publisher.

Secondary Stakeholders. Groups which have a less formal connection to the organization, such as environmentalists community activists and the media.

Second-injury Fund. State funds paying the excess amount of benefit awarded an employee for a second injury if the disability is greater than that caused by the second injury if the disability is greater than that caused by the second injury alone. Its purpose is to encourage employers to hire handicapped workers.

Second-level-communication. Communication that customers make only when their first attempt to gain satisfaction proves fruitless.

Second-tier Subsidiaries. Subsidiaries that report to a tax heaven subsidiary.

Secrecy. A characteristic of an accounting system which implies that companies do not disclose much information about accounting practices.

Secret Partner. A partner who assumes an active role in the business but is not known to the public as a partner.

Section 1244 Stock. Stock that offers some tax benefits to the stockholders in case of corporate failure.

Section 401 (k) Plan. A qualified profit-sharing or thrift plan that allows participants the option of putting money into the plan or receiving the funds as cash. The employee can voluntarily elect to have his or her salary reduced up to some maximum limit, which is then invested in the employer's section 401 (k) plan.

Section 482. The U.S. department of treasury regulations governing transfer prices.

Sector Fund. Such fund invests only in stocks belonging to a specific industry. Sector funds usually aim for growth and while this can be very lucrative if the sector is doing well. The corresponding risk is also higher. Sector funds are generally considered to be among those at the greatest risk among equity funds.

Secular Totalitarianism. A dictatorship not affiliated with any religious group or system of beliefs.

Secular Trend. Long-term growth or decay.

Secular Trust. A trust agreement applied to funds held to finance a nonqualified retirement benefit to a favored employee. A secular trust is owned by the employee.

Secured Debt. Debt that in the event of default has first claim on specified assets.

Secured Premium Notes (SPN). It is a secured debenture redeemable at a premium, *i.e.* at a price higher than the purchase (or face) price. It is a medium to long-term debenture, zero interest debenture (ZID) or zero coupon bonds that do not carry an explicit rate of interest. The difference between the face value of the bond and its purchase price is the return of the investor.

Security. Price of paper that proves ownership of stocks, bonds and other investments.

Securities Act of 1934. Main provisions of this act set up securities and Exchange Commission and gave Federal Reserve Board the authority to set margin requirements for buying stocks.

Securities Analysts. Related financial analysts.

Securities and Exchange Commission (SEC). A U.S. government agency that regulates securities brokers, dealers and markets.

Securitization. It is the process by which illiquid assets are packaged, converted into tradable securities and sold to the third party investors. Currently securitization transactions in the country cover car receivables, truck receivables, receivables from the department of telecommunications and housing loan receivables.

Security Agreement. An agreement between the owner trustee and the indenture trustee whereby the owner trustee assigns title to the equipment, the lease and rental payments under the lease as security for amounts due to the lenders. The same as an indenture of trust or mortgage.

Seed Financing. Money invested in a new venture prior to or during, start-up to underwrite operations, assets, or business development.

Segment. Any line of activity or part of an organization for which separate determination of costs and sales is wanted.

Segment Margin. The contribution margin for each segment less all separable fixed costs both discretionary and committed, a measure of long run profitability.

Segmentation Strategy. The strategy of subdividing a market into distinct subsets of customers that behave in the same way or have similar needs.

Segmented Market Hypothesis. The hypothesis that bonds with different maturates are not substitutable for one another, their yields are determined independently of one another.

Seignorage. The profit from creating money and a source of revenue to the government.

Selection. It is the process of picking individuals who have relevant qualifications to fill jobs in an organization.

Selective Buying Motives. The motives which enter into the final determination of the specific product which is purchased.

Self Concept. Person's self perception as a physical, social and spiritual being.

Self Contained Tasks. Independent work units consisting of members of previously interdependent groups.

Self Directed Work Team. An intact group of employees who are responsible for a whole work process or segment that delivers a product or service to an internal or external customer.

Self Efficacy. Belief in one's ability to do a task.

Self Esteem. One's overall self-evaluation.

Self Fulfilling Prophecy. People's expectations determine behavior and performance.

Self Insurance. Designating part of a firm's earnings as a cushion against possible future losses.

Self Managed Teams. Groups of employees granted administrative oversight for their work.

Self Management Leadership. Process of leading others to lead themselves.

Self Monitoring. Observing one's own behavior and adapting it to the situation.

Self Reinforcement. The reinforcement or punishment of one's own behavior.

Self Service Layout. A type of retail store design that gives customers direct access to merchandise.

Self Serving Bias. Taking more personal responsibility for success than failure.

Self Serving Biases. The tendency to interpret information in a way that puts the perceiver in the best light.

Self talk. Evaluating thoughts about oneself.

Self-actualization. It is the striving of an individual to reach the highest level of potential.

Self-directed Work Team. A group of employees who supervise their own work and are given broad discretion over the direction of their work.

Self-funding. It occurs when an employer sets aside funds to pay health claims in excess of the amount provided by funding agency in lieu of insurance coverage.

Self-insurance. When a firm retains enough funds to cover a specific loss.

Seller's Pricing Discretion. The difference between the direct variable costs of producing, marketing and distributing the product and the highest price that buyers are willing to pay for the product.

Sellers Costs. The costs that the seller incurs to provide the products or service to the buyer.

Selling Agent. Sells the entire output of a manufacturer and represents him on a continuous basis.

Selling Hedge. Anyone who owns a commodity in the actual market and who is considered long simply sells a contract in the futures market (that it becomes a short).

Semantic Congruency Effect. When judging which number in a pair is largest, people find the task easier when both numbers are large than when both are small. The opposite is true when people have to decide which item is smaller.

Semantics. The different uses and meanings of words, often influencing the effectiveness of a message.

Semi Strong from Market Efficiency. Asserts that no publicly available information will help predict future asset prices or returns better than the last known value of the asset.

Semiconductor Silicon Chip. A small computational device made of silicon material that is a key component of computers and other forms of electronic technology. (*See* Microprocessor.)

Sender. The person who wishes to relay or share particular information and meaning and initiates the communication process.

Senior Debt. It derives its name from its position in the hierarchy of capital structure. In a liquidation scenario, senior debt is repaid in full prior to making any payments to the subordinated debt and/or equity holders, provided the firm has a strong base of equity to which an appropriate amount of debt can be added, senior debt could be the next source of short and long-term capital.

Sensitivity Analysis. Measuring how the basic predicted results will be effected by variations in the critical data inputs that will influence those results.

Sensitivity Index. An index that measures the relationship between sales of a product and changes in disposable personal income.

Sensitivity Training. A form of training based on behavior of persons in groups and through undirected group interchange, designed to make these persons more aware of the feelings and the feelings of others towards them.

Separable Cost. A cost directly identified with a particular segment.

Separate Account. Variation of the deposit administration pension plan arrangement in which pension funds are segregated so that account assets are not commensurate with insurance company's general assets and can be invested separately.

Separate Entity Approach. A system for taxation of corporate income in which each unit is taxed when it receives income, with the result being double taxation.

Sequential Interdependence. The interdependence that exists when one group must complete certain tasks before another group can complete its tasks.

Sequestration. The term refers to the act of seizure of property or other assets by the courts until a dispute has been settled.

Serendipity. The faculty for making desirable discoveries by accident.

Servant Leadership. Articulating a vision for the organization and giving employees what they need to carry out that vision.

Servant Leadership. Focuses on increased services to others rather than to oneself.

Services. Activities which are offered for sale or are offered in connection with sale of goods.

Service Benefits. Health insurance benefits that pay hospital charges or payment for care received by the insured directly to the hospital or providers of care. The plan provides service rather than cash benefits to the insured.

Service Bureaus. Firms that use their computer systems to process data for business customers.

Service Corps of Retired Executives (SCORE). An SBA-sponsored group of retired executives who give free advice to small businesses.

Service Departments. Those departments that exist solely to aid the production departments by rendering specialized assistance with certain phases of the work.

Service Exports. International received earnings other than those derived from the exporting of tangible goods.

Service Mark. A legal term indicating the exclusive right to use a brand to identify a service.

Service Organizations. Organizations that transform inputs into intangible products.

Service Sector. The broad group of companies that provide some sort of service to customers.

Service Selling. The type of selling in which a salesperson assists a consumer in completing a purchase where the consumer has already decided to make purchase.

Service Society. A society in which the provision of services rather than the production of material goods, dominate work and employs the largest proportion of the labour force.

Services Accounts. The part of a country's current account that measures travel, transportation and tourism fees and royalties.

Settlement. It refers to the scrip-wise settlement of trades by a broker after the trading period is over.

Settlement Date. After trade has been executed, securities and money must change hands within five business days (excluding Sundays and holidays). For example, if trade is made on Wednesday, it is settled on the following Wednesday.

Settlement Guarantee. Settlement guarantee is the guarantee provided by the clearing corporation of settlement of all trades even if a party defaults to deliver securities or pay cash.

Settlement of Transaction in Non-specified Securities. Transactions in non-specified securities are for delivery, unless they are offset by opposite transaction in the course at the settlement period itself. The exchange issues delivery orders and receives orders for all transactions entered into, during the settlement period which are not offset by opposite.

Settlement Options. Ways in which life insurance policy proceeds can be paid other than in a lump sum, including interest, fixed period, fixed amount, and life income options.

Settlement Period. The stock exchanges divide the period of one year into settlement periods. The settlement period in specified shares as well as non-specified shares is generally a week.

Severance Pay. A special payment made to an employee of a firm to compensate an unexpected permanent layoff.

Sex Role Stereotype. Beliefs about appropriate roles for men and women.

Sexual Harassment. Unwelcome sexual advances and sexual conduct that must be tolerated as a condition of employment or basis for employment decisions, that unreasonably interferes with the employee's work performance or that creates a hostile working environment.

Segmentation Variables. The parameters used to distinguish one form of market behavior from another.

SEZ. Special Economic Zone.

Shadow Price. Measures the value (that is, contribution to the objective function) of one additional unit of a resource. It is equivalent to the dual variable.

Shaping. Reinforcing closer and closer approximations to a target behavior.

Shareholders Derivative Suit. A lawsuit initiated by one or more stockholders that attempts to recover damages suffered by the company due to alleged action of the company's management.

Share Split. A share split is a method to increase the number of outstanding shares through a proportional reduction in the par value of the share. A share split affects only the par value and the number of outstanding shares, however the shareholders total fund remains unaltered.

Shareholder. *See* Stock-holder.

Shareholder Proposal. A proposal made by a stockholder and included in a corporation's notice of its annual meeting that advocates some course of action to be taken by the company.

Shareholder Suit (Individual). A lawsuit initiated by one or more stockholders that attempts to recover damages they (as stockholders) personally suffered due to alleged actions of the company's management.

Shareholder Wealth. A measure of the value of a firm. Shareholders' wealth is equal to the value of a firm's common stock, which, in turn, is equal to the present value of all future cash returns expected to be generated by the firm for the benefit of its owners.

Shipper's Export Declaration. A shipping document that controls exports and is used to compile trade statistics.

Shopping Centre. A group of different kinds of stores located in a single area sharing a common parking lot and usually advertising as a group.

Shopping Goods. A goods in which price and quality comparisons are usually made before purchase. The price is usually a sizable amount and purchasing is made infrequently. This goods is also widely advertised.

Short Hedge. A future or option position to protect against a possible decrease in prices.

Short Range Plan. A plan that governs a firm's operations for one year or less.

Short Rate Table. Schedule used by insurers to refund premiums on policy cancellation. It refunds less than a pro rata amount to cover insurer's expenses in issuing and printing the policy and to offset adverse selection.

Short Selling. Selling a stock and then buying it back at a later date in order to make a profit.

Short Term Assets. Assets in debt market which mature in one year or less from the date of issue.

Short Term Investment. A temporary investment in marketable securities of idle cash.

Short Term Lease. Generally refers to an operating lease.

Short Term Liabilities. Borrowed money that must be repaid within 12 months.

Shortage. Situation where quantity demanded exceeds quantity supplied.

Short-rate Cancellation Schedule. The short-rate cancellation schedule applies when an insured cancels a property insurance policy. The short-rate are higher than pro rata cancellation rates to allow the insurer to recover the acquisition expenses and give reorganization to the potential for adverse selection. For example, the short rate may credit the insurer with earning 5 per cent of the premium after one day of coverage.

Short-run Aggregate Supply (SRAS). Characterizes the supply side of the macro economy in the short-run, *i.e.* summarizes the total quantity of goods and services that an economy will produce at various price levels holding constant such things as the prices of inputs, taxes and stock of physical capital available to firms and the level of technology.

Short-run Macroeconomic Equilibrium. The determination of equilibrium interest rate price level and level of real GDP corresponding to the inter-section of aggregate demand and short-run aggregate supply.

Short-run Performance Margin. The contribution margin for each segment less separable.

Side Effect. *See* Externally.

Sight Draft. A commercial bill of exchange that requires payment to be made as soon as it is presented to the party, obligated to pay.

Signora. The profit from creating money and a source of revenue to the government.

Silent Language. The way variety of cues other than formal language by which messages can be sent.

Silent Partners. Business partners who typically contribute money instead of being involved in day-to-day operations.

Simple Deposit Multiplier. The multiple by which deposits increase in reserves.

Simple Differentiated Structure. A flat structure in which a manager coordinates work through direct supervision.

Simple Interest. Interest earned only on the original principal amount invested.

Simple Quantity Theory of Money Demand. Views transactions as the primary motive for holding money.

Simple Random Sample. Each item in a business has an equal and known chance of being selected for the sample.

Simple Structure. A structure with few departments, arranged by function, headed by an entrepreneur/owner and with few technical support staff.

Simple Undifferentiated Structure. A structure with no departments or hierarchy.

Simplex Method. A step-by-step mathematical procedure for finding the optimal solution to a linear-programming problem.

Simplified Employee Pension (SEP). An employer-sponsored individual retirement account that meets certain requirements. Paperwork is reduced for employers who wish to cover employees in a retirement plan. Under current law, the employer can make a maximum annual tax-deductible contribution equal to 15 per cent of the employee's compensation or $30,000, whichever is lower.

Simply Fund. The clearing house has ample protection against default as a result of its original and variation margin requirements. Margin deposits, however, form only the foundation for the resources that make it possible for the clearing house to guarantee all cleared contracts for both delivery and payment. As a further safeguard and as a condition at membership a clearing member contributes to the guarantee fund at the clearing-house.

Simulation. Experimentation performed on a system model that has been designed to capture the critical realities of a decision-making situation.

Single Premium Whole Life Insurance. A single life insurance that provides lifetime protection with a single premium payment.

Single Entry System. A checkbook system of accounting reflecting only receipts and disbursements.

Single European Act. A 1987 act of the EU (then the EC) allowing all proposals except those relating to taxation workers' rights and immigration to be adopted by a weighted majority of member countries.

Single Limit. The total amount of insurance applies to the entire accident without a separate limit for each person.

Single Line Store. A store which carries a wide variety of one line of merchandise.

Single Premium Deferred Annuity. A retirement annuity that is purchased with a single premium with benefits to start at some future date.

Single Segmentation Strategy. A strategy that recognizes the existence of several distinct market segments but focuses on only the most profitable segment.

Single Step Income Statement. One that groups all revenue together and then lists and deducts all expenses together without drawing any intermediate subtotals.

Single Taxation. Under this system, shareholders' earnings are taxed only once at the corporate level. Dividends received by shareholders are exempt from tax. India currently follows this system and companies in India pay tax on their profits at 35 per cent and they will have to pay additional tax of 10 per cent on the after-tax profits distributed as dividends to shareholders. Shareholders, both individuals and corporations do not pay taxes on the dividend income. However, they do pay tax on capital gains. The marginal personal tax is 30 per cent and capital gain tax rates 20 per cent. Under this system, an investor will prefer dividends over capital gains.

Single Use Plans. Plans that are used once and then discarded.

Single-step Profit and Loss Account. It records all the revenue items first and then the expense items. The total expenditure is subtracted from the total revenue to obtain the net income or net profit.

Sinking Fund. It is a fund created out of fixed payments each period to accumulate to a future sum after a specific period.

Sinking Rate Fund. The rate of interest allocated to a sinking fund set aside for future payment of taxes (generally applicable only in leveraged leases).

Situational Approach to Leadership. The approach that studies leadership on the premise that is strongly influenced by the situation from which the leader emerges and in which he or she operates.

Situational Leadership Theory. A leadership model whose premise is that a leader's style should be contingent on a subordinates' competence and commitment.

Situational Theories. Propose that leader styles should match the situation at hand.

Sized Out. It occurs when a broker cannot cross stock at a block trader's price because another broker is offering a larger number of shares at the trader's prices, making the other broker's offer more attractive.

Skill. Specific capacity to manipulate objects.

Skilled Based Pay. Adjusting compensation levels to reflect the blocks of skills and individual acquires, rather than job titles.

Skilled-nursing Facility. Daily nursing and rehabilitative care, ordered by a physician. This level of care is performed under the supervision of skilled medical personnel.

Skimming Price Strategy. A marketing approach that sets very high prices for a limited period before reducing them to more competitive levels.

Skimming Prices. It is a strategy of putting a high initial price followed by several price drops. Skimming allows the seller to attract as many buyers as possible at the highest price before dropping the price some more, which attracts more buyers at the next level.

Slack Resources. Buffers that are created between groups to reduce sequential inter-dependence.

Slack Variable. A variable that represents the difference between the right-hand side and left-hand side of a left hand or equal to inequality constraint. It is added to the left-hand side of the inequality to convert the constraint to equality. It measures the amount of an unused or idle resource.

Slippage. Underperformance of a start-up company. Slippage may lead Sweet Equity.

Small Batch Production (SBP). A manufacturing technology that involves producing goods in small quantities tailored to customer specifications.

Small Batch Technology. The production of small numbers of goods in response to a specific customer request.

Small Business. Any business that is independently owned and operated, not dominant in its field and meets size and standards that vary based on the industry.

Small Business Administration. An agency of the federal government created to assist, encourage and protect.

Small Business Development Centers (SBDCs). University-affiliated centers offering consulting, education, and other support to small business.

Small Business Innovation Research. The primary US government agency established to assist small business ventures with direct loans, loan guarantees, consulting, market assistance, management advice and a variety of other services.

Small Business Investment Companies (SBICs). Privately owned banks, regulated by the small business administration, that supply capital to small businesses.

Small Business Investment Corporation. A company chartered by the US government specifically to help underwrite small businesses with equity and debt financing. The program is limited to companies with less than $6 million in net worth and less than $2 million in after-tax earnings averaged over the previous two years.

Small Business Marketing. Business activities that identify a target market, determine market's potential and prepare, communicate and deliver a bundle of satisfaction to the market.

Smithsonian Agreement. A 1971 agreement among countries that resulted in the devaluation of the U.S. dollar, revaluation of other world currencies a widening of exchange rate flexibility and a commitment on the part of all participating countries to reduce trade.

Smoot-Hawley Act. Enhanced in 1997, act adopted by members of the European community. The member countries formed an economic union.

Snake. It is the popular term for the European system that links the and currencies: the Belgian-French francs, the Danish kroner, the Irish punt, the Dutch guilder, the German Dutch mark and the Italian lira.

Snap Quote. The snap quote feature allows a trading member participant to get instantaneous market information as any desired security descriptor. This is normally used for descriptors that are not already as displayed in the market watch window. The information presented is same as that of market watch window.

Social Accounting. A system of record keeping that reports economic and financial activity for the whole economy and/or between the principal sectors of the economy.

Social Audit. A systematic examination of the objectives, strategies, organization, and performance of the social reasonability function.

Social Class. Divisions within a society having different level of social prestige.

Social Contract. In international business, an unwritten agreement usually derived from business discussions with government and community leaders that a firm in a host nation will serve the needs of that nation's people in a responsive manner so that mutual interests and benefits will develop from the relationship.

Social Democrats. Those committed to achieving socialism by democratic means.

Social Emotional Cohesiveness. Sense of togetherness based on emotional satisfaction.

Social Forces. The relationship of people to each other within a particular culture.

Social Forecasting. An attempt to estimate major social and political trends that may affect a company's operations and environment in the future.

Social Insurance. Government insurance programs with certain characteristics that distinguish them from other government insurance programs. Programs are generally compulsory; specific earmarked taxes fund the programs; benefits are heavily weighed in favor of low-income groups and programs are designed to achieve certain social goals.

Social Involvement. *See* Corporate social involvement.

Social Learning Theory. Theory that states most people learn how to behave by observing models.

Social Loafing. Doing less than one's share of work on the assumption that the group's results will not indicate one's failure to contribute.

Social Market Economy. An economic system in which there is heavy government spending and high taxation to pay for such social services as health care, education subsidized, housing for the poor, and unemployment benefits but the prices of products are determined by supply and demand rather than by government fiat.

Social Mobility. The extent to which individuals can move out of the social strata into which they are born.

Social Overhead Costs. Public and private investments that are necessary to prepare the environment for effective operation of a new business or another major institution.

Social Partnership. A temporary or permanent coalition of pluralistic interest groups who cooperate for the purpose of addressing or resolving some social problem.

Social Power. Ability to get things done with human, informational and material resources.

Social Regulations. Regulations intended to accomplish certain social improvements such as equal employment opportunity or on the job safety and health.

Social Report. Information about an organization's social performance, often contained in a company's annual report to stockholders and sometimes prepared as a special report to management or the general public.

Social Responsibility. The obligation a business assumes to maximize its negative impact on society.

Social Responsibility. *See* Corporate social responsibility.

Social Responsibility of Managers. The responsibility of managers, in carrying out their socially approved missions, to be responsive to, to be congruent with, to interact and live with the forces or elements of their social environment.

Social Responsiveness. The viewpoint that business social responsibility is satisfied when business pursues, profit legally, reacts in demands and acts to prevent future wrongs and problems.

Social Responsiveness. *See* Corporate social responsiveness.

Social Strata. Hierarchical social categories often based on family background.

Social Democrats. Those committed to achieving socialism by democratic means of occupation and income.

Social Structure. The basic social organization of a society.

Social Support. Amount of helpfulness derived from social relationships.

Social Support System. The circle of people who care about a person.

Socialism. A political philosophy advocating substantial public involvement, through government ownership in the means of production and distribution.

Soft Arbitrage. The term implies the movement of funds between the money markets and bank deposits to benefit from the difference in interest rates.

Socialization. The process by which an individual learns the norms, values, goals, and expectations of the organization.

Socialized Power. Directed at helping others.

Society. A broad grouping of people having common traditions, institutions and collective activities and interest; the term nation-state is often used in international business to denote a society.

Society. The people, institutions and technology that make up a recognizable human community.

Socio-cultural Dimension. The aspect of the general environment that includes the demographics and the values of the society within which an organization operates.

Socio-economic System. The combined and interrelated social, economical and political institution's characteristics of a society.

Sociology. The behavioral science that studies group behavior. It seeks general laws to explain inter-group and intra-group behavior.

Socio-technical System. A system viewed as an interconnection of physical (technical) and social elements in an organization.

Soft Arbitrage. The term implies the movement of funds between the money markets and bank deposits to benefit from the difference in interest rates.

Soft Budget. A financial condition in which an enterprise excess of expenditure over earnings is compensated for by some other institution typically a government or a state controlled financial institution.

Soft Currency. *See* Weak currency.

Soft Rationing. The situation that occurs when units in a business are allocated a certain amount of financing for capital budgeting.

Software. A computer program or set of commands that instructs a computer to perform various operations such as reading, analyzing, or storing data in a specified location.

Sogo Shosha. Japanese trading companies that import and export merchandise.

Sola. A bill of exchange that does not have a duplicate as in bills in a set.

Soldiering. The systematic slowdown in work by labourers, with the deliberate purpose of keeping their employers ignorant of how fast the work can be done.

Sole Proprietorship. A form of business in which ownership resides with one person only who has unlimited liability for operations and debts.

Solicitation Method. A method of selling federal agency securities in which orders are taken from buyers and the securities are priced and delivered to investors after the order book is closed.

Solid Waste. Any solid waste materials resulting from human activities such as municipal refuse and sewage industrial wastes and agricultural wastes.

Solid Waste Pollution. Trash and garbage that are not properly disposed of to avoid pollution.

Solvency. It refers to the firm's ability to meet eventually all its long-term and short-term debts.

Source Documents. The original records of any transaction, internal or external, that occurs in the entity's operation.

Sources and Uses Statement. A financial statement indicating wherefrom a firm obtained funds and how they were used (spent) during a specific period of time.

Sources of Cash. A firm's activities that generate cash.

Sourcing. The act of searching out products or components needed for sale or integration into the production process.

Sourcing Decisions. Whether a firm should make or buy component parts.

Sourcing Strategy. The strategy that a company pursues in purchasing materials, components and final products. Sourcing can be from domestic and foreign locations and from inside and outside the company.

South-Eastern Underwriters Association (SEUA) Case. Legal landmark decision of 1944 over-ruling the Paul V. Virginia ruling and finding that insurance was interstate cummerce when conducted across state lines and was subject to federal regulation.

Southern African Development Community (SADC). An organization endeavouring to counter the economic influence of South Africa in the region by focusing on economic objectives, such as regional cooperation in attracting investment.

Sovereignty. Freedom from external control, especially when applied to a body politic.

Span of Control. The number of subordinates who report to a superior. The span of control is a factor that affects the shape and height of an organization structure.

Special Drawing Rights (SDRs). A unit of account issued to countries by the International Monetary Fund to expand their official reserves bases.

Special Purpose Equipment. Machines design to serve specialized functions in the production process.

Special Purpose Property. Property which is uniquely valuable to the lessee and not valuable to anyone else except scrap.

Specialization. The division of work into jobs that are limited in terms of tasks and responsibilities and different from one another significantly.

Specialized Asset. An asset designed to perform a specific task whose value is significantly reduced in its next-best use.

Speciality Store. A store which offers a limited variety of merchandise but an extensive assortment of goods which are stocked.

Specialty Goods. Goods which have some unique quality or characteristic or have a higher degree of brand identification which causes consumers to make a concerted effort to purchase them.

Specific Duty. A duty (tariff) assessed on a per-unit basis.

Specific Identification. This inventory method concentrates on the physical tracing of the particular items sold.

Specific Tariff. Tariff levied as a fixed change for each unite of goods imported.

Speculating. The purchase and sale of stock quickly with the intent of making a profit in a short period of time. There is a considerable risk in speculation.

Speculation. The buying or selling of foreign exchange with the objective of earning a profit.

Speculative Motive. The part of Keynes' theory of money demand depends on interest rates because of the effects of capital gains and losses on bonds.

Speculative Risk. An exposure to loss that could result in a loss or gain or no change as a result of fortuitous circumstances. Investment in common stocks creates a speculative risk.

Speculators. Those who buy and sell in the forward market. Not to hedge a position but to intentionally take a risky position in the market.

Speed of Adjustment. Determines how quickly expectations adjust to past errors in expectations.

Spending Variance. Basically, a price variance applied to variable overhead. However, other factors besides price may influence the amount of the variance.

Spill Over Model. Describes the reciprocal relationship between job and life satisfaction.

Spillover Effects. Situations in which the marketing programme in one country results in awareness of the product in other countries.

Spin-off Organization. A company now operating almost independently of the parent because its activities do not fit easily with the parent's existing competencies.

Spin-offs. New ventures separated into subsidiaries, divisions or independent businesses by corporations to pursue corporate innovations.

Splintered Authority. The situation where the total authority to accomplish a given result rests in more than one position and must be pooled, or combined to make the required decision.

Split Capital Trust. Type of trust that is issued by an investment trust company, with fixed winding up date on which the investors are paid the surplus assets. Holders of income shares receive payment throughout the life of the trust.

Split Limits. The amount of insurance for body injury liability and property damage liability are stated separately.

Split Rating. It occurs when two bond rating services give the same issue two different ratings.

Split-dollar Life Insurance. A method of paying for permanent life insurance converge in which two parties (often an employer and employee) each pay a portion of the annual premium with one party paying an amount equal to the increase in cash value in a given year (the employer) and the other party (the employee) paying the balance.

Split-off Point. The juncture of the production where the joint products become individually identifiable.

Splitting/Consolidation. The problem of splitting shares high face value into shares of a lower face value is known as splitting. The reverse process of combining shares that have a low face value into one share of higher value is known as consolidation.

Sponsor. A manager who is committed to an idea or recommendation, uses his or her own political power to support it.

Sponsorship. An investment in special event cause for the purpose of building awareness of the company and its products.

Spontaneous Current Liabilities. Accounts payable and bills payable and other types of accruals arise spontaneously out of the firm's operations are therefore called spontaneous current liabilities.

Spontaneous Financing. Short-term debts, such as account payable, that spontaneously increase in proportion to a firm's increasing sales.

Spot Advertisement. The advertiser can broadcast his message over one or many stations at various times by having the stations sent out his message separately.

Spot Exchange Rate. The current value of one unit of a currency in terms of a second currency.

Spot Market. Spot markets are markets for immediate delivery.

Spot Price. The price on some asset for immediate delivery.

Spot Trading. Trading by delivery of shares and payment for the same on the date of purchase or in the next day.

Spread. A spread is a trade involving the purchase of one option and the sale of another, both on the same stock.

Spread Order. Orders may be good for a specified period at time or they may be open that is, effective until explicitly cancelled by the customer. An order may be entered to be good for a day, a week, a month or a year cancelled.

Spreadsheet Program. Application software that allows users to perform accounting and other numerical tasks on an electronic worksheet.

Squaring up Transactions. A client settles his contract of sales by purchase and purchase by sales and by cross contracts within the settlement period. This is known as (i) squaring up transactions or (ii) complete the contract by delivery of shares or payment of cash, as the case may be.

SSAP 21. The UK accounting standard, "Accounting for leases and hire-purchase transactions", issued by the Accounting Standards Committee. Under the standard finance, leases should be capitalized by the lessee. It also has detailed provisions for lessor accounting.

Stability of Dividends. Stability of dividends sometimes means regularity in paying some dividend annually.

Stable Dollar Dividend Policy. A policy wherein a firm alters its cash dividend payment only when it feels the new dividend can be sustained.

Stable Environment. An environment in which stakeholders demands, and specifically customer desires, are well understood and relatively stable over time.

Stable External Environment. An environment in which there is little unpredictable change.

Staff. A relationship in an organizational position where an incumbent's task is to give some other person advice or counsel.

Staff Activities. Activities that support 'line' activities.

Staff Authority. The authority to advise but not to command. It may be exerted laterally or upward.

Staff Functions. Activities that contribute indirectly to the creation of the organization. Ordinarily, staff personnel advise line personnel.

Staff Personnel. Provide research, advice and recommendations to the line mangers.

Staffing. Fill and keeping filled, the positions in the organization structure with competent people. This is done through: (1) defining work-force requirements, (2) inventorying the people available, (3) recruiting, (4) selecting candidates for positions, (5) placing candidates, (6) promoting, (7) appraising, (8) planning the career of, (9) compensating and (10) training or otherwise developing people.

Staged Equity. A lease financing where the lessor does not put up its full equity investment initially but pays this amount over a period of time in the lease.

Stages in Succession. Phases in the process of transferring leadership from parent to child in a family business.

Stakeholder Audit. Systematic identification of all parties likely to be affected by the organization.

Stakeholder Map. A representation of the organization's stakeholders and their stakes.

Stakeholders. The collection of groups including stockholders, employees, customers and society at large, that a company must satisfy to survive.

Stand Alone Principle. Evaluation of a project based on the project's incremental cash flows.

Standard Absorption Costing. That type of product costing in which the cost of the finished unit is calculated as the sum of the costs of the standard allowances for factors of production, including fixed factory overhead, without reference to the costs actually incurred.

Standard and Poor's 500 Stock Average. An index of stock prices comprised of 425 industries, 50 utilities and 25 rails.

Standard Cost. A carefully predetermined cost that should be attained, usually expressed per unit.

Standard Deviation. A measure of dispersion around the expected value of a probability or frequency distribution; the square root of the variance.

Standard Direct Costing. That type of product costing in which the cost of the finished product is calculated as the sum of the costs of the standard allowances for the factors of production excluding fixed factory overhead which is treated as a period cost, and without reference to costs actually incurred.

Standard Industrial Classification (SIC) Code. US government code used to classify a firm by its type of business operations.

Standard Interest Rate. The interest rate expressed in terms of the interest payment made each period. Also quoted interest rate.

Standard Lookback Option. At the maturity of the option, the payoff for a call option depends on the difference between the spot price of the underlying asset and the minimum value of the asset price over the life of the option. The payoff for a put option depends on the difference between the maximum value of the asset price over the life of the option and the spot price of the underlying asset.

Standard of Deferred Payment. The function that money performs when it is used as the standard for calculating payments deferred to a latter date.

Standard of Living. A measure of wealth of a nation: total production of the nation divided by total population.

Standard Operating Procedure. An established method of conducting a business activity.

Stare Decision. To abide by already decided cases. This legal principle providing continuity to legal decisions. The decision of the count when it first encounters a particular set of circumstances sets a present for deciding future case involving similar circumstances.

Stars. Those businesses that have high market shares and operate in industries experiencing major growth.

Startup. Creating a new business from scratch.

State Banking Commissions. Control the formation of state banks and examine state banks that are not members of the Federal Reserve or the FDIC. Regulations of these commissions vary from state to state.

State Banks. Banks chartered by the appropriate agency in various states.

State Constitutions. Documents of the individual states that prescribe the form and power of state government within the limits set by the federal constitution.

State-directed Economy. An economy in which the state plays a proactive role in influencing a direction and magnitude of private sector investments.

State Statutes. Legislation passed by the state legislatures.

State Wide Branching. Practice that allows banks to freely open branches throughout the state.

Stated Interest Rate. The interest rate expressed in terms of the interest payment made each period. Also *quoted interest rate.*

Stated Value. A nominal value of a stock certificate that is usually far below the actual cash invested. *See* Par value.

Statement of Cash Flows. A firm's financial statement that summarizes its sources and used of cash over a specified period.

Statement of Changes in Financial Position. A formal explanation of the sources and uses of resources, usually sources and uses of working capital.

Statement of Financial Condition. A synonym for balance sheet.

Statement of Profit and Loss. The income statement.

Statement of Retained Earnings. A financial statement that analyzes changes in the retained earnings.

Statement of Sources and Applications of Funds. *See* Statement of changes in financial position.

States of Nature. Synonym for events. *See* States.

States. Synonym for events.

Static Budget. A budget prepared for only one level of activity and, on subsequently, one that does not adjust automatically to changes in the level of volume.

Static Hedge. A hedge that consists of buying/selling securities that are held until the maturity date of the derivative being hedged.

Static Theory of Capital Structure. Theory that a firm borrows up to the point where the tax benefits from an extra dollar in debt is exactly equal to the cost that comes from the increased probability of financial distress.

Statistical Discrepancy. Measures the amount by which the balance of payments accounts do not really balance.

Statistical Map. Data presented according to geographic divisions.

Statistical Process Control. An alternate form of screening control that employs control charts to continuously track performance variation overtime.

Statistical Process Control. The use of statistical methods to assess quality during the operation process.

Statistics. The techniques used for collecting, organizing, summarizing, interpreting, analyzing numerical data, making predictions and from the data.

Status. Is the relative social ranking an individual has in a group or organization.

Status Consensus. The agreement of group members about the relative status of members of the group.

Status Hierarchy. The ranking of group members within the group, that is, the prestige rank order of group members.

Statute of Limitations. A law defining a specific period of time during which a lawsuit can be brought. For example, the law may allow an injured party three years from the time an injury was discovered to file suit. If the injured party does not begin the lawsuit with in the specified time period, the right to bring the suit lost.

Step Debt. Debt in connection with a leveraged lease, arranged in tiers with different maturates of amortization to improve the lessor's cash flow and reduce the lessee's costs.

Step-down Method. Allocation of service department costs to other departments as well as production departments. Once a department's costs are allocated to other departments, no subsequent department costs are allocated back to it.

Stepped Rentals. Rental payments which vary from one another in a structured lease. Usually done for specific cash flows and for tax reasons.

Step-variable Costs. Those variable costs that change abruptly at intervals of activity because their acquisition comes in indivisible chunks.

Stereotypes. A standardized and oversimplified mental picture of a group.

Stereotyping. A type of perceptual organization in which one categorizes people into groups based on certain characteristics such as race, sex, or educational level, and then make generalizations about them according to their group.

Stipulated Loss Value. The same as insured value.

Stock Certificate. A document specifying the number of shares owned by a stockholder.

Stock Certificate. The evidence of ownership in a corporation.

Stock Dividend. (1) A distribution to stockholders of additional shares of any class of the distributing company's stock without any payment to the company by the stockholders. (2) A dividend paid to a common stock in units of additional share of the stock. (3) A payment to stockholders in the form of shares of stock instead of cash.

Stock Exchange. The market-place where securities are traded.

Stock Index Arbitrage. The program trading strategy in which professional traders look for underpricing or overpricing of stock-index financial futures contracts compared to the cash market (spot) prices of comparable stocks, simultaneously buying (selling) stocks and selling (buying) futures contracts to profit from any temporary relative mis-pricing of these two financial instruments.

Stock Index Futures. A futures contract written on a stock market index.

Stock Insurance Company. An insurer organized as profit making venture with owners who are not necessarily policy holders.

Stock Insurer. A proprietary insurer owned by stockholders who elect board of directors.

Stock Market. The buying and selling of stocks for the purpose of making money for the buyers and sellers of the stock.

Stock Market Bubble. When the stocks defy gravity and reach their peak levels, which do not confirm to the fundamentals, it results in a stock market bubble. The market shows irrational exuberance and stocks move up at an exponential speed. The bubble is supported by a P/E ratio, which is not justifiable in such cases. The dot.com boom in early part of 2000 is the best example. Dot.com companies were valued higher than the established brick and mortar companies off the same field. When such a Stock Market Bubble bursts, it leads to a sharp roller coaster ride in the stock prices, which happened in the later part of the year with most of these dot.com companies plunging 70-80 per cent from their peak in 2000.

Stock Market Index. A portfolio of common stocks.

Stock of Foreign Direct Investment. The total accumulated value of foreign-owned asses at a given time.

Stock Option. It gives an employee the right to buy stock in the company, usually at the fixed price for a period of time. In order to motivate employees and managers and to build the spirit of ownership in the organization stock options are offered. Key managers and employees are offered shares in the venture depending upon several factors like seniority, participation.

Stock Split. A situation in which a company changes the number of outstanding shares of common stock by issuing to each existing shareholder a multiple number of units of the shares originally held. The issuance of additional shares for no consideration and under conditions indicating that the objective is to increase the number of outstanding shares for the purpose of reducing their unit market price.

Stockbroker. Acts as the middleman between buyers and sellers of stocks.

Stockholder. A person group or organization owning one or more shares of stack in a corporation.

Stockholders' Equity. The excess of assets over liabilities of a corporation.

Stocks. The term is used synonymously with the ordinary shares (or with ordinary shares and fixed interest securities collectively) in the USA. However, ordinary shares are called common stocks. The term is used quite generally with reference to ordinary shares. In U.K., the term is usually used in reference to a fixed interest security issued and quoted in units of 100 pounds.

Stop Transfer. The instruction given by a registered holder of shares to the company to stop the transfer of shares as a result of theft, loss, etc. Shares belonging to A are sold to B who gets them transferred in his name and sells them to C. Now C sends these shares to the company and gets them transferred to his name. Meanwhile A discovers that his share certificates were stolen and fraudulently sold by some one else. He gets a court order restraining the company from further transferring the shares and attaching them (currently in possession OFC). This is known as "Stop transfer".

Storage Costs. The costs of storing a commodity.

Storage Unit. The memory of the computer where data are stored for future reference.

Store of Value. A means of storing today's purchasing power for use of tomorrow. An important function of money.

Storming Stage. The stage when conflict casually occurs and in which group members begin to assert their roles, jockey for leadership positions and make known their feelings about a task.

Strangle. An option portfolio consisting of a long call and a long put option with the same exercise price and exercise date.

Straight Debentures. The non-convertible debenture (NCD) is also known as a straight debenture.

Straight Deductible. Deductible in an insurance contract by which the insured must pay a certain number of dollars of loss before the insurer is required to make a payment.

Straight Voting. Procedure in which a shareholder may cast all votes for each member of the board of directors.

Straight-line Method. An accounting method for depreciating assets that spreads the depreciation equally over the estimated useful life of the asset.

Strategic Acquisition. A purchase in which the value of business is based on both the firm's stand alone characteri-stics and the synergies that the buyer thinks can be created.

Strategic Alliance. An organizational relationship that links two or more independent business entities in a common endeavor.

Strategic Business Units (SBUs). A distinct form of organization, usually employed within a larger company, constructed around a product or service, so that it will receive the attention normally given a complete product or project organization structure. These units are expected to be handled as though the units are expected to be handled as though they were independent businesses.

Strategic Commitment. A decision that has a long-term impact and is difficult to reverse, such as entering a foreign market.

Strategic Constituency. Any group of people with a stake in the organization's operation or success.

Strategic Control. A form of control whose purpose is to ensure that the organization effectively understands and responds to the realities of its environment.

Strategic Decision. A decision regarding the direction a firm will take in relation to its customers and competitors.

Strategic Flexibility. Ability to adapt to new objectives.

Strategic Goals. Goals set by higher managers that deal with such general topics as the firm's growth, new markets, or new goods and services.

Strategic Information. Information about a firm's competitors, customers and market that affects its ability to compete.

Strategic Intent. An objective that gives an organization cohesion over the long term while it builds competitive viability.

Strategic Management. Develops the mission, objectives and strategies of the entire organization, the top-level decision makers in the organizations.

Strategic Options. Options for future related business products or strategies.

Strategic Plan (or Long Range Plan). A firm's overall plan for the future. A long-term plan involving major commitments.

Strategic Planning. A systematic way of analyzing and responding to competitive environment.

Strategic Right Sizing. Eliminating functions and positions that are not critical to a firm's strategic success.

Strategic Use of IT. The use of information to better position a company to compete with its industry.

Strategies. General programmes of action and deployment of resources to attain comprehensive objectives. The programme of objectives of an organization and their changes, resources used to attain these objectives and policies governing the acquisition, use and disposition of these resources.

Strength Perspective. Assumes that the strength of corporate culture is related to a firm's financial performance.

Stress. Behavioral, physical, or psychological response to stressors.

Stressor. The stimulus that causes stress.

Strict Liability. Liability without fault. A rule of law creating a heavy burden for defendants in liability suits.

Strike. Action of an employee to stop work until a labor management conflict is settled or a contract is signed. Workers stay off the job, stopping work, to gain their demands, the most effective weapon of labour unions.

Strike Price. The price at which the underlying asset may be purchased or sold when an option is exercised.

Stringent Credit Policy. When a firm sells on credit on a highly selective basis only, to those customers who have proven credit worthiness and who are financially strong in the firm is following stringent credit policy.

Strip Debt. Debt, in connection with a leveraged lease, arranged with different maturities and amortization to improve the lessor's cash flow and reduce the lessee's costs.

Stripped Securities. Interest-bearing financial instruments (usually bonds) that have been split up into multiple discount securities, each composed of one interest payment (known as an IO) or one promised principal payment (known as a PO).

Strong Form Market Efficiency. Asserts that no current information either publicly available or not, can improve on using the most recently known value of an asset price to predict the future value of the asset price.

Structural Change. A planned change of the formally prescribed task and authority relationships in an organization's design.

Structured Interview. It is conducted using a set of standardized questions that are asked all applicants for a job.

Structured Settlements. In negligence cases, instead of the defendant paying a lump sum to a plaintiff, the defendant (using the service of an insurer) promises a series of annuity payments to the injured party.

Sub Optimization. A situation where one department of a business, acting in its own self-interest, hurts or inhibits the performance of another department. Leading to less effective outcomes for the business overall.

Subcontracting. Exists when a contractor enters into another contract with a firm to perform part of the function he has contracted to perform.

Subjective Risk. Uncertainty based on one's mental condition or state of mind.

Sub-lease. A transaction in which leased property is re-leased by the original lessee to a third party and the lease agreement between the two original parties remains in effect.

Subordinated. A creditor claim is junior to other creditor claims.

Subordinated Bond. A bond whose claim on the assets of the issuer—the borrower—is subordinate to a claim by another bond.

Subordinated Debenture. *See* Subordinated bond.

Subrogation. The substitution of one party (the insurer) for another party (the insured) in that party's right. The substitution occurs because the first party has made a payment for which another is responsible. In insurance, subrogation occurs when the insurer pays a claim while the insured has a right of action against a third party for causing a loss. After making the claims payment, the insurer is subrogated to the insured's right to sue the third party.

Subsidiarity. A principle which implies that EU interference should take place only in areas of common concern and that the policies should be set at the national level.

Subsidiary. A corporation owned or controlled by a parent company, through the ownership of more than 50 per cent of the voting stock.

Subsidies. Sum paid (usually by government) to companies in certain industries to enable them to sell their goods or services at a price close to the prevailing market price. It is also used to provide financial support to commercial or quasi-commercial activity that would otherwise not be viable in narrow profit and loss term, usually to sustain broader economic or social benefits.

Substitutes. Goods or services that are related in the sense that when the price of one increases, the demand for the other increases because people substitute towards the one that is relatively cheaper.

Substitutes for Leadership. Theory identifying situations in which traditional leadership behaviors are irrelevant.

Substitution Drawbacks. A provision allowing domestic merchandise to be substituted for merchandise that is imported for eventual export, thus allowing the U.S. firm to exclude the duty paid on the merchandise in costs and in sales prices.

Substitution Effect. As the return on an asset increases people will substitute go away towards the one with the relatively higher returns.

Sub-system. Any system that is part of a larger one.

Subunit Autonomy. Possession of decision-making power by managers of subunits of an organization.

Successful Business. Any business that excels over a long period of time.

Suicide Clause. Contractual provision in a life insurance policy stating that if the insured commits suicide within two years after the policy is issued, the face amount of insurance will not be paid, only premiums paid will be refunded.

Sum of the Digits Method. An accounting method for depreciating assets providing for the largest depreciation to be taken at the beginning of the asset's life and the smallest depreciation to be taken in the later year.

Sum-of-the-years'-digits Depreciation (SYD). A popular form of accelerated depreciation where the sum of the digits is the total of the numbers representing the years of life.

Sunk Costs. Unavoidable costs that do not result in marketable assets and that do not add to the net worth of a business.

Super 301. A clause in U.S. tariff legislation permitting U.S. trade negotiators to threaten more restrictive import regulations to get other countries to lower their restrictions against U.S. make products or services.

Supermarket. A store which emphasizes low prices on fast-moving merchandise and offers some customer services.

Supervisors. Same as managers, but ordinarily used to apply to managers as the lowest level or first line of managing.

Supplemental Major Medical Insurance. Group health insurance plan that supplements the benefits provided by a basic medical expense plan. It provides more comprehensive benefits with higher limits and is designed for a catastrophic loss.

Supplementary Medical Insurance. Part B of the Medicare program that covers physicians' fees and other related medical services. Most eligible Medicare recipients are automatically included unless they voluntarily refuse this coverage.

Suppliers. Organizations and individuals who provide resources to other organizations.

Supply Curve. A schedule showing the relationship between the price of a good or services and its quantity supplied.

Supply Function. Describes the relationship that exists during some period of time between the number of units of a good or service that producers are willing to place on the market and a given set of conditions that influence the willingness to place those units on the market such as prices of the resources used to produce the commodity and the available technology which can be used to produce the commodity.

Supply Side Economics. An approach to economic policy which argues that the nation's economic policy should be directed towards increasing productivity and the supply of goods in order to combat inflation.

Supportive Communication. A style of communicating that delivers a message accurately while supporting and enhancing the relationship between the parties to the communication.

Supportive Selling. Selling efforts in which salespersons try to generate goodwill and provide specialized service rather than trying to get orders.

Surely Insurance. Insures against loss from one party to a contract not fulfilling its obligation.

Surety. Party who agrees to answer for the debt, default, or obligation of another in the purchase of a bond.

Surety Bond. Bond that provides monetary compensation if the bonded party fails to perform certain acts.

Suretyship. Type of primary insurance that covers loss of money through fraud or dishonesty.

Surgical Expense Insurance. Health insurance that provides for payment of physicians' fees for surgical operations performed in a hospital or elsewhere.

Surplus. Situation where the quantity supplied exceeds quantity demanded.

Surplus Budget Unit. An individual or business firm or unit of government whose current income receipts exceeds its current expenditure and therefore is a new lender of funds to the money and capital markets.

Surplus Fund. The clearing house has various margin, requirements original margin and small fee for clearing the member's trades. These sources of revenue become the surplus fund and helps to cover costs. Money in this fund is invested in government securities and interest earned is applied to the operating expenses of the clearing house.

Surplus Line Broker. Specialized insurance broker licensed to place business with a non-admitted insurer (a company not licensed to do business in the state).

Surplus Line. Insurance on an exposure for which no coverage is available in the normal market.

Surplus Variable. A variable that represents the difference between the right-hand side and left-hand side of a greater than or equal to inequality constraint. It is subtracted from the left-hand side of the inequality to convert the constraint to an equality. It measures the amount of a product (or output) in excess of the required amount.

Surrender Cost Index. Method of measuring the cost of insurance policy to an insured if the policy is surrendered at the end of some specified time period where time value of money is taken into consideration.

Survey Feedback. The gathering of data through questionnaires and or personal interviews and the return of that data to employees in a structured form to facilitate discussion and problem solving.

Survival of the Fittest. A phrase derived from the idea of Charles Darwin and Herbert Spencer which means that only the strongest and most capable individual is able to survive and excel in life's competitive struggles.

Survivor Income Benefits. Monthly benefits paid to an eligible surviving spouse or children for a limited period following the disabled worker's death.

Survivor Life Insurance. (Also known as second-to-die life insurance.) A life insurance policy covering two lives that provides a death payment at the second death. If more than two lives are coverd, payment is made at the last death. Survivor life insurance is frequently used in estate at the first death to the surviving spouse, with life insurance proceeds providing liquidity for estate taxes at the second death.

Sushi Bond. It is a Japanese bond demonstrated in Eurodollars.

Sustainable Competitive Advantage. A competitive advantage that competitors can not duplicate easily.

Sustained Competitive Advantage. A strategy for value creation that competitors cannot match. When an organization has a sustained competitive advantage, other organizations cannot erase that advantage by copying it.

Sustained Risk of Forfeiture. In non-qualified benefit plans, a legal doctrine determining when an employee is deemed to be in constructive receipt of compensation. Constructive receipt does not occur if the employee faces a substantial risk of forfeiture.

Swaps. Two companies lend each other different currencies (currency swaps) or at different interest rates, one fixed and one floating (interest rate swaps).

Swaption. An option on a swap.

Sweetening Debt. Warrants help to make the issue of equity and debentures attractive. If the company is doubtful about the full subscription of the debenture issue, warrants are used to sweeten the issue by giving the investors an opportunity to participate in capital gains when the share price appreciates.

Sweetening Fixed Income Securities. Investors generally prefer fixed interest, convertible debentures over non-convertible, because this enables them to earn a definite and fixed income with the chance of making capital gains. Hence, the convertibility feature 'sweetens' the issue. Also the company may offer relatively low interest rate on convertible debentures because of the value of the conversion feature as compared to a non-convertible debenture.

Switching Between Offers. The switching of acceptances between different offers is not possible. The offer once accepted by a shareholder cannot be withdrawn. To enable the shareholders to be in a better position to decide as to which of the substituting offers is better and also not to cause last minute decisions/ confusions. The offer price is effectively frozen for 7 working days up to the closing date of the offer. Shareholders would be advised to wait till the commencement of that period to be aware of upward revision in the offer price of either offer (initial and competitive).

SWOT Analysis. The evaluation of organization's internal strengths and weaknesses and the opportunities and threats associated with the firm's external environment.

Symbiotic. A conglomerate financial firm that frequently merges insurance sales, security brokerage, real estate brokerage, financial counseling and credit services within the same organization.

Symmetric Information. In the loan market, when borrowers and banks have the same information about whether a loan will be repaid.

Syndicate. A group of underwriters formed to share the risk and to help sell an issue.

Syndication. Cooperation by a lead bank and several other banks to make a large loan to a public or private organization.

Synergy. The ability of the whole system more than the sum of its parts.

Synthetic Derivative. A portfolio of traded securities that duplicates the cash flows and payoffs to a derivative.

Synthetic Fuel (Synfuel). Fuel produced by converting naturally occurring hydrogen and carbon compounds such as coal and shale rock into useful forms of energy such as coal gas, coal liquid fuel and shale oil.

Synthetic Process. A production process that combines raw materials to produce a product.

Synthetic Replication. The process of forming a synthetic derivative.

System. A formal means of gathering data to aid and coordinate the process of making decisions.

System Messages Window. This window is for broadcast of messages from the exchange to all the trading members/ participants.

System Software. Programs that control the internal functioning of computer.

System, Definition of. A set or assemblage of things connected or interdependent and interacting so as to form a complex unity a whole composed of parts in orderly arrangement according to some scheme or plan. For any system there must be boundaries that separate it from its environment.

System's Approach. An approach to management theory that views organizations and the environments within which they operate as sets of interrelated parts to be managed as a whole in order to achieve a common goal.

System-4 Linker's. People-oriented organization design, which emphasized open communication, supportive-ness, inputs from employees to managers and general supervision. The extreme opposite of System-4 is System-1 organization design.

Systematic and Rational Allocation. It deals with those costs which expire to generate revenue during a period but cannot be directly associated with the specific revenue. Depreciation is an example of such costs.

Systematic Risk. The portion of the total risk of an investment that is associated with the market as a whole. Systematic risk cannot be diversified away.

Systematic Risk Principle. The expected return on a risky asset depends only on that asset's systematic risk.

Systems, Boundaries. The demarcation lines or area definition separating a given system from its environment.

Systems, Closed. Not having interactions with the system's environment.

Systems, Open. Having interaction with the system's environment and exchanging information, energy, or material with that environment.

T

T+5 Rolling Settlement System. In this system, Monday's trades are settled on Monday.

Table. A method of presenting statistical data more clearly.

Tactics. Action plans by which strategies are implemented.

Taft-Hartley Act. The labour Management Relation Act of 1947 which among other features, outlines unfair labour practices of labour unions and provides for court injunctions to prevent strikes.

Tag Along. This is an agreement between the entire capitalist and key employees. This is a protection offered to important employees in the event of a merger or a takeover. The representative of the fund agrees to a certain employees into the new organization.

Takeover. When an acquirer takes over the control or management of the target company, it is termed as takeover.

Taking Inventory. The action of counting all inventory on hand as of a specific time.

Tall Pyramid Structure. A structure that fosters narrow span of control, a large number of management levels, and more centralized decision making.

Tangible Assets. *See* Tangible Fixed Assets.

Tangible Fixed Assets. Tangible fixed assets include land, building, machinery, furniture, etc. These are normally recorded at cost. Cost of tangible fixed assets are allocated over their useful lives. The amount so allocated each year is called depreciation. Cost of tangible fixed assets are reduced every year by the amount of depreciation.

Tangible Resources. Organizational resources that are visible and easy to measure.

Tangible Rewards. Exists in the form of pay, better working conditions, fringe benefits, etc.

Tape Dancing. Unethical methods of manipulating share prices in the USA in which a dealer reports a deal inclusive of his commission. This seems to make the share prices rise.

Taraniwalla. The taraniwalla may be a jobber or specialist who specializes in specified stocks. He trades in and out of the market for a small difference in price and as such is an important factor in making a market, *i.e.* maintaining a continuous and liquid market in stocks in which he specializes. The taraniwalla specializes in stocks that are relatively not so active.

Target. In terms of monetary policy, a goal or variable that the policy maker cannot directly control.

Target Company. The target company is a company whose shares are listed on stock exchange(s) and whose shares or voting rights are acquired/being acquired or whose control is taken over/being taken over by the acquirer.

Target Dividend Payout Ratio. A dividend policy wherein the firm seeks to pay out a specified percentage of sustainable earnings.

Target Elements of Change. Components of an organization that may be changed.

Target Payout Ratio. A firm's long-term desired dividend-to-earnings ratio.

Target Rate. Often used in capital budgeting as either the minimum desired rate of return or the budgeted rate of return.

Tariff. A tax on improved product.

Tariffs. Charges made in return for goods or services.

Task. It is a distinct identifiable work activity composed of motions.

Task Centered Leader Behavior. An effort to lead employees by focusing on work and how well employees perform.

Task Depth. The degree of accountability or responsibility required by a job.

Task Environment. The dimensions of the environment that directly interact with and influence the organization.

Task Group. A formal group of individuals working as a unit to complete a task.

Task of the Manager. *See* Manager's, task of.

Task Roles. Task oriented group behavior.

Task Scope. The amount of variety in job's activities.

Task Structure. The degree of structure imposed on a job. The job may be routine or non-routine. If the job is routine, it will be spelled out in detail. An inspector on the assembly line has a structured task, while the job of the research scientist has relatively little task structure.

Tax Anticipation Notes. Short-term debt obligations issued by state and local governments to provide for immediate cash needs until tax revenues come in.

Tax Asymmetries. Most of the economies have varieties of taxes and tax incentives which cause tax asymmetries. Tax asymmetries make security transactions more beneficial to some. A number of financial transactions may create additional wealth because of tax differences.

Tax Benefit Transfers (TBT). A TBT lease, made possible in the US by the 1981 Tax Act (ERTA), was limited by the 1982 Act (FERA). The transaction is set up so that the lessee is also the lender under a leveraged lease arrangement and all payments except an initial sum paid by the lessor (tax benefit buyer) cancel each other out. That is, one company effectively pays another a fee for the tax benefits associated with capital investment.

Tax Effect of Salvage Value. The company will make a profit if the asset's salvage value is more than its book value. Capital gain is equal to salvage value minus original value of the asset, capital gains are generally taxed at a rate lower than the ordinary income.

Tax Exemption Securities. Debt securities issued by the state, city, country and other local units of government or by other qualified borrowers whose interest income is exempt from federal taxation and from most state taxes as well.

Tax Haven Countries. Countries with low income taxes or no taxes on foreign sources income.

Tax Haven Subsidiary. A subsidiary of a company established in a tax haven country for the purpose of minimizing income tax.

Tax Holiday. The period in which a startup company does not need to pay any taxes.

Tax Indemnity Clause. Clause inserted into a tax based lease providing for increases in rentals in the event of legislation which adversely affects the lessor's ability to claim tax benefits on the equipment.

Tax Risk. The risk of changes in the tax treatment of interest income.

Tax Saving Fund. Such funds allow to claim a rebate u/s 99 of the Income Tax Act. The maximum allowable rebate in any year in r/s 2000 hence, the maximum that one can invest in a tax saving fund locks investors funds is for a period of three years otherwise the rebate is lost.

Tax Shield. Usually defined as non-cash items (*e.g.* depreciation) charged against income, thus protecting that amount from tax.

Tax Treaty. A treaty between two countries that generally results in the reciprocal reduction on dividend with-holding taxes and the exemption of taxes or royalties and sometimes interest payments.

Tax Variation Clause. A clause in lease agreement in the UK which allows the lessor or vary the rentals if either the rate of tax or the tax system changes.

Tax Written Down Value. The value of an asset after deducting the total capital allowances claimed from the cost of the asset.

Team. Small group with complementary skills who hold themselves mutually accountable for common purpose, goals and approach.

Team Based Pay. Linking pays to teamwork behavior and or team results.

Team Building. A change technique that focuses on the interaction within a group to identify and solve problems and implement changes.

Team Viability. Team members satisfied and willing to contribute.

Technical Analysis. Charting or plotting historical data and asset prices.

Technical Elite. Highly trained and technically specialized members of an organization who may exercise great influence on policies and decisions from a purely technical point of view.

Technical Learning. A stage in the development of social responsiveness within a company during which a person with specialized knowledge helps the organization learn more about some social problem and how to cope with it.

Technical Management Skill. The skill of working with the resources and knowledge in a specific area. Such skill is important to first-level and middle managers.

Technical Salesperson. Specialist who provides technical expertise in installing and servicing equipment such as computers.

Technical Skills. The ability of a manager to work with things.

Technological Change. A planned change in the machinery, equipment or techniques that are used to accomplish organizational goals.

Technology. The branch of knowledge that deals with applied science and industrial arts. Knowledge in science or industry.

Technology Absorbing Capacity. The ability of a recipient to work effectively with technology particularly in relation to the need for training and equity in order to effect a transfer.

Technology Assessment. An analytic attempt to understand beforehand if possible the economic and social effects of new technology particularly the unintended, indirect and possible harmful impacts that may occur.

Technology Transfer. A business sharing its advanced technology, including patents and operating know-how with another business or government.

Techno-structure. Members of an organization who possess and use specialized technical knowledge in a group decision-making process.

Tectonic Change. Moderate but significant change that builds on existing elements of the organization's identity.

Telecommuting. A situation where a person can work at home at the computer terminal instead of commuting to work by car, public transportation of other means.

Telecommuting. Performing knowledge work and transmitting the results of that work by means of computer terminal to an organization's central data bank and management centre, while the employee works at home or at some other remote location.

Teleconference. A meeting of organization's employees who are in widely separated locations that is made possible by two-way television transmission.

Telemarketing. A form of distribution of goods coupled with promotion using the telephone to make sales.

Temporal Method. A method of translating foreign currency financial statements used when the functional currency is that of the parent company.

Term Insurance. Type of life insurance that provides temporary protection for specified number of years. It is usually renewable and convertible.

Term Loan. Money loaned for a five-to-ten-year term, corresponding to the length of time the investment will bring in profits.

Term Premium. The compensation required to induce investors to purchase an asset with a different term to maturity than their preferred one.

Term Structure of Interest Rates. The relationship between the yields of otherwise identical financial assets and their term to maturity.

Terminal Cash Flows. Cash flows at the end of the terminal year.

Terminal Emulation. A communication mode that allows personal computers to exchange information with mainframes.

Terminal Reserve. In life insurance, the reserve at the end of any given policy year.

Terminal Value. *See* Residual value.

Termination. Permanent separation from the company.

Termination Schedule. Leases, sometimes contain provisions permitting a lessee to terminate the lease, during the lease term in the event the leased equipment becomes obsolete and surplus to its needs. The liability of the lessee in the event of such termination is set forth in a termination schedule which values the equipment at various times during the lease term. If the equipment is sold at a price lower than the set forth in the schedule, the lessee pays the difference.

Terms of Sale. Conditions under which a firm sells its goods and services for cash or credit.

Terms of Trade. The quantity of imports that can be bought by a given quantity of a country's exports.

Test Market. Selling a new product in one city to test sales of a product for projection to the entire market.

Test Marketing. Selling a product/ service in certain select markets to see what customers think.

TFE. Toronto Futures Exchange, Canada.

The Money Option. An option with a strike price equal to the current market price of the underlying asset.

Theft. A broad term describing the taking of other's property. Burglary and embezzlement are types of theft.

Theocratic Law System. A legal system based on religious precepts.

Theocratic Totalitarianism. A dictatorship lead by a religious group.

Theory. The systematic grouping of interdependent concepts and principles which give a grime-work to, or tie together, significant knowledge.

Theory of Country Size. The theory which holds that countries with large land areas are more apt to have varied climates and natural resources and therefore generally are nearly self-sufficient than smaller countries.

Theory of Justice. An approach to decision making that assumes decisions should be guided by equity, fairness and impartiality.

Theory of Rights. An approach to decision making which assumes that there are certain individual rights that must always be protected.

Theory X and Theory Y. Assumption about the nature of people as suggested by Douglas McGregor. For example, theory X suggests that people dislike work and will avoid it if they can. On the other hand, Theory Y suggests, for instance, that the expenditure of physical and mental effort in work is as natural as play or rest.

Theory Z. Several authors proposed theories using the letter 'z'. In general, theory Z refers to selected Japanese managerial practices adapted to the environment of the United States as suggested by William Ouchi, for example, one of the characteristics of Type Z organizations is the emphasis on inter-personal skills needed for group decision making.

Theta. A measure of change in an option premium with respect to a one-day change in time-to-maturity.

Theta Neutral. A portfolio position that has a theta of zero.

Third Country Bills. Bankers' acceptances issued by banks in one country that finance the transport or storage of goods traded between two other countries.

Third Market. Mechanism through which securities listed on a stock exchange are traded off the exchange in the over-the-counter-market.

Third Wave. A period of widespread social change characteristic of high tech-nology, service oriented knowledge based societies.

Third World Nations. Developing nations as distinguished from more developed free world nations and communist nations.

360 Degree Feedback. Comparison of anonymous feedback from one's superior, subordinates, and peers with self perceptions.

Third Country Nationals. Expatriate employees who are neither citizens of the country in which they are working nor citizens of the country where the company is headquartered.

Third World Countries. Developing countries or those not considered as socialist or non-socialist industrial countries.

Throughput. The amount of work that can be done by computer in a given amount of time.

Tick Size. The smallest price change allowed for trading an asset.

Ticker. The ticker displays information about a trade as and when it takes place.

Tie-in Provisions. Stipulations in licensing that require the license to purchase or sell products from or to the licensor respectively.

TIFFE. Tokyo International Financial Futures Exchange.

Tight Credit Policy. Tight credit policy means rejection of certain types of accounts whose credit worthiness is doubtful. This results into loss of sales consequently, loss of contribution. This is an opportunity loss to the firm. As the firm starts loosing its credit policy, it accepts all or some of those accounts which the firm had earlier rejected. Thus the firm will recapture lost sales and thus, lost contribution. The opportunity cost of lost contribution excludes with the loosening of credit policy.

Time Adjustment. The process of adjusting the value of a cash flow (or stream of cash flows) to reflect its value at another point in time.

Time Adjusted Rate of Return. *See* Internal rate of return.

Time and Motion Study. Formal analysis of the basic movements used to carry out a task and the time required for each movement.

Time Deposits. Savings accounts in commercial banks or savings and loan association.

Time Draft. A commercial bill of exchange calling for payment to be made at some time after delivery.

Time Element Coverage. *See* Business income (interruption) insurance.

Time Interest Earned Ratio. The ratio of operating income to interest changes.

Time Limit on Certain Defenses Provision. Provision in a health insurance policy that prohibits the company from canceling the policy or denying a claim on the basis of a preexisting condition or misstatement in the application after the policy has been in force for two or three years, with the exception of fraudulent misstatement.

Time Series Analysis. The easiest way to evaluate the performance of a firm. Compare its present ratios with the past ratios over a period of time. It is known as time series analysis. It gives an indication of the direction of change and reflects whether the firm's financial perfor-mance has improved, deteriorated or remained constant over time.

Time Spread. Having same exercise price if a trade involves purchase options and sale options both on the same stock but one expires later than the other, it is called time spread.

Time Study. The process of determining the appropriate elapsed time for the completion of a task or job. This process was developed as part of Frederick W. Taylor's effort to determine a fair day's work.

Time Value. The amount of money that option buyers are willing to pay for an option in anticipation of change in the underlying asset price that will cause the option to increase in value. An option's premium is the sum of time value of intrinsic value. The amount by which an option's premium exceeds the option's intrinsic value is the option time value.

Time-at-the-day Order. A time-at-the-day order is one that must be executed at a specific time or at specific intervals during the trading session.

Time-utility. A good or service that must be available at the time when it is demanded to satisfy a want.

Timing Difference. Difference between the periods in which transactions affect pretax income for reporting to income tax authorities and the period in which they enter into the determination of pretax income for reporting to shareholders.

Timing Option. The right to deliver a bond on any day in the delivery month of treasury bond futures contract.

Title V 11. It is that portion of the 1964 Civil Right Act prohibiting discrimination in employment.

TNC. *See* Transnational Corporation.

Tobin's Q. Tobin's Q is the ratio of the market value of firm's assets to its assets replacement costs. It is argued that firms will have an incentive to invest when Q is greater than 1. They will be reluctant to invest once Q becomes equal to 1.

Token Coins. Coins such as U.S. pennies nickels dimes and quarters, which resemble commodity money coins but which are fiat money. The face value of these coins exceeds their value as a commodity.

Tombstone. An advertisement announcing a public offering.

Tontine. A money transfer scheme, now illegal in the United States, where all money transferred to a pool is given to the last survivor(s) of the pool.

Top Down Investment. An investment strategy that first takes a view on the economy and then the industry scenario before looking into the potential performance of a company this is opposite to the bottom up techniques.

Top Management. The top level of an administrative hierarchy. Managers at this level coordinate the work of other managers but do not report to a manager.

Tort. A civil wrong independent of a contract.

Total Asset Turnover. The ratio of sales to the total assets, showing the efficiency with which a firm's assets are used to generate sales.

Total Cost. The sum of cost of goods sold, selling expenses and over head costs.

Total Credit. Sales during the period or average level of accounts receivable during the period.

Total Defensive. Assets/projected daily operating expenditures.

Total Deficit. The difference between all government spending (both primary spending and interest pay-ments) and tax collections.

Total Disability. Condition of an insured that makes him or her completely unable to perform all duties of the insured's own occupation or unable to perform the duties of any occupation for which the insured is reasonably fitted by training, education, and experience.

Total Factor Productivity. The ratio of outputs to all the resources used to create them.

Total Fixed Costs. Costs that remain constant at the quantity produced or sold varies.

Total Liabilities/Total Assets.

Total Product. The total level of output produced with a given quantity of an input.

Total Project Approach. A method of comparing two or more alternative courses of action by computing the total expected inflows and out-flows of each alternative and then converting these flows to their present value by applying some predetermined minimum rate of return.

Total Quality Control. An approach to quality in organizations that seek to achieve continuous quality improvements through the involvement and commitment of all employees.

Total Quality Management (TQM). The process that a company uses to achieve quality where the goal is elimination of all defects.

Total Reserves. They include foreign currency reserves and SDRs.

Total Self Direction. The assignment of virtually every employee in the organization to a self-directed work team.

Total Variable. Costs that vary with the quantity produced or sold.

Totalitarianism. A political system characterized by the absence of widespread participation in decision making.

Toxic Chemicals. Any type of chemical that is harmful to marine life animals or humans.

Toxic Substances. Any substance used in production or in consumer products that is poisonous or capable of causing serious health problems for those persons exposed (compare with hazardous waste).

TQM. *See* Total Quality Management.

Tracker Bond. It is lump sum amount invested in equities that guarantees capital and often guarantees also a minimum return.

Trade Associations. An organization that represents the business and professional interest of the firm or persons in a trade, industry or professions; for example medical doctors, chemical manufacturers or used car dealers.

Trade-credit Agencies. Privately owned organizations that collect credit information on businesses.

Trade Credit. Credit extended by suppliers and vendors on purchases of materials, inventory and services.

Trade Diversion. A situation in which exports shift to a less efficient producing country because of preferential trade barriers.

Trade Dress. Elements of a firm's distinctive image not protected by trademark, patent or copyright.

Trade Guarantee. Trade guarantee is the guarantee provided by the clearing corporation for all trades that are executed on the exchange. In contrast the settlement guarantees the settlement of trade after multilateral netting.

Trade Marks and Trade Names. They are the exclusive rights granted by the government to use certain names, symbols, designs, etc.

Trade Related Aspects of Intellectual Property Rights (TRIPS). A provision from the Uruguay round of trade negotiations requiring countries to agree to enforce procedures under their national laws to protect intellectual property rights.

Trade Secret. Private company information not available to others, that is useful to the company business but could be harmful if known to others, especially competitors.

Traded Options. Create a legal right to buy or sell a financial asset at an agreed upon price for specific time period.

Trademark. A name or logo distinguishing a company or product.

Trade-offs Economic and Social. An attempt to balance economic and social gains against economic and social costs when it is impossible to achieve all that is desired in both economic and social terms.

Trader Work Stations. Trading is done by members and their authorized representative from their trader work stations installed in their offices through the BSE on line trading system.

Trading Company. An organization that acquires goods in one country and sells them to buyers in another country.

Trading Electronically. Clients who use electronic trading service enter orders on-screen to trade with fund managers, brokers, market makers and exchange specialists around the world. These clients see live orders coming through internet and negotiate or execute any order they choose. Regardless of a client's size or location, they have an equal opportunity to respond to each other. In more traditional markets where electronic trading is not available, clients can trade by telephone through transaction desk.

Trading for Delivery. Trading conducted with an intention to deliver the shares as opposed to a position that is squared off within the settlement.

Trading on the Equity. Using borrowed money at a fixed interest rate and/or using funds provided by preferred stockholders with the aim of enhancing the rate of return on common stockholders' equity.

Trading Range. Price range between highest and lowest prices at which a stock is traded.

Trading Strategy. A portfolio position that can change over time.

Traditional Costing. *See* Absorption costing.

Traditional Net Cost Method. Traditional method of determining cost to an insured of a life insurance policy, determined by subtracting the total dividends received and cash value at the end of a period from the total premiums paid during that period.

Training. It is a learning process whereby people acquire skills, concepts, attitudes or knowledge to aid in the achievements of goals.

Training and Experience Form. An application device that presents a small number of the important tasks of a job and asks the applicants whether they have ever performed or been trained in each of the activities.

Trait Appraisals. Appraising people, whether managers or non-managers, on the basis of personality traits and work-oriented characteristics.

Trait Theory. Attempts to specify which personal characteristics (physical, personality, mental) are associated with leadership effectiveness. Trait theory relies on research that relates various traits to effectiveness criteria.

Transaction. An event that effects the financial position of an entity and requires recording.

Transaction Accounts. Deposits (such as a checking account or other accounts offered by financial institutions) that can be used to make payments for purchases of goods and services.

Transaction Costs. The costs involved in buying or selling an asset.

Transaction Exposure. Foreign exchange risk that occurs because the parent company must translate foreign-currency financial statements into the reporting currency of the parent company.

Transaction Motive. The desire to hold money because it is useful in making purchases.

Transaction Processing System. An information system that handles routine, recurring transactions.

Transaction Support System. An information system that handles routine business transactions.

Transactional. An organization in which different capabilities and contributions among different country operations are: (1) shared and integrated; (2) multinational enterprise; (3) company owned and managed by nationals from different countries.

Transactional Corporation (TNC). A company owned and managed by nationals in different countries also may be synonymous with multi-national enterprise.

Transactional Leadership. A more traditional approach in which managers engage in both task and consideration oriented behavior in an exchange manner.

Transfer. The reassignment of a current employee to another job at the same level as the regional job.

Transfer Deed. A transfer deed is a form that is used for effecting transfer of shares or debentures as is valid for a specified period. It should be sent to the company along with the share certificate for registering the transfer. The transfer deed must be duly stamped and signed by on behalf of the transferor and transferee and complete in all perspectives. The transfer deed is an important document of transfer and the form is prescribed by the Companies Act 1956. It has to be date stamped by the prescribed authority. It is valid for 12 months from the date of stamping by the prescribed authority or till the date on which the register of members are closed for the first time after the date stamping by the prescribed authority whichever is later.

Transfer of Ownership. Traditionally the final step in conveyance of power from parent to child—that of distributing ownership of the family business.

Transfer Payments. Funds given to private individuals without a *quid pro quo* exchange.

Transfer Price. The amount charged by one submit of an organization for a product or service that it supplies to another submit of the same organization.

Transferred-in-costs. In process costing, costs incurred in a previous department that have been received by a subsequent department.

Transformational Leadership. A style that goes beyond mere exchange relationships by inspiring employees to look beyond their own self-interests and by generating awareness and acceptance of the group's purposes and mission.

Transit Float. Funds tied up during the time necessary for a deposited check to clear through the commercial banking system and become usable to the company.

Transition State. The period during which the organization learns the behavior needed to reach the desired future state.

Transmission. It is the lawful process by which the ownership of securities is transferred to the legal heirs of the deceased.

Transnational Labour Relations. Labour activities conducted across national boundaries by organized labour.

Transparency. A characteristic of an accounting system that implies the companies to disclose a great deal of information about accounting practices more common in Anglo Saxon countries (United States, United Kingdom).

Treasury Bill Auction. The formal process by which the US Treasury sells new issues of treasury bills.

Treasury Bill Futures. A futures contract written on treasury bills.

Treasury Bills. Short-term debt instruments used by the U.S. government to obtain funds. T-bills are sold at a discount from face value. Pay no explicit interest payments, and have maturities of 3, 6 or 12 months.

Treasury Bond. A coupon bond issued by the US government with maturity less than ten years.

Treasury Bond Futures. A futures contract written on treasury bonds.

Treasury Note Futures. A futures contract written on treasury notes.

Treasury Notes and Bonds. Long-term bonds issued by the US Treasury to finance the national debt and other federal government expenditures.

Treasury Stock. Outstanding stock that has subsequently been repurchased and not cancelled by the company.

Treasury Strips. A synthetic zero-coupon bond constructed from treasury notes and bonds.

Treaty Reinsurance. Type of reinsurance in which the primary company must cede insurance to the re-insurer and the re-insurer must accept. The ceding company is automatically reinsured according to the terms of the reinsurance contract.

Tree Harvesting Problem. The maximization of Net Present Value would depend on when trees are harvested. The net future value of trees increase when harvesting is postponed; but the opportunity cost of capital is incurred by not realizing the value by harvesting the trees. The NPV will be maximized when the trees are harvested at the point where the percentage increases in value equals the opportunity cost of capital.

Trend Analysis. In financial analysis the direction of changes over a period of time is of crucial importance. Time series or trend analysis of ratios indicate the direction of change.

Trespasser. A person who enters or remains on the owner's property without the owner's consent.

Triad Strategy. A strategy proposing that an MNE should have a presence in Europe, the United States and Asia (especially Japan).

Triangular Arbitrage. Taking advantage of discrepancies between the spot exchange rate between two currencies and the exchange rate that can be obtained by trading one of the two currencies first for a third currency. And then trading that third currency for the other of the two currencies.

Trips. *See* Trade Related Aspects of Intellectual Property Rights.

True Lease. A true lease, in the US, is a transaction which qualifies as a lease under the Internal Revenue Code so the lessee can claim rental payments as tax deductions and the lessor can claim tax benefits of ownership as depreciation and ITC. Since the 1981 Tax Act, alternative "safe harbour" rules have been available regarding what constitutes a lease (now more limited in application).

Trust. Reciprocal faith in other's intentions and behavior.

Trust Certificate. Document evidencing the beneficial ownership of a trust estate of an equity participant (or owner participant trust or owner) in an owner trust.

Trust Companies. Companies that receive money and invest it for the benefit of a third party.

Trust Fund Plan. A type of pension plan in which all pension contributions are deposited with a trustee who invests the funds according to a trust agreement between employer and trustee. Benefits are paid directly out of the trust fund.

Trust Receipt. A title to goods which remains with a financial institution when it has lent a business some money.

Trustee. A bank or trust company which holds title or a security interest in leased property in trust for the benefit of the lessee, lessor, and/or creditors of the lessor. A leveraged lease often has two trustees—owner trustee and indenture trustee.

Trustee Fee. Fees due either to the owner trustee or the indenture trustee.

Trustee Owner. The lessor under a leveraged lease holding trust certificates evidencing their beneficial interest as owners under the owner trust. A trust or owner is the same as an equity participant or owner.

Truth in Lending. A law passed by the US Congress in 1968 that requires covered lenders to disclose fully all the relevant terms of a personal loan to the borrower and to report a standardized loan rate (known as the APR or annual percentage rate).

TSE. Toronto Stock Exchange, Canada.

Turbulent Environment. An environment wherein the customer or stakeholder demands are continuously changing or the primary technology of the firm is constantly being improved and updated.

Turnaround Strategy. A strategy in which the firm attempts through such measures viz., cost-cutting, quality enhancement or the elimination of management positions to restore economic strength in a declining business.

12b-l fees. Relating to the distribution costs of mutual fund shares.

26 Receivables turnover. The number of times receivables are turned over during a specified period of time.

Turnkey Operation. An operating facility that is constructed under contract and transferred to the owner when the facility is ready to begin operations.

Turnover. It is the process in which employees leave the organization and have to be replaced.

Turtle Blood. It is a stable security with no volatility and a price that is not expected to increase quickly.

Twisting. An illegal replacement of life insurance based on incomplete or deceptive comparisons between existing and proposed policies.

Tying Contacts. An agreement that requires a customer to agree to buy all future needs of a product from the seller as a condition of current purchasing.

Type A Ideas. Startup ideas centered around providing customers with an existing product not available in their market.

Type A Behavior Pattern. Aggressively involved in a chronic and determined struggle to accomplish more in less time.

Type B Ideas. Startup ideas, involving new technology, centered on providing customers with a new product.

Type C Ideas. Startup ideas centered on providing customers with an improved product.

U

U.S. Canada Free Trade Agreement. *See* Canada U.S. Free Trade agreement.

U.S. Shareholder. For U.S. tax purposes a person or a company owning atleast two per cent of the voting stock of a foreign subsidiary.

U.S. Terms. The practice of using the direct quote for exchange rates.

Uberrima Fides. Utmost good faith. The standard of behavior imposed on the insured by an insurance contact. The requirement that the insured deals with the insurer without making material mis-representations concealing material facts.

U-from Organization. Organizational design based on functional departmentation, often for a single-product strategy.

Ultimate Net Loss. The total amount that the insured is legally obligated to pay.

Umbrella Liability Policy. A policy, usasally with large limits covering losses in excess of the limits provided by the underlying liability insurance. For example, a personal umbrella liability insurance policy provides people with excess converge over the liability coverage provided by their homeowners and autonomy insurance.

Umbrella Prospectus. Under an umbrella prospectus the issuing company does not need to seek the approval of the market regulator each time it hits the market.

Unadjusted Rate of Return. *See* Accounting rate of return.

Unaided Analytic. Analysis is limited to processing information in one's mind.

Unamidable Cost. The opposite of avoidable cost.

Unanticipated Inflation. The amount of inflation that is different from the expected inflation rate.

Unbiased Expectations Hypothesis. A theory of the yield curve which contends that the curve's shape is determined exclusively by investor expectations regarding future interest rate movements.

Unbilled Revenue. Fees earned in a given period but for which no bills have been sent to the customer.

Uncertainty. A situation in which individuals cannot estimate probabilities over outcomes. Either because they cannot list the possible outcomes or because they cannot estimate the probabilities to assign to the various outcomes.

Uncertainty Decisions. Decision situations in which no past experiences or historical data are available. Any one of a number of criteria is employed, depending upon the personality of the manager.

Unchanged Issues Index. It is useful to examine not only the number of stocks that advance and decline but also the number that remain unchanged. When a higher than normal percentage of stocks remain unchanged in price, the market is likely getting a top. The index is calculated each day by dividing the number of issues which are unchanged in price by the total number of stocks traded.

Uncovered Option. Writing a call or a put on an underlying asset not owned by the writer.

UNCTAD. UN Conference on Trade and Development.

Under capitalization. Lack of funds to operate a business normally.

Underemployment. The result of taking a job that requires less education, training or skills than possessed by a worker.

Underfunded. A pension plan that does not have sufficient funds to meet all future promised payments.

Underinsured Motorists Coverage. Coverage that can be added to the personal auto policy. Coverage pays damages for a bodily injury to an insured caused by the ownership or operation of an underinsured vehicle by another driver. The negligent driver may have insurance that meets the state's financial responsibility or compulsory insurance law requirement, but the amount carried is insufficient to cover the loss sustained by the insured.

Underwriter's Spread. The difference between the gross proceeds and the net proceeds.

Underapplied Factory Overheads. The excess of actual factory overheads over the factory overheads applied to products.

Underemployed. Those people who are working at less than their capacity.

Underground Economy. That part of the economy that is unrecorded in official measurements of economic activity because it consists of illegal activities and un-recorded cash transactions.

Underinsurance. Having less insurance than is required by the policy provisions, especially the coinsurance provision. *See* Insurance.

Underinsured Motorist's Insurance. An automobile insurance policy option providing payment when the insured is injured by a negligence motorist having less insurance than the insured and because of the defendant's inadequate coverage the insured cannot recover for all damage sustained.

Underlying Values. Unarticulated ethical beliefs that provide a foundation for ethical behavior in a firm.

Underlying. The specific security/asset, which an option contract is based.

Under-water Option. Stock options offered to the US employees. The shares are normally offered at a discount on the market rate, but when the market price falls below the grant price, the option goes under-water.

Underwriters. Investment firms that act as intermediaries between a company selling securities and the investing public.

Underwriting Cycle. A pattern that the profits, in the P&C industry, tend to follow.

Underwriting. The functional process of an insurer that involves the evaluation of risk and the acceptance of risk in accordance with the insurer's underwriting philosophy by rating (calculating a premium) applicants for insurance.

Undistributed Earnings. *See* Retained income.

Undue Influence. When assent is not voluntary because of the nature of the relationship of the parties to the contract.

Unearned Premiums. Reserves set aside that contain the portion of a premium that has been paid before insurance coverage has been provided.

Unearned Premiums. The percentage of an advance premium not yet earned by the insurer by the passage of time. For example, if an insured pays a one-year premium in advance, after the policy has been in force for two months, ten-twelfths of the premium remains unearned.

Unearned Revenue. *See* Deferred revenue.

Unemployment Rate. The ratio of the number of people classified as unemployed to the total labor force.

Unexpired Costs. Any expenditure benefiting the future. Any asset, including prepaid expenses, normally appearing on balance sheet.

Unfair Labour Practice. Management or labour union acts prohibited by federal legislation.

Unfavourable Balance of Trade. An indication of a trade deficit which means imports are greater than exports.

Unfounded Debt. The portion of national debt that is in the form of fixed-term securities. It consists of the floating debt, listed securities and small-scale savings.

Unfounded Plan. Pays pension benefits out of current income to the organization.

Unfreezing. The disruption of forces maintaining the existing state (state A) or level of behavior.

Unified Banking. System where banks serve both as commercial banks and investment banks.

Unified Tax Credit. Tax credit that can be used to reduce the amount of the federal estate or gift tax.

Uniform Commercial Code. A group of statutes that are recommended to provide some conformity between states' commercial laws.

Uniform Franchise Offering Circular (UFOC). A document accepted by the Federal Trade Commission as satisfying its franchise disclosure requirements.

Uniform Reserve Requirements. Identical reserve requirements for commercial banks savings and loans and credit unions.

Uniform Transfer Tax. The combination of the federal gift and estate taxes.

Unilateral Contract. Only one party makes a legally enforceable promise.

Unilateral Transfer. In the balance of payments accounts, the transfer of funds or goods for which no payment is expected in return.

Uninsured Motorists Coverage. That part of the personal auto policy designed to insure against bodily injury caused by an uninsured motorist, a hit-and-run driver, or a driver whose company is insolvent.

Uninsured Plan. It is one which the benefits at retirement are determined by the employer based upon calculations that considers the age of the employee and years worked.

Union. Union is a formal association of workers that promotes the welfare of its members.

Union Shop. A worker must join the labour union within a stipulated period of time after his employment in order to continue working in that periods.

Unique Risk. A risk that affects at most a small number of assets.

Unisex Rating. A rating system in which the pooled loss experience of both sexes is used to determine the rates charged.

Unit Bank. *See* Unit banking.

Unit Banking. Restricting a bank to have only one office or to service a single location.

Unit of Account. A measure in which prices or values of goods and services are stated. An important function of money.

United Nations (UN). An international organization of countries formed in 1945 to promise world peace and security.

United Nations Conference on Trade and Development. An UN body that has been especially active in dealing with the relationship between developing and industrialized countries with respect to trade.

Unity of Command. Having each subordinate report to only one superior. The principle of unity of command implies only that the more an individual reports to a single superior, the less the problem of conflict in instructions and the greater the feeling of personal responsibility for results.

Universal Copyright Convention. A multilateral agreement to protect copyrights.

Universal FI. An FI that can engage in a broad range of financial service activities.

Universal Life Insurance. A type of life insurance policy allowing the insured flexibility in choosing premium payment and death benefits during the contract period.

Universalistic Approach to Organization Design. A set of ideas which concludes that there exists only one effective design for all organizations regardless of setting.

Universality of Management. The concept that basic management science, theory, principles and concepts are applicable in any culture even though application in practice may vary depending on cultural differences, contingencies or situations.

Universalization. The belief that there are commonly shared business standards and principles that are accepted throughout the world.

Unlimited Liability. The individual responsibility for all debts incurred. Creditors have a claim for these debts and can exercise it against both the business assets and personal assets so the proprietor.

Unlimited Liability. This exists in forms of business ownership that allow judgment against not only what the owner has invested in the business but all the rest of his assets.

Unlimited Material Deduction. A provision of the federal estate tax allowing the first spouse to transfer an unlimited amount of assets to the serving spouse without incurring an estate tax liability.

Unoccupied. A situation arising when an insured leaves possessions in residence but is temporarily absent from the premises not to be confused with vacant, which means both property and persons have been moved from the premises.

Unregimented Strategy. Strategy that defines the total market as the target market.

Unrelated Diversification. The action of diversifying into any business that is potentially profitable for the organization.

Unrequired Transfer. *See* Unilateral transfer.

Unsatisfied Judgment Fund. Fund established by a state to compensate accident victims who have exhausted all other means of recovery. As of date of publication, only five states have such laws.

Unsatisfied Need. The starting point in the process of motivation. It is a deficiency of something within the individual that provides the spark that leads to behavior.

Unseasoned New Issue. A company's first equity issue made available to the public.

Unsystematic Risk. A risk that affects at most a small number of assets.

Unusual, Customary and Reasonable Charges (UCR). Amounts payable for health care referring to the physician's normal charge for a specific procedure, the amount charged for the same procedure by physicians with similar training in the same geographical area and the amount considered reasonable if the physician's usual charge does not exceed the customary charge.

Up-and-in Option. For up-and-in option, an upper level (barrier) is specified for the asset price on which the option is written. For an up-and-in call (put) option, the contract becomes a standard call (put) option if the price of the underlying asset never goes above the barrier during the life of the contract, otherwise the contract expires worthless.

Up-and-out Option. For up-and-out option, an upper level (barrier) is specified for the asset price on which the option is written. For a up-and-out call (put) option, the contract ceases to exist if the price of the underlying asset goes above the barrier. If the price of the underlying asset never goes above the barrier during the life of the contract, the contract expires as an ordinary call (put) option.

Up-date Lease. Up-date lease is intended to prospect the lessee against the risk of obsolescence. The lessor agrees to replace obsolete asset with new one at a specified rent.

Upfront Fee. The fee charged for making funds available through a loan commitment.

Upper Managers. Those who make decisions about the overall performance and direction of the organization.

Upside Gain and Downside Loss. The profits a business can make and the losses it can suffer. The amount of money it takes in if everything goes well. The amount it will gross if operations are "as expected" or the amount it will lose if things do not work out well.

Up-tick Rule. A rule in the stock market that prohibits short sales except when the last transaction in the stock had a price increase.

Upward Communication. Communication that flows from individuals at lower level of an organization structure to those at higher level. Some of the most common upward communication flows are suggestion boxes, group meetings and appeals or grievance procedures.

US Treasury Bills. A debt obligation, one year or less to maturity, issued by the United States Government.

Usage Variance. Efficiency variance pertaining to materials or direct labour.

User-friendly. A term that describes computers and programs designed to be easily understood and used.

Usury. An excessively high interest rate.

Usury Laws. Laws that restrict the interest rate that can be charged on loans and credit card balances.

Utilitarian Philosophy. A philosophy where believers seek the greatest satisfaction for the largest number of individuals.

Utilitarianism. An approach to decision making that assumes decisions producing the greatest good for the greatest number of stakeholders are ethical.

Utility. The power of a good or service to satisfy a human want.

Utility (Social). A concept used in ethical reasoning that refers to the net positive gain or benefit to society of some actions or decisions.

Utility Patent. Registered protection for a new process or a product's function.

UV. Disclosed value orders allow the trading member to place an order which gets activated only when the security crosses a threshold price, until then the order does not enter the market. In the case of an OS sell order, the order gets triggered if the last traded price is less than or equal to the OS sell order price.

V

Vacant. Empty, without contents. *See* Unoccupied.

Valence. The importance of each potential outcome to the individual.

Validity. A "test" actually predicts what it says.

Value Added Network (VAN). A subscription service network for communicating with other firms and/or customer.

Value Added Tax. A tax that is a percentage of the value added to a product at each stage of the business process.

Value Chain. An organization's activities that are interdependent and contribute to the creation of value, consisting of inbound logistics.

Value Engineering. The analysis of the operation of a product or service, estimating the value of each operation, and attempting to improve the operation by trying to keep costs low at each step or part.

Value Marginal Product of Deposit. The marginal product of deposits multiplied by the market interest rate on loans, indicates the additional revenue, a purely competitive bank gets from an additional $ 1 of deposits.

Value System. The system of activities that links the activities of suppliers, producers, distribution channels and ultimate buyers.

Value-additivity Principle. It implies that if we know the NPVs of separate projects, the value of the firm will increase by the sum of their NPVs. The firm's value can simply be found by adding their values.

Value-at-risk. A measurement of risk in terms of future financial loss on current investment portfolio. It represents the worst-case future financial loss one can expect to incur on a portfolio within a given time frame (95 per cent confidence level). In the table below, there is a user portfolio and the S&P 500 portfolio. While both portfolios have equal market value, the use of portfolio's higher VaR Numbers indicate that it carries significantly more risk than the S&P 500 portfolio. For example, one can say with 95 per cent confidence that on any given day in future, the currently-held user portfolio could lose up to $ 1,159, and the S&P 500, up to $ 776. Since the user portfolio's daily VaR is presented "with 95 per cent confidence", the user must understand that on any given day in the future there is a 5 per cent probability of maximum financial loss exceeding $ 1,159.

Valued Policy. A type of insurance policy in which the insurer agrees to pay the face amount in the event of a total loss, regardless of the actual damage sustained. Valued insurance policies are often used to insure artwork and similar items, regarding which the market value at the time of loss may be difficult to estimate when the insurance policy begins.

Valued Policy Laws. Laws requiring payment to an insured of the face amount of insurance if a total loss to real property occurs from a peril specified in the law, even though the policy may state that only actual cash value will be paid.

Values. Fundamental and enduring beliefs about the most desirable conditions and purposes of human life.

Vandalism. The malicious destruction of another's property.

Vanishing Premium Policy. A whole life policy in which the premium vanishes or disappears after a number of years.

Variable Annuities. Investment opportunities similar to mutual funds sold by insurance companies.

Variable Budget. *See* Flexible budget.

Variable Budgeting. A form of budgeting that targets expected costs at various output levels.

Variable Cost. A cost that changes in relation to output.

Variable Cost Percentage. The variable expense ratio expressed as a percentage.

Variable Cost Ratio. *See* Variable expense ratio.

Variable Expense. An expense that changes in relation to output. When production is low, the expense does so; examples include cost of materials and labor.

Variable Expense Ratio. All variable expenses divided by revenues.

Variable Inspection. The determination of product acceptability based on a variable such as weight or length.

Variable Interval Schedule. A pattern whereby the period of reinforcement varies between one reinforcement and the next.

Variable Life Insurance. A type of cash value life insurance policy giving the insured flexibility in choosing the underlying investment media.

Variable Pay. Compensation based on achievement of certain goal (such as sales or profits).

Variable Price. A method of pricing in which the buyers and sellers negotiate the price.

Variable Pricing Strategy. A marketing approach that sets more than one price for goods in order to offer price concessions to certain customers.

Variable Rate Mortgage. Home mortgage loans carrying an interest rate that varies during the term of a loan generally depending on the movement of interest rates in the open market.

Variable Ratio Schedule. A pattern whereby the behavior required for reinforcement is varied.

Variable Working Capital. The extra working capital needed to support the changing production and sales activities is called fluctuating or variable or temporary working capital.

Values

VaR-Parameters	User Portfolio	S&P 500 Portfolio
Market value of portfolio (as of latest market closing)	$95,910	$95,910
Daily value at risk	$1,159	$776
Monthly value at risk	$5,311	$3,557
Annual value at risk	$18,399	$12,322

Variance. (1) A probability—weighed sum of the squared deviations of potential out-comes from their mean. (2) The deviation of actual results from the expected or budgeted result.

Variation Call. *See* Main-tenance margin.

Variation Margin. The additional funds the trader must deposit is called the variation margin. The gains or losses on open futures contracts calculated by marking the contracts to the market price at the end of each trading day (or session). These gains or losses are credited or debited by the clearing house to each clearing member's account and by members to their respective customer's accounts.

Variety Store. This store carrier a wide range of relatively inexpensive goods for the household.

Varying Cost of Capital. In reality opportunity cost of capital is not constant over time. Hence various oppor-tunity costs are applied to, while taking decisions of investment.

VAT. *See* Value added tax.

Vega. The change in the option's value for a unit change in the volatility.

Vega Neutral. A portfolio position that has a vega of zero.

Vehicle Currency. A monetary unit of a nation that is not only the standard of value (unit of account) for domestic transactions but is used to express the prices of many goods and services traded between nations as well.

Velocity. The number of times the average unit of money changes hands in one year.

Vending Machine. A method of distributing through machines merchandise which has high demand and high frequency of sale.

Vendor. Manufacturers of equipment could use a lessor as the third party to market the leasing of the period.

Venture Capital Firm. A corporation that invests in risky businesses with high growth potential. Usually in exchange for considerable shares of the ownership.

Venture Capital. Type of financing sought by early-stage companies seeking to grow rapidly.

Venture Capitalist. A private individual or company that usually invests in ventures with higher risk-return possibilities than average. Most venture capitalists invest through equity instruments. Some states have venture capital funds for underwriting new ventures, and most security trading firms have funds set aside for high-risk portfolio investments.

Venture Capitalist. An investor or investment group that commits money to a new business ventures.

Venture Fund. A specialized fund that invests in distressed loans.

VER. Voluntary Export Restraints.

Verbal Communication. Words spoken through various channels to convey information and meaning.

Verbal Threshold. A suit for damages is allowed only in serious cases such as death, etc.

Verifiability. *See* Objectivity.

Vertical Bear Spread. Buy a call (put) option and sell a call (put) with a lower strike price. All options have the same maturity.

Vertical Bull Spread. Buy a call (put) option and sell a call (put) with a higher strike price. All options have the same maturity.

Vertical Company. The term refers to a company when buys life assurance policies from people with a long term or terminal illness.

Vertical Coordination. The integration of succeeding levels of the organization.

Vertical Differentiation. The centralization and decentralization of decision-making responsibilities.

Vertical Information Systems. Computer systems that provide managers with information about the organization's performance.

Vertical Integration. The control of the different stages as a product moves from raw materials through production to final distribution.

Vertical Option Spread. Buying and selling call or put options with the same expiration date but different strike prices.

Vertical Specialization. The division of labor at different levels of management into different tasks of planning, organizing, leading and controlling.

Vested. The period of time an employee must work before he or she is eligible to receive pension benefits. And data among computers in more than one location.

Vested Benefit. The right of an employee to the employee's contribution to a person plan. Federal law specifies vesting schedules for qualified pension plans.

Vestibule Training. Training which is given in an area away from the job.

Vesting. It is the right of employees to receive benefits from their pension plans.

Vicarious Liability. Legal liability arising out of another's actions. For example, a contractor may have liability if a subcontractor injurs another party.

Vice President. A top manager who is responsible for a specific area of the company.

Video Screen. Where the output of a computer is displayed.

Video-conferencing. The transmission of real-time images.

Videodisc. A disc on which television signals have been recorded for the purpose of storing digital data that may be played back.

Virtual Reality. A three-dimensional computer generated environment that gives the user a sensation of being part of that environment.

Virtual Team. Combining the talent and ideas of people worldwide by using technology to communicate in addressing business problems and opportunities.

Visible Exports. Merchandise exports.

Visible Imports. Merchandise imports.

Vision. Long-term goal describing 'what' an organization wants to become.

Voice Mail. Telephone messages stored by a computerized system.

Volatility. The standard deviation of an asset's return.

Volume Variance. *See* Production volume variance and sales volume.

Voluntary Bankruptcy. Bankruptcy that occurs when a owner asks the court to declare the business unable to meet financial obligations and to provide it with protection from creditors.

Voluntary Chain. A group of retailers who voluntarily associate themselves with a wholesaler to take advantage of volume purchases and discounts.

Voluntary Export Restraints (VER). A negotiated limitations of exports between an importing and an exporting country.

Voyage Policy. It is related to marine policy that is valid only for a single, specific voyage.

VRAs. Voluntary Restraints Agreements.

Vroom-Yetton Theory. A situational theory of leadership that attempts to identify the appropriate leadership style for a given set of circumstances or situations. The leadership styles are defined by the extent to which the subordinates participate in decision making.

Vulnerable Derivative. A derivative for which there is risk that the writer of a derivative might default.

W

Wage. Payments made to workers on an hourly rated basis.

Wage and Salary Administration. It is a group of activities involved in the development, implementation and maintenance of a base pay system.

Wage and Salary Survey. A study that tells the company compensation paid by comparable firms for specific jobs the firms have in common.

Wage Rate. The level of wages paid by employees.

Wage Rigidity. Nominal wage stickiness or slow adjustment, due to formal and informal contracts.

Wagner Act. The National Labour Relations Act of 1935 which outlined unfair labour practices of management.

Waiver. Voluntary relinquishment of a known legal right.

Waiver-of-premium Option. An extra-cost of life insurance policy provision made for the insurer to insurer to forgo collection of premiums while the insured is permanently disabled, despite the forgone premiums, the policy remains in force with benefits calculated as if premiums had been paid.

Wall Street. A customary way of referring to the financial community of banks, investment institutions and stock exchanges centred in the wall street area of New York city.

Wall Street Journal. The most familiar business newspaper.

Wall Street Rule. A common practice among corporate stockholders of voting their shares of stock to support the company's management or selling the stock if they disagree seriously with management policies.

War Clause. Restriction in a life insurance policy that excludes payment if the insured dies as a direct result of war.

Warehouse Receipts. Receipts for goods stored in a warehouse.

Warehouse Showroom. A retailing operation which includes in one building a large warehouse used for storage and a showroom for displaying samples of each piece of brand-name merchandise handled. Furniture and catalogue showrooms are two major users of this retailing method.

Warehousing. On the stock markets, using funds invested in insurance or unit trusts to buy shares that are falling in price, usually as a precursor to a takeover bid.

Warranties. Promises or guarantees to consumers, assuring certain performance or product quality and usually specifying replacement of defectives or repairs.

Warranty. A seller's promise or statement of fact about a product.

Wash Lease. US jargon, particularly under 1981 Tax Act, same as grip lease. This sale of TIC benefits indepen-dently of depreciation benefits to lessors requiring specifically short term shelter.

Water Pollution. Low levels of oxygen, low or high pH, temperature or toxic chemicals in water that harm marine life or human.

Watered Stock. Stock that has become a smaller percentage of a company's total share capital because of subsequent share issues.

Weak Currency. A currency that is not fully convertible.

Weak Form Market Efficiency. Claims that the best prediction of next period's asset price is this period's price.

Wealth. The value of assets minus the value of debts owned by an individual or institution.

Wealth Effect. During periods of prolonged asset price rise or a bull phase in the stock markets, consumption patterns may also show an increase, this increase is known as the wealth effect. During the boom period, asset holders reap larger returns from their holdings in stocks and property and hence consume more. Even those who do not hold to many assets tend to jump on the consumerist bandwagon. This also results in a fall in savings.

Web-Peomerene Export Trade Act. Legislation allowing selected American firms desiring international trade to form monopolies in order to compete with foreign cartels.

Web Browser. Communi-cations software designed to access and display information at internet websites.

Website. A firm's location on the world wide web.

WEC. World Energy Council.

Weekend Game. Name given to the policy of lowering deposit balances on Fridays, since that day's figures count three times for reserve accounting purposes.

Weighted Cost of Capital. The cost of capital adjusted to reflect the relative costs of debt and equity financing.

Weighted-Average Cost. This inventory method assumes that all items available for sale during the period are best represented by their weighed average cost prices.

Weighted-average Cost of Capital. An average of the component costs of the individual sources of capital employed by the firm. The term is sometimes shortened to average cost of capital.

Wellness Programs. Organization-sponsored programs designed to promote employee health and well-being.

West African Economic Community. A regional economic group involving Benin, Burkina Faso, Coted'Ivoire, Mali, Mauritania, Nigeria and Senegal.

Western Hemisphere. Literally the earth's area between the zero and 180th meridian but usually indicates the continents of the American and adjacent islands excluding Greenland.

Wheel Network. Communication network in which information flows from a single person.

When-issued Securities. Commitments to buy or sell securities before they are issued.

Whipsaw. Violent movements (or series of movements) in the prices of any market.

Whistle Bowling. An employee's disclosure (to the public) of alleged organizational misconduct.

White Square Defence. In a takeover situation a target company may place significant number of its shares with a friendly party in order to prevent the raider from acquiring them.

White-collar Crime. Crimes of the business world other than budget and robbery.

Whole Life Insurance. A type of life insurance in which a person is insured as long as he pays premiums and collects only at death.

Wholesale Bank. A bank that focuses its business activities on commercial banking relationships.

Wholesale Price Index. The Wholesale Price Index (WPI) covers all commodities, *i.e.* primary goods, power, fuel, manufactured goods and services. Each of these is given a different weightage in the index, according to its importance. The WPI is not intended to capture the effect of price rise on the consumer as it takes the wholesale prices.

Wholesaler. The middleman between the producer and final consumer in the channel of distribution.

Wholly Owned Subsidiary. A domestic or foreign operation that is completely owned and operated by a parent organization.

Wide Span of control. A situation where large number of people (six or more) report to a supervisor.

Wide Area Network. A network in which computers are linked by telephone lines or long-range communications devices.

Wildcard Option. The right to deliver on a futures contract after the closure of trading but before the start of the next trading day.

Wildcat Bank. Banks in the early 1800s that would purposely issue excessive notes and locate in remote places to make redemption difficult.

Wildcat Scheme. It is a speculative investment that is not expected to succeed.

Window of Opportunity. A time horizon during which opportunities exist before something occurs to eliminate them.

Withdrawal Behavior. Avoidance of the work situation as a result of job dissatisfaction.

With-holding Tax. Payable on the rentals received from many cross border leases depending on the double taxation arrangements between the countries involved may be prohibitively high.

Word-processing Program. Application software that allows users to create, manipulate, print text and graphics on a computer.

Work Design. The function of organizing tasks and responsibilities.

Work Ethic. The belief that human labour and work are inherently worthwhile, admirable and both personally or socially valuable. The work ethics is sometimes called "the protestant ethic" or "the protestant work ethic" due to its origin among early protestant theologians.

Workforce Diversity. The movement of people from different demographic, ethnic backgrounds and values orientations into the organizational mix.

Work Group. It is a collection of individuals brought together to perform organizational work.

Work in Process Inventory. Those products that are partially completed or in transit.

Work Measurement. The careful analysis of a task its size and the methods used in its performance.

Work Teams. Groups of employees with freedom to function without close supervision.

Work/Family Conflict. The sense that work and family demands interfere with each other.

Worker's Compensation. Payment designed to help employees who have job-related illness or injured.

Workers' Compensation Insurance. Coverage that obligates the insurer to pay employees for injury or illness related to employment.

Workforce Demographics. Statistical profiles of adult workers.

Workforce Diversity. Difference among employees in terms of such dimensions as gender, age and race.

Working Capital. Funds used in the daily operations of the business for such purposes as payrolls, raw materials and accounts receivables. Also it is excess of current assets over current liabilities.

Working Capital Cycle. The daily flow of resources through a firm.

Working Capital Management. The management of current assets and current liabilities.

Working Capital Provided by Operations. Revenues less all operating expenses requiring working capital.

Working Partners. Business partners who play a role in day-to-day operations.

Workstations. Powerful personal computers stable to carry out more than one function at time.

World Bank. Financial organization established and supported by the industrialized nations to loan money to underdeveloped and developing countries; formerly known as the International Bank for Reconstruction and Development.

World Intellectual Property Organization (WIPO). A multilateral agreement to protect patents.

World Trade Organization (WTO). A voluntary organization through which groups of countries negotiate trading agreements and which has authority to oversee trade disputes among countries.

World Wide Product Division Structure. Business organizational structure based on product divisions that have world wide responsibility.

Worldwide Transaction Desks. Instinet transaction desks are located in eight of the world's key financial centres and staffed by professionals with many years of experience in their local market. Their trading professionals are available around the clock to discuss trading strategies, place orders, check executions and provide other services that one may require.

WPG. Winnipeg Commodity Exchange, Canada.

Writer. A person who issues a derivative security.

Writing the Rules. The competitive technique called writing the rules, a company works with the government or a trade association to establish the technical standards and other rules that will govern competition of the industry.

Written Communication. Information transferred as recorded words, such as memos, reports, and electronic mails.

Written Down Allowance. A depreciation allowance where each year's allowance is based on a percentage of the written down value at the end of the previous year. Cars and assets leased to tax paying bodies are all subject to 25% annual writing down allowances and those leased abroad to 10% writing down allowances.

Wrongful Death Lawsuits. Litigation arising when the defendant's alleged actions resulted in the plaintiff's death.

WTO. *See* World Trade Organization.

X

XXX Add Back Method. The practice of beginning a statement of changes in financial position with net income and then adding or deducting income statement items not affecting working capital.

Y

Yellow Book. Popular term for a publication entitled admission of securities, listing, issued by the London Stock Exchange Council, setting out regulations of admission to the official list and the obligations of the securities admitted.

Yellow-dog Contract. The requirement by an employer that employees agree not to join a union as a condition of employment. This action is prohibited by labour legislation today.

Yield. The yield-maturity of a bond.

Yield Curve. The relationship between interest rates on identical financial assets and their term to maturity.

Yield to Maturity. The interest rate at which the amount used to purchase a financial asset, like a bond, would have to be invested in order to grow to the face value paid at maturity.

Y-network. Communication network in which information flows upward and downward through the hierarchy, widening to encompass the employees reporting to a supervisor.

Z

Zaibatsu. Large family owned Japanese business that existed before World War II and consisted of a series of financial and manufacturing companies usually held together by a large holding company.

Zai-tech. Japanese and the US stock market practice of borrowing money in order to invest in stocks and bonds.

ZBB. Symbol for zero base budgeting.

Zerial Bond. It is a stripped treasury bond or other zero-coupon debt instrument issued in serial form.

Zero Defects. The elimination of defects which results in the reduction of manufacturing costs and an increase in consumer satisfaction.

Zero Discharge. An abstract unattainable environmental goal that would involve the elimination of all industrial and agricultural pollution.

Zero Sum Gain. A situation in which one party's gain equals to another party's loss.

Zero-balance Account. A disbursement account in which the firm maintains a zero balance, transferring funds from a master account only as needed to cover checks presented for payment.

Zero-base Budgeting. Budgeting in which enterprise programmes are divided into 'packages' comprising goals, activities needed resources and costs calculated for each package from the ground up.

Zero-coupon Bond. A bond that makes no interest or coupon payments.

Z-score. The result obtained from solving a linear discriminated problem.

Z-trench: High Pay-out Clientele. Investors who prefer near dividends to future dividends are high payout clientele. They prefer dividends than capital gains. They wish firms to pay high dividends than retention of profits.